Furry Tales

ALSO BY FRED PATTEN

Furry Fandom Conventions, 1989–2015
(McFarland, 2017)

Furry Tales

A Review of Essential Anthropomorphic Fiction

FRED PATTEN

Foreword by Kyell Gold

McFarland & Company, Inc., Publishers
Jefferson, North Carolina

The author died on November 12, 2018,
shortly after completing this manuscript.

ISBN (print) 978-1-4766-7598-5
ISBN (ebook) 978-1-4766-3704-4

LIBRARY OF CONGRESS AND BRITISH LIBRARY
CATALOGUING DATA ARE AVAILABLE

© 2019 Sherrill C. Patten. All rights reserved

No part of this book may be reproduced or transmitted in any form or by any means, electronic or mechanical, including photocopying or recording, or by any information storage and retrieval system, without permission in writing from the publisher.

Front cover image © 2019 Dmitriy Trubin/Shutterstock

Manufactured in the United States of America

*McFarland & Company, Inc., Publishers
Box 611, Jefferson, North Carolina 28640
www.mcfarlandpub.com*

To the pioneers (or maybe just the weirdos)
who created furry fandom

Acknowledgments

I would like to thank several people for their help with this book.

Mary E. Lowd, a veteran furry fan and head of the Cóyotl Awards committee, for reading and commenting on parts of my manuscript.

All the furry specialty publishers who sent me high-resolution scans of their logos.

John Batteiger of DonMarquis.com, and John Radcliffe of The Kipling Society, for providing details about the first editions of Marquis' *archy and mehitabel* books and Kipling's two *Jungle Books*.

Lori McLeod of the Toronto Public Library's Osborne Collection of Early Children's Books for also providing details about the first editions of some books.

JJ Jacobson, Cherry Williams, Eric Milenkiewicz, and Zayda Delgado of the University of California, Riverside's Rivera Library, and its Eaton Collection of Science Fiction and Fantasy; my friend Roz Gibson, and my sister Sherrill, for supplying the book cover scans to illustrate this.

Layla Milholen, my editor at McFarland, and the others there for agreeing that my book is a worthwhile addition to their books on literature and popular culture, and for their help in shaping its format.

Table of Contents

Acknowledgments
vi

Foreword by Kyell Gold
1

Preface
7

Introduction
9

THE TEXTS
13

Appendix 1: Nonfiction Works
201

Appendix 2: Author and Chronological Lists
202

Appendix 3: Awards
205

Appendix 4: Furry Specialty Publishers
211

Index
217

Foreword by Kyell Gold

In the early 1990s, I discovered that there was a community for people who liked books with animal characters. Fred Patten was already there.

The "furry fandom" coalesced in the 1980s, and while these fans aren't fans of a specific media work, there are several core works that influenced many of the people who joined. Some may have read most of the pre–1980 books on Fred's list, some may have read only one, but it's fair to say that nearly everyone in this fandom is aware of many of the books here.

For my own part, *Watership Down* was the first complex novel I read with wholly animal characters, and I loved it. I'd read *The Wind in the Willows*, *Alice in Wonderland/Through the Looking-Glass*, and many other books with animal characters, but *Watership Down*, a full, character-driven story with adult themes, expanded the world of what was possible. I pushed it on several friends, none of whom seemed as enthusiastic about it as I was, and in those pre–Internet days, I had nobody else to talk to about it.

In the 1980s, Fred was present in the southern California scene generally credited as the birthplace of furry fandom. He already had a great deal of experience in bringing an interesting subculture to the attention of more people, as he had worked to bring anime to the U.S., an endeavor he would continue for many years (in 1980 he received the Inkpot Award at Comic-Con for this work). He was also starting to become aware of fans in science fiction circles who, like me, loved furry literature and didn't have anyone else to discuss it with. These fans formed a small community, first at other science fiction conventions, and later at their own meets. Many of them made art and comics, and the mindset they brought to the furry fandom of contributing creatively to your community has persisted to this day. The discussions about favorite works that everyone shared took place not just in face to face meetings, but also in the pages of the work they created.

Early on, the only way for members to share their creative output was through an Amateur Press Association, or APA. An APA was a fanzine by and for the fans. Each contributing member would produce enough copies of their work for everyone in the group and then mail those pages to the editor. The editor took all the mailings, collated them into issues of the zine that included everyone's contributions (often with help; the gatherings to put together issues with page counts that numbered anywhere from ten to a hundred became social events in and of themselves), and mailed them back out to the members.

One of the earliest APAs in furry fandom (perhaps the second after the early *Vootie!*) was *Rowrbrazzle*, a collection that focused on art and comics but also included stories.

In 1989, Fred took over editorship of *Rowrbrazzle* and was running it when I first heard about it.

In the science fiction fandom, professional publication is the goal of many fans. The early furry fans knew that there was no professional market publishing the kind of stories they were interested in (*Watership Down*, *The Architect of Sleep*, the *Chanur* series, and *Ring of Swords* being examples of the frustratingly rare exceptions). Instead, as I joined the fandom, *Rowrbrazzle* was held up as the only work created by furry fans for furry fans. We weren't just talking about the books we loved; we were creating comics and stories of our own.

Many early comics had their start in *Rowrbrazzle*, and my friends and I, seeing these comics appear with the intriguing tagline "featured in the pages of *Rowrbrazzle*," wondered not just how one got to join it, but how we on the outside could ever see one of the issues (as they were distributed to members only). At the time, there was a long, long waiting list to join, and it's not overstating the importance of *Rowrbrazzle* to say that it was the most important publication in furry fandom for several years.

As the furry fandom grew, so did the number of APAs, and eventually the fandom added some fanzines that were sold to the public at large, so when I finally started writing stories, there were many other venues to send them to. I never joined *Rowrbrazzle* personally, but I got stories published in other fanzines. Printing technology improved and the fandom continued to grow, and more professional venues sprung up for furry fans to publish their stories. As they did, of course Fred got involved with those as well.

One of the first projects I associate with him was Sofawolf Press's book *Best in Show*, later reprinted as *Furry! The World's Best Anthropomorphic Fiction* by iBooks. I believe this was Fred's first anthology in the furry fandom, but it would by no means be his last. What he envisioned for this book was a collection of all the stories that had been printed in fanzines over the years he'd been in the fandom, not just in *Rowrbrazzle* but in any publication he'd run across—and he had copies of most of them. He also had an encyclopedic memory for the stories (in later years, he reached farther back into SF to reprint furry stories from decades ago that he still remembered), and it was important to him that these stories, originally printed in fanzines with very limited circulation, be made more available to the fandom at large. Only two of the twenty-six stories in *Best in Show* were from his years at *Rowrbrazzle*; overall they represented a sampling of most major fanzines in the first fifteen years of furry fandom.

This is all by way of telling you that if anyone was going to provide a retrospective of furry literature and boil it down to the most important 100 books, it would have to be Fred Patten.

And I believe this retrospective is important. These hundred books, which include those that inspired a worldwide community as well as some created by the community, represent a continuum of human experience through the lens of how we anthropomorphize animals. So I'm going to talk a little more about the furry fandom.

The word fandom usually indicates a community built around a creative work—like *Star Trek*—but those communities are also built around a philosophy or set of ideas in that work. What draws someone to the gritty reality of George R.R. Martin's *Game of Thrones* series rather than the romantic swashbuckling *Star Wars* movies? People gravitate to experiences and messages that are meaningful to them.

So what to make of the furry community, often called a "fandom" because the community resembles a fan community even though it lacks a central work? I and others have said in the past that furries are fans of an aesthetic rather than a work, of a means of expressing themselves that isn't terribly common in mainstream society (a close parallel might be the steampunk fandom, whose fans love the aesthetic of Victorian adventure stories and the philosophy of independence and discovery). Through the lens of animal characters, furry fans tell the stories they want to tell, about themselves or about the world.

The furry community began as a bunch of people, mostly cartoonists, with a love of funny animal cartoons and comics. It's expanded to a worldwide group of more than a hundred thousand people as of 2010, and the modern-day furry community includes people in just about any creative field you can imagine: art, writing, video games, music, dance, and more. What they all have in common is some kind of connection to animals.

Furry fans often identify themselves with a particular animal or animals, a choice that can change over the years as the person grows and changes. This identification sometimes represents the person they feel they are, and sometimes the person they want to be. For example, a furry identifying with a wolf might be focused on the strength and sociability of wolves; a furry identifying with a bear might identify with physical size and general amiability. What they may not realize is that the associations they make between the person they identify as and the animal character they choose have their roots in centuries of storytelling.

These animal characters that furry fans connect to are built not only from the real animals they're based on (the physicality of the real animals is often part of the fandom) but also from centuries of popular culture. Myths and stories have grown up around animals based partly on observation and partly on the desire of humans to build stories around their world. Prior to the first written stories, we find prehistoric cave paintings and the animal-headed gods of Egypt, and almost as soon as stories were being written, they began to feature animal characters. Aesop's stories of trickster foxes informed the medieval *Roman de Reynard*; the Br'er Rabbit stories informed Bugs Bunny. Jack London romanticized wolves in American culture, associating them with the fierce independence of the frontier and making them more palatable by reinforcing their connection with domestic dogs in *The Call of the Wild* and *White Fang*, preparing us for Jim Brandenburg's 1987 photo-journalism covering arctic wolves which, though nonfiction, does possess a degree of anthropomorphism.

So the historical record of novels tracing the changes in the perception of animals in popular culture is an exceedingly interesting one for people specifically interested in animals, but also for people outside that fandom simply interested in how human-animal relationships have been represented over the years in works intended for a larger audience. Animal characters continue to be popular in mainstream culture, and though some of the books represented here may be little known by today's standards, they certainly influenced works that we do know today.

The second part of this collection, the works produced by small press publishers specifically for the furry community, is just as interesting. The 2000s, as Fred notes, saw the rise of on-demand publishing and niche markets for books that could not be expected to sell thousands of copies but might sell hundreds—too small a run for a large publisher, but now within the reach of specialty presses.

This in turn allowed for a discourse to take place in the furry community. With no central work being published by a large company, the only ways for furry fans to share their work with each other had been through fan-generated media, which was unreliable and limited. The most prestigious publications, the APAs, couldn't be seen by the majority of the fandom. Eventually, more fanzines appeared, but it was hard to get complete novels out unless they were published completely on the Internet.

I missed Paul Kidd's first novel sale, but I remember hearing about his novel *A Whisper of Wings*, published by a small furry press that was mostly putting out professional-looking fanzines at the time. It felt like a sea change in the fandom: rather than read a friend's copies of an APA or wait to buy fanzines at the one or two yearly conventions, here was a novel not only written by a member of our fandom but published by one as well.

Around that same time, I was frustrated by the lack of markets for the stories I wanted to write, and a friend of mine, similarly frustrated, did a lot of research into on-demand printing. We both wanted to provide a professional venue for stories, and in 1999 we founded Sofawolf Press with that goal in mind.

There were other small presses around at that time, and more cropped up every year. Artwork, short fiction, and longer fiction became easier to find in the fandom. You could buy some books from Amazon, or you could find the press's home page and buy them there. The fiction that had appeared in photocopied fanzines now filled professional publications for sale to everyone; publishers kept back catalogs so that new patrons could fill in their collection. The discourse of storytelling in the community grew stronger and more vibrant.

Novels were of course slower to follow. Many novels were serialized online or self-published through early print-on-demand sites like Lulu. But as the 2000s went along, more and more small publishers added novels to their catalog. A look at the fandom's first literary awards, the Ursa Major Awards, shows the shift: in their first five years the candidates for Best Anthropomorphic Novel came more often from non-fandom publishers than fandom publishers and the Internet/self-publishing combined. From 2006 on, the ratio flipped: fandom publishers outnumbered non-fandom and Internet/self-publishing (which stayed about the same) combined.

Over the last fifteen years, the writing scene in the furry community has continued to grow stronger and stronger, and so has the discourse in the novels. Stories respond to other stories and authors develop worlds and work with each other. There are conversations about how to build worlds for the fandom, there are writing workshops for the fandom, and more and more books coming out every year.

There are good old-fashioned adventure stories, there are personal journeys of discovery, there are space operas and mysteries and romance. The community is exploring and discovering what it means to tell these stories with animal characters and how that can change the expectations of the stories.

As part of that community, I'm naturally drawn to it, but I think that watching any young community grow, exchange ideas, and show off their creativity is fascinating. So even if you're not in the furry fandom, this collection of reviews offers something interesting for you.

I mentioned that Fred had compiled the best stories from the first fifteen years of furry fandom into a collection, published in 2003. That was only the beginning of his work with the fandom. As novels came out, Fred did his best to read and review every single one of them. Certainly I have not had a novel published that Fred didn't review, and every time I sought out a review of a furry-published book, one of Fred's reviews came up. When one news site shut down or stopped responding to him, he'd find another one. In 2005 he suffered a stroke, but a year or so later he was back to requesting copies of books from publishers as they came out and writing reviews.

As the number of publishers grew, Fred found more homes for his anthology project ideas. "Edited by Fred Patten" became a staple of anthology covers, and many furry writers remember him as the editor who accepted their first story. Fred's comprehensive knowledge of the history of anthropomorphic literature meant not only that he was an excellent judge of stories, but that he was excited to find any story that was doing something new, something different, something that would expand the ideas in the furry community and spark other writers to go to new places. His focus was on sharing the work he was passionate about with everyone, whether by writing reviews that would encourage people to pick up new books or by discovering new stories to share with the world.

With all that in mind, I think it is eminently fitting that this is the last book Fred completed before his death in November 2018 (he had also just completed work on a compilation of winners of furry fandom's newer literary award, *The Coyotl Awards Anthology*, to be released by FurPlanet in 2019). He loved history and the furry fandom and so a book showing the winding path of popular books that led to the last thirty-ish years of the furry community's stories seems like the perfect work to remember him by. It's hard to imagine the furry writing community without the fatherly figure who encouraged us and supported us, but I'm very glad that Fred lived to see how active and exciting the community grew to be.

These hundred books of anthropomorphic literature are a wonderful collection, reviewed and fit into their place in history by the foremost historian of anthropomorphic literature. I'm just as excited to see the next hundred. I wish Fred would be able to see them as well, because just as the early books in this collection laid a foundation for the books that came later, Fred himself has laid the foundation for many books yet to come.

Kyell Gold has won 12 Ursa Major awards for his stories and novels, and his novel Out of Position *co-won the Rainbow Award for Best Gay Novel of 2009. He helped create RAWR, the first residential furry writing workshop, and has instructed at each of its sessions through 2018. More information is at http://www.kyellgold.com.*

Preface

I have been an enthusiast of one form or another of science fiction and fantasy for my whole life. I was born in Los Angeles, California, on December 11, 1940, and I discovered science fiction when I was nine years old, when my father brought Robert A. Heinlein's newly-published *Sixth Column* from the L.A. Public Library. Public libraries did not accept paperbacks during the 1950s when many original paperback sf novels, anthologies, and collections were published, so I started a personal "library for books that other libraries won't have" during my adolescence. I attended UCLA from 1959 to 1963, graduating with a BS in history in 1962 and an MLS in library science in 1963; my MLS thesis was on the books of sf author Andre Norton.

In 1960, while a student at UCLA, I attended my first meeting of the weekly (Thursday evening) Los Angeles Science Fantasy Society (established 1934), and I have been a participant in sf and related fandom activities ever since. I published my first mimeographed fanzine, *Foofaraw*, in 1961, and had my first book review published in 1962. I was employed as a librarian from 1963 to 1990, mainly as a cataloguer in Hughes Aircraft Company's Company Technical Document Center from 1969 to 1990. From 1991 to 2002 when it went out of business, I was the first employee of Streamline Pictures, specializing in the licensing and dubbing of Japanese animation (anime) for American theatrical, TV, and home video sales.

During that time, I was an active hobbyist in many sf and fantasy fandoms. I became active in comic-book fandom as well as sf fandom in the 1960s, writing ¡*Supermen South!* about Mexican comic-book superheroes, for the comics fanzine *Alter-Ego* in 1965. During 1972–1975, I was the co-owner (with Richard Kyle) of Graphic Story Bookshop in Long Beach, California, an early sf/comics specialty bookshop and the first in America to import foreign comics including Japanese manga. It was through this shop that I discovered Japanese manga and anime. I co-founded (with Mark Merlino) the Cartoon/Fantasy Organization (C/FO) in May 1977, the first anime fan club in the U.S. and Canada. In 1980 I received the San Diego Comic-Con's Inkpot Award for helping to introduce Japanese anime to America. (I and other early anime fans claim credit for introducing the Japanese fan word "cosplay" to America, which today has almost completely replaced "costuming" and "masquerading" even outside of fandom.) I have been on many sf convention organizing committees, including several times as chairman. In 2006 I received a special Life Achievement Award from the World Science Fiction Convention, "in recognition of a lifetime of service to the fandom."

From 2002 to 2005, I was a freelance writer specializing in Japanese anime. I had monthly columns for three anime and comics specialty magazines, *Animation World Network*, *Comics Buyer's Guide*, and *Newtype USA*, when I had a major stroke in March 2005. Since then I have been paralyzed, living in a convalescent hospital bed in Southern California, where I communicate with the outside world through a MacBook Pro computer.

I have become more and more involved in furry fandom since 1980. During the 1980 World Science Fiction Convention in Boston, I participated in the first events that led to the evolution of furry fandom—the meeting with Steve Gallacci at that convention's Art Show, and the informal gatherings around him at other sf and comics conventions to discuss funny animals. I was a founding member of *Rowrbrazzle*, the quarterly furry Amateur Press Association, in 1984, publishing a pioneering furry fanzine, *Lettres de Coquefredouille*, for it. I became *Rowrbrazzle*'s Official Editor from 1989 until my stroke in 2005. I was at the first furry convention in January 1989, and was an attendee of practically every furry convention on the West Coast of America and several "Back East" until my stroke. I co-founded the annual Ursa Major Award for the best anthropomorphic work in (currently) twelve categories, and I am still on its organizational Anthropomorphic Literature and Arts Association (ALAA; http://www.ursamajorawards.org/). I was elected to the Australian Fandom Conventions' global Furry Hall of Fame in 2011, and I am a current member of the Furry Writers' Guild (FWG; http://furrywritersguild.com/).

Besides writing two books about animation (*Watching Anime, Reading Manga: 25 Years of Essays and Reviews* [Stone Bridge Press, September 2004] and *Funny Animals and More: From Anime to Zoomorphics* [Theme Park Press, March 2014]), and one about furry fandom (*Furry Fandom Conventions, 1989–2015* [McFarland, 2017]); I have specialized in editing fifteen anthologies of furry short fiction, including the first anthology of furry fiction, *Best in Show: 15 Years of Outstanding Furry Fiction* (Sofawolf Press, July 2003). The latest is *Exploring New Places* (FurPlanet Productions, July 2018). I have been a furry literary book reviewer since January 1990, at first for paper magazines like *Yarf! The Magazine of Applied Anthropomorphics* (69 issues, 1990–2003), and later for several online magazines, currently for *Flayrah* and *Dogpatch Press*. I have also reviewed non-furry books for the online *AmoXcalli*, and written a weekly animation column for *Cartoon Research* from 2013 to 2017. I have written numerous articles on furry history including "An Illustrated History of Furry Fandom, 1966–1996" and "Funny Animals in World War II Propaganda." When I had my stroke in 2005, my collection was donated to the University of California, Riverside, forming the Fred Patten Special Collection on Science Fiction and Animation, a part of the UCR Library's Eaton Collection of Science Fiction and Fantasy. My holdings of furry literature, fanzines, and ephemera have given the UCR Library the most extensive collection of furry material in the world.

Introduction

The subculture of furry fandom started in the early 1980s. Anthropomorphic literature goes back further. How much further depends upon how "talking animal literature" is defined.

Do the talking animals in some of *Aesop's Fables* (ca. 580 BCE orally) make them the oldest anthropomorphic literature? The earliest surviving comedy, the anonymous *Batrachomyomachia* (*The Battle of Frogs and Mice*) from ca. 330 BCE, has some dialogue. It is a short parody of the *Iliad* about a one-day war between opposing armies of mice and frogs, with the mice wearing armor of bean-pods and nutshells while the frogs have reed spears, plant-leaf shields, and snail-shell helmets. The earliest work that was a written novel is the risqué *Metamorphoses* by Apuleius (Lucius Apuleius Madaurensis), dated to around 160 CE, better known as *The Golden Ass* (renamed by St. Augustine around 400 CE). In it a young man, also named Lucius, tries to turn himself by magic into a bird for erotic reasons, but mistakes the spell and ends up as a donkey but with his human brain. The novel relates Lucius' picaresque adventures as he searches as an ass for the antidote that will turn him human again.

Around the mid- and late-12th century, the Northern European tales of Baron Reynard the fox in the anthropomorphic animal court of King Nobel the lion—a parody of then-current human nobles and aristocrats—were written down, by Nivardus of Ghent, Pierre de Saint-Cloud, and others. In China, there were the folk tales around the actual seventeen-year journey from China to India and back by the Buddhist monk Xuán Zàng from 629 to 645, that were novelized as *Journey to the West* by Wu Cheng'en (died 1580) in his later years, emphasizing Xuán Zàng's mythical supernatural bodyguards, especially Sun Wu-kung the Monkey King, and Zhu Bajie ("Pigsy"), a humorous half-man, half-pig monster.

But these were not novels in the modern form. European literary novels and talking animals came together in the late 18th century. Before about the 1750s, common European attitudes toward animals were about the same as toward inanimate objects. Children were allowed, if not encouraged, to treat pets and other animals as breakable toys. As an aspect of the Age of Enlightenment, such tormenting of dumb beasts began to be considered as cruel. One result of this was the development of uplifting children's literature. Books were written for parents to give to their children for their moral edification, as didactic lessons of virtue and kindness to animals.

The first novels featuring anthropomorphic animals were published as cheap pamphlets that could be given to young children, or read to them by a nursemaid or mother.

The Life and Perambulation of a Mouse by Dorothy Kilner (1784), narrated by Nimble the mouse, is his life story of escaping torture by thoughtless children. The similar *Fabulous Histories* by Mrs. (Sarah) Trimmer (1786), renamed *The Story of the Robins* in 19th century editions, is about the nest of Mr. and Mrs. Robin and their chicks Robin, Dicksy, Flapsy, and Pecksy; and the two human children on whose home their nest is, who observe them. Good things happen to the good chicks and the young Bensons; bad things happen to Robin and to the Bensons' human playmates who are thoughtless and use small animals as toys. The animals can talk, but are otherwise not anthropomorphized.

The earliest novel with fantasy animals to be enjoyed by adults, as well as children, was Lewis Carroll's *Alice's Adventures in Wonderland* (1865), and its sequel, *Through the Looking-Glass, and What Alice Found There* (1871). The White Rabbit who wears a waistcoat and pocket watch, the Cheshire Cat who fades into and out of existence, the hookah-smoking caterpillar, the Pigeon who accuses Alice of being a serpent, and others—plus all the human characters accepting these human-sized, talking animals as normal—made animal fantasies respectable. It was soon followed by the two *Jungle Books* of Rudyard Kipling (1894 and 1895). H.G. Wells' science-fiction novel *The Island of Dr. Moreau* (1896), about trying to turn animals into humans through vivisection, was an animal fantasy for adults only.

A few animal fantasies for adults followed into the 20th century. *Animal Farm* by George Orwell (1945) merged the animal fantasy with political satire. (The Axis' sole example, *Van Den Vos Reynaerde* (*About Reynard the Fox*) by Robert Van Genechten (1941), with evil rhinoceroses that are blatant parodies of greedy Jewish merchants, was never translated into English. It probably could not be published today, because of most nations' laws against hate literature.) The real impetus for talking-animal fantasies for adults was *Watership Down* by Richard Adams (1972). Its rabbit religion and language were considered brilliant. By the end of the 20th century, there were "*Watership Down–type*" novels about cats, horses, squirrels, moles, honeybees, puffins, salmon, and more, who had their own vocabularies and religions.

The first members of furry fandom read many of these. When they coalesced at sf conventions and comics conventions in the early 1980s, they discovered that many of their favorite fantasy movies (usually animated), TV cartoons and comic books, and children's novels like *The Rescuers* by Margery Sharp, featured intelligent, talking animals. Their favorite sf novels and short stories featured animal-like aliens. One of the oldest was "A Martian Odyssey" by Stanley G. Weinbaum (*Wonder Stories*, July 1934). Its protagonist is Dick Jarvis, an American explorer on Mars, but the character that readers remember is Tweel, the ostrichlike Martian native who befriends him. "A Martian Odyssey" was reprinted in sf anthologies for decades, so many readers over generations were familiar with it. Another was the 1930s–'40s *Lensman* magazine series by Edward Elmer "Doc" Smith, novelized in the 1950s, about the Galactic Patrol, an interstellar police force. Its main characters were all humans, but there were several memorable friendly aliens among the supporting characters; notably Worsel the Velantian (a heroic reptilian "dragon").

During the 1990s, the more literary-minded furry fans started amateur magazines that were published and sold within the fandom: *Anthrolations, FurryPhile, Mythagoras, Pawprints Fanzine, Zoomorphica*, and more. Some lasted only one issue, while the longest-lived of these, *Yarf! The Journal of Applied Anthropomorphics*, ran for 69 issues from January 1990 to September 2003, with a furry book review column. Other fans wrote the short stories for these furry magazines and Internet distribution.

In describing the influences that some of these anthropomorphic novels and stories have had on the creation of furry fandom, the term *proto-fans* refers to those who remembered being influenced by books and stories before 1980. *Early furry fans* are those who talked about the then-current stories they were reading between 1980 and 2000.

The development of do-it-yourself book publishing technology, making the publishing of very small print runs practical, appeared in the early 2000s. Furry writers who could not sell anthropomorphic-animal fantasies to major publishers could afford to have their own books published by CreateSpace, Lulu Press, AuthorHouse, and others, for sale at furry conventions and on the Internet through the new Amazon mail-order service. More ambitious fans could start their own furry-specialty small presses, and get their manuscripts from furry writers. United Publications, Vision Books, Sofawolf Press, Anthropomorphic Dreams Publishing, FurPlanet Productions, and others appeared during the first decade of the 2000s. Still more such as Goal Publishing and Thurston Howl Publications appeared during the 2010s. As with everything else, some only published a few titles and disappeared, while others have flourished.

By the early 2010s, furry fandom had built up its own literature of original novels and short fiction, written by furry-fandom authors and published by the furry specialty presses. New reprint anthologies of short fiction with intelligent animals from the sf magazines of the 20th century, the favorite stories of the early furry fans, appeared. According to FurPlanet Productions, one of the largest furry specialty publishers with sales tables at a half dozen conventions or more a year across the U.S., sales have been primarily of electronic editions ordered from its online catalogue, and of paper editions at conventions through impulse buying. (Due to international trade restrictions, U.S. publishers have not had sales tables at the growing Canadian furry conventions.)

During this time, many fan artists have become prominent through exhibiting in convention art shows, painting convention souvenir-book covers, and displaying their work on Internet art sites like DeviantArt and FurAffinity. The new furry publishers have commissioned them to paint the covers for their books. So a book from a furry specialty press may exhibit a cover by a notable furry-fandom artist, as well.

The rise of electronic publishing, especially Amazon's Kindle books, has complicated things. I have decided to limit these 100 anthropomorphic fiction books and their sequels to those on paper editions (although many also have electronic editions). This is partly because there are no really important anthropomorphic books that do not have a paper edition. Also, hardcover and softcover paper books are kept today by those trying to build a large library, while electronic editions are more for those who only want to read a work but not keep it permanently.

There is no formal list of the most important works of anthropomorphic literature. This book has been compiled by studying the growth of furry fandom. It includes the works before 2000 that have influenced those who became the first furry fans. When furry fandom coalesced at sf and comics conventions in the early 1980s, these were the novels and short stories that the fans recommended to each other (along with many children's fantasies, such as the *Dr. Dolittle* novels by Hugh Lofting, the *Freddy the Pig* series by Walter R. Brooks, *The Mouse and the Motorcycle* and its two sequels by Beverly Cleary, and others). Naturally enough, the recommendations at sf conventions were heavy on adult science-fiction that contained memorable non-human protagonists. As furry fandom grew, so did the recommendations. Many that were briefly recommended, such as the 1985 British *The Singing Tree* by Brian Parvin (the U.S. edition was titled *The White*

Fox), were quickly forgotten, but those that have continued to remain popular are included here.

The earliest furry-fandom novelist is Paul Kidd in Perth, Western Australia. He serialized his unsold *Mus of Kerbridge* and *Fangs of K'aath* manuscripts in his *Rowrbrazzle* fanzine, *Barking Mad*, beginning in 1989. When his *Mus of Kerbridge* finally appeared as a cheap paperback in 1995, it was cheered as the first novel sale by a member of furry fandom. When the first furry specialty small presses appeared in 1999 and 2000, Kidd's novels were their first titles. Here are the first anthology in 2003 of short fiction from furry magazines; the first novels and anthologies of short fiction to win furry fandom's first literary award; and the novels, anthologies, and collections published by the furry small presses since then that furry fans have recognized as their best.

Many adolescents entering furry fandom today think that anthropomorphic literature goes back no further than the furry specialty publishers of the 21st century. Here are a hundred classic and award-winning anthropomorphic novels (and their sequels) and anthologies that today's furry fans are reading and enjoying, plus their sequels. Many have influenced the work of today's furry authors. These can be recommended to new fans for pleasure reading. They can be studied by academics interested in the development of anthropomorphic literature.

The subculture of furry fandom began in the 1980s. Serious nonfiction studies of furry fandom have begun to be published since the 2010s. Four of these are also added.

The Texts

Top-of-page running headers reflect the first title in a series.

The Abandoned • by Paul Gallico

New York: Alfred A. Knopf, September 1950, hardcover, 315 pp. Published in the UK as Jennie. London: Michael Joseph Ltd., October 1950, hardcover, 268 pp.

    Paul Gallico (1897–1976) wrote many popular stories that featured animals, such as *The Snow Goose* (1941). Only three were anthropomorphic fantasies: *The Abandoned* (1950); *Thomasina, the Cat Who Thought She Was God* (1957); and *Manxmouse* (1968). *The Abandoned* is the best of these. Ironically, it's the only one that hasn't been made into a movie. It's good that the novel is being kept in print.

    The Abandoned tells the story of those cats who do not live with human companions and must survive as alley strays. The eponymous abandoned are Peter Brown, an 8-year-old London boy who is transformed into a white cat's body after an accident, and Jennie Baldrin, a street-wise tabby who teaches Peter to be a cat:

> Peter guessed that he must have been hurt in the accident though he could not remember very much from the time he had left the safety of Scotch Nanny's side and run out across the street to get to the garden in the square, where the tabby striped kitten was warming herself by the railing and washing in the early spring sunshine.

It starts with Peter running away from his Scottish nursemaid and dashing into London traffic to play with a tabby kitten stray. Peter is immediately identified as an upper-class child (his parents can afford a nursemaid) who loves cats. The next four pages establish that Peter really, *really* wants a pet cat. He has been asking for one since he was four, but his mother says he cannot have one. Every time he sneaks a stray home, his callous nursemaid throws it out. Peter's father is an Army colonel who is stationed abroad, "and his mother was always busy and having to dress up to go out, leaving him with Nanny," so he is essentially a rich but emotionally abandoned child. Peter's transformation into a cat, and his adoption by the motherly Jennie Baldrin, gives him a real mother for the first time he can remember.

    Presumably there is a connection between Peter's running into the street to see a tabby kitten, and Jennie Baldrin's being a tabby cat. *The Abandoned* is full of subtle references and connections, such as Jennie Baldrin's name, "baudrons" being a late Middle English (ca. 1400–1450 Scots dialect) word for a cat; Peter's Scottish Nanny and Jennie's coming from Glasgow. Gallico had a sharp eye for the behavior of cats, and considerable knowledge of their history, which Jennie relates to Peter:

"Someone named Julius Caesar is supposed to have brought some of us to Britain in 55–54 B.C. But that wasn't *our* branch of the family. *We* were in Egypt two thousand years before that when, as you've no doubt read, cats were sacred. A lot of people try to be or act sacred, but we actually were, with temples and altars, and priests to look after us. I suppose you have noticed how small my head is. Egyptian strain. And then of course *this*."

And here Jennie rolled over on her flank and held up her paws so that Peter could inspect the under sides of them. "Why, they're quite black," Peter said, referring to the pads. He then looked at his own and remarked: "Mine are all pink."

But mostly the story is about cat behavior. *The Abandoned* may be the best novel ever written for rationalizing and explaining their habits:

"When in doubt—any kind of doubt—wash! That is rule No. 1," said Jennie.... "If you have committed an error and anybody scolds you—wash," she was saying. "If you slip and fall off something and somebody laughs at you—wash. If you are getting the worst of an argument and want to break off hostilities until you have composed yourself, start washing. Remember, every cat respects another cat at her toilet. That's our first rule of social deportment, and you must also observe it."

Or:

Here she crouched down a few feet away from the dead mouse and then began a slow waggling of her hind quarters from side to side, gradually increasing the speed and shortening the distance of the waggle. "That's what you must try, to begin with," she explained. "We don't do that for fun, or because we're nervous, but to give ourselves motion. It's ever so much harder and less accurate to spring from a standing start than from a moving one. Try it now and see how much easier it is to take off than the other way."

There are many of these lessons throughout the novel.

The Abandoned is also the story of Peter's life as a cat in the slums of London and Glasgow, and of his and Jennie's experiences as ship's cats in getting to Glasgow and back again. It is a mixture of fantasy-adventure for older children and a romance for adults, as Peter matures physically and emotionally in his husky tomcat's body from a frightened child under Jennie's motherly guidance into her mature lover and protector from other toms. The setting of London rebuilding after the wartime bombing is dated today, but the characterizations of cat personality types are timeless.

There is debate as to whether the U.S. or the British edition should be considered the true first edition. *The Abandoned*, the U.S. edition, was published in September 1950; *Jennie*, the British edition, was published in October 1950. September 1950 obviously comes before October, but by only one month; and the British setting and language (trucks are lorries) implies that it was originally intended to be published in England first. There have been many reprints over the years, under both titles, although some have been as adult novels and some as "children's classics." Since this is considered "literature," many public libraries have it.

Albert of Adelaide • by Howard L. Anderson. Map by Jim McMahon.

New York: Hachette Book Group/Twelve, July 2012, hardcover, 233 pp.

Australia today is not what it used to be. Imported animals like sheep, foxes, and rabbits have replaced the older native animals. Kangaroos and wallabies are tolerated as "cute," but other native animals have been relegated to zoos where they are penned in and stared at by humans. But there is a legend that somewhere in Australia, far from the human-settled southeast, isolated in the vast desert, there is a place where things haven't changed and the original animal inhabitants live freely:

> In the early morning of a day long after the war, a small figure walked slowly along one of the winding tracks somewhere to the east of Tennant Creek. On close examination, the figure didn't look any different from most of his kind. He was about two feet tall and covered with short brown fur. He had a short, thick tail that dragged the ground when he walked upright and a ducklike bill where any other animal would have a nose.
>
> The only thing that set Albert apart from any other platypus was that he was carrying an empty soft drink bottle. It was his possession of a bottle, coupled with the fact that he was hundreds of miles north of any running water, that made him different.

Albert the platypus is staggering about in the parched desert next to the South Australia Railway tracks near Tennant Creek, somewhere north of Alice Springs. Albert has escaped from the Adelaide Zoo and is searching for ... what?

> The stories had been vague at best ... *somewhere in the desert ... a place where old Australia still existed ... keep going north ... the Promised Land.* Those descriptions had sounded good in Adelaide, but they were worthless in a desert where every direction looked the same.

Albert of Adelaide by Howard L. Anderson (Hachette Book Group/Twelve, July 2012). A colorful and unique picaresque fantasy featuring Australian animals in a 19th-century outback setting. Cover art by Marc Burckhardt.

Albert had tried to prepare for his search by stockpiling a small hoard of food and water from his cage in Adelaide, but it had lasted only long enough to reach Tenant Creek. "Now, he was out of food, out of water, and out of plans."

Resolved to die as far north of Adelaide as possible, Albert stumbles into the camp of Jack the wombat. Jack has never heard of where Albert is looking for:

> "What I meant was, is this the place where things haven't changed and Australia is like it used to be?"
>
> The wombat thought for a long time before he answered. "If you mean somewhere animals run around without any clothes on while being chased by people with spears and boomerangs, the answer is no. It's not bloody likely that you'd find old Jack in a place like that."

Albert follows Jack to Ponsby Station, a ramshackle general store in a half-played-out mine site. The proprietor is "a large red kangaroo wearing an apron and a dirty silk shirt with garters on the sleeves. A pair of wire-rimmed spectacles rested on his nose." The customers are two bandicoots wearing canvas overalls.

Albert is naïve but he is no softy. When he runs into anti-platypus prejudice from the marsupials, he gets ready to fight:

> As both bandicoots and the kangaroo stared at Albert, he could feel the spurs on his hind legs start to extend themselves. The more they stared, the more they reminded Albert of the people at the zoo,

and with each look the anger in Albert's soul burned brighter. At the zoo there was nothing he could do, but here he might be allowed the luxury of a violent act.

Albert of Adelaide is a picaresque novel. Albert's wanderings take him into and out of many potentially fatal situations. It is similar to another classic picaresque novel, Twain's *The Adventures of Huckleberry Finn*. It's full of rough-and-tumble small towns that Albert has to leave in a hurry after a shootout. In fact, one of the next friends and role-models he meets is Terrance James Walcott, a raccoon holdup artist and claim jumper from the California gold camps who escaped from San Francisco barely ahead of a Vigilance Committee mob.

By now the reader will have realized that *Albert of Adelaide* has segued from current people-inhabited Adelaide and the modern continent-spanning South Australian Railway to a 19th-century Northern Australian landscape of frontier mining camps inhabited by anthropomorphic Aussie animals; marsupials who aren't familiar with a platypus from the Murray River and who don't trust strangers. Albert, at first an outsider unsure whether he should abandon his search for Old Australia, becomes the leader of the odd group of animals opposing the scoundrelly Bertram, the white tuxedo-wearing wallaby and Theodore, his murderously psychotic possum henchman who are tricking the citizens of Barton Springs into making them constable, then mayor, and finally general of the marsupial community, out to exterminate the dingo aborigines.

Albert of Adelaide is a fine anthropomorphic novel, with a rich cast of Australian animals and one raccoon immigrant. Like Grahame's *The Wind in the Willows*, the animals segue confusingly between being clothes-wearing imitation humans and natural animals, and being their real sizes and all human-sized. Individual clothes-wearing kangaroos hop, but a town full of them walk like humans. But the animals' natural abilities figure in many scenes. The desert-dwelling marsupials are unfamiliar with platypuses, and on several occasions Albert's poison spurs prove to be a powerful secret weapon.

Albert of Adelaide is an excellent animal fantasy. Unfortunately, Anderson has said on Amazon that it was the first novel of a planned *Old Australia* trilogy, but the publisher rejected the sequels when *Albert* didn't sell. Anderson has self-published the second novel, *The Famous Captain Walcott*, in 2017, but only in an electronic edition. He said, "*The Famous Captain Walcott* is the middle book of a trilogy that began with *Albert of Adelaide*. *Lily* the third book in the series has been written and will be published if there is sufficient interest."

Alice's Adventures in Wonderland • by Lewis Carroll. Illustrated by John Tenniel.

London: Macmillan and Co., 1866 [November 1865], hardcover, 202 pp.

Through the Looking-Glass, and What Alice Found There • by Lewis Carroll. Illustrated by John Tenniel.

London: Macmillan and Co., 1872 [December 1871], hardcover, 236 pp.

The earliest talking-animal fantasy that people still read for pleasure is *Alice's Adventures in Wonderland*, or *Alice* and its sequel—they are often published together as one book today. *Alice* is more than just a talking-animal fantasy, it is also the first novel—designed for all ages, even if Carroll wrote it for a young girl's amusement—with memorable talking, anthropomorphized animals (the White Rabbit, the Cheshire Cat, the March Hare, Bill the Lizard, the Dormouse, the Caterpillar, etc.) who did not appear just to deliver a moral lesson.

Both stories are presented as Alice's dreams, although the dream world is so vivid that it quickly overwhelms the reader. Alice is a lively, seven-year-old, mid–Victorian girl, bored with her older sister's pictureless book while outdoors on a riverbank on a sunny May afternoon. Alice (whom the reader may assume has fallen asleep) sees a talking White Rabbit wearing a waistcoat and holding a pocket-watch, worrying that he will be late. Alice follows him into his burrow, which leads to the underground Wonderland. It is filled with fantasy, from the size-changing drinks and foods to all the talking animals. Notable examples (along with bizarre humans like the Mad Hatter) are a mouse and his long tale/tail, the Dodo's Caucus-Race, Bill the Lizard and his ladder, the hookah-smoking Caterpillar, a Pigeon who accuses her of being a serpent because her neck has grown long and sinuous, and she admits that she eats eggs, fish- and frog-footmen, the Cheshire Cat, the "mad" tea party at the March Hare's house with the March Hare and the sleepy Dormouse, the living playing cards, and the Mock Turtle and the Gryphon.

Through the Looking-Glass, the sequel, was published seven years later (it was written immediately after but publication was delayed until Tenniel finished the illustrations), but is set only six months later. Alice, playing indoors alone on a snowy winter afternoon, imagines that she goes through a large wall-mounted mirror and returns to Wonderland. Most of the fantastic characters such as Tweedledee and Tweedledum are human, and chess-related, but Alice also meets a garden of live flowers, a talking sheep, and the Lion and the Unicorn. Alice has two poems recited to her with anthropomorphic characters; the Walrus and the Carpenter, and the Jabberwocky, which includes the Jubjub Bird and the Bandersnatch.

Alice is the first fantasy that presents its animals (including talking plants) on an equal social level with its humans instead of condescending to them, and often in a half-human form rather than as just natural animals with the ability to talk. This begins immediately when Alice sees the White Rabbit:

> when suddenly a White Rabbit with pink eyes ran close by her.
> There was nothing so *very* remarkable in that; nor did Alice think it so *very* much out of the way to hear the Rabbit say to itself "Oh dear! Oh dear! I shall be too late!" […]; but, when the Rabbit actually *took a watch out of its waistcoat-pocket*, and looked at it, and then hurried on, Alice started to her feet, for it flashed across her mind that she had never before seen a rabbit with either a waistcoat-pocket, or a watch to take out of it, and burning with curiosity, she ran across the field after it, and was just in time to see it pop down a large rabbit-hole under the hedge.

In Wonderland, Alice has constant conversations with the animals:

> "Please come back and finish your story!" Alice called after it. And the others all joined in chorus "Yes, please do!" But the Mouse only shook its head impatiently, and walked a little quicker.
> "What a pity it wouldn't stay!" sighed the Lory, as soon as it was quite out of sight. And an old Crab took the opportunity of saying to her daughter "Ah, my dear! Let this be a lesson to you never to lose your temper!" "Hold your tongue, Ma!" said the young Crab, a little snappishly. "You're enough to try the patience of an oyster!"
> "As if it wasn't trouble enough hatching the eggs," said the Pigeon; "but I must be on the look-out for serpents, night and day! Why, I haven't had a wink of sleep these three weeks!"

> "I'm very sorry you've been annoyed," said Alice, who was beginning to see its meaning.
>
> "And just as I'd taken the highest tree in the wood," continued the Pigeon, raising its voice to a shriek, "and just as I was thinking I should be free of them at last, they must needs come wriggling down from the sky! Ugh, Serpent!"
>
> "But I'm *not* a serpent, I tell you!" said Alice. "I'm a—I'm a—"
>
> "Well! *What* are you?" said the Pigeon. "I can see you're trying to invent something!"
>
> "I—I'm a little girl," said Alice, rather doubtfully, as she remembered the number of changes she had gone through that day.
>
> "A likely story indeed!" said the Pigeon, in a tone of the deepest contempt. "I've seen a good many little girls in my time, but never *one* with such a neck as that! No, no! You're a serpent; and there's no use denying it. I suppose you'll be telling me next that you never tasted an egg!"
>
> "I *have* tasted eggs, certainly," said Alice, who was a very truthful child; "but little girls eat eggs quite as much as serpents do, you know."
>
> "I don't believe it," said the Pigeon; "but if they do, why then they're a kind of serpent, that's all I can say."
>
> "'In *that* direction,' the Cat said, waving its right paw round, "lives a Hatter: and in *that* direction," waving the other paw, "lives a March Hare. Visit either you like: they're both mad."
>
> "But I don't want to go among mad people," Alice remarked.
>
> "Oh, you can't help that," said the Cat: "we're all mad here. I'm mad. You're mad."
>
> "How do you know I'm mad?" said Alice.
>
> "You must be," said the Cat, "or you wouldn't have come here."

There seems little point in recommending *Alice's Adventures in Wonderland* and *Through the Looking-Glass, and What Alice Found There*, because you've already read them. You must have. Everyone has.

The Alien Dark • by Diana G. Gallagher. Illustrated by Clive Caldwell.

Lake Geneva WI: TSR Books, December 1990, paperback, 309 pp.

> A shudder rippled along Tahl's shoulders as an image of the enigmatic Riitha f'ath rose in his mind. A sheen of soft, silver down covered her four petite breasts, belly, arms, and lower legs. The black long fur streaming from her head, muzzle, and shoulders and shagging from her hips and thighs gleamed with the rich luster of meticulous grooming. Like most of the crew, Riitha usually wore only a vest and fringed loin cloth in the climate-controlled confines of the ship. Thick, silver-tipped black lashes ringed large amber eyes that always shone with a mysterious light when she seduced and then rejected the *shtahn*.

This is the first extended description of the *ahsin bey*, the catlike space explorers who are the cast of *The Alien Dark*. It is clear from the beginning that the characters are not humans, but just what they are is revealed slowly. At first there are only brief glimpses: "Tahl's silver-tipped pointed ears" and "The short hairs on Chiun's light brown muzzle bristled with expectation"; "The short hairs covering Riitha's face, lower arms, belly, and lower legs bristled at Tahl's patronizing tone. She stiffened slightly, then hesitated, all too aware that Tahl's gaze had shifted to the small mounds of her four, milkless breasts"; "Tahl dug his foot-claws into the foam floor and grabbed a handhold suspended from the low ceiling…"; "Hane's lip curled back in a snarl, exposing sharp fangs"; and "Lish's sparse brown fur bristled with the urgency of her mating cycle."

The spaceship *Dan tahlni*, with a crew of thirty *ahsin bey*, have spent decades traveling twelve light-years from their own homeworld of Hasu-din to the Chai-te stellar system to explore it for colonization. They find Chai-te's outer planets and asteroid belt rich in the plasmas and minerals they need, but due to a restriction against settling in any system where intelligent life already exists, they have to make sure that the inner planets are also devoid of sapient life. But they do not have time to explore these thoroughly:

> The *Dan tahlni* was very close to failure by default because of lack of time and fuel. The alien sun, Chai-te, was not only brighter and hotter than Chai-din, its planetary system was more expansive. Extra fuel had been allotted for this contingency, but not enough. Because of this, the crew had not been able to explore the inner planets as thoroughly as they had those in the outer system. In addition, several large equipment pods, including the interstellar transmitter that was their only link to Hasu-din, had been left in orbit around Chai-te Five to conserve what fuel remained.

An additional reason for failure is the psychological nature of the *bey*. They are divided into two classes; the dominant *du-ahn* who have rigidly analytical/logical mentalities, and the minority *venja-ahn* who are emotional and imaginative:

> In any hopeless situation, fear triggered the death-wish mechanism in *du-ahn*. Unable or unwilling to suffer or fight in the face of futility, their minds shut down their bodies. Du-ahn fell into a catatonic state of deep hibernation where the normal awakening reflexes stimulated by seasonal change, hunger, or alarm were not operative. They slept and peacefully starved to death.

The interstellar mission of the *Dan tahlni* is already so risky, with the odds against their survival until a colony ship from Hasu-din can arrive decades later, that most of the du-ahn aboard are fatalistically primed to go into death-wish sleep at any hint of failure.

A superficial scan shows that they are apparently in luck. Chai-te Two is a verdant wilderness without any life more advanced than small lizards, while Chai-te Three is a lifeless ball of overheated murky carbon dioxide. Tahl d'jehn, the expedition's *shtahn jii* (leader; he can go into a thought-trance to apply logic to forecast/predict the success or failure of any proposed plan) is ready to declare Chai-te devoid of any intelligent life. But Riitha f'ath, the *venja-ahn* biologist, insists that they investigate more closely.

The novel's cover blurbs give away that they discover that the third planet was once inhabited by intelligent beings that became extinct a hundred million years ago. What happened to these humans, whether it poses a threat to the *bey*, and whether they can afford to explore more thoroughly, throws the explorers into an emotional turmoil that Tahl must control despite feuding cliques and sabotage lest so many of the crew go into death-wish that the rest cannot survive.

The Alien Dark is partly the drama of what happened to the third planet and its long-extinct humans, partly the "impossible" romance between *du-ahn* Tahl and *venja-ahn* Riitha, and partly the suspense story of whether the *Dan tahlni* and its crew will survive or not. It is unusual in being told almost completely from the viewpoint of furry aliens ("Stocha's claws kneaded the smoke-gray shag on his thighs. The silver-tipped long-fur gracing his muzzle and ears bristled" [*ibid.*]), although the human story—a hundred-million-year-old flashback—is extensive once it gets started. The *ahsin bey* are constantly described in inhuman terms—"The stench of fear and rage was thick and ominous"; they have more powerful scent: "Lish winced as the throbbing pain intensified. The compulsion to satisfy the mounting passion within her had been denied. Soon she would reach the peak of the hormonal drive, and the unrequited desire would torment her for the twenty days of her fertilization cycle. Despondency overwhelmed her, and she fell into a defeated crouch"; their breeding is more undeniably instinctual—all of which makes *The Alien Dark* a truly furry novel.

The Alien Dark was widely read and highly recommended by furry fans when it was published in 1990. Unfortunately, it was a cheap paperback that went out of print almost immediately, and Gallagher went on to write authorized TV novels (*Star Trek Voyager*, *Buffy the Vampire Slayer*, *Sabrina the Teenage Witch—Salem's Tails*, *Charmed*, etc.) and Young Adult girls' romances without returning to the setting of *The Alien Dark*. It is worth seeking out.

Already Among Us: An Anthropomorphic Anthology • edited by Fred Patten.
Birmingham, AL: Legion Publishing, June 2012, hardcover, 398 pp.

The theme of *Already Among Us* is that intelligent animals may already be here:

> People have tried over the centuries to prove that some animals are equal in intelligence with humans. There have been numerous attempts to teach human languages to dogs, cats, horses, or apes, from scientific to entertainment purposes; or, fictionally, to learn the languages of these animals.... *Already Among Us* presents fourteen stories in which humans are confronted by animals of obvious equal intelligence [Introduction].

This is the first anthology to reprint the short stories from science-fiction magazines that early furry fans had recommended to each other. The first six of these had been favorites of proto-fans in reprint sf anthologies of the 1950s to the 1980s, that were themselves out of print by 2012. The last eight were from sf magazines and original-fiction fantasy anthologies published after 1980, most of which had never been reprinted before.

The fourteen stories, published in chronological order from 1942 to 2006, are: "The Star Mouse," by Fredric Brown; "Number Nine," by Cleve Cartmill; "Socrates," by John Christopher; "The Model of a Judge," by William Morrison; "Yo Ho Hoka!," by Poul Anderson and Gordon R. Dickson; "Dr. Birdmouse," by Reginald Bretnor; "Dog's Life," by Martha Soukup; "River Man," by Michael H. Payne; "Schurman's Trek," by Roland J. Green; "MacGregor," by Paul DiFilippo; "Doggy Love," by Scott Bradfield; "The Fate of Mice," by Susan Palwick; "All the Pigs' Houses," by Mickey Zucker Reichert; and "Killer Kitty," by Harding Young.

Nine of these are nominally sf, and five are pure fantasies. They range from humor to drama, pathos, horror, and literary parody.

These are all enjoyable as talking-animal stories, although some of the older stories are clearly dated. "The Star Mouse" (1942), a comedy, was written during World War II, with its stereotypical European refugee Jewish scientist in the U.S. Herr Professor Oberberger catches a mouse and names him Mickey, but with his thick German accent it comes out as Mitkey. Mitkey is rescued from a rocket experiment by super-aliens who raise his intelligence to human level. Mitkey proposes that they make all mice super-smart, who would then take over Australia for their Lebensraum:

> "Ve vould call it Moustralia instead of Australia, und ve vould instead of Sydney call der capital Dissney, in honor of—"

"The Model of a Judge" (1953) is set in the future on a moon of Saturn that has been colonized by humans; but the business leaders, scientists, and politicians are all men, while the women are secretaries and housewives. Ronar, a wolflike alien predator with enhanced senses, is scientifically "reformed" and, with his superior taste, made the judge of a cake-baking contest:

> "My dear, he has the most exquisite sense of taste!"
> "I still don't understand."

"It's superhuman.... We could mix all sorts of spices—the most delicate, most exotic herbs from Venus or Mars, and the strongest, coarsest flavors from Earth or one of the plant-growing asteroids—and he could tell us everything we had added, and exactly how much."

"Dr. Birdmouse" (1962) is an exaggerated farce about any two species becoming able to breed with each other, resulting in characters like Mr. Snakepig, Miss Cowturtle, and Miss Moosevulture. But when the chuckles are over, it can make beginning furry writers think about the results of interspecies marriages.

"Shurman's Trek" (1994) is a drama of a colony of bioengineered elephants on a new homeworld who are forced to undertake a grueling trek to escape an interstellar war. Dr. Roberta Schurman, the human scientist in charge of "the Hathi project," and Clan-Mother Drini, the Hathis' matriarch, are the trek's unprepared leaders. Elephant herds have a matrilineal society, and this story features two strong female protagonists.

"MacGregor" (1994) is a savage parody; a combination of Beatrix Potter's gentle children's tales with futuristic ultra-bleak dystopian dramas:

Already Among Us: An Anthropomorphic Anthology **edited by Fred Patten (Legion Publishing, June 2012). The first reprint anthology of anthro animal stories from the sf magazines, with many of the stories that influenced early furry fans. Cover art by Roz Gibson.**

> His perch was high on a hill in the Lake District, near the village of Sawrey, in the western bioregion of the European Community.... To the south Peter could see the grounds of the Beatrix Potter epcot, otherwise known as the Garden.
>
> The two years—a fifth of his warranted lifespan—since his flight into the arms of the CLF had been packed with activity. On death's very doorstep from lack of diet-supplements, he had stumbled upon the London nucleus of the CLF just in time.

"Doggy Love" (2003) is a satire about pet dogs using their humans' home computers when they aren't looking, to establish a canine dating service. It's a condensed version of such feline novels of the time as *Feline Online* by Elyse Cregar, and *Cats in Cyberspace* by Beth Hilgartner (both 2001), which furry fans were discussing.

When I began selecting stories for *Already Among Us,* my goal was to include all of the sf magazine stories that furry fans had been recommending to each other for years. The only omission was one that was among the most popular of all; "Jerry Was a Man," by Robert A. Heinlein (1947). The Heinlein estate refused reprint permission; possibly because it was just about to be reprinted in a new edition of Heinlein's 1953 collection *Assignment in Eternity* (Baen Books, July 2012).

I edited a similar reprint anthology three years later, *An Anthropomorphic Century;*

Stories from 1909 to 2008 (FurPlanet Productions, 2015). Its 20 stories run from "Tobermory," by Saki (1909) to "The Wishing Tree" by Renee Carter Hall (2008), taken from sf and non-sf magazines, newspapers, original-fiction anthologies, and the Internet.

The Animal Fable in Science Fiction and Fantasy • by Bruce Shaw. Foreword by Van Ikin.

Jefferson, NC: McFarland, 2010, paperback, 268 pp.

This scholarly study, #20 in McFarland's *Critical Explorations in Science Fiction and Fantasy* series, edited by Donald E. Palumbo and C.W. Sullivan III, presents a literary and historical analysis of the theme of intelligent animals in modern (20th century) science fiction and fantasy:

> Though animal stories and fables stretch back into the antiquity of ancient India, Persia, Greece and Rome, the reasons for writing them and their resonance for readers (and listeners) remain consistent to the present. This work argues that they were essential sources of amusement and instruction—and were also often profoundly unsettling. Such authors in the realm of the animal fable as Tolkien, Freud, Voltaire, Bakhtin, Cordwainer Smith, Karel Čapek, Vladimir Propp, and many more are discussed [back-cover blurb].

Shaw begins with a brief discussion of the Beast Fable and the Animal Fable, from prehistoric times through Lucius' *The Golden Ass* (late 2nd century CE), the medieval *The Romance of Reynard the Fox* (12th century), Geoffrey Chaucer's "The Nun's Priest's Tale" (1386–87), Wu Ch'eng-en's *Monkey* (1590s), the animal fables of Jean de La Fontaine (17th century), and lots of 19th and 20th-century examples. Shaw next lists the scholars who have analyzed these fables and the importance of intelligent animals in literature: Mikhail Bakhtin, Vladimir Propp, Karel Čapek, and J.R.R. Tolkien. In the chapter "Philosophies of Laughter," he summarizes their arguments, concentrating upon "dialogism versus monologism, polyglossia, and carnivalization" (p. 19), with an emphasis upon the latter:

> Carnival, a word derived from the Italian, which in free translation means "to leave off eating meat" (*carne* = meat; *vale* = farewell –that is, "goodbye to flesh food") is associated with the popular Medieval festivals that took place immediately prior to Lenten fasting. During such festivities the authorities allowed a relaxation between the traditional social hierarchies so that commoners might make fun of their lords, kings and clerics without fear of the severe reprisals they could expect at other times of the year. Hence Carnival is associated with a relaxation of taboos, the dissolution of inequalities, and the subversion of authority that is brought about by turning accepted modes of conduct on their heads. Kings become commoners, the sacred becomes profane, and opposites, such as heaven and hell, fantasy and fact, are mingled (Selden 18–19) [p. 32].

Hence, stories with intelligent, talking animals rely heavily upon carnivalization; the acceptance of the fantastic reversal of the natural order, to make a philosophical point, or for pure amusement.

The chapters "The Lineage of the Animal Fable," "Recasting the Animal Fable: Short Stories," and "Recasting the Animal Fable: Novels and Novellas" briefly mention 19th and 20th-century examples in general literature such as Lewis Carroll's *Alice's Adventures in Wonderland* (1865), Anatole France's *Penguin Island* (1906), Saki's short story "Tobermory" (1909), and Franz Kafka's *The Metamorphosis* (1917); some previous related studies (Eugene La Faille's 1984 "Pawprints Across the Galaxy: Dogs in Science Fiction"); and lots and *lots* of sf stories with intelligent animals. David Brin, Philip K. Dick, and Andre Norton are frequently cited. Other authors include Poul Anderson (*Brain Wave*, 1954), Kirsten Bakis (*Lives of the Monster Dogs*, 1997), Fredric Brown ("Star Mouse," 1942), Kenneth Cook (*Play Little Victims*, 1978), Lester del Rey ("The Faithful," 1938), Gordon Dickson ("Dolphin's Way," 1964), Daniel Keyes ("Flowers for Algernon," 1959), William Kotzwinkle (*Doctor Rat*, 1976), Anne McCaffrey (*Decision at Doona*, 1969), Ian McDonald ("Floating Dogs," 1991), J.T. McIntosh (*The Fittest*, 1955), Will Self (*Great Apes*, 1997)—too many to list.

Though many authors and stories are mentioned, Shaw focuses upon six to examine in depth: Mikhail Bulgakov and *The Heart of a Dog* (1925), Karel Čapek and *War with the Newts* (1936), Olaf Stapledon and *Sirius: A Fantasy of Love and Discord* (1944), Peter Goldsworthy and *Wish* (1995), Clifford D. Simak and *City* (1952), and Cordwainer Smith and "The Dead Lady of Clown Town" (1964). Shaw first presents a chapter of biographies of these authors, placing them within their societies, and then analyzes—you might say dissects—each of these works. For example, in his analysis of *City* by Clifford D. Simak, Shaw says:

The Animal Fable in Science Fiction and Fantasy by Bruce Shaw (McFarland, 2010). A study of 20th-century sf and fantasy featuring intelligent animals. Cover art by Howard V. Brown, reprinted from *Startling Stories*, November 1939.

> There is an aesthetic appeal in Simak's style that makes many stories in *City* moving and satisfying to read. *City* contains allegory, parody, and some elements of the carnivalesque in the ways by which so many accepted ideas and practices are inverted, mainly gently in comparison to the violence in the works of Linebarger, Stapledon and Čapek, or Čapek's boisterousness, or the *canus agonistes* of Stapledon's character Sirius [p. 197].

These chapters run for over 120 pages of this 260-page book.

The focus of *The Animal Fable in Science Fiction and Fantasy* might be called academic rather than popular, with its scholarly concentration upon the 20th-century—in practical terms, before the existence of the "furry fandom" subculture. Yet Shaw does refer briefly to "The only bibliography [of animal-human tales in science fiction and fantasy] of greater comprehensiveness, to my knowledge, is one published on the Internet by Dan Lorey of Cornell University. Lorey (1–2) finds what he calls 'furry novels'—that is, novels 'containing at least one furry character/plot thread'" (p. 47). Shaw identifies this bibliography in his bibliography (p. 231) as having appeared on alt.fan.furry on March 20, 1995. So this study does contain a vague awareness of furry fandom—yet none regarding the literature produced by furry fandom.

As is de rigueur for any critical analysis, there is an extensive bibliography (16 pages) and an index (22 pp.). *The Animal Fable in Science Fiction and Fantasy* is well worth reading as a survey of intelligent-animal adult fantasy outside of and before the furry specialty press, which in practical terms meant the science fiction and fantasy genre.

Animal Farm: A Fairy Story • by George Orwell.

London: Secker & Warburg, August 1945, hardcover, 91 pp.

If there is one classic above all others in anthropomorphic literature, it is inarguably *Animal Farm*. This fable of how a group of animals revolts against their human masters, and develops their own (deeply flawed) civilization, has never been out of print since it was published in 1945. It was written by George Orwell (Eric Blair) as a parable of Stalin's betrayal and corruption of the Soviet revolution; but for enthusiasts of anthropomorphic fiction it stands as the definitive description of intelligent animals creating a joint society and trying to coexist with humans.

The animals of Manor Farm are oppressed by Mr. Jones, their drunken owner. Old Major, the ancient boar whom they all consider their philosophical mentor, argues that humans are a parasite which they can do without. But when Old Major dies, the animals continue to suffer until the night that Mr. Jones forgets to feed them and then beats them in a drunken frenzy. The animals revolt and chase every human from the farm, then are frightened yet giddy at their own success. They rename Manor Farm as Animal Farm, and determine to put into practice Old Major's goal of a society of animal equals, painting on the barn their Seven Commandments including "No animal shall kill any other animal" and "All animals are equal." A group of clever and enthusiastic pigs led by Napoleon and Snowball gradually emerge as the leaders of Animal Farm. When the neighboring farmers try to restore human mastery, Snowball leads the animals in the successful Battle of the Cowshed. Yet while Snowball is organizing grandiose projects to improve Animal Farm, Napoleon works on his own secret project of raising puppies into attack dogs loyal to him alone. He drives Snowball from the Farm, then presents himself as the savior of the animal's revolution from Snowball's treachery. Gradually the animals' equality is whittled down, the Seven Commandments are mysteriously changed (No animal shall kill any other animal *without cause*"), and the pigs' leadership is built up:

> Napoleon was now never spoken of simply as "Napoleon." He was always referred to in formal style as "our Leader, Comrade Napoleon," and the pigs liked to invent for him such titles as Father of All Animals, Terror of Mankind, Protector of the Sheep-fold, Ducklings' Friend, and the like.
>
> Years passed. The seasons came and went, the short animal lives fled by. A time came when there was no one who remembered the old days before the Rebellion, except Clover, Benjamin, Moses the raven, and a number of the pigs.... The farm was more prosperous now, and better organized: it had even been enlarged by two fields which had been bought from Mr. Pilkington.... But the luxuries of which Snowball had once taught the animals to dream, the stalls with electric light and hot and cold water, and the three-day week, were no longer talked about. Napoleon had denounced such ideas as contrary to the spirit of Animism. The truest happiness, he said, lay in working hard and living frugally.

This leads ultimately to the replacement of The Seven Commandments with the one well-known:

> ALL ANIMALS ARE EQUAL
> BUT SOME ANIMALS ARE MORE EQUAL THAN OTHERS

And the pigs teaching themselves to walk upon two legs, at which point the other animals can no longer tell them apart from their human oppressors.

Hundreds, if not thousands, of literary analyses of *Animal Farm* have been written since 1945 to point out the allegorical parallels: Old Major is a combination of Karl Marx and V.I. Lenin; Napoleon is Josef Stalin, who made himself the dictator of the Soviet Union and ruthlessly purged his rivals and enemies; Snowball is Leon Trotsky, whose early goals for the peoples' revolution were suppressed and whose propaganda turned into the peoples' enemy; Squealer, the pig who is Napoleon's news-announcer, is V.M. Molotov, the early editor of *Pravda*, the Communist Party's newspaper, who constantly rewrote history into whatever Stalin wanted it to say; Boxer, the cart horse who believes, "If Comrade Napoleon says it, it must be right," represents the Soviet masses who blindly trust Stalin, Mr. Pilkington of Pinchfield Farm and Mr. Frederick of Foxglove Farm, Animal Farm's off-again, on-again friends and enemies whom Napoleon plays off against each other are Great Britain and Nazi Germany; and so forth and so on. These are all true; yet they are incidental to *Animal Farm*'s status as a great story of intelligent animals of many species building their own society. Napoleon, Snowball, Squealer, Maximus and the other pigs; Boxer, Clover, and Mollie the horses; Benjamin the donkey; Muriel the goat; the sheep bleating, "Four legs good, two legs bad"—these are among the best-known characters in anthropomorphic literature. *Animal Farm* is a brilliant parable to those who get the 1910s to 1940s real-world references, and an equally riveting story to today's readers.

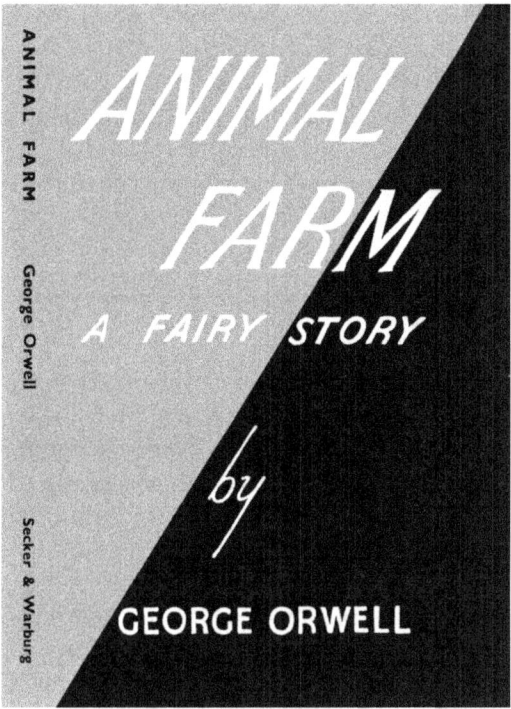

Animal Farm: A Fairy Story by George Orwell (Secker & Warburg, August 1945). The "some animals are more equal than others" classic that influenced many proto- and earliest furry fans. Cover art uncredited.

The story behind the novella (not a novel; it is only 30,000 words) is also well known. Orwell wrote it during 1944, but it was rejected by Britain's major publishers because it was such an obvious anti–Stalin polemic and the Soviet Union was still a wartime ally. Secker & Warburg, a minor publisher, finally accepted it, but because of wartime paper shortages it was not published until August 1945, and then in an edition of only 4,500 copies. It was an instant success, getting rave reviews and selling out within a month. Secker & Warburg rushed another 10,000 copies into print in November, as soon as they could get more paper; it became an American Book of the Month Club selection the next year; and it has gone on to one success after another.

Fans of *Animal Farm* may want to read two notable and very unauthorized pastiches. *Anarchist Farm* by "Jane Doe" (III Publishing, August 1996, 190 pages), is a pro-anarchist parable; "Pancho," a white pig (obviously Snowball incognito) escapes from Animal Farm to nearby Anarchist Farm where all animals are truly equal with no leaders. *Snowball's Chance* by John Reed (Roof Books, November 2002, 137 pages), is a cynical sequel in which Snowball returns and convinces the animals to replace socialism with capitalism, with both proving equally corrupt.

Animal Land: The Creatures of Children's Fiction • by Margaret Blount. Illustrated.

London: Hutchinson, October 1974, hardcover, 336 pp.

Today there are many academic studies of talking animals in children's literature. *Animal Land* was one of the first, and remains one of the best. Whether you look for the original British edition, the American edition (New York: William Morrow & Co., March 1975, hardcover, 336 pp.), or a reprint, *Animal Land* is worth reading. You may think you are already familiar with all the stories covered in it, but Margaret Blount has profiles of dozens that will be new to even talking-animal connoisseurs.

The book is divided into three parts: "Animal Fable," "Animal Fantasy," and "Animal Edens." "Animal Fable" discusses the primitive beginnings of talking animal tales. "The folklore story abounds in talking animals, clever animals that have an ambiguous or helpful role, or even appear to have private lives and families on the human model while coexisting with human masters, owners, or acquaintances. No one knows the origins of such stories, apart from the obvious racial strains which make a Japanese story different from an African, Danish, Scottish or English one." Blount considers the animal fable as basically a cautionary or moral parable. "There is not always an obvious moral either, but usually a certain rough justice, plenty of cruelty, deaths, mutilations and revenge." Tales of animal revenge against humans for specific to abstract cruelties range from "The Traveling Musicians" to Daphne du Maurier's/Alfred Hitchcock's *The Birds*. Blount traces the evolution of the animal fable from rough, anonymous folktales to cultured literary updates (Charles Perrault's "Puss in Boots"), and their artificial imitations by such authors as Hans Christian Andersen.

Stories discussed or analyzed in detail include Joel Chandler Harris' tales of Br'er Rabbit; the medieval Reynard the Fox fable, in particular as told by Chaucer ("Turn this story into Robin Hood, without any pretence of the hero being a 'good' character, and the feel is much the same"); and 19th century editions of Aesop's Fables as children's books, with Christian morals overlaid. This leads Blount to original 18th and 19th century stories for children in which talking animals preach didactic moral lessons: *Divine and Moral Songs for Children* by Isaac Watt, 1715 (parodied in *Alice's Adventures in Wonderland*), *Tommy Trip's History of Birds and Beasts* by John Newbery, 1760, *The Life and Perambulation of a Mouse* by Dorothy Kilner, 1784, *Fabulous Histories Designed for the Instruction of Children, Respecting Their Treatment of Animals* by Mrs. Trimmer, 1786 ("Mother Robin is rather a snob [...]"), etc., etc. Blount traces these to both better-told late 19th century moral stories such as Anna Sewell's *Black Beauty*, 1877, and to their 20th century equivalents.

"Four Satires" examines Jonathan Swift's *Gulliver's Travels*, 1726, Karel Čapek's *Insect Play*, 1923, George Orwell's *Animal Farm*, 1945, and Erich Kästner's *The Animals' Con-

ference, 1955. This is followed by "People with Heads," some stories with, or illustrated with, humans with animal heads; though Blount's examples also include some fantasy animals such as Carroll's Cheshire Cat and White Rabbit. "Most stories in this genre are lighthearted, some merely strange, and there is often a feeling that the medium has run away with the writer and the device was more interesting and important than the message." These range from *The Headlong Career and Woful Ending of Precocious Piggy* by Thomas Hood, 1859, to the later 19th century works of Edward Lear and Lewis Carroll, the animal-headed protagonists of British 20th century children's magazines such as the Bruin Boys and Rupert Bear, Don Marquis' archy the cockroach, and Walt Disney's classic anthropomorphic stars.

In "Animal Fantasy," Blount concentrates on famous literary works that depend upon talking animals. Many of these star the famous fantasy animals of mythology who interact with modern children, such as the fiery Phoenix in E. Nesbit's *The Phoenix and the Carpet*, 1904, and almost too many Unicorn children's novels to list. Blount includes here the then-popular British newspaper comic strip *Flook*, drawn by Wally Fawkes, 1948 to 1984, which featured a magical cute animal in adult satires on human foibles. To mention only highlights, further chapters cover "Dragons" (J.R.R. Tolkien's *Farmer Giles of Ham*, 1949), "Dressed Animals and Others" (Kenneth Grahame's *The Wind in the Willows*, 1905), "Lilliputian Life: The Mouse Story" (Margery Sharp's *The Rescuers*, 1959, and its sequels), "Only Toys" (A.A. Milne's *Winnie the Pooh*, 1926, and its sequels), "If Only They Could Speak: The Pet Story" (Hugh Lofting's *The Story of Dr. Dolittle*, 1922, and its sequels).

To list everything that Margaret Blount covers would make for an *extremely* long review. A few other highlights are Beatrix Potter's many animal books, Rudyard Kipling's *Jungle Book* tales and his *Thy Servant, a Dog*, Michael Bond's *Paddington Bear* series, E.B. White's *Stuart Little* and *Charlotte's Web*, Jean de Brunhoff's Babar the Elephant, Ernest Thompson Seton and "the humanized 'Nature' story," Dodie Smith's *One Hundred and One Dalmatians*, Tove Jansson's Moomintroll series, Maurice Sendak's *Where the Wild Things Are*, and "Fallen and Redeemed: Animals in the Novels of C.S. Lewis." For every novel or series Blount devotes several pages to, there are dozens of others briefly mentioned in less than a page. *Animal Land* contains over fifty illustrations taken from these stories, including classics such as John Tenniel's *Alice's Adventures in Wonderland* and Pauline Baynes' Narnian illustrations, and many others that will delight talking animal fans. Since this is a scholarly study, the book includes both a bibliography and an index.

If you want to read a book *about* talking animals rather than fiction starring them, and an excellent comprehensive survey of the genre (though a bit Anglocentric), *Animal Land* is definitely the place to start.

Anonymous Rex: A Detective Story • by Eric Garcia.
New York: Villiard Books, August 1999, hardcover, 276 pp.

Casual Rex: A Novel • by Eric Garcia.
New York: Villiard Books, March 2001, hardcover, 337 pp.

Hot and Sweaty Rex: A Dinosaur Mafia Mystery • by Eric Garcia.
New York: Villiard Books, March 2004, hardcover, 336 pp.

You have to admire an author who can make his novel compellingly readable when it ought to be ludicrously silly. The premise of *Anonymous Rex* and its sequels is that dinosaurs did not become extinct, but are still living in modern civilization, disguised as humans. Vincent Rubio, a seedy Los Angeles private investigator in the Sam Spade/Mike Hammer–style, is really a Velociraptor in a full-body human suit. A friend of his, a L.A.P.D. detective, is a Brontosaur in disguise. A Brontosaur passing as a human? That must be a *really good* full-body costume!

Unbelievable? Surely. But this book's publisher was also the publisher of Gary Wolf's second Roger Rabbit novel. You've heard of Roger Rabbit? That was also over-the-top fantastic. But it was very cleverly developed to carefully build plausible drama and suspense upon that outrageous scenario. Garcia's three *Dinosaur Mafia Mystery* novels are also that good. Those who will pretend to swallow the premise will find that it leads to a consistent, intelligent story that supports good drama:

> The Evolution Club—gotta be a dino joint, no two ways about it. We love shit like that, little in-jokes that make us feel oh-so-superior to the two-legged mammals with whom we grudgingly share dominance over the earth. My usual haunt is the Fossil Fuels Club in Santa Monica, but I've logged in some classically blurry early morning hours at the Dinorama, the Meteor Nightspot, and mid city's very own Tar Pit Club, just to name a few. The last Council estimate laid the dinosaur community out at about 5 percent of the American population, but I have a hunch we own a disproportionate amount of nightclubs in this country.

Rubio visits a patient at a hospital:

> "I'll have to—"
> "Announce me. I know." Standard protocol. Ward F is a special wing, set up by dino administrators and doctors who designed it so that our kind might have a sanctuary within the confines of a working hospital. There are dino health clinics all over the country, of course, but most major hospitals contain special wards in case one of us should be brought in for emergency treatment, as Mr. Burke was last Wednesday morning.
> The official story on Ward F is that it is reserved for patients with "special needs," a scope of circumstances ranging from religious preferences to round-the-clock bedside care to standard VIP treatment. This is a broad enough definition that it makes it easy for dino administrators to classify all their nonhumans as "special needs" patients, and thus move them and only them into the ward. All visitors—doctors included—must be announced to the nurses on staff (dinos in disguise, every one), ostensibly for privacy and security, but in actuality in defense against an accidental sighting. It sounds like a risky system, and every once in a while you'll hear some dino raise the roof about the chances that we take, but the whiners never come up with a better solution than the system we have now.

Garcia does try to keep the concept from being too implausible by postulating that, in the millions of years since the dinosaurs were "last seen," they have also been evolving, and they no longer are the behemoths shown in museums' paleontological recreations (which are themselves exaggerated due to deliberately faked fossil evidence by the dinos):

> A few moments after Vallardo buzzes his receptionist, we are joined by two Brontosaurs in human guise, introduced to me as Frank and Peter. Their costumes designate them as twins, and so far as I can tell from their comparable enormity, they may very well have been actual littermates as well. The evolutionary process that shrank the rest of us dinosaurs into somewhat manageable heights—some of us too manageable—didn't have as much an effect on Brontosaurs, resulting in their current status as the largest dinosaurs on earth. It is no wonder that so many of them play for the National Football League.

These three examples out of context may make *Anonymous Rex* look exposition-heavy and light on action and drama, but in context the novel moves briskly along. Once the rules of Rubio's world have been established, the story flows smoothly:

"Tell me something," she says, coming closer, hot breath on my throat. "Why do you find it necessary to stir up trouble?"

"Am I stirring? I thought it was more of a shake."

A pause. Will she kiss me or spit at me? Neither—the Coleophysis backs away. "You went to see Dr. Emil Vallardo, is that correct?"

"Considering your goons picked me up outside the medical center, I'd say you know it's correct." Without asking permission—enough with the permission—I squat up and down, up and down, trying to get feeling back in my legs. The Coleo pays my impromptu workout no mind.

"They're not my goons." Then, a moment later: "Dr. Vallardo is a twisted man, Vincent. Brilliant, but twisted. It would be better if you left him to work on his bastardization of nature by himself."

As that passage should hint, *Anonymous Rex* is more than a standard murder mystery with cute references that many of the characters are dinos in disguise. The scenario of a secret dinosaur society hidden within humanity, determined to keep its secret at all costs despite both curious humans and renegade dinos; and of characters with individualized dino-species attributes which they can take advantage of, is paramount to the case. This is a 'morphic novel in the best sense. I agree fully with whoever reviewed this book for *Publishers Weekly* (July 3, 1999, pg. 62): "You might not believe any of this 30 seconds after you close the covers, and at odd moments the narrative veers into shtick, but while it's going on you're mostly going to be dazzled by Garcia's energy and chutzpah."

Garcia's two other *Dinosaur Mafia Mysteries* are *Casual Rex* in 2001, and *Hot and Sweaty Rex* in 2004. *Casual Rex* was the winner of the first Ursa Major Award in the Best Novel category. It got Garcia invited to be the Guest of Honor at ConFurence 2002, which had "furry noir" as its theme.

archy and mehitabel • by Don Marquis. Illustrated by George Herriman.
New York: Doubleday, Page & Co., December 1927, hardcover, 206 pp.

archys life of mehitabel • by Don Marquis. Illustrated by George Herriman.
New York: Doubleday, Doran & Co., December 1933, hardcover, 190 pp.

archy does his part • by Don Marquis. Illustrated by George Herriman.
New York: Doubleday, Doran & Co., December 1935, hardcover, 280 pp.

the lives and times of archy and mehitabel • by Don Marquis. Illustrated by George Herriman.
New York: Doubleday, Doran & Co., July 1940, hardcover, 3 vol. in 1, 676 pp.

Don Marquis (1878–1937) was a popular and humorous author and newspaper/magazine columnist of the 1910s through the early 1930s. He was most famous for his columns about Archy the Cockroach and his associates, developed for the New York City newspaper *The Evening Sun* in 1916. As Marquis reported it in the opening of *archy and mehitabel*:

We came into our room earlier than usual in the morning, and discovered a gigantic cockroach jumping about upon the [typewriter] keys.

He did not see us and we watched him. He would climb painfully upon the framework of the machine and cast himself with all his force upon a key, head downward, and his weight and the impact of the blow were just sufficient to operate the machine, one slow letter after another. He could not work the capital letters, and he had a great deal of difficulty operating the mechanism that shifts the paper so that a fresh line may be started.

Since Archy could not operate the shift key, he became popular as "archy." All of his associates he wrote about—Mehitabel, the alley cat who claimed to be the reincarnation of Egyptian Queen Cleopatra, Freddy the rat who ate Archy's poems as literary criticism, Warty Bliggens the egomaniacal toad, Pete the pup, and others—became popular through Archy's lower-case writings.

Marquis wrote about other things in his daily column for *The Evening Sun* and later *The New York Tribune* in the 1920s, but his most popular columns were those about Archy and his associates. They were sometimes illustrated by the equally popular George Herriman, creator of the *Krazy Kat* comic strip. In 1927 Marquis collected the best of these into a book, *archy and mehitabel*. Later, Marquis moved from his newspaper columns to magazines like *Collier's* and *The Saturday Evening Post*, taking Archy and company with him. He wrote in his Introduction to *archys life of mehitabel*:

> A few years ago I collected a number of Archy's communications into a book, and this volume surprised me by selling thirty thousand copies at a time when "books were not selling." The characters appeared for two years in *Collier's Weekly* also, and they must have met with a response in that journal, for the editors insisted that I do them every week.

Marquis got two more books out of Archy, *archys life of mehitabel* in 1933 and *archy does his part* in 1935. The three books were reprinted together as *the life and times of archy & mehitabel* in 1940, which replaced all three. Marquis and his lively vermin lost their popularity toward the end of the 20th century, but many proto- and early furry fans were influenced by *the life and times of archy & mehitabel*.

Archy as the reincarnation of a free-verse poet allowed Marquis to express himself in that form. Most of Archy's free-verse poems in the three books are five to ten pages long. Archy often commented on then-topical events in Marquis' newspaper and magazine columns, but Marquis avoided most of these in the collections:

> i see things from the under side now
> thank you for the apple peelings in the wastepaper basket
> but your paste is getting so stale i can t eat it
> there is a cat here called mehitabel I wish you would have
> removed she nearly ate me the other night why don t she
> catch rats that is what she is supposed to be for
> there is a rat here she should get without delay

Most of Archy's "poems" describe the comings and goings of himself and the rats, frogs and other cockroaches around him, but every so often he rages as a cockroach against humanity, as in "the return of archy":

> where have i been so long
> you ask me
> i have been going up
> and down like the devil
> seeking what i might devour
> i am hungry always hungry
> and in the end i shall
> eat everything

> all the world shall come at
> last to the multitudinous maws
> of insects
> a civilization perishes
> before the tireless teeth
> of little little germs
> ha ha i have thrown off the mask
> at last
> you thought i was only
> an archy
> but i am more than that
> i am anarchy
> where have i been you ask
> i have been organizing the insects
> the ants the worms the wasps
> the bees the cockroaches
> the mosquitoes
> for a revolt against mankind
> i have declared war
> upon humanity
> i even i shall fling
> the mighty atom
> that splits a planet asunder
> […]

Fans were most impressed by this pre–1945 reference to the atom in warfare.

The first two books were the favorites. *archy does his part* is mostly Archy's topical comments on 1930s events such as the end of Prohibition and the beginning of FDR's presidency, which might be considered boring compared to the earlier books; but proto-fans did enjoy Archy's reference to Disney's 1933 *Silly Symphonies* cartoon *The Three Little Pigs* in "the big bad wolf":

> i went to a movie show
> the other evening in the cuff
> of a friends turned up trousers
> and saw the three little pigs
> and was greatly edified by the moral lesson […]

Bambi: A Life in the Woods • by Felix Salten. Translated by Whittaker Chambers. Foreword by John Galsworthy. Illustrated by Kurt Wiese.

London: Jonathan Cape; New York: Simon & Schuster, July 1928, hardcover, 293 pp.

Bambi's Children: The Story of a Forest Family • by Felix Salten. Translated by Barthold Fles; edited by R. Sugden Tilley. Illustrated by Erna Pinner.

Indianapolis, IN: Bobbs-Merrill, December 1939, hardcover, 315 pp.

Bambi: A Life in the Woods by Felix Salten (Siegmund Salzmann) was originally published as *Bambi: Eine Lebensgeschichte aus dem Walde* in Vienna in 1923. It is one of the novels that almost all proto- and early furry fans read that led to their being part of furry fandom. It is also one of the novels that is only arguably anthropomorphic, because the animals talk among themselves but are otherwise realistic.

This nature fantasy describes the birth and youth of a roe deer in a Central European forest. Bambi at first associates only with his mother:

> Once he asked, "Whom does this trail belong to, Mother?"
> His mother answered, "To us."
> Bambi asked again, "To you and me?"
> "Yes."
> "To us two?"
> "Yes."
> "Only to us two?"
> "No, " said his mother. "To us deer."
> "What are deer?" Bambi asked, and laughed.
> His mother looked at him from head to foot and laughed too. "You are a deer and I am a deer. We're both deer," she said. "Do you understand?"

Bambi listens to birds talking. Soon his mother leads him out of the forest to a meadow.

> "Walking on the meadow is not so simple," his mother went on. "It's a difficult and dangerous business. Don't ask me why. You'll find that out later on. Now do exactly as I tell you to. Will you?"
> "Yes," Bambi promised.
> "Good," said his mother. "I'm going out alone first. Stay here and wait. And don't take your eyes off me for a minute. If you see me run back here, then turn round and run as fast as you can. I'll catch up with you soon." She grew silent and seemed to be thinking. Then she went on earnestly, "Run anyway as fast as your legs will carry you. Run even if something should happen ... even if you should see me fall to the ground.... Don't think of me, do you understand? No matter what you see or hear, start running right away and just as fast as you possibly can. Do you promise me to do that?"
> "Yes," said Bambi softly. His mother spoke so seriously.

Bambi talks with a grasshopper and a butterfly. He meets a Hare who addresses him as a young prince. He and his mother meet his aunt Ena and her fawns Faline and Gobo. They gambol and play together. They are awestruck by the sight of adult stags.

Months pass, and summer turns to autumn. The mother deer leave their fawns to live alone while they go to the stags. Bambi, Gobo, and Faline console themselves together. The mothers return, but the fawns learn to become self-reliant. Bambi sees his father, the old Prince, but he is confused when all the other animals express fear of Him:

> Bambi looked around. His mother was no longer there.
> "What are they talking about now?" thought Bambi. "I can't understand what they are talking about. Who is this 'He' they talk about? That was He, too, that I saw in the bushes, but He didn't kill me."

Winter comes, beautiful but very cold:

> But Bambi soon stopped being pleased with the snow. For it grew harder and harder to find food. He had to paw the snow away with endless labor before he could find one withered little blade of grass. The snow crust cut his legs and he was afraid of cutting his feet.

All the animals get into a blind panic when "He" comes. After, Gobo is gone and "Bambi never saw his mother again."

Spring comes, and leaves and grass grow again. Bambi develops antlers. As spring turns to summer, the young bucks spar instead of playing together, and Bambi and Faline develop feelings for each other. Gobo reappears; he explains that He rescued him during the winter, and that they have nothing to fear from Him. But when a jay cries danger and Gobo refuses to flee with the others, he is killed.

The seasons change again. Bambi becomes solitary:

> Bambi kept silent. But a gentle anxious curiosity was stirring in him, too. He wanted to ask about Faline, about Aunt Ena, and Ronno and Karus, about all his childhood companions. But he kept silent.
> The squirrel still sat in front of him, studying him. "What antlers!" he cried admiringly. "What antlers! Nobody in the whole forest, except the old Prince, has antlers like that."

At the conclusion, the old Prince gives way to Bambi. Bambi meets two newborn fawns who remind him of Faline and himself when they were fawns. The reader will recognize them as Bambi's and Faline's children.

Many Americans are more familiar with *Bambi* through the 1942 Walt Disney animated film, which turns the setting into a North American forest and Bambi into a North American white-tailed deer. But a deer is a deer, and *Bambi: A Life in the Woods* feels at home on both continents.

Salten followed his first *Bambi* with *Bambi's Children: The Story of a Forest Family*. Now Bambi and Faline are the adult deer who educate their twin fawns, Geno and his sister Gurri. They talk with other forest animals, and learn more about Him; the differences between hunters and poachers, and gamekeepers and others who protect the deer. But it was not published until eleven years later, and is not as well-known as the first.

Barsk: The Elephants' Graveyard • by Lawrence M. Schoen.

New York: Tom Doherty Associates/Tor Books, December 2015, hardcover, 384 pp.

The Moons of Barsk • by Lawrence M. Schoen.

New York: Tom Doherty Associates/Tor Books, August 2018, hardcover, 430 pp.

In the very far future, civilization has spread throughout the galaxy, but there are no longer any humans. Humanity has been replaced by the descendants of uplifted animals.

Chapter One, "A Death Detoured," features Rüsul, an elderly Fant, alone and naked, on a raft six days at sea. He is on his death journey, the traditional final rite of passage of every Fant on the world of Barsk. Rüsul expects to sail alone until he dies. He does not expect to be picked up by a spaceship of Cans (canines; Dogs) commanded by a Cheetah, Nonyx-Captain Selishta. She tells her Cans, "'Maybe this one will know something useful about whatever shrubs and leaves the drug comes from. Hold him here a moment while the rest of the crew secures his flotsam, and then put him below in one of the vacant isolation cells."

The importance of Barsk's drug, koph, is explained in Chapter Four, "Solutions in Memory," in this description of Lirlowil the Otter and her ability to talk with the dead:

> Beautiful by Otter standards, she'd spent the last few years enjoying the peaks of privilege earned not by any acts of her own, but by the random chance that gifted her with being able to both read minds and talk with the dead. Unless you had the misfortune to be one of those disgusting Fant on Barsk, you could go your entire life without encountering a Speaker. The drug that triggered the ability was fiendishly expensive, and rarely worked the first few times. Alliance science had yet to determine what genetic markers resulted in the talent. Off Barsk, Speakers were unlikely, though hardly uncommon. True telepaths though, people who could effortlessly slip inside the mind of other beings and sample their memories and knowledge as easily as flipping the pages of a book, were orders of magnitude more rare.

The number of individuals with both sets of abilities would make for a very small dinner party indeed. Lirlowil's mental gifts emerged with puberty and elevated her social status a thousand-fold. The discovery that her talents included Speaking occurred a couple of years later when she'd sampled some koph at a party and began seeing nefshons over the next hour's time.

Nefshons are the "shimmering subatomic particles of memory," the relics of personality that constitute what is left of the dead. Taking koph enables those with the genetic ability to become a Speaker to pull together those nefshons from the dead and talk with them. Speakers are very sought after in galactic society by all who want to contact the dead: relatives who want to speak to loved ones, law enforcement officers who need to speak with the fatal victims of crimes, historians who want to interview illustrious deceased notables. Speakers are notable themselves, and they can charge almost anything for their talents. They need koph to energize those talents. Therefore koph is "fiendishly expensive." And it is found only on Barsk, which is inhabited by the disgusting Fant, who are disgusting because of their enormous size, because of their ugly, wrinkled, furless skin (furlessness alone is enough to render anyone hideously ugly in this galactic society), and because of those horrible long, prehensile noses and great, flapping ears that only the Fant have.

Everyone wants koph, and since only the despised Fant can deliver it, some among the galaxy's Bears, Elk, Yak, Prairie Dogs, Cats, and other peoples (all furred) will do anything to get it. Nonyx-Captain Selishta, the Cheetah, is one who will fly down to proscribed Barsk to kidnap Fant and try to force them to reveal the origins of koph—which none of her victims know. Lirlowil the Otter, a pampered Speaker, is grabbed by galactic bureaucracy and made to use her Speaker talent to call up the nefshons of deceased Fant that may know how koph is made, so it can be manufactured for the benefit of society. And on Barsk, the Fant Speaker Jorl and the crippled Fant child Pizlo each tries in his own way to unlock the secrets of koph, nefshons, and the dead.

It's a vast and colorful galactic society:

> Jorl's head turned so quickly toward this voice that his trunk nearly slapped the third Dog in front of him, causing that one to flinch, duck, and fall onto his ass. Jorl frowned. Cans were fiercely loyal and disciplined; they made up the bulk of the Patrol, but they were almost never in charge. Standing now in the gate, the source of the responding question, was a Cheetah. Unlike the Dogs, she wore neither hood nor mask. The blue of her gear proclaimed her officer status, and the molded insignia at her elbows, distinct to the initiated but easily missed if you didn't know to look, marked her rank.
>
> Urs-Major Krasnoi bent at the knees and staggered, pulling away from the senator's aide. A trio of gleaming metal talons extended just beyond her fingertips for an instant before vanishing back within her clothes. The Bear's eyes bulged as he fell back onto the snowy ground, dead.
>
> "You and you," Bish [a Yak] pointed at the two nearest Ailuros. "See to this body and carry it to my personal ship. Druz [a Sloth], take charge of cleaning up this mess. I want any sign that we were ever here to be gone."

Barsk is unusual in being an interstellar novel from a major science-fiction publisher, Tor Books, that began as two stories in a furry fanzine almost thirty ago. "Of Storm and Furry: Peals and Vents" in *Mythagoras* #2, Summer 1990, and "Of Storm and Furry: Contemporary Past" in *Mythagoras* #3, Autumn 1990. From two short stories in a tiny fanzine to a well-received hardcover book is an impressive step; and *Barsk* is an impressive anthropomorphic book. It was a SFWA 2015 Nebula Award finalist, and it won the 2015 Cóyotl Award for Best Novel.

The Moons of Barsk presents a wider scope: the hatred of the other 85 species of the

Alliance for the Fant, their determination to kill them all, and the effort of the Fant to survive, as seen through Jorl and Pizlo. There is one more *Barsk* novel to come.

The Bees • by Laline Paull. Frontispiece, bee illustrations from Meyers Konversations-Lexikon 1897.

New York: HarperCollinsPress/Ecco, May 2014, hardcover, 340 pp.

> The man stared through the trees, not listening.
> "There—thought for a moment it had vanished."
> An old wooden beehive stood camouflaged against the trees. The woman drew back.
> "I won't come any closer," she said. "I'm a bit funny about insects."

The reader knows from the beginning that the orchard hive is on an old, out-of-business farm being sold, to be demolished so its land can be added to a light-industrial complex. But the bees in the old wooden beehive don't know it.

Flora 717 has just been born, in a shabby Arrivals Hall meant for the hive's lower-class workers:

> Row upon row of cells like hers stretched into the distance, and there the cells were quiet but resonant, as if the occupants still slept. Immediately around her was great activity, with many recently broken and cleared-out chambers and many more cracking and falling as new bees arrived. The differing scents of her neighbors also came into focus, some sweeter, some sharper, all of them pleasant to absorb.
> With a hard, erratic pulse in the ground, a young female came running down the corridor between the cells, her face frantic.
> #"Halt!"# Harsh voices reverberated from both ends of the corridor and a strong astringent scent rose in the air. Every bee stopped moving except the young female, who stumbled and fell across Flora's pile of debris. Then she clawed her way into the remains of the broken cell and huddled in the corner, her little hands up.
> Cloaked in a bitter scent that hid their faces and made them identical, dark figures strode down the corridor toward Flora. Pushing her aside, they dragged out the weeping young bee. At the sight of their spiked gauntlets, a spasm of fear in Flora's brain released more knowledge. They were police.
> #'You fled inspection.'# One of them pulled at the girl's wings so another could examine the four still-wet membranes. The edge of one was shriveled.
> "Spare me," she cried. "I will not fly; I will serve in any other way—"
> #"Deformity is evil. Deformity is not permitted."#
> Before the young bee could speak the two officers pressed her head down until there was a sharp crack. She hung limp between them and they dropped her body in the corridor.
> #"You."# Their peculiar rasping voice addressed Flora. She did not know which one spoke, so she stared at the black hooks on the backs of their legs. #"Hold still."# Long black calipers slid from their gauntlets and they measured her height. #"Excessive variation. Abnormal."#
> "That will be all, officers." At the kind voice and fragrant smell, the police released Flora. They bowed to a tall and well-groomed bee with a beautiful face.
> #"Sister Sage. This one is obscenely ugly."#
> #"And excessively large—"#
> "It would appear so. Thank you officers, you may go."
> Sister Sage waited for them to leave. She smiled at Flora.

Bees are controlled so much by instinct that it is very difficult to realistically anthropomorphize them. But it has been done, in *A Hive for the Honeybee*, by Soinbhe Lally (original Irish edition, February 1996; U.S. edition, March 1999), and the award-winning 1998–1999 five-issue comic book *Clan Apis* by Dr. Jay Hosler, a neurobiologist specializing in the study of honeybees, collected into a 158-page graphic novel in January 2000. And now there is Laline Paull's complex dystopian *The Bees*.

Although the bees do not know that their hive is in danger from humans, they are aware of other, natural threats such as a season of excessive cold and rain.

Every bee in the hive has its place and its occupation from birth. "Accept, Obey, and Serve" is their mantra. The bees accept this without thinking, and the hive's police ruthlessly kill any who deviate from the norm physically or mentally. Flora 717, born to be a lowly sanitation worker, is one of those deviates; but before the police can weed her out, she is taken under the protection of Sister Sage, a high-ranking member of the hive's Melissae priesthood. (In pre-Christian Greece, one of the goddess Aphrodite's attributes was Melissa, the Queen bee, and her priestesses were called the Melissae. *The Bees* contains references to more than just the scientific study of bees.)

Sister Sage excuses her defense of Flora 717 by saying that she needs her for an experiment. Due to the bees' unquestioning obedience, she is never asked to explain. Flora's differences include the ability to wonder and question beyond a sanitation worker's usual duties. These are usually forbidden, but Sister Sage recognizes that her ability to learn, plus her courage and strength, are assets that the hive needs during this unusually cold and damp summer, so she is permitted to survive. When the experiment is ended, Flora is still protected by Sister Sage's sponsorship. She begins to live her own life, and to take on different roles within the hive.

But there is one difference that cannot be permitted. When Flora feels the urge to produce fertile eggs after her meeting with the hive's drones, breaking the commandment that only the Queen may bring future life to the hive, she knows that she must lay them and mix them in with the royal brood in secrecy lest she be torn apart. This becomes harder and harder as her larvae are discovered.

The Bees mixes episodes of Flora's adventures outside the hive—escaping from bee-eating crows, attacks by vicious wasps, a deadly hailstorm, the dangers of a nearby human city, the theft of their honey by a human beekeeper—with her surreptitious laying of her forbidden eggs.

Flora's personal championship of her child becomes submerged within the apocalyptic chaos of the death of the old Queen, the ritual fight for supremacy of two princesses to become the new Queen, a civil war between two worker castes, and more. *The Bees* is an anthropomorphic fantasy based on realistic bee behavior—and, as is well-known, realistic nature ain't pretty. *The Bees* was a finalist for the 2014 Cóyotl Award for Best Novel.

Best in Show: Fifteen Years of Outstanding Furry Fiction • edited by Fred Patten. Illustrated.

St. Paul, MN: Sofawolf Press, July 2003, paperback, 455 pp.

Furry! The Best Anthropomorphic Stories Ever • edited by Fred Patten.

New York: iBooks, February 2006, paperback, 445 pp.

Best in Show (2003) is the first anthology of short fiction from the fanzines and amateur magazines of the new furry fandom. It was published by Sofawolf Press, one of the first of the new furry specialty small presses. Patten's seventeen pages of Introduction, Afterword, and Bibliography provided the first history of furry fandom and a detailed

Internet "where to find it" list. (The latter is now very dated, but it was valuable at the time.)

The book was a major sensation in the subculture when it first appeared. It won the 2003 Ursa Major Award in the Best Anthropomorphic Other Literary Work (not a novel or short fiction) category. The book's cover by Ursula Vernon also won a 2003 Ursa Major Award, in the Best Anthropomorphic Published Illustration category.

It presents twenty-six short stories from the first fifteen years of furry publications, 1987 to 2002. (Actually the earliest story was from *FurVersion* #16, May 1989. No stories from *FurVersion* #1, May 1987, to #15 were considered good enough to reprint.) Practically all of the short-lived furry magazines of the 1990s, the amateur press associations, and the new Internet are represented: *Alternate Realms, Anthrolations, The Ever-Changing Palace, Fang, Claw, & Steel, Fantastic Furry Stories, FurryPhile, FURthest North Crew, Historimorphs, Morphic Tales, Mythagoras, North American Fur, Pawprints Fanzine,* Raven Blackmane's *Raven's Lair* website, *Rowrbrazzle, Tales from the Tai-Pan Universe, Yarf!,* and *Zoomorphica.*

Best in Show: Fifteen Years of Outstanding Furry Fiction edited by Fred Patten (Sofawolf Press, July 2003). The first anthology of stories from the furry fanzines and magazines. Winner of the 2003 Ursa Major Awards for Best Other Literary Work and Best Published Illustration. Cover art by Ursula Vernon.

Most of the authors then in furry fandom are also represented. Except for the fact that most literary magazines, including the sf magazines, did not accept stories with talking animals, these stories were good enough to be professionally sold. At least a half-dozen of the authors have gone on to write multiple books and magazine stories.

Best in Show is a high-quality showcase for the authorship in furry fandom during the 1990s. It is divided into three sections: "Living Together: Furries and Humans," "Living Apart: Alternate Furry Worlds," and "Living Within: Transformation." Each section has a new Introduction, by Tim Susman, Gene Breshears, and Phil Geusz.

"Living Together," about humans and anthropomorphic animals living in a joint civilization, contains ten stories: "To the Magic Born" by Brian W. Antoine, "Foxy Lady" by Lawrence Watt-Evans, "The Color of Rain" by Gene Breshears, "Crucible" by Kim Liu. "How George Miles Almost Saved the World" by Watts Martin, "Canis Major" by

Michael H. Payne, "A Snapshot from Fayetteville" by Mick Collins, "Wings" by Todd G. Sutherland, "Respect the Sea" by Jeff Eddy, and "The Boar Goes North" by Matt Posner.

"Living Apart," about civilizations of anthropomorphic animals alone, has twelve stories: "Port in a Storm" by Robert K. Carspecken, "Rosettes and Ribbons" by M.C.A. Hogarth, "Painted Memories" by Conrad Wong, "Recruiting" by Elizabeth McCoy, "Rat's Reputation" by Michael H. Payne, "Whimper's Law" by Craig Hilton, "Beneath the Crystal Sea" by Brock Hoagland, "Secret Weapon" by Allan Kitchen, "Mercy to the Cubs: A Tale of the Furkindred" by Chas. P.A. Melville, "Messenger" by Mel. White, "Castlefail" by Jefferson P. Swycaffer, and "Repas du Vivant" by Axel Shaikman.

"Living Within: Transformation," about humans turning into anthropomorphic (or at least thinking) animals, has four stories: "Graduation Day" by Phil Geusz, "Top of the Mountain" by Ben Goodridge, "Find the Beautiful" by Tim Susman, and "Little Monster" by Tom Turrittin.

Ten of the stories are illustrated with their original magazine illustrations, by Conrad Wong, Dave Bryant, Kylen Christine Miles, Jennie Hofer, Margaret Carspecken, Vicky M. Wyman, Jonathan Kaufman, and John Nunnemacher.

The twenty-six stories run the gamut from humans and anthropomorphic animals living together peacefully, to humans oppressing anthropomorphic animals as a subservient class, anthropomorphic animals dominating humans, anthropomorphic animals of many species living together, animals divided by their species, humans turning into anthropomorphic animals against their wills, and humans deliberately turning themselves into animals. *Best in Show* was meant as leisure reading, but it was also an example in 2003 of Do It Yourself writing for any furry fans who might assume that professional-quality anthropomorphic writing had to come from "real" authors in mainstream publications.

One aspect of furry fandom that *Best in Show* inadvertently illustrated was that the subculture had not yet adopted its emphasis on fursona identities. The stories are written under their authors' real names (or, in a couple of cases, realistic-sounding pseudonyms). The vogue for flamboyantly exaggerated pseudonyms would come a few years later.

Best in Show went through three printings almost immediately, via Sofawolf Press' online catalogue and at convention sales tables. It was the first furry press book reprinted for the general public. That publisher, iBooks, licensed it for a mass-market edition, retitled *Furry! The Best Anthropomorphic Stories Ever* (the cover had a variant title: *Furry! The World's Best Anthropomorphic Fiction!*) in 2006, with new introductory matter by Patten for the general public rather than the furry fan, and without the interior art. Unfortunately, the owner of iBooks was killed in a traffic accident seven months before its publication. *Furry!* was the last book that iBooks released before declaring bankruptcy and going out of business permanently. But *Furry!* had been shipped before iBooks disappeared, and for years it could be bought on Amazon, or in bookshops throughout the world.

The *Furry!* edition is still available as of this writing, while the 2003 *Best in Show* has become a sought-after collectable.

Bête • by Adam Roberts.
London: Gollancz, September 2014, hardcover, 311 pp.

> As I raised the bolt-gun to its head the cow said: "Won't you at least Turing-test me, Graham?"
>
> "Don't call me Graham," I told it. "My wife calls me Graham. My mum calls me Graham. Nobody else."
>
> "Oh, *Mister* Penhaligon," the cow said, sarcastically. We'll have to assume, for the moment, that cows are capable of sarcasm. "It won't much delay you. And if I fail, then surely, go ahead: bye-bye-*bos-taurus*. But!"
>
> "You're not helping your case," I said, "by enunciating so clearly. You don't sound like a cow."
>
> "Moo," said the cow, arching one hairless eyebrow.

Graham Penhaligon is a farmer. Farmers traditionally slaughter their cattle and serve them at family meals. So Farmer Penhaligon kills his cow, despite its pleading to him to spare it. And finds himself arrested for maybe-murder. Which he expects.

Bête is set in the near future, when the animal-rights movement—specifically an organization called Deep Blue Deep Green (DBDG)—is going about surreptitiously raising some animals' intelligence to force the courts to decide whether an animal with artificially raised intelligence is a legal person. The courts have declared a moratorium on the killing of such animals while the legal debate goes on; which has been going on for seemingly forever.

Farmer Penhaligon is a quietly angry man. He is at least a third-generation farmer. His parents and grandparents were farmers before him. It's what society has taught him is approved and Right. He resents being caught up in a social movement to make him a villain and Wrong. And to be expected to put his whole way of life on hold while the courts dither for years. So he does what he has always done: kills and butchers the cow:

> I was halfway through this procedure when the police arrived. I suppose the DBDG Environmentalists had alerted them, or maybe the chip had called them direct. At any rate, there were two officers leaning on the gate, and they were polite in that disdainful way unique to British coppers. They called my name, and then they called it again, and I stomped out of the shed to face them. Inevitably disconcerting to be interviewed by the police when you're wearing oilskin overalls that are literally covered in dripping gore.
>
> Was I aware (that ponderous law enforcement voice) that Parliament had legislated? That slaughter of the so-called "canny cows" was to be suspended? Pending the decision of the Supreme Court on the legality or otherwise of, etc., etc.? I said I followed the news.

Since the courts are still dithering, killing an intelligent cow isn't murder, yet. At worst, Penhaligon is guilty of "breaching the terms of the Canny Cow Stay of Execution Order; a fine, if you're cooperative, but two months in prison if you're not." Penhaligon expects to pay his fine, or to serve his short sentence, and to get on with his farmer's life. But it's too late for that:

> My case had generated some media interest. A picket of Radical Vegetarians booed me as I left the police station. At least I *think* they were booing me. They may have been mooing at me. My phone, when the Law returned it to me, was clogged with messages from papers and iZines keen for a soundbite or an interview. It was a hot-button issue, I suppose. I was in no mood to talk to anybody; I got into the car too furious to drive, and Rosemary steered us both home.

Bête—in the book, the word comes to mean an intelligent animal, though in reality, it means "stupid" in French—covers many years. Penhaligon keeps his farm as long as is economically possible, and finally sells it to a woman who is murdered three months later, apparently by a rat bête. Penhaligon takes a series of odd jobs, is divorced, becomes a wandering loner. The novel becomes both his personal story and his story of the changing society around him:

> I remember having lunch in a pub. The news was being displayed on a screen that all the animals in London Zoo had been chipped. Eco-activists had smuggled chips into Monkey World, in Dorset,

tucked into pallets of bananas. The chip was barely visible to the naked eye, and moved from the mouth to the roof of the mouth whilst the animals chewed, and implanted itself far back, afterwards growing calcium connective filaments that webbed into the brain. This latter process took a week or so, but soon enough the monkeys all became talkative bêtes. Three circuses had closed because their performing animals were, quote, making inappropriate invitations to audience members, unquote. A man was put on trial in Newcastle for bestiality: he had been having sex with his pet Irish setter, which was illegal under the meaning of the act. His barrister was able to call the dog as a witness; its paws hooked over the top of the witness box, its hindlegs shaking a little with the effort of standing. The hound confirmed its consent in the matter. The man walked free. On the court steps he made a long speech about the love that dare not bark its name, and of the need to petition Parliament to make the marriage between a human and a canny bête legal.

Bête is a marvelously inventive novel, keeping you wondering how far society in general and Graham Penhaligon in particular will go. It is well worth finding out.

Bête may seem more like fantasy than science fiction because of all the talking animals. Raising an animal's intelligence to human level would not give it the vocal apparatus to talk. Roberts has thought of that: "My mouth is a lot more flexible than yours," said the cow. "My tongue is longer and much more maneuverable. Plus I have a four-compartment stomach designed to release cud for rechewing, so I can augment breath sounds with gastric gas release sounds. Human phonemes are a doddle." Rats can't talk, of course, but monkeys, dogs—you'd be surprised at what an animal can do once it puts its mind to it.

Bête is Adam Roberts' fifteenth novel since 2001. He has been nominated for the Arthur C. Clarke Award three times, and has won both the BSFA (British Science Fiction Association) Award for Best Novel, and the John W. Campbell Memorial Award. *Bête* was a finalist for the 2014 Cóyotl Award for Best Novel.

Black Beauty: His Grooms and Companions. The Autobiography of a Horse. Translated from the Original Equine • by Anna Sewell. Frontispiece by C. Hewitt.

London: Jarrold and Sons, November 1877, hardcover ("2/—in cloth boards, ⅔ in extra board, gilt edges"), 247 pp.

When furry fandom started, it was common for fans to ask each other, "What books have you read?" Most fans were animal-lovers who had read the same literary classics and sf books, whether the animals had been anthropomorphized or not. Almost everyone had read *The Call of the Wild* (1903) and *White Fang* (1906) by Jack London, which clearly were not.

But what about fantasies where the animals talked to each other but were otherwise realistic, like *Black Beauty* by Anna Sewell (1877) or *Bambi: A Life in the Woods* by Felix Salten (1928)? Fans disagreed over whether they should be considered anthropomorphic or not; but everyone had read them, and they were beloved.

Black Beauty is written as an autobiography of a domesticated horse in Victorian England:

> The first place that I can well remember was a large pleasant meadow with a pond of clear water in it. Some shady trees leaned over it, and rushes and water-lilies grew at the deep end. Over the hedge on one side we looked into a ploughed field, and on the other we looked over a gate at our master's house, which stood by the roadside; at the top of the meadow was a plantation of fir trees, and at the bottom a running brook overhung by a steep bank.
>
> Whilst I was young I lived upon my mother's milk, as I could not eat grass. In the day time I ran

by her side, and at night I lay down close by her. When it was hot, we used to stand by the pond in the shade of the trees, and when it was cold, we had a nice warm shed near the plantation.

[The floating semicolon (;) is deliberate. It was a peculiarity of the first publisher.]
　The horses talk from almost the start:

One day, when there was a great deal of kicking, my mother whinnied to me to come to her, and then she said:
　"I wish you to pay attention to what I am going to say to you. The colts who live here are very good colts, but they are cart-horse colts, and, of course, they have not learned manners. You have been well bred and well born ; your father has a great name in these parts, and your grandfather won the cup two years at the Newmarket races; your grandmother had the sweetest temper of any horse I ever knew, and I think you have never seen me kick or bite. I hope you will grow up gentle and good, and never learn bad ways ; do your work with a good will, lift your feet up well when you trot, and never bite or kick even in play."
　I have never forgotten my mother's advice ; I knew she was a wise old horse, and our master thought a great deal of her. Her name was Duchess, but he often called her Pet.

When he is four years old, Beauty is broken by Squire Gordon to be used as a gentle carriage horse. There are many adventures, such as a stable fire and a nighttime ride for a doctor. But Beauty is sold to a progression of masters, or entrusted to different grooms, some of whom are better than others. His life goes downhill:

The farrier ordered all the litter to be taken out of my box day by day, and the floor kept very clean. Then I was to have bean mashes, a little green meat, and not so much corn, till my feet were well again. With this treatment I soon regained my spirits, but Mr. Barry was so much disgusted at being twice deceived by his grooms, that he determined to give up keeping a horse, and to hire when he wanted one. I was therefore kept till my feet were quite sound, and then was sold again.

Beauty becomes a London cab-horse, then a cart-horse of a master who does not take care of him:

One day I was loaded more than usual, and part of the road was a steep uphill: I used all my strength, but I could not get on, and was obliged continually to stop. This did not please my driver, and he laid his whip on badly. "Get on, you lazy fellow," he said, "or I'll make you."
　Again I started the heavy load, and struggled on a few yards ; again the whip came down, and again I struggled forward. The pain of that great cart whip was sharp, but my mind was hurt quite as much as my poor sides. To be punished and abused when I was doing my very best was so hard, it took the heart out of me. A third time he was flogging me cruelly, when a lady stepped quickly up to him, and said in a sweet, earnest voice—
　"Oh ! pray do not whip your good horse any more ; I am sure he is doing all he can, and the road is very steep, I am sure he is doing his best."

Beauty is overworked until he falls in the street:

In the evening I was sufficiently recovered to be led back to Skinner's stables, where I think they did the best for me they could. In the morning Skinner came with a farrier to look at me. He examined me very closely and said—
　"This is a case of overwork more than disease, and if you could give him a run off for six months, he would be able to work again ; but now there is not an ounce of strength in him."
　"Then he must just go to the dogs," said Skinner, "I have no meadows to nurse sick horses in—he might get well or he might not ; that sort of thing don't suit my business."

Beauty is finally sold to a kindly farmer, whose groom recognizes Beauty from having cared for him as a lad. Beauty is given a peaceful retirement.
　Black Beauty has many equine conversations, most often between Black Beauty and

his stablemates Merrilegs and Ginger, and sometimes other horses. Captain, a former military charger, tells his personal experience of the Charge of the Light Brigade at Balaclava in the Crimean War. The book is anthropomorphic enough for most fans.

The Blood Jaguar • by Michael H. Payne.

New York: Tom Doherty Associates/Tor Books, December 1998, hardcover, 256 pp.

Rat's Reputation • by Michael H. Payne. Illustrated by Louvelex.

St. Paul, MN: Sofawolf Press, July 2015, paperback, 367 pp.

The earliest story from the pioneering furry fanzines of the late 1980s and 1990s that is in *Best in Show* (2003), the first anthology of short fiction for furry fandom, was Michael H. Payne's "Rat's Reputation" from *FurVersion* #16, May 1989. *Rat's Reputation* the novel is Payne's fixup and expansion of all his "*Around About Ottersgate*" short fiction featuring Rat and his neighbors of the animal community of Ottersgate and environs. It's also his second novel in the "*Around About Ottersgate*" world, following *The Blood Jaguar* (Tor Books, December 1998; reprinted Sofawolf Press, June 2012).

> The rustling grew louder, seemed to come closer, and Alphonse [a gypsy squirrel] stopped as the ground started to shake.
> An earthquake? He'd been through a couple when the caravan traveled out west, but here?
> The shaking grew more violent with each passing second, and he was huddling down, glad he was out in the woods where nothing could really fall on him, when with a crash like a landslide, something tore out of the ground ahead, molten rock fountaining all fire-red and ash-black up over his head to smash into the trees, cracking and falling in a perfect circle around the pit of lava that yawned open, a sudden sulfurous stink plastering Alphonse's face.
> Then everything froze, Alphonse blinking to clear his eyes, a lumpy mass of darkness rising from the pit, its vast golden eyes swinging around to fix on Alphonse. The silence went on and on until a voice spoke, soft and rough as a step into sandy soil: "I reckon you know who I am, son."
> Alphonse could only nod.

When the High Ones call you, you come. When the High Ones give you a duty, you do that duty. Alphonse's duty is to find the baby rat on the streambank and raise him up. Except that the rat isn't a baby; he's four years old.

The story skips to when Rat is an adolescent. He's miserable. He doesn't have a name; the gypsy squirrels consider him unique enough among them that Rat is sufficient. He can't talk High Sciurid properly; his mouth is shaped wrong: "He tried to say 'beautiful,' but as usual his tongue got in the way of his teeth, making him cringe with sudden pain." He gets blamed for everything. Mostly it's prejudice due to the bad reputation that rats have always had: "She gave a sniff. 'Rats are nothing but pirates and thieves; my daddy and all my storybooks say so.'"

Rat's Reputation covers most of Rat's very confused growing up. Since he's an orphan raised at different times by squirrels and mice, is he a squirrel, or a mouse, or a rat, or none of the above; in which case, what is he? Since nobody likes him. why did a High One save him? Those who have read *The Blood Jaguar* know that Rat does make three close friends—well, two friends and an acquaintance—Fisher, Skink, and Bobcat. This tells how he meets them.

Rat's Reputation is variously a religious experience, a psychological exploration, a romance, a murder mystery, a tragicomedy, a coming of age narrative, and a travelogue. Payne's writing is in the mystic tradition of Kenneth Grahame" *The Wind in the Willows*. Is the animal cast wearing clothes or in their natural fur, feathers, and scales? Do they live in urban-style buildings or in burrows and nests? The combination comes across as less of an inconsistency than as a rich and exotic blend.

In one of the novel's longer passages, "Roaming," Rat goes into a seven-year self-imposed exile from Ottersgate; a walkabout that takes him throughout the world. *Rat's Reputation* presents a whole WORLD designed for all species of animals:

> Rat thanked her, tied the pouch around his neck, and left by the back door. A block and a half brought him to a second-hand shop, and he spent most of the coins on two vests—one black and the other green plaid—three faded bandannas, and an oilskin backpack.
>
> They helped him blend in, but … more than just these strange new rats, there were more different sorts of folks here than he had ever seen in one place before in his life. Skiffs and lighters sliding in and out of the docks; buildings of wood and brick and stone packed along the waterfront walk and every side street; fish and spices and the massed exhalations of so many lungs: it all made him a little dizzy. If he hadn't been heading somewhere, he might've stopped, but…
>
> Even at double speed it took two days to cross the place, but at last the pampas began to give way, sandy soil here and there, spreading, taking over, the wagons emerging into the desert. Cheering, the haulers let their chant fly, the ramparts of the Dyhari mountains growing from nubs to spikes to full-fledged peaks over the next few hours, the walls and towers of Kazirazif nestled against the foothills.
>
> Meerkats with capes, hats, and spears stopped them at the city's south gate, checked their paperwork, and guided the wagons through the narrow streets to the marketplace in the square outside the caliph's palace. "Right, then!" AlTrent [the fox wagonmaster] yelled. "Tayo, the ropes!"

The Blood Jaguar and *Rat's Reputation* make an attractive matched pair. Both are among the very best of anthropomorphic literature. *The Blood Jaguar* was written before furry fandom started its first literary award, but *Rat's Reputation* was a finalist for the 2015 Cóyotl Award for Best Novel.

The Book of Lapism • by Phil Geusz.

Birmingham, AL: Legion Printing & Publishing, January 2015, hardcover, 351 pp.

The Book of Lapism is the second collection of Phil Geusz's Lapist stories. The earlier *The First Book of Lapism* (ANTHRO Press, June 2009) is not only out of print, it lacks the two most recent stories. This new book is complete.

Phil Geusz's Lapist stories are set in the unspecified near future, maybe a hundred years from now, when materialism, greed, and a callous fuck-you-Jack/I've-got-mine society are making more thoughtful people despondent about whether there is anything worth living for. The philosophy/religion of Lapism grows up; a true brotherhood whose adherents have themselves physically bioengineered into anthropomorphic rabbits to show their friendly, gentle, caring nature. The Lapists have a very rocky and insecure first few years, as covered in these six stories. More rocky than they'd probably like to admit. There are serpents in Paradise.

Each of the six stories has a different narrator; four Lapists and two humans. "Drama Class," the first story, features the dilemma of Blueberry Longleaper Rabbit, a Lapist high-schooler. He doesn't face prejudice (his classmates think that having a cute rabbit-boy amidst them is great!), but the others don't really understand what Lapism is about. Should Blueberry accept the *status quo* (his drama class decides to put on "Alice in Wonderland" as their play just so he can be the White Rabbit), or should he proselytize and risk creating trouble? Worse, his parents had the whole family genengineered into humanoid rabbits when Blueberry and his younger brother Digger were little more than infants, and Digger has grown up *hating* being a bunny-boy. Is it youthful rebellion, or is Digger's antipathy more basic? More urgently, can Blueberry keep Digger out of serious legal trouble?

"Schism" is set earlier, when Lapism is just getting started. Sweetgrass, the founder of Lapism, has been assassinated, and his son-in-law Silkfur (father of Blueberry and Digger) reluctantly takes his place. Will the killer come after him next? A convert dies while being genengineered into a rabbit, and her father sues the Lapists for $30 million; enough to bankrupt the Lapists. But the worst threat comes from within the Lapists themselves. Well-meaning Church Elder Oaktree wants to proselytize aggressively to enlarge the Church as quickly as possible, while Silkfur believes in growing very slowly and accepting only those who truly understand and embrace the philosophy of Lapism. The schism threatens to tear the tiny movement apart.

"Full Immersion" features Jeremy, a human boy whose greedy foster parents have him genengineered into Bluegrass Spelunker Rabbit as a carny show attraction. Jeremy must decide whether it's better to join in the hoax, to become human again as soon as possible—or to really study Lapism and enter its brotherhood. They offer a better "family" than anything that he's known. ("Schism" and "Full Immersion" were reversed in the earlier collection.)

"In the Beginning" is set the earliest of all, before Lapism exists. The previous stories tell that Lapism came about because of the moral bankruptcy of humanity. "In the Beginning" shows that spiritual deadness. Dr. Thomas Aaron is materially successful, as one of the developers of the costly genengineering process that can turn humans into part-animals. But he doesn't care and is drinking himself to death. His wife has become a cultist who despises him and is divorcing him; his "friends" are all materialists who care only for making money; the public has become totally self-centered and is lawsuit-happy; all those who show any sign of spiritual concerns are emotionally weak; and he is depressed because the humans he transforms all choose cats, wolves, lions, and other popular aggressive predators. "In the Beginning" tells of Dr. Tom's moral conversion that will lead to Lapism.

The Book of Lapism by Phil Geusz (Legion Printing & Publishing, January 2015). The complete collection of Geusz's popular Lapism stories. Cover art by Micheal Day.

"Prodigal Son," one of the two new stories, is told by Gary Johnson, the workaholic leader of a national TV network's news crew who usually covers disasters, riots, and is just back from a story about a teenage school shooter who left fifteen dead. Gary is assigned against his will to do a feel-good story about people who *don't* go bad: the Lapists at their first father-son summer camp, Camp Oaktree. The Lapists will only let Gary come if he brings his teenage son, so he pressures his ex-wife to loan him his kid for a weekend. To his surprise, the ex agrees. Gary Junior is turning into a juvenile delinquent, and maybe the camp will help him. Gary assumes that his biggest problem will be to keep his son from calling the Lapists "bunny-fags" to their faces, but the situation is worse than he expects. The Lapists are hostile to being used to get TV ratings, and Gary Junior is deeper into trouble than he realizes. Gary's efforts to turn the situation around lead to more than he plans on.

The narrator of "Chosen People" is Juniper Lawkeeper Rabbit, a former human marksman who has converted to Lapism, become a rabbit, and been hired as sheriff of Oaktree Village, the first planned Lapist city. Juniper expects most of his duties to involve protecting the humanoid rabbits from troublemakers or criminals among the humans of the nearby towns. Instead, he becomes uneasily aware that many of the Lapists, with their smug *we're so much better than the humans* attitude, may be encouraging the growing bad feelings against Oaktree Village. As Silkfur points out in "Prodigal Son," the morphed Lapists are still 95 percent human, with most human failings still intact. When crime does finally occur, and Juniper is ordered by the mayor to ignore clues and investigate only the humans because no Lapists could possibly be guilty, what is he to do?

Geusz's writing is smooth and sharp at the same time. In "Prodigal Son" he has to show that the unpleasantly cynical, work-obsessed narrator is blind to his own faults, at the same time making him seem appealing enough to capture the reader's sympathy. Geusz makes it look easy:

It's impossible not to wonder what might happen in the Lapists' future, in another hundred or two hundred years; but Geusz has no current plans to continue the series. Republishing *The First Book of Lapism* with these two newer stories implies that there are no plans for "The Second Book of Lapism." So if you missed *The First Book of Lapism* before, don't miss *The Book of Lapism* now.

Charlotte's Web • by E.B. White. Illustrated by Garth Williams.

New York: Harper & Brothers, October 1952, hardcover, 184 pp.

Practically all furry fans read many talking-animal books when they are children. But there is something about White's writing that has made *Charlotte's Web* an all ages classic, not to be relegated to just "a children's book." Indeed, as 1952 sinks further into the past, its rural setting seems as fantastic as its talking animals are.

Fern Arable, an 8-year-old farm girl, asks her father where he is going with an ax. The answer is to kill a newborn weakling piglet. Fern demands to be allowed to save it. She nurses it like a human baby. When Wilbur is five weeks old, he has grown large enough to be sold to Fern's uncle, Homer L. Zuckerman, who has a larger farm.

When Wilbur goes to live on the Zuckermans' farm, the animal conversations start:

> "When I'm out here," he said, "there's no place to go but in. When I'm indoors, there's no place to go but out in the yard."
>
> "That's where you're wrong, my friend, my friend," said a voice.
>
> Wilbur looked through the fence and saw the goose standing there.
>
> "You don't have to stay in that dirty-little dirty-little dirty-little yard," said the goose, who talked rather fast. "One of the boards is loose. Push on it, push-push-push on it, and come on out!"

"What?" said Wilbur. "Say it slower!"
"At-at-at, at the risk of repeating myself," said the goose, "I suggest that you come on out. It's wonderful out here."

Wilbur soon wanders beyond the barn and the little yard outside it to explore throughout Mr. Zuckerman's farm. He meets and talks with many animals.

The news of Wilbur's escape spread rapidly among the animals on the place. Whenever any creature broke loose on Zuckerman's farm, the event was of great interest to the others. The goose shouted to the nearest cow that Wilbur was free, and soon all the cows knew. The lambs learned about it from their mothers. The horses, in their stalls in the barn, pricked up their ears when they heard the goose hollering, and soon the horses had caught on to what was happening. "Wilbur's out," they said. Every animal stirred and lifted its head and became excited to know that one of his friends had got free and was no longer penned up or tied fast.

Wilbur's closest friend is Templeton the rat, who isn't very close at all:

Sadly, Wilbur lay down and listened to the rain. Soon he saw the rat climbing down a slanting board that he used as a stairway.
"Will you play with me, Templeton?" asked Wilbur.
"Play?" said Templeton, twirling his whiskers. "Play? I hardly know the meaning of the word."
"Well," said Wilbur, "it means to have fun, to frolic, to run and skip and make merry."
"I never do those things if I can avoid them," replied the rat, sourly. "I prefer to spend my time eating, gnawing, spying, and hiding. I am a glutton but not a merrymaker. Right now I am on my way to your trough to eat your breakfast, since you haven't got sense enough to eat it yourself."

Wilbur gets a friend that he doesn't know about:

Darkness settled over everything. Soon there were only shadows and the noises of the sheep chewing their cuds, and occasionally the rattle of a cow-chain up overhead. You can imagine Wilbur's surprise when, out of the darkness, came a small voice he had never heard before. It sounded rather thin, but pleasant. "Do you want a friend, Wilbur?" it said. "I'll be a friend to you. I've watched you all day and I like you."

The small voice comes from Charlotte A. Cavatica, a spider in a web high overhead at the top of the barn doorway. Over the next months Wilbur tries to emulate Charlotte. He tries to spin a web with a string he gets Templeton to tie onto his tail. It doesn't work, but gradually Wilbur, Charlotte, and Templeton bond with each other.

Farm pigs traditionally grow up and are butchered for dinner, or are sent to the slaughterhouse. Charlotte decides to help Wilbur avoid that:

On foggy mornings, Charlotte's web was truly a thing of beauty. This morning each thin strand was decorated with dozens of tiny beads of water. The web glistened in the light and made a pattern of loveliness and mystery, like a delicate veil. Even Lurvy [the hired man], who wasn't particularly interested in beauty, noticed the web when he came with the pig's breakfast. He noted how clearly it showed up and he noted how big and carefully built it was. And then he took another look and he saw something that made him set his pail down. There, in the center of the web, neatly woven in block letters, was a message. It said:
SOME PIG!
Lurvy felt weak. He brushed his hand across his eyes and stared harder at Charlotte's web.

Mr. Zuckerman and Lurvy think it's a miracle meaning that Wilbur is a special pig. Soon all Mr. Zuckerman's neighbors for miles around come to look at Charlotte's web and the wondrous pig. Charlotte calls all the animals together to brainstorm new words for her web to keep the humans worked up:

"Furthermore," said Mr. Zuckerman, "I want you to start building a crate for Wilbur. I have decided to take the pig to the County Fair on September sixth. Make the crate large and paint it green with gold letters!"

"What will the letters say?" asked Lurvy.

"They should say *Zuckerman's Famous Pig*."

Wilbur is groomed for the County Fair that autumn. Charlotte continues to weave words like RADIANT and HUMBLE to keep up the interest. She and Templeton go along secretly to the Fair. But a spider's life is short. Charlotte lays 514 eggs, fashions an egg sac for them, lives long enough to see Wilbur win a special prize, and dies of old age. The book has a bittersweet ending, with Wilbur getting Templeton to bring Charlotte's egg sac back with them, and Charlotte's children hatching next spring. Most fly away on web-balloons, but there are always a few of Charlotte's daughters, granddaughters, and great-granddaughters that stay in Zuckerman's barn to keep Wilbur company for the rest of his life.

Claw the Way to Victory • edited by AnthroAquatic.

Capalaba, Queensland, Australia: Jaffa Books, January 2016, paperback, 285 pp.

Claw the Way to Victory is an anthology of eleven short stories "each showcasing a different sport and [showing] just how the instincts of an animal matched with the intelligence of a human can help or hurt a player" (blurb). Jaffa Books is the first Australian furry small press, although this book was printed and sold by editor AnthroAquatic in the U.S.

In "Descent" by TrianglePascal (gliding), Anthony, a mallard TV reporter, interviews Lacy Gallant, a golden eagle who is about to attempt the first unassisted thousand-foot descent off a cliff into a sheer gorge—without a parachute. The mammals in the sports camera crew think she's crazy. Anthony, as a bird but not a hunter-diver, can dimly appreciate what she feels when she's gliding.

"Discus Dog" by James L. Steele (discus) features Greg Rett, a young wolf in his first Major League Discus game, like football but much more brutal. Of the two nine-animal teams one is a mix of three canines, four felines, and two reptiles; the other is all wolves. Greg, in the excitement of the game, bites a rival player's throat out. The National Discus League officials question him. The press questions him. No police question him. Everybody agrees that these things happen in the passion of the game, and Greg is a rookie who hasn't yet developed self-control, so it's okay. Greg feels that he committed murder (or at least manslaughter), and he can't believe that he's getting off so easily…

"Bottom of the Ninth" by PJ Wolf (baseball) is narrated by "six-year-old me," the batter at the bottom of the last inning of Game Three of the Super Series. We never do find out who or what "six-year-old me" is, but we find out so much else about animal baseball that it doesn't matter.

"A Knight's Tale" by Eric Lane (tournament swordsmanship) is narrated by Jacob Harper a.k.a. Sir Michael Hemsworth, a coyote knight dueling a boar for the lordship of a modern renaissance fair. When he is gored, he loses his nerve even after he heals. His otter best friend helps him get it back again. This is a well-written story (although Lane misuses a couple of medieval technical terms), with the knight-reinactors taking advantage of their animal traits.

"Ping Pong Diplomacy" by Huskyteer (ping pong) is about an internationally-prestigious table-tennis tournament between teams led by Tux, a U.S. cat, and a Communist Chinese team led by a tiger. Tux has always been a fan and player of table-tennis, which is why he is chosen for the U.S. team invited to China. But the Chinese have developed table-tennis into a cross between a science, an art form, and a religion; and they are helped here by their animal nature:

> Only then did Tux have time to work out what was off-kilter about the game.
> Jun *wasn't using a paddle*. He was simply hitting the ball with the enormous pad of his paw, easily as broad as a competition paddle, and, Tux thought, remembering the pawshake, with just the right combination of firmness and flexibility, like a layer of rubber.

Tux takes advantage of his own feline instincts to stay glued to the bouncing ball. Huskyteer mixes the game competition with low-grade diplomatic espionage.

In "After the Last Bell's Rung" by Patrick Rochefort (boxing), Balus Bubalis is an Asian water-buffalo but also a Texas native. He was a Heavyweight Champion twenty-five years earlier, but he never went professional, retiring instead to help his dirt-poor family. He later became a physiotherapist specializing in treating sports injuries. The unnamed narrator interviewing him for his life's story focuses upon how having thick horns affects boxing. There's no drama in this story, but a lot of heart. Balus is the sort of quiet man who was featured in "The Most Unforgettable Character I've Ever Met" stories.

Claw the Way to Victory edited by AnthroAquatic (Jaffa Books, January 2016). A furry sports theme anthology. The first Australian furry specialty publisher. Cover art by Jenn "Pac" Rodriguez.

"A Leap Forward" by Mikasi-Wolf (running) isn't about a formal sport as much as it is about using running training to stay ahead of the police. Lesaut (civet) and Liam (angora cat) are parentless street youths who have their own society, The Movement, on the rooftops of their city. The older Liam asks Lesaut to mentor a newcomer, the 16-year-old horse Snoss, to The Movement. He doesn't tell Lesaut that the police in the streets and subways below are looking for Snoss.

"A Gentleman of Strength" by Dwale (sumo wrestling) is a polite translation of *rikishi*, a sumo wrestler, usually translated just as "strong man." This is the story of the final tournament of Ame, an aging honey bear sumo wrestler. The story describes sumo wrestling in depth, adding such animal traits as whether a plantigrade or a digitigrade stance is better for a sumo wrestler, the disadvantages of having a long tail, and so on.

"Nightball" by TrianglePascal (basketball) contrasts the playing of day animals and night animals. Never the twain shall meet—until a day animal, a cat, goes out for a nocturnal team. The attributes of the nocs (a skunk, an owl, a deer, etc.) are illustrated. The story is why the cat wants to play with them.

"Eight Seconds and the Grace of God" by Patrick Rochefort (rodeo) is set in the macho world of cowboy poker players and rodeo contestants, where both the stallion and steer riders and their mounts are sentient. Barroom fights and fights in the rodeo ring. Bradley Shoulders and Cameron McKenzie, both steers, are not friends. Cameron is friends with Dawson Chinook, the mutt. Dawson is hot to ride Bradley in the rodeo and win, to square up for his pal getting sucker-punched. But the hulking steer is three times Dawson's size.

"Marge the Barge" by Mary E. Lowd (ice skating) is a large Newfoundland dog. Marge suffered an injury that ended her hockey-playing days. Her only hope for staying on the ice is to learn to become a figure skater. But a huge Newfie amidst all those dainty animals performing graceful ballerina twirls and the like? Will Marge's determination be enough?

The stories in *Claw the Way to Victory* all hold your interest even if you don't care about their sports. The anthology was a finalist for the 2016 Ursa Major Award in the Other Literary Work category, and "A Gentleman of Strength" and "Marge the Barge" were both finalists in the Short Fiction category. "A Gentleman of Strength" was also a finalist for the 2016 Cóyotl Award in the Short Story category.

Decision at Doona • by Anne McCaffrey.
New York: Ballantine Books, April 1969, paperback, 254 pp.

Crisis on Doona • by Anne McCaffrey and Jody Linn Nye.
New York: Ace Books, March 1992, paperback, 328 pp.

Treaty Planet • by Anne McCaffrey and Jody Lynn Nye.
London: Corgi Books, February 1994, hardcover, 441 pp.

Treaty at Doona • by Anne McCaffrey and Jody Lynn Nye.
New York: Ace Books, September 1994, paperback, 342 pp.

Doona • by Anne McCaffrey and Jody Lynn Nye.
New York: Ace Books, February 2004, paperback, 585 pp.

Decision at Doona by Anne McCaffrey is an encouraging example of the basic plot of humans and furry aliens learning to live and work together in harmony. Published in 1969, it was one of the favorite novels of the earliest furry fans in the 1980s.

Two future civilizations are unaware of each other; humanity and the felinoid

Hrrubans. Both face catastrophic overpopulation, the exhaustion of natural resources and food, public apathy, and so on. Officials fear a complete collapse in just a few more generations.

Both species have had traumatic experiences with alien cultures in the past. The humans are governed by the Principle of Non-Cohabitation that resulted from "the terrible Siwannah tragedy.... And never, since the mass suicide of the gentle Siwannese, had a colony been set up where another intelligent species had been discovered by Spacedep."

Ken Reeve has been looking forward to emigrate from Earth to a wide-open colony planet:

> Home! [Earth, the leader of the Amalgamated Worlds.] A planet so overpopulated you married at sixteen to get on the list to have one of the two children allowed you before you were thirty—that is, if you could prove that you had no hereditary genetic faults or handicapping recessive traits. A planet so crowded for space there were only twelve Square Miles of international backyard remaining. He'd been eighteen before he had touched dirt, seen grass or smelled a pine tree. A trip to the local Square Mile had been his cherished award for being top man in Section Academy. The poignant memory of the experience had motivated and sustained him during the frustrating years of intensive study necessary to qualify for immigration under Colonial Department jurisdiction.

Ken is overjoyed when he is approved to become a colonist with his family on the newly approved (which automatically means uninhabited) idyllic world of Doona. Setting up the colony means a long spaceship journey, and spending eighteen months on Doona clearing land to construct their frontier town. Ken and the other colonists work happily and enthusiastically to build their new home. The colonists have just finished their town and are waiting for the spaceship bringing their families and farm animals when Ken and another colonist return from exploring with unbelievable news:

> "We're not alone on Doona, Lee," Ken cried, waving the quick-prints at the startled sociologist. "We're not alone!"
> "You're round the bend, man!"
> "No, he's not," growled Sam Gaynor, his face set in hard, bitter lines. "There's a village across the river in that grove of porous wood trees, where the river widens below the falls. A big village, full of furred, tailed cats that walk on their hind legs and carry knives."

The Hrrubans are described in greater detail later:

> Close up, the resemblance to cats was uncanny, Reeve thought, returning the solemn stares solemnly.
> The great green eyes regarded him from under straight wide brows, dark pupils narrowed against the orange sun. Flattish noses were broad at the nostril over lipless wide mouths. The chins were short bridges in the middle of the wide hinged jaw. The lobeless ears had tufted tips. Each child—for their very appearance and attitude cried youth to Reeve—wore a belt around his middle. A short sheathed knife hung from it without covering their obvious maleness. Their skins were a light fawn, like a soft velour, but their heads were covered with a darker tan mop of hair that hung to their ear tips. Visible between their spraddled legs were short, tufted tails, stuck straight out behind them in surprise.

There is general consternation. Nobody knows how the government's exploration team could have missed the felinoid natives, but their existence is undeniable. And by the Principle of Non-Cohabitation, this means that the humans have to give up their colony and return to Earth. But the spaceship with their families and livestock arrives before the Earth government can be informed. The natives are friendly, teaching the humans their language, and constructing an impressive bridge to link their two villages. None of the women want to return to overcrowded Earth, either. Why can't they stay despite the

Principle of Non-Cohabitation, since the Hrrubans are clearly not traumatized by the humans into committing mass suicide?

There are mysteries of where the Hrrubans had been until they appeared with their villages all set up, where their settlements on Doona other than nearby small villages are, and what their real plans for the humans are? Ken does not want to turn down their too-good-to-be-true friendship, but he cannot bring himself to fully trust it, either, especially since all the Hrrubans politely change the subject when asked for more information about their culture. Faster-than-light homing capsules from Earth bring contradictory panicked officious orders from the three bureaucracies involved; Alreldep (Alien Relations Department), Codep (Colonial Department), and Spacedep (Space Department).

The humans and the Hrrubans form individual friendships and closer social relations. Ken's six-year-old son Todd charms the Hrrubans by making himself a rope tail like theirs and following them around everywhere. Todd and a Hrruban boy, Hrriss, form an inseparable friendship. Todd becomes practically an adoptive Hrruban, "going native" more fully than any of the humans.

The colonists, now under Ken's unofficial leadership, decide that even knowing the Hrrubans are technologically advanced, they trust them more than the Earth government. There is a tense confrontation between the three Earth bureaucracies, the Hrruban liberal and xenophobic factions among their executive leadership, and the human and Hrruban governments, in which the colonists must try to be more than helpless pawns. Thanks to Ken and the headstrong Todd, all ends happily.

The existence of the two sequels (written with Jody Lynn Nye) gives away that all ends well. *Crisis on Doona* and *Treaty at Doona* (British title: *Treaty Planet*) are set twenty-five and thirty-two years later, with Todd and Hrriss as adults. Furry fans politely acknowledged the two sequels, but they were never considered the influential classics that *Decision at Doona* was.

Dogs of War • edited by Fred Patten.

Dallas, TX: FurPlanet Productions, January 2017, paperback, 455 pp.

Dogs of War II: Aftermath • edited by Fred Patten.

Dallas, TX: FurPlanet Productions, December 2017, paperback, 478 pp.

Solicitations from furry fandom specialty publishers for original short fiction for a theme anthology usually get about twenty usable submissions, or 150,000 words. The call for *Dogs of War* got twice that number, or enough good stories for two books. So they became two anthologies, debuting at two furry conventions at the opposite ends of 2017; Further Confusion in San Jose in January, and Midwest FurFest in Chicago in December. FurPlanet Productions, the publisher, sells online and through Amazon, and has sales tables at from six to twelve other fan conventions across the U.S. a year. Its books are also on sale at furry conventions in Australia and Germany.

Sales of the two *Dogs of War* anthologies have been better than usual. Who knew that stories about anthro animal soldiers and warriors (of all species) would be so popular? The books also demonstrate the growth of furry fandom, and of furry small-press publishing.

Dogs of War contains twenty-three stories; "Nosy and Wolf" by Ken McGregor,

"After Their Kind" by Taylor Harbin, "Succession" by Devin Hallsworth, "Two If by Sea" by Field T. Mouse, "The Queens' Confederate Space Marines" by Elizabeth McCoy, "The Loving Children" by Bill McCormick, "Strike, but Hear Me" by Jefferson P. Swycaffer, "End of Ages" by BanWynn Oakshadow, "Shells on the Beach" by Tom Mullins, "Cross of Valor Reception for the Raccoon, Tanner Williams, Declassified Transcript" by John Kulp, "Last Man Standing" by Frances Pauli, "Hunter's Fall" by Angela Oliver, "Old Regimes" by Gullwolf, "The Shrine War" by Alan Loewen, "The Monster in the Mist" by Madison Keller, "Wolves in Winter" by Searska GreyRaven, "The Third Variety" by Rob Baird, "The Best and Worst of Worlds" by Mary E. Lowd, "Tooth, Claw and Fang" by Stephen Coughlan, "Sacrifice" by J.N. Wolfe, "War of Attrition" by Lisa Timpf, "Fathers to Sons" by MikasiWolf, and "Hoodies and Horses" by Michael D. Winkle.

"From a rabbit army's training camp, to a human army turned into wolves, praying mantises in spacesuits, rattlesnake troops, prejudice against uplifted rat sailors, multi-tailed fox warrior priestesses, and more; these are stories for your imagination and enjoyment" (blurb). The authors range from "greymuzzles" who were writing for free for furry magazines in the 1990s to young fans making their first paid published sales. They come from seven countries: Australia, Canada, Germany, New Zealand, Singapore, Sweden, and the U.S. The twenty-three names are divided into seventeen real names (or plausible pseudonyms) and six obvious fursonas. They include fourteen men, eight women, and one who refuses to reveal "its" gender.

Dogs of War won the 2017 Ursa Major Award in the Best Anthropomorphic Other Literary Work category. Its cover by Teagan Gavet was a finalist in the Best Anthropomorphic Published Illustration category.

Dogs of War II: Aftermath contains twenty stories: "Dog, Extended" by Cairyn, "Remembrance" by Alice "Huskyteer" Dryden, "Scars" by Televassi, "The Surface Tension" by Dwale, "My Brother's Shadow" by M.R. Anglin, "Close to Us" by MikasiWolf, "Lime Tiger" by Slip-Wolf, "Umbra's Legion: The Destruction of Ismara" by Geoff Galt, "Umbra's Legion: Charon's Obol" by Adam Baker, "The Call" by Lord Ikari, "Every Horse Will Do His Duty" by Thurston Howl, "Matched Up" by K. Hubschmid, "The Son of Goulon Stumptail" by NightEyes DaySpring, "Noble" by Thomas "Faux" Steele, "Trial by Error" by Jaden Drackus, "The Night the Stars Fell" by KC Alpinus, "Tears of the Sea" by Mikasi-Wolf, "The Pack" by Argyron, "Red Engines" by Kris Schnee, and "Going Home" by Miles Reaver.

"From bioengineered military dogs with Artificial Intelligence to a fawn trying to prove he is a stag, a horse sailor on a warship, a canid-ape space war, a self-aware robot bird, a fox soldier passed over for a deserved promotion, reindeer Vikings, animal Sea Bees constructing an island airstrip, and more; these are stories for your imagination and enjoyment" (blurb). Add Great Britain and Slovenia to the countries represented.

Three stories in *Dogs of War* take place in the settings of their authors' previous novels or short fiction series (Angela Oliver, Madison Keller, and Mary E. Lowd). One more is in *Dogs of War II* (M.R. Anglin).

Many of the stories are dependent upon the anthropomorphic-animal nature of their characters. "Nosy and Wolf" by Ken McGregor is about rabbits training to overcome their traditional timidity:

> "The big rabbit had deep gouges crisscrossing his face, most of them over his left eye—the missing one. None of them knew his real name. It was like he never had one." He went on.
>
> "But, that was a long time ago. Ancient history. Today's rabbit is a fighter. A warrior." He walked

the line, stopping at each young rabbit and holding their gaze. "You, all of you, will be warriors, too. If you survive training." He shrugged. "Some don't."

"Two If by Sea" by Field T. Mouse pits herbivores against carnivores:

Emerson's whiskers twitched. He lowered his arms and gripped his knees.
  "How did you escape your cell? I doubt anyone let you out."
  "It's a long story," was the slow, evasive reply.
  The predator looked left, then right. "We seem to have plenty of time."
  The mouse gave him a withering side-glance. "I'd rather not relive it."
  "Typical prey. You cannot handle reality, so you pretend it does not exist. You live in denial, the whole lot of you. If your kind would only acknowledge that predators are superior in—"

There are several stories about humans creating bioengineered intelligent animal soldiers, or intelligent animal soldiers replacing mankind. In "War of Attrition" by Lisa Timpf, uplifted animal soldiers worry that they will be treated like traditional animals in warfare:

"'They wouldn't,' I snarled, showing my teeth.
  "They have before," Emmitt replied in his smooth voice, favoring me with a glare from his yellow-green eyes. He licked his paw and groomed his right ear, as though striving for a casual air. "Didn't they leave animals behind on the battlefield in their so-called World Wars?"
  Yuma, a border collie and likely the smartest among us even without the AI implant, closed her eyes and checked her memory. 'It's true,' she said, her features solemn."

The *Dogs of War* pair are two of the most popular anthologies produced by and for furry fandom. The first was a finalist for the 2017 Leo Literary Award in the Best Anthology category.

Duncton Wood • by William Horwood.
London: Country Life, September 1980, hardcover, 543 pp.

Duncton Quest • by William Horwood.
London: Century, August 1988, hardcover, 717 pp.

Duncton Found • by William Horwood. Map.
London: Century, July 1989, hardcover, 779 pp.

Duncton Tales • by William Horwood. Map.
London: HarperCollins U.K., July 1991, hardcover, 454 pp.

Duncton Rising • by William Horwood. Map.
London: HarperCollins U.K., October 1992, hardcover, 499 pp.

Duncton Stone • by William Horwood. Map.
London: HarperCollins U.K., April 1993, hardcover, 689 pp.

Duncton Wood

The six novels of William Horwood's *The Duncton Chronicles* series are a sometimes awesome, sometimes horrifying, often emotionally exhausting epic saga of warfare and religious persecution among the mole communities of the English countryside. To confuse matters, the last three novels are both *The Duncton Chronicles* parts 4 to 6, and *The Book of Silence* volumes 1 to 3. When put together, the six add up to 3,681 pages.

Horwood originally wrote *Duncton Wood* as a stand-alone novel. The other five novels did not start following until eight years later, so it may be convenient to read just the first, and then stop—if you can.

"*Duncton Wood* is the story of a quest into the nature of love and greed, of oppression and liberty, of integrity, grace, and of the power of the spirit," a blurb begins. "Here, in an epic fantasy of the highest order, William Horwood bestows upon the world of moles a mythic history that overflows with richness and fascination, involving the same momentous struggles between Good and Evil that have always plagued humankind."

Duncton Wood is one of the oldest and largest of the mole communities that dot the British countryside:

> No mole knew the whole system—it was too large—but all knew and loved its center: Burrow Vale. Here the elder burrows lay, and in early spring white anemones glistened between the trees before the bluebell carpet came, mirroring a clear spring sky.
>
> At Barrow Vale a pocket of gravelly soil caused the oaks to thin out, creating a natural open space warmed by the sun in summer, white and silent in the snow of deep winter, always the last place of light in the wood at nightfall. Being worm-scarce because of the poor soil, its tunnels were communal and everymole went there without fear. It was a place of gossip and chatter, where young moles met to play and venture out, often for their first time, onto the surface. It was relatively safe from predators, too, for the tunnels that radiated from it to all parts of the system made for early warning of an approaching danger long before it arrived.

There are pages and pages of such descriptions. Duncton Wood is the home of moledom's greatest library, the Holy Burrows of Uffington, and the center of moledom's peaceful Stone religion, based upon "the great Stone, the curious isolated standing stone that stood silent and huge at the highest point of the wood. It was tens of millions of years old and it looked its age—hard, gnarled and gray."

But secular power in Duncton Wood has been seized by the savage wanderer Mandrake of Siabod:

> The first that came to him he hardly seemed to touch, yet down he fell, not only dead but torn to death; the second died of a talon thrust so powerful that it seemed to start at his snout and end at his tail; the third turned to run even before he attacked, but too late. A mighty lunge from Mandrake caught him too, and he lay screaming, his black fur savaged open, red blood glistening. And as Mandrake passed by, he coldly crushed his snout and left him there arced out in a bloody, searing, ruthless death. Then they backed before him this way and that, chattering in fear, running away, taking to surface routes in their fright.

However, Mandrake is only the most visible problem. For generations the moles of Duncton Wood have been losing interest in and forgetting the traditions of their Stone religion. This novel is the story of the lovers Bracken and Rebecca (Mandrake's own daughter), and how they not only raise a rebellion against Mandrake, but against Rune, one of Duncton's former leaders who has become Mandrake's second in command and tries to seize Mandrake's power. They return Duncton Wood to the ancient religion of the Stone.

Horwood skillfully blends human and mole mannerisms:

> Cairn ran on, laughing, snouting over his shoulder to see how far ahead he was and drawn on by such a sweet wildflower smell ahead. When, Oh! And a tumble. And a snarl. And Rebecca. Rebecca and

Cairn. Tense and staring at each other, Rebecca's talons hard in the ground and Cairn looking to see and snouting to scent if there were other males about.

"Not since *Watership Down* and *The Lord of the Rings* has a fictional world been so imaginatively crafted," the blurb goes on; and the continuing following in Britain for *The Duncton Chronicles* tends to bear this out.

A blurb for *Duncton Quest*, the second novel, is: "Out of the chilly north have swarmed the grikes—a bloodthirsty tribe of warrior moles…. They are fanatical followers of the 'Word,' a harsh creed which demands that they convert or kill all believers in the sacred Stone." In *Duncton Found*, the sadistic grikes destroy the sanctuaries of the Stone, but Bracken's and Rebecca's son Tryfan escapes and fathers a child, Beechen, who is the prophesized Stone Mole. The last three novels, *The Book of Silence* series, are set a century later. The Newborn, an intolerant sect, grows within the peaceful Stone faith itself. Privet, a withdrawn scholar, protests against the perversion of the Stone teachings, and is forced to flee. A resistance of Stone believers and disillusioned Newborners grows around her.

The Duncton Chronicles is an epic series, but readers may have to order it through Amazon.co.uk. It has always been more popular in Great Britain than in America.

Earthman's Burden • by Poul Anderson and Gordon R. Dickson. Illustrated by Edd Cartier.

New York: Gnome Press, July 1957, hardcover, 185 pp.

Star Prince Charlie • by Poul Anderson and Gordon R. Dickson.

New York: Putnam, April 1975, hardcover, 190 pp.

Hoka! • by Poul Anderson and Gordon R. Dickson. Illustrated by Victoria Poyser, Nicola Cuti, Lela Dowling, & Phil Foglio.

New York: Simon & Schuster/Wallaby, October 1983, paperback, 219 pp.

Hoka! Hoka! Hoka! • by Poul Anderson and Gordon R. Dickson.

Riverdale, NY: Baen Books, November 1998, paperback, 307 pp.

Hokas Pokas! • by Poul Anderson and Gordon R. Dickson.

Riverdale, NY: Baen Books, February 2000, paperback, 278 pages, $6.99.

The Sound & the Furry: The Complete Hoka Stories • by Poul Anderson and Gordon R. Dickson.

New York: Science Fiction Book Club/SFBC, March 2001, hardcover, 406 pp., sold to SFBC members only.

Humorous science fiction is all too rare. One of the most successful humorous series during the late 20th century was the *Hoka* stories of Poul Anderson and Gordon R. Dickson. They began in the short-lived *Other Worlds Science Stories* in May 1951, moved to *Universe Science Fiction* after *Other Worlds* ceased publication, then to *The Magazine of Fantasy and Science Fiction* when *Universe* bit the dust. By 1957 there were almost enough Hoka stories to fill a book. Anderson and Dickson added one original story and a short "Interlude" after each to tie them all together into a novel, and *Earthman's Burden* was the result.

The 1950s were the postwar era with the Marshall Plan and the sparklingly new United Nations, when idealistic America was trying to pull the whole world up to Western levels of prosperity and democracy. The *Hoka* stories carried these ideals into space. By the 25th (?) century, the galaxy is being explored and politically united in the Interbeing League (IL), benevolently led by Earth (which is led by America). Unfortunately, a few totalitarian planets are out to sabotage the League so they can engage in old-fashioned empire building. One of the newest planets discovered is Toka, inhabited by two rival intelligent species, the reptilian Slissii and the mammalian Hokas. The Slissii, roughly humanoid tyrannosaurs, are cruel and cunning, while the friendly Hokas look like three-feet-tall, tubby, golden-furred teddy bears. Unfortunately, the Hokas are disunited and—childlike. They have a hard time taking anything seriously. Worse, they cannot distinguish between fact and fiction, and the IL's serious manuals on good government are ignored in favor of the more exciting Earth fiction: Westerns, pirate sagas, jungle ape-man thrillers, and so on. Each Hoka nation has picked its own genre of colorful fiction to model itself after. Young Ensign Alex Jones of the Terrestrial Interstellar Survey Service finds himself the IL's new envoy to Toka, to be officially neutral but unofficially to make sure that the chaotic Hokas win out over the better-organized Slissii, and remain unconquered by hostile alien invaders.

"The Sheriff of Canyon Gulch" brings Alex Jones to Toka as a marooned Survey Scout, to a small Hokan town that has taken the pulp-fictional cowboys and Indians uncritically as its role-model. The green-skinned Slisii are, of course, the Injuns. The Hokas hope at first that Alex is a Lone Stranger–type hero, but after he naïvely fouls up trying to live up to the stereotype, they demote him to the post of Sheriff—everyone knows that the Sheriff is the biggest blunderer of the community. Alex, figuring that he can't sink any lower, gets thoroughly drunk on the Hoka's rotgut and accidentally leads them to victory over the Slissii.

"Don Jones" moves to an IL hostel on Earth, where a "Tokan ursinoid" delegation has been brought to consider the advantages of IL membership. Alex Jones is appointed their Official Host because he has more hands-on experience than anyone else with the Hokas. Alex and his girlfriend Tammi Hostrup try to follow the IL's officious guidelines, despite the pettiness of Alex's superior, Hardman Terwilliger; the jealousy between Tammi and Terwilliger's secretary Doralene Rawlings; and the six Hokas who, after an evening at the opera, have decided that they have become Don Giovanni and Company: the unstoppable lecher and invincible swordsman; the crafty servant; the arrogant soldiers; etc.—especially The Ghost of the murdered Commandant (the Hokas are looking for someone to pour whitewash over to draft as the ghost). Alex manages to maneuver the resulting farce into a bureaucratic victory, and he is appointed the permanent resident Plenipotentiary to Toka.

The remaining four stories—"In Hoka Signo Vinces," "The Adventure of the Misplaced Hound," "Yo Ho Hoka!," and "The Tiddlywink Warriors"—take place over a dozen years on Toka. Alex, now married to Tammi and living in the new planetary capital of

Mixumanu, is forced every few years by some crisis or other to travel to a different Hokan community to resolve the matter. He becomes drafted in each to play an important but powerless sidekick role. In the Space Patrol, he is the senior Coordinator; in Sherlock Holmes' London, he is Watson; in the Royal Navy of Napoleonic times, he is the pirate Captain Greenbeard; and in the Foreign Legion he is the raw recruit who is expected to die nobly for *la belle France*. The stories are all nonstop burlesque.

The *Hoka* stories were rollicking good fun, and readers in the mid–1950s could not get enough of them. Anderson and Dickson wrote three more short stories or novelettes in the 1950s, in the settings of "Casey at the Bat" baseball, mid–20th-century secret agentry, and "The Jungle Book" (starring not Alex but his and Tammi's young son as Mowgli). There was a Young Adult novel, *Star Prince Charlie*, in 1975. Finally, the last new story was published in 1983, in which warlike space aliens are opposed only by a Hoka Napoleon Bonaparte and his *Grande Armée* of Hokan grenadiers. "Joy in Mudville," "Undiplomatic Immunity," "Full Pack (Hokas Wild)," and "The Napoleon Crime" were collected into the paperback *Hoka!* in 1983. After these had been out of print for years, in 1998 *Hoka! Hoka! Hoka!* republished everything in *Earthman's Burden* plus the first two stories from *Hoka!*; followed by *Hokas Pokas!* in 2000 with the last two stories from *Hoka!* plus *Star Prince Charlie*. At last, in 2001, the Science Fiction Book Club brought everything together into one 399-page volume, *The Sound & the Furry: The Complete Hoka Stories*. For many years until furry literature became more common, *Earthman's Burden* and the later *Hoka* books were favorites of the sf fans who later became furry fans.

Fabulous Histories. Designed for the Instruction of Children, Respecting Their Treatment of Animals • by Mrs. [Sarah] Trimmer.

London: T. Longman, G.C.J. and J. Robinson, and J. Johnson, 1786, pamphlet (2 volumes), 238 pp.

The modern era of talking animals in literature is generally believed to start with Lewis Carroll's *Alice's Adventures in Wonderland* (1865). That is the oldest novel still commonly published today, and the earliest that people (both children and adults) read voluntarily for pleasure. Yet there were quite a few stories in the late 18th century with talking animals, usually as didactic moral lessons to teach children to be kind to animals.

One of the most influential was Mrs. Trimmer's *Fabulous Histories* (1784), about a mother and father robin who build their nest in the home of Miss Harriet Benson, age 11, and her brother Master Frederick, age 6. The children watch the robins and their hatchlings avidly, and learn from them under their mother's guidance. The birds talk, but only to each other: "In a hole which time had made, in a wall covered with ivy, a pair of Redbreasts built their nest."

The mother Redbreast lays four eggs, which their father views with pride but concern:

> We may promise ourselves much delight in rearing our little family, said he, but it will occasion us a great deal of trouble; I would willingly bear the whole fatigue myself, but it will be impossible for me, with my utmost labour and industry, to supply all our nestlings with what is sufficient for their daily support; it will therefore be necessary for you to leave the nest occasionally, in order sometimes to seek provisions for them.

Eventually the four eggs hatch into father Redbreast's "little darlings, to whom, for the sake of distinction, I shall give the names of Robin, Dicksy, Flapsy, and Pecksy." The children are eager to feed the birds, which their mother allows them to do but not too wastefully, "as it is not right to cut pieces from a loaf on purpose for birds, because there are many children who want bread, to whom we should give the preference. Would you deprive a poor little hungry boy of his breakfast, to give it to birds?"

Meanwhile the birds are getting along in their nest:

> The hen bird, as I informed you, repaired immediately to the nest; her heart fluttered with apprehension, as she entered it, and she eagerly called out, Are you all safe, my little dears?—All safe, my good mother, replied Pecksy, but a little hungry, and very cold.—Well, said she, your last complaint I can soon remove; but in respect to the satisfying your hunger, that must be your father's task, for I have not been able to bring anything good for you to eat; however, he will soon be here, I make no doubt.

The narrative is full of incidents as seen from the robins' point of view of human children carelessly or maliciously using them as playthings, to be casually discarded when they "break." Other menaces are acknowledged, such as a hawk, but it is made clear that these are natural predators merely following their instincts. Only humans know the difference between right and wrong, and mistreat animals through deliberate cruelty. The Benson children are contrasted with their thoughtless playmates who bring nests of baby birds home, at best not meaning to hurt them but invariably resulting in their starving to death; and who throw rocks and do worse to any cats, dogs, or domestic fowl that they catch, pull the wings off of flies, and so on. A different example is that of rich but lonely Mrs. Addis, who coos over her beloved pet parrot, parakeet, macaw, squirrel, and others, but who relegates her own young children to the back rooms and her servants' indifferent care. Her daughter Augusta is understandably jealous of the pampered animals. Mrs. Benson points out to Harriet that it is just as wrong to spoil animals as to mistreat them. "The lap-dog is, I am sure, a miserable object, full of diseases, the consequences of luxurious living."

In the robins' scenes, the baby birds grow up. The boys Robin and Pecksy are adventurous, while Dicksy and sister Flapsy are more timorous. These scenes are just as didactic; Robin, the bad example, greedily eats all the worms himself, and is scolded by father Redbreast for not sharing with his siblings. Mrs. Trimmer wrings these scenes for as much pathos as she can cram into them: "Oh! cried he [Robin], that I had but followed the advice and example of my tender parents, then I had been safe in the nest, blest with their kind caresses, and enjoying the kind company of my dear brother and sisters! but now I am of all birds the most wretched!"

Robin is crippled and believed by his family to be lost, but is rescued by Master Frederick. When the other robins find him, they are encouraged by the kindness shown to him to enter Frederick's room themselves. Frederick is rewarded by seeing the robins explore his room and come and go freely through the open window, in comparison to the sterile life of Mrs. Addis' caged pets.

Ultimately, the Redbreasts grow up free and happy as wild birds should be. What happens to the humans is also summarized; Harriet and Frederick Benson become pleasant and well-liked adults, while the others in the story meet fates that are foretold by how kind or cruel toward animals they have been.

Fabulous Histories was reprinted for about a century, usually retitled *The Story of the Robins*. Its popularity ended around the 1880s, when less condescending children's literature became available; social customs described in the story became blatantly outdated; and society generally evolved from rural to urban, making the be-good-to-animals message largely irrelevant.

FANG

Volume 1 edited by Alex Vance. Amsterdam: Osfer's Joint Publications, September 2005, paperback, 349 pp.; Volume 2 edited by Alex Vance. Amsterdam: Osfer's Joint Publications, November 2005, paperback, 267 pp.; Volume 3 edited by Alex Vance. Amsterdam: Bad Dog Books, July 2007, paperback, 267 pp.; Volume 4 edited by Skip Ruddertail and Graveyard Greg. Dallas, TX: Bad Dog Books, January 2012, paperback, $331 pp.; Volume 5 edited by Ashe Valisca. Dallas, TX: Bad Dog Books, January 2014, paperback, 291 pp.; Volume 6 edited by Ashe Valisca. Dallas, TX: Bad Dog Books, July 2015, paperback, 249 pp.; Volume 7 edited by Ashe Valisca. Dallas, TX: Bad Dog Books, July 2016, paperback, 366 pp.; Volume 8 edited by Ashe Valisca. Dallas, TX: Bad Dog Books, June 2017, paperback, 330 pp.; Volume 9 edited by Ashe Valisca. Dallas, TX: Bad Dog Books, (forthcoming), paperback.

ROAR

Volume 1 edited by Ben Goodridge. Amsterdam: Bad Dog Books, July 2007, paperback, 277 pp.; Volume 2 edited by Buck C. Turner. Amsterdam: Bad Dog Books, January 2010, paperback, 312 pp.; Volume 3 edited by Buck C. Turner. Amsterdam: Bad Dog Books, February 2011, paperback, 260 pp.; Volume 4 edited by Buck C. Turner. Dallas, TX: Bad Dog Books, June 2012, paperback, 300 pp.; Volume 5 edited by Buck C. Turner. Dallas, TX: Bad Dog Books, July 2014, paperback, 325 pp.; Volume 6 edited by Mary E. Lowd. Dallas, TX: Bad Dog Books, July 2015, paperback, 394 pp.; Volume 7 edited by Mary E. Lowd. Dallas, TX: Bad Dog Books, July 2016, paperback, 377 pp.; Volume 8 edited by Mary E. Lowd. Dallas, TX: Bad Dog Books, June 2017, paperback, 284 pp.; Volume 9 edited by Mary E. Lowd. Dallas, TX: Bad Dog Books, July 2018, paperback, 297 pp.

CLAW

Volume 1 edited by K.C. Alpinus. Dallas, TX: Bad Dog Books, July 2018, paperback, 265 pp.

Bad Dog Books began in 2005 as Osfer's Joint Publications (renamed BDB in 2006) when Alex Vance started his small press in Amsterdam, specializing in literate furry homosexual erotic fantasy. *FANG* was subtitled "The Little Black Book of Furry Fiction," and blurbed as "the beginning of a new era in furry publishing, and this first issue was dedicated to bringing the finest modern homoerotica to the anthropomorphic reading public."

ROAR was originally intended as *FANG* volume 4, but Bad Dog Books began getting so much non-erotic fiction that it was decided to publish it as an all-ages companion volume, subtitled "The Little White Book of Furry Fiction." Both *FANG* and *ROAR* are magazines in a paperback book format. They initially appeared erratically.

The two were marketed in the U.S. by FurPlanet Productions. Beginning with their second volumes, each *FANG* and *ROAR* have had a theme. But Vance had health problems, and most of Bad Dog Books' sales were in the U.S. In December 2011, Vance sold Bad Dog Books to FurPlanet Productions, with the stipulation that FurPlanet continue to use the Bad Dog imprint on *FANG* and *ROAR*, and that it continues to publish new paper volumes annually.

FurPlanet has done so, in addition to making Bad Dog Books its imprint for electronic editions. By 2018, there have been nine volumes of each. They are currently released at each Anthrocon convention, in Pittsburgh over the July 4 weekend. *FANG*'s annual themes have been Horror, Fantasy, Life After High School, Best Enemies, the Victorian Era, Las Vegas, Paradise, and Bad Romance. *ROAR*'s themes have been Games, Moments, Fame, Secrets, Scoundrels, Legendary, Paradise, and Resistance. In 2018, FurPlanet added *CLAW*, for stories of furry lesbian relationships.

FANG and *ROAR* have incidentally marked the appearances in furry literature of fursona names. Before about 2005, furry authors used their real names or plausible pseudonyms. After that, names such as NightEyes DaySpring, Angelwolf, and Searska GreyRaven have become common. Also, before theme anthologies from furry fandom's specialty presses became common, *FANG* and *ROAR* established themselves as two of the best publications of themed anthropomorphic short fiction. *Goodreads* called *FANG* volume 1 "a "Who's Who" of the furry writing community."

Neither *FANG* nor *ROAR* have ever won awards, but many of the stories in *ROAR* have been Cóyotl or Ursa Major Award finalists, and "Chasing the Spotlight" by Tim Susman in *ROAR* volume 4 won the 2012 Cóyotl Award for Best Short Story. Teagan Gavet's cover for *ROAR* volume 6 was a UMA finalist in the 2015 Best Anthropomorphic Published Illustration category, and *ROAR* volume 8 was a 2017 UMA finalist in the Other Literary Work category. It is too early to tell about *CLAW*.

"Chasing the Spotlight" presents an alternate world's furry story. The narrator is Alex Roberts, the one-man reporter/editor/producer of the WhispOWorld computer news feed, one of the top 50 North American online news sites. Alex gets a tip leading him to a guy who has had himself surgically made into a furry—faint fur all over, pointed ears, a drooping tail. "Lon" talks about it being part of a plan for a horror movie actor, but Alex senses that Lon is just saying what he's been ordered to say. The group who performed Lon's drastic surgery are being too secretive, and Lon seems frightened of saying too much because he isn't the first artificial furry; but the others have "disappeared." Alex wonders what if there are more furry fans willing to undergo surgical modification than anyone suspects? What if this "industry" is ruthless enough to make its mistakes "disappear"? If Alex breaks the story, he could be famous—or dead…

In addition to "Chasing the Spotlight" by Tim Susman, *ROAR* volume 4 contains "The Savior of Dragondom" by Sarina Dorie and "St. Kalwain and the Lady Uta" by Mary Lowd; the former a finalist for the 2012 Cóyotl Award and the latter for the 2012 Ursa Major Award for Short Fiction. *ROAR* volume 5 contains "The Wharf Cat's Mermaid" by Mary E. Lowd, a 2014 Ursa Major finalist. *ROAR* volume 7 contains both "Old-Dry-Snakeskin" by Ross Whitlock and "The Torch" by Chris "Sparf" Williams, 2016 Cóyotl Award finalists; and *ROAR* volume 8 contains "Behesht" by Dwale, both a 2017 Cóyotl Award and an Ursa Major Award finalist.

Both *FANG* and *ROAR* are always worth reading, especially *ROAR*.

Fangs of K'aath • by Paul Kidd. Illustrated by Monika Livingstone.

Keston, England: United Publications, April 2000, hardcover, 367 pp.

Fangs of K'aath II: Guardians of Light • by Paul Kidd. Illustrated by Monika Livingstone.

Keston, England: United Publications, January 2006, paperback, 337 pp.

The first notable author of novels in furry fandom was Paul Kidd. He joined *Rowrbrazzle*, the furry amateur press association, in April 1989, and began serializing his unsold manuscripts of two novels, *Mus of Kerbridge* and *Fangs of K'aath*. The reasons for rejection were always the same. These were novels featuring fantasy and talking animals, but they were written for adults, not children, and there was no market for talking-animal novels for adults.

When the first furry fandom specialty presses appeared, Kidd's unsold novels finally were published as books. *Fangs of K'aath*, an Arabian Nights fantasy, was the first book of English fan Martin Dudman, who started United Publications to publish anthropomorphic literature and games, and to import them and Japanese fantasy manga into Great Britain. It was an attractive hardcover with a dust jacket and illustrations by popular American fan artist Monika Livingstone. Kidd's pseudo–Middle Eastern dimension of Aku-Mashad is described with a wealth of detail and color. He suspensefully sets up dramatic scenes—the attack of the assassins at Emir Caïd's estate—and fills them with dazzling action:

Fangs of K'aath by Paul Kidd (United Publications, April 2000). One of the first novels in furry fandom, serialized in a fanzine in 1989, and one of the first furry specialty press books. Cover art by Monika Livingstone.

> In the Kingdom of Osra, by the banks of the Amu Daja, lay the ancient capital city Sath, a tarnished jewel in a comfortable crown. The great river meandered past the city walls, fondly caressing the worn old stones, while domes and minarets lay sleepily beneath the setting sun, bleached and tired by the endless heat…. The people of Sath were a riot of clashing shapes; Jackal, Tiger, Cat and Fox, scurrying Mice and Rabbits in their slave chains. Fur and tails and endless chatter turned the crowded streets into a melting pot where all races mingled. The city was a place of tangled alleyways, of fortress walls and gaping market squares. Minarets hurtled themselves proudly up to God while the slums sank down into the dust; mosaic tiles and marble clashed with fading white wash…. For those with wealth, life was good. There were slaves and jewels, wines and luscious drugs; uncounted sensual pleasures to while away the hours.

Fangs of K'aath is the romance of Raschid (Jackal), a Prince, and Sandhri (Bat), a marketplace storyteller. Raschid is the scholarly son of the Shah of Osra's first wife. But he is the Shah's second son, since the Shah's second wife gave birth first. Raschid is happy with this, since he would rather spend his time in the palace library studying, and leave the pompous glitter and backstabbing of court intrigue to his arrogant half-brother Abbas.

Raschid meets Sandhri when he decides to go incognito among the commoners to record their old folk tales. His attention quickly shifts to Sandhri herself; a peasant from the mountains, uneducated but obviously quick-witted, sparkling with joy and spontaneity that is so different from the haughty, stultifying court life. Raschid's first folk-tale expedition turns into regular trips to the marketplace to spend time with Sandhri, who believes that he is a student from a distant city.

Unfortunately, Raschid is too important to avoid the court intrigue. His mother, Lady Shiraj, is constantly scheming to have him replace Abbas as Shah Marwan's leading son and heir. Raschid's interest in Sandhri is diverting him from her plans to promote him socially among the nobility. Abbas and his mother, Lady Farasche, have no intention of letting Raschid become a serious rival, and hurting Sandhri would be one way to hurt him. When Shah Marwan callously puts the untrained Raschid in command of a military expedition to settle a rebellion between feuding desert nobles and nomad raiders, he is forced to bring Sandhri with him to protect her. Their adventures in the desert bring them closer together, and also temper them to face their adversaries at court more effectively.

Fangs of K'aath is the sort of Arabian Nights extravaganza popularized by Hollywood, full of exotically costumed nobles, gossamer-veiled dancing girls, scimitar-waving palace guards, crowded bazaars, a fanatic priesthood, wizened sorcerers, disguised assassins, cruel desert tribes, and more. And they are all anthropomorphic animals. The royal dynasty are jackals, the Grand Vizier is a tiger, two Emirs are a cat and a fox, the harem mistress is a rabbit, and so forth. The major surprise is that the bats in this world do not have wings, and the reason that they are wingless has to do with the demon-goddess K'aath.

The novel was popular, and Kidd followed it up six years later with the further adventures of Shah Raschid, Sandhri the storyteller, Yariim the dancer, and Itbit the gamin, and their friends, plus many new friends—and enemies, specifically Tsu-Khan, a warlord-necromancer (arctic fox) who plots to destroy not just Osra, but all Aku-Mashad. To quote the opening of one of Sandhri's parables (in her Hill Country accent):

> Long ago, after Adamah and Ewah left the garden of Eden, many off the animals also ate from the Tree of Life. The bats persuaded the others, and so t'ey all came to eat the sacred fruit. Everything v'ith furf and paws came scuttling up the tree to take part of the power that had made Adamah and Ewah lords of the Earth.
>
> Still! Some animals missed out on the whole experience! The hooved animals and the fish could not climb the tree, and the birds slept late and missed the whole affair. The insects v'ere perfectly happy as they v'ere, and also refused to eat from the tree. But the other animals changed and grew. T'ey rose up onto two feet, and they knew lust and fear, passion and glory. But t'ey also knew love, and for this, God treasured t'em even though t'ey had disobeyed his command.
>
> God could not release t'ese new Peoples of the Tree onto the Earth, and so he made a new v'orld for them, "Aku Mashad." A gate v'as opened, and all the animals who had eaten of the tree v'ere sent forth from Eden to found new lives.

This is why canines, felines, ursines, mustelids, rodents, and most other non-hooved mammals became humanoid and of comparable size for a joint civilization, but not the beasts of burden.

Fangs of K'aath and its sequel have held up well, as furry fandom has become filled with newer anthropomorphic novels.

Felicia: The Night of the Basquot • by Chas. P.A. Melville. Illustrated by the author.

Seattle, WA: CreateSpace, September 2017, paperback, 257 pp.

"So!" crowed Felicia happily. And then she frowned. "So," she repeated, more uncertainly. And then, in puzzlement, "So." Her ears flicked as she turned to stare at the rising sun. "So, what's a 'Basquot' anyway?"

Felicia cla di Burrows, the vixen renegade sorceress blackballed from the Magi Council, first appeared as an enigmatic background character when Melville began self-publishing *The Champion of Katara* comic book, #1 dated August–September 1987.

Spiteful and egocentric, all that was really clear was that Felicia had been horribly mistreated as a child. She began studying sorcery—including forbidden black magic—to gain revenge against those who had destroyed her family. But her heart was not really in being evil, and she kept using her magic to help others while postponing her vendetta against her family's enemies. As a flawed "good guy" and a colorful, charismatic character, Felicia became the most popular of Melville's anthro animal cast. Felicia's most dramatic and complex adventure was the 184-page graphic novel *Felicia: Melari's Wish* (August 1994).

Melville later brought Felicia back in a series of text novelette booklets, with illustrations every few pages, published by CaféPress. These continued the lighter stories in the 1990s comic book *ZU*. Felicia became a professional sorceress-for-hire/detective who got involved with finding and dispelling ancient evils, or preventing their escape to wreak havoc in Katara and its neighboring animal kingdoms of Dogonia, Bruinsland (bears), Scentas (skunks), Rodentia (mice), and others. Melville wrote five of these from 2004 to 2008. One, *Felicia and the Tailcutter's Curse* (June 2004), won that year's Ursa Major Award in the Best Short Fiction category. All five were republished as a single book, *The Vixen Sorceress* (CreateSpace, December 2008).

Melville began producing a Felicia webcomic, *Felicia, Sorceress of Katara*, in December 2007, but for nine years there were no Felicia text adventures. Finally in 2017, Felicia reappeared in her first novel.

Felicia: The Night of the Basquot is her origin story, and an introduction to her world (which might be described as Tolkien lite, with funny animals). It begins when Felicia emerges in Katara from a mysterious seven-year disappearance, crackling with magic energy and ready to join the all-powerful Magi Council (a.k.a. the Brotherhood of the Candle) as its newest and youngest sorceress. Instead, she is shocked and infuriated to learn that she has been rejected:

> There was a liquidly pop, and somebody stepped through into the middle of Manwa Katdu's private office.
>
> Felicia swept her cloak out of the way and marched in, looking furiously about before centering her sights upon the wizard. "You!" she snapped, angrily advancing upon him. She pointed at him, her fist still grasping an official letter. "Are you Manwa Katdu? I want to speak to you!"
>
> Manwa [a cat wizard] lowered the still-sparking mace, but kept a tight grip upon it. 'Who are you?" he demanded indignantly. "How dare you just barge in to my sanctuary this way? Do you have any sense of proper decorum?" *More to the point*, he wondered, *how did you break through a series of protective spells set in place by a committee of the most powerful Magi?*
>
> "Blow it out of your peaked hat," snapped the vixen shaking the letter at him. "I want to know what this means!"
>
> [...]
>
> Felicia resumed glaring at him and continued her harangue. "How can you possibly dismiss my application so casually? Don't meet your minimum standards? Why, you've no idea *what* I'm capable of!"
>
> "That is precisely the point," Manwa told her. "We *don't* know." He studied her more carefully. "You

are Felicia, correct? The old Sorceress' apprentice? Then you know as well as anyone should how careful the Council is in accepting applicants to its order, even from among its own brotherhood."

Felicia's determination to keep how she learned her magic a secret (part of her planned revenge against the powerful wolf nobleman who murdered her family when she was a child) keeps the suspicious Council from accepting her. This world has two gods, or a god and a demon, the good Aln and the evil Murk; and the Magi Council will not admit anyone to its ranks until they are certain that the applicant is not an agent of the Murk. Felicia is obviously powerful enough, but she will not reveal her training or the source of her magic.

Before the matter of her rejection by the Council can be resolved, this world undergoes a major attack by the minions of the Murk. The wizards and sorceresses of the Council rush to oppose it, while Felicia is sidetracked by the enemy who killed her family:

> *It's too soon*, a voice in the back of her mind warned. *You're not ready yet!* "I should have known," she growled to herself. "From the very beginning, I should have known. When I first saw the tray! Only *he* would have had access to it and all of the other property stolen from my parents!" She pulled on the reins, forcing the horse to take a fork that led along a deep stream. Startled night creatures scattered at her approach, chittering as they fled into the high grass. *You're not ready yet!* her inner voice reminded her firmly. *It's too soon! This isn't according to the plan! First, you get established and make a name for yourself! Remember? Then, you slowly, slowly, acquire friends among the powerful, until you have enough to worry him. When it's time, you move your friends against him. But you need time!*
>
> "I don't have time!" she snarled aloud, and snapped the reins again to urge the horse faster. "He's up to something *now*, and he's using my parents' wealth to do it! By Aln! I'll make him suffer for this!"

Felicia: The Night of the Basquot is a fast-paced mixture of drama and humor, well-blended although occasionally descending into silliness, as when Felicia wins the dubious support of the Toy Pooch Patrol, a band of miniature dog warriors, or with names like Bill Sneakyshoes. On the whole, though, if you like Disney-fairy-tale–type desperate battles of funny-animal knights against monsters, good versus evil wizards and sorceresses, noble sacrifices and tragic deaths, you will enjoy *Felicia: The Night of the Basquot*. Melville presents a broader picture of his animal world, and the mood is generally more serious than in his novelettes like *Felicia and the Cult of the Rubber Nose* with its mime assassins.

Felidae • by Akif Pirinçci. Translated by Ralph Noble.
New York: Villard Books, February 1993, hardcover, 292 pp.

Felidae on the Road • by Akif Pirinçci. Translated by Anthea Bell.
London: Fourth Estate Ltd., July 1994, hardcover, 246 pp.

"A novel of cats and murder," is the cover tagline beneath a headshot of a glowering cat. "If you really want to hear my tale," the novel opens, "—and I strongly urge you to do so—you must get used to the fact that it's not going to be pleasant." It isn't. But it is tensely suspenseful, and is unique in being a serious, grisly murder mystery for adults in which the entire main cast—victims, suspects, and detectives—are intelligent cats.

"It all began when we moved into that damned house." Gustav Löbel, a "simple-minded" human, moves with the narrator, his cat Francis, from their apartment into an old house which is cheap because it badly needs fixing up. "The front of the building, embellished with a number of cracked, ornamental plaster baubles, resembled the visage of a mummified Egyptian king. Gray and weathered, it glowered at you as if it had demonic intentions for the living." And so on, at considerable length. Francis' "detective noir" descriptions are always lengthy, picturesque, and depressing. The events in *Felidae* are horrific enough, but even before they occur, you get the impression that Francis is the type of character who could not describe a six-year-old's birthday party without making it sound like a horror movie.

The novel is full of realistic feline behavior such as flehming and marking territory:

> Since I had just moved in, however, the status of ownership was now clear; naturally, I insisted upon my right to obliterate all previous signatures with my own. And so, swiveling 180 degrees, I concentrated with all my might and fired away.
>
> The environmentally safe, all-purpose jet that shot out from between my rear legs inundated the spot where my predecessor had left his calling card. Order had once again been established in the world.

As soon as he begins to explore his new neighborhood, Francis finds a corpse:

> What I saw there was, so to speak, my welcoming present. Under the tall tree, half-covered by shrubbery, lay a black brother with all his limbs stretched out. Only he wasn't sleeping. I could hardly imagine that he would ever engage in any activity again, whether active or passive. He was, as people of lesser finesse might say, as dead as a doornail. More specifically, this was a member of my species whose corpse was already in an advanced state of putrefaction. All his blood had gushed from his neck, which had been torn completely into shreds, and formed a large pool that was now a dry stain. Excited flies circled over him like vultures over slaughtered cattle.

This is the fourth cat that has died violently. As Francis meets the other neighborhood cats in the next few days (they all refer to their humans as "can openers" since opening cans of cat food is the only purpose of humans, in their opinion), and corpse #5 is found, Francis realizes that all the victims were sexually active males. He begins to investigate.

Francis soon discovers that the uninhabitable top floor of his new home looks like the ruins of a scientific laboratory. It is also a meeting place of a crazily ominous feline religion:

> What I saw below could have made a photojournalist into a multimillionaire overnight with just one snapshot. It was an unbelievable sight. About two hundred brothers and sisters had pushed, shoved, and squeezed into the middle of a filthy room, where the frayed wire ends of two loose electric cables met and crossed, spraying sparks. An elderly brother with white, billowing fur, the one who drooled out the holy tirade I had heard earlier, pressed down one of the cables with his paw so that it sprang up and down, creating intermittent electric contact. One after the other, brothers and sisters were jumping over the wires where they touched and exploded into fiery bright sparks. This gave them powerful shocks that scorched their fur and made them scream at the top of their lungs. The shocks threw them to the floor, dazed and exhausted; nevertheless, some of the really crazy ones apparently didn't get enough and wanted to submit themselves to the torture all over again. Unfortunately, there were other mental cases standing behind them who hadn't had their laughs for the day and pushed the ones who had just gotten shocked aside to get to the front themselves.
>
> "In the name of Brother Claudandus!" drubbed the preacher to his little lambs. "In the name of Brother Claudandus, who sacrificed himself for our sakes and who became God! Claudandus, O holy Claudandus, hear our suffering, hear our voices, hear our prayers! Accept our sacrifices!"

Females begin to be victims. Francis gradually learns what sadistic experiments were conducted on cats in the house eight years previously. He discovers an ancient underground catacomb where a mad Persian, Jesaja, has been duped into disposing of hundreds of dead cats for the murderous feline "Mister X" over the years. Nightmares featuring the victims, the faceless killer, the now-dead human scientist, and genetics pioneer Gregor Mendel offer clues just beyond understanding. Francis gains two allies who help him investigate; the foulmouthed, battered tomcat Bluebeard, and the elegant, erudite Pascal who is computer-literate and creates a data base with all the clues. Francis calls a Christmas Day open meeting of all the cats in the neighborhood at which shocking new clues are revealed, and Francis realizes that the killer has been in their midst all along.

Felidae, "der Katzenkrimi," was first published in 1989 in Germany (*Felidae*; Munich, Wilhelm Goldmann Verlag, July 1989). It was a major hit. A faithful (but condensed) animated feature by TFC Trickompany Filmproduktion GmbH was released in October 1994. Its home video release in America was shown on the program of furry fandom conventions for the next ten years. Seven sequels have been published in Germany (*Francis—Felidae II*, Goldmann, September 1993; *Cave Canem—Ein Felidae-Roman*, Goldmann, August 1999; *Das Duell—Ein Felidae-Roman*, Eichborn, October 2002; *Salve Roma!—Ein Felidae-Roman*, Eichborn, March 2004; *Schandtat—Ein Felidae-Roman*, Diana, May 2007; *Felipolis: Ein Felidae-Roman*, Diana, September 2010; and *Göttergleich: Ein Felidae-Roman*, Heyne, September 2012), but only *Francis—Felidae II* (as *Felidae on the Road*) and *Felidae V: Salve Roma!* have been published so far in English.

Flight of the Godkin Griffin • by M.C.A. Hogarth. Illustrations, map by the author.

St. Paul, MN: Sofawolf Press, June 2012, paperback, 247 pp.

The Godson's Triumph • by M.C.A. Hogarth. Illustrations; map by the author.

St. Paul, MN: Sofawolf Press, June 2014, paperback, 235 pp.

Flight of the Godkin Griffin is told in the form of the diary of Mistress Commander Angharad Godkin, 48 years old, from the eve of her long-awaited retirement after thirty-four years in the army of the Godkindred Kingdom; at once obviously an inhuman army on another world. She has been recuperating at Fort Endgame after being wounded at the battle for Glendallia; a Pyrrhic victory in which she lost most of her cavalry unit and half of her command staff. She is just packing to leave when she is summoned to the office of the Fort's commander:

> The Mistress General hovers behind a desk, overlooking several maps and emitting a palpable air of tension. She has never elucidated her bloodlines to me, though to be named Godkin she must be the product of the interbreeding of at least ten species, as I am. In appearance, she is mostly mammalian, leaning toward genet or marten with rounded ears and a striped tail.
> "Mistress General, you wanted to see me?" I ask.
> "Yes," she says curtly. "Angharad Godkin, you are hereby assigned to replace the provincial governor of the newly pacified province of Shraeven, on orders of the Godson."
> My beak drops open in shock. Any soldier in the Godson's army can retire … unless they're on active duty.
> Casandre sighs. 'Sit, Angharad."
> I refuse. 'I'm retiring tomorrow."
> "Not anymore," she says. "I'm sorry, Angharad, truly, but the Godson himself sent the orders. It's time for Governor Chordwain to step down."

In just the first two pages, Hogarth establishes that this is another world (with three moons), that Angharad can fly (her wings were injured in the battle for Glendallia; also, "A warm breeze presages spring and sweeps my fine hair off my shoulders, tickling my wings."—Angharad wears a backless blouse with breeches), that the creatures of this world can interbreed and do not look like each other, and that the royal court is *really* anxious for the politically inexperienced Angharad to take command of the large province of Shraeven (until its conquest an independent kingdom) as soon as possible. She is promised all the additional troops she wants, a new support staff, an almost unlimited expense account—but she, personally, has to be the new Governor. Angharad suspects that the "newly pacified province" is in fact a hellhole, and that she is expected to fail— but who wants her, personally, to be a scapegoat?

This is basically a semi-medieval political fantasy thriller. "'Shraeven,' [Silfie] says, "is an impossible province because it has so many ethnicities with such extremely different religions and customs that no one has been able to unite them long enough to convince them they've been conquered." Angharad, a military veteran but with no political experience, must educate herself fast in the internecine court and church intrigues of Shraeven; and deduce how this leads back to the Godson's court. "Angharad quickly finds herself the central piece in a game being fought on too many levels, all of them very foreign to her nature and background. But if she's being forced to play, she's going to play to win; and everyone may come to regret having gotten her into the game" (blurb).

Of important added interest, there are constant references to this planet's unique biology: "I have time to turn and recognize the lean figure jogging toward me as Gavan from the Third Moon Plain, one of my infantry captains, a stalwart veteran of two of my campaigns and a Fourblood of mostly predator lines: there's bear in his ears and nose and wolf in the tail, certainly" and "The door crashes open, expelling a page and a man on his heels. My first glance suggests wolf's ears, ram's horns, a coyote's muzzle, the spots of an ocelot, the stripes of a zebra."

This biology also figures into the social and political intrigue. "Angharad believes that her race is moving toward divinity by breeding many different species together; her own ten-species bloodline places her near the Godson in rank and makes her choice of mate difficult" (blurb). Angharad is an old lover (lesbian) of her new second-in-command, the vixenlike Silfia Fiveblood of the Dale, "who'd broken my heart when she allowed her family to dictate whether she should dally in a non-productive union instead of wedding someone who would produce the child Sixblood of the Dale." The myriad religions in Shraeven range from those that encourage interbreeding with anything that moves, to those that encourage interbreeding just among intelligent beings, to those that want to kill all the mixed breeds, much less the human-animal mongrels. One cult even worships the winged interbreeds like Angharad as gods. "'Perfection,' I murmur. 'Just what I need. A following.'"

And all the above is just in the first chapter! This all results in a novel of political intrigue in which the furry element is especially important. There is no human vs. furry conflict; everyone is a furry of one kind or another, with many more blends than Earth has species. It is almost immediately evident that in this context, "man" means anyone who is sentient. And the further they get into Shraeven, the more Angharad finds that it is not at all like she has been led to expect.

The reader should not be surprised to find that *Flight of the Godkin Griffin* frustratingly ends with Angharad and her army only nearing the capital of Shraeven, because

Sofawolf Press' publicity warns, *"Flight of the Godkin Griffin* is the first of a two-book series detailing Angharad's entry into Shraeven and her growing awareness of the challenges, both political and personal, that lie ahead of her." The conclusion, *The Godson's Triumph*, is just as imaginative. *Flight of the Godkin Griffin* was a finalist for the 2012 Ursa Major Award in the Best Anthropomorphic Novel category.

The Fox of Richmond Park • by Kate Dreyer.

London: Unbound, July 2017, paperback, 287 pp.

> If the Animals of Farthing Wood had lived in London and hated each other a little bit more, their story may have been a lot like this one. *"Get out of the way or get an antler up the arse, yeah? I'm sick of these glorified donkeys"* [blurb].

Almost all the (British) reviewers have compared this British novel to Colin Dann's 1979 classic *The Animals of Farthing Wood*. In that, the woodland community of Farthing Wood is paved over by human developers. The wildlife inhabitants, led by Fox, undertake a dangerous trek together to the safety of the distant White Deer Park nature reserve. *The Animals of Farthing Wood* is a Young Adult novel. All the animals act together in brotherhood. No one eats anybody.

The Fox of Richmond Park is an Adult novel. Richmond Park is a large wildlife park in London that Wikipedia says is known for its deer. In this talking-animal novel, the deer are the arrogant elite class of the Park's fauna. When the deer decide they want the lakeside area where several foxes have had their dens for generations, they just tell the foxes to move out. Most accept the order without protest. Vince does not.

> "Why I should leave," Vince snarled as he prowled back and forth in the semi-circle of bare earth that marked the entrance to his den, black ears flat to his head, "just because some over-entitled deer want to be near the lake?"
>
> "It's not like that. And you can dig a new, bigger den in a day or two. I don't see what the problem is. Other animals have moved without a fuss." Edward tilted his antlers towards the small skulk of foxes several leaps away, who had gathered at the edge of the woodland to wait for the sun to set. "And your friends are being very cooperative."
>
> "That's because you've told them a load of scat about how great the cemetery is." Vince said, the copper fur on his back bristling. He'd had every intention of talking this through civilly with the stag, but his temper had other ideas. Just like last time."

The other foxes privately agree with Vince, but why bring on an animal war? It's easier to move. Vince goes on arguing until he says he'd rather leave the park altogether than move to an inferior neighborhood, just because the deer order it.

> "But I'm not your enemy, Vince [Edward says]. This park is a wonderful place where we can all live together in safety, where humans respect us and take care of us. But there are rules. Just follow the rules like everyone else and you can stay. The last thing we want is to drive anyone away. Be serious, Vince. Do you really want to leave this place and live among humans? Dodging their cars, being kept awake by their incessant noise, eating their leftovers out of bins? Especially after what happened to your father."

Vince won't back down. Besides, he'd always wondered where his grandparents had lived before they came to Richmond Park. Now he's free to find out. He's not alone, either. Rita the magpie wants to join him.

> "Why do you want to come? I don't even know where I'm going."
> "I want to travel with you. See London. Have an adventure!"

"I'm not going on an adventure. I'm just looking for my grandparents' old home."

"Sounds like an adventure to me. Come on, I've spent too many seasons in this place. There's nothing for me here and I'm getting old…. I want to see the city! Fly to new places and taste new food and hear new birds!"

So Vince and Rita venture from Richmond Park, where they have always led a sheltered, protected life, into the London metropolis. They have to dodge cars, learn how to cross streets with traffic lights, discover the difference between human pedestrians with cell phone cameras who just want to take their pictures and animal welfare officers who want to trap Vince, and more. A running joke is Vince's frustration to find out what a poodle is.

Their search for Vince's grandparents' den takes them from Richmond Park to Hyde Park, Regent's Park where the London Zoo is, and further afield. They meet many animals like Sid the badger, Oswald the swan, Frank and Roger the geese, Socks the cat ("Official Feline Administrator of the Hammersmith area"), G, Jonny, and Ra-Ra, the rat gourmets of Soho, Arthur the hedgehog, and more. Some are helpful. Some are murderous. There is comedy, suspense, violence, and tragedy. Vince and Rita are gradually joined by others.

There are hints of romantic complications. Vince has left a vixen, Sophie, back in Richmond Park. Sophie has recently mated with another tod, Jake, but she and Vince still have feelings for each other. Vince and Rita meet another vixen, Laurie, an urban fox, on their travels. Will Vince mate with Laurie, or return to Richmond Park for Sophie? How far will Jake go to ensure that Vince does not return to Richmond Park?

There is also the constant plot to kill Vince before he can find his grandparents' home.

"Why bother? [asks Kara the owl] He's already gone."

"His death will be a warning to everyone here [answers Edward]. They need to be reminded that the city is dangerous and that Richmond Park is the best home they'll ever have. I have little doubt that Vince will fail on his own, but I'm not risking it. I can't have him sending messages back, encouraging others to flout the rules or leave or … worse. Park Watch would fall apart. I've spent seasons making this park what it is and I won't have that flea-ridden creature ruin it for me."

Dreyer refers at one point to *Watership Down*, but it's obvious before then that she is familiar with it. However, *The Fox of Richmond Park* is completely original. It is a top-quality addition to any library of talking-realistic-animal fantasies.

Foxhunt! • by Rich Hanes.

Everett, WA: Arkham Bridge Publishing, June 2009, paperback, 337 pp.

This is furry space opera, set in the Wildstar Universe of genetically-engineered human-like animals.

The interstellar peoples of the galaxy are all modified Earth mammals based upon dogs, foxes, raccoons, wolves, and more, although humans do exist. And the animals don't like each other. Interstellar warfare is strictly regulated through a Mercenary Command, and restricted to small mercenary companies rather than large national armies. Captain Sebastian Valentino, a humanoid fox, is the leader of the Star Rangers, the most successful mercenary company in the galaxy; 300+ mostly canids such as his Senior Lieutenant Corey Delzano, a jackal, and Junior Lieutenant Patricia Darling, a painted dog.

The Star Rangers usually are hired by the government of Valentino's own Star Alliance, and their target is usually the Alliance's traditional rival, the Canis Dominion.

All this is background that the reader will pick up in the first thirty or forty pages. The story is that Captain Sebastian Valentino is having an extremely bad day. Or bad week. Or bad months. First, his Assistant Captain and best friend Adrian Miller is killed in a botched raid that Sebastian blames himself for. Second, Adrian's extremely formal Rite of Passage (funeral) is also botched, which Sebastian (who is having a brief nervous breakdown) also blames himself for. Sebastian's new Assistant Captain, Corey Delzano, talks him out of it, incidentally giving the reader a smooth background course in Volpa history, language, and religion.

The third reason is the most important:

> Sebastian sighed and looked up over the top of his hefty tome on modern naval combat. A dingo with green general-duty epaulets approached him. "You're interrupting the Battle of Morswood, Collins," Sebastian said. "This better be important."
>
> "Extremely. See, we just got into orbit, and—"
>
> "Out with it, Sydney."
>
> Librarian Collins thrust a freshly printed newspaper into Sebastian's paws. "You'd better read this."
>
> Sebastian was long used to the strange texture and appearance of shipboard paper. The translucent sheets glittered when the metal threading in its pressed pulp surface caught the light. Limitations in ink forced grayscale only, and a limited lifespan, but ship life has its concessions. It was a far better solution than shutting the crew out of external news.
>
> Right now, Sebastian was concerned with the newspaper's cover: crosshairs super-imposed over a photograph of himself.
>
> "What is this?" He read the headline. "Fox on the Run?"
>
> "It's the National Informer—"
>
> Sebastian slammed the paper down atop the reading table with a dull smack. "I can see that, I'm not blind! I mean the caption, 'Number one mercenary becomes number one target.'"
>
> "We just got it over Lafayette's newswire, it's dated yesterday. I got it to you as soon as I could."
>
> Sebastian mumbled, sought out the associated story, and began to read. "Dateline, Sirius, 9 Ares. Canis Dominion officials stunned the galaxy today by proclaiming a bounty upon the head of Captain Sebastian Valentino, founder and commander of MerCom's highest ranked unit, Valentino's Star Rangers. The unprecedented announcement came just three triads after the destruction of an unidentified research installation in the Monterrey system, presumed to have been the work of the Star Rangers. This is the first time in history that a state has issued a bounty on a unit sanctioned by the Mercenary Command, and at a total payout of 3,000,000D, by far the largest ever offered for a single head."

The bounty may be irregular or even illegal, but it's been issued by a large government, and anyone who wants to collect it can count on being safe in the Canis Dominion. Sebastian is very devoted to traditional Volpa customs, and cannot be dissuaded from going personally to Adrian's family on the planet Wexford II to pay his condolences, despite the huge bounty on his head. At least he goes in disguise. The conversations, TV newscasts overheard, and so on will give the reader more background on the fox-dominated Star Alliance. Instead of saying "etc., etc., etc.," the foxes say "bark bark bark." The Alliance is concerned about the declining vulpine birth rate. Other interstellar nations mentioned in passing are the Pan-Atlantica Federation, the Balkany Democratic Republic, and the Lupine Order.

All of this is cited to show how much background there is. It is well-integrated into the novel. Sebastian is on Wexford II to see Adrian's parents. He's in disguise as a civilian, and is also taking a needed vacation after his recent breakdown. He stays in regular communication with Corey and his Rangers in his warship, the Favored Sky, in orbit. Everything is fine—until they aren't.

The huge bounty on him makes hiring his Rangers politically unacceptable for the Alliance. Someone tries to hire the Star Rangers themselves to assassinate him. Corey is tempted—with Sebastian dead, he would become the permanent leader of the Rangers. There is a precognition of doom, a tragic romance, and betrayal. Sebastian gives risky orders that, considering his earlier breakdown, make the Rangers doubt his emotional stability. Again, Corey is tempted—removing his Captain on mental grounds would be another way to take over the Rangers. The #2 mercenary company in the galaxy, the Disintegrators commanded by red wolf Commander Duke Thompson of the registered mercenary warship *Indeterrable*, attacks the Rangers to collect on the bounty: "You are a wanted war criminal, Valentino. It is my duty as a member of civilized society to place you under arrest."

Thing go from bad to worse. There are even one-on-one battles in titan combat armor (anime giant robots)! And the characters (aside from the odd human) are all furry. The dialogue contains many vulpine-specific references. "I can smell your lies…" "And now I get the stiff-tail?" "So that's it," he said, "after all my loyal service to the Alliance, it's goodbye, good luck, don't catch your tail in the door?" There are also references to the canid species in the Star Rangers:

> "Is it that time of year?"
> Corey scowled and bared his teeth. "No!"
> Patricia shrugged. "Well, how should I know? You look like you'd be helped by the company of a nice jackal woman, if there is such a thing."
> A snicker ran up from the bridge crew.
> "It is not mating season for jackals, you insufferable whelp!" Corey said.

For wolf fans, there is a lengthy sequence among the Lupine Order. *Foxhunt!* is superior both as space opera and as anthropomorphic literature.

Francis • by David Stern. Illustrated by Garrett Price.

New York: Farrar, Straus and Co., October 1946, hardcover, 226 pp.

Francis Goes to Washington • by David Stern. Frontispiece by Garrett Price.

New York: Farrar, Straus & Co, September 1948, hardcover, 255 pp.

The *Francis* novel is really the revised "Francis the talking-flying mule" short stories that Stern wrote for *Esquire* magazine (he turned Frances, a female, into Francis, a male, and connected the separate stories into a single novel) while serving on an Army newspaper in Honolulu during World War II. During America's participation in World War II, the only talking-animal wartime novel was *Mr. Limpet* by Theodore Pratt; but the magazine short stories kept the American home front entertained with wartime funny animals. (The *Mr. Ed* humorous fantasies by Walter R. Brooks, about Wilbur Pope and his often-drunken talking horse, were not war-related.)

The stories are narrated by a nameless second lieutenant (dubbed Peter Stirling in the sequel and in the movies, which is actually the pseudonym Stern used for the magazine stories during wartime) who finds himself rushed through an East Coast college's ROTC and sent to fight the "Japs" in the mountainous Burmese countryside. In the first story, he gets lost from the platoon he is supposed to be leading, and is caught between the shelling of both sides:

> I'd half-risen to make a run for it when I heard the whine of a shell. With the instinct one learns quickly in battle, I dove, rolled over three times, and came to a stop sitting up.
> I was at the bottom of a slight ravine surrounded by low banyan trees. I looked around.
> Standing a few feet from me was a runt of an Army mule, as sad a creature as ever hauled a load away. His head hung low and his back hung lower. The animal's hide was bespattered and anointed with what appeared to be a collection of all that was worst in Burma.
> I scanned the ravine.
> Except for the mule, it was empty.
> I began feeling myself all over to discover if I was injured. When I came to my posterior I winced. Nothing serious, but tender.
> "Isn't this one hell of a mess?" I must have spoken aloud.
> "You said a mouthful," said a voice.
> I leaped to my feet. Frantically I searched the ravine, following my gaze with the muzzle of my carbine.
> "I suggest you pull your head down," said the voice, "or you'll get it blown off."
> "Who said that?" I demanded.
> "I did." The voice was close.
> "Where are you?" I swung completely around.
> "Right in front of you."
> I could see nothing except the mule.
> "I can't see you," I said. "Come out or I'll shoot."
> "I am out," said the voice. "And you better put up that gun before you hurt somebody."

Most of "I Meet Francis" consists of the lieutenant slowly being convinced in the midst of an artillery barrage that he is really talking with a mule, and Francis' arguing that Army mules are more important than second lieutenants:

> "Next step," said the mule, "I calculate I am worth exactly seven of you."
> "What!"
> "You heard me, lieutenant. I'm worth to the Army exactly seven of you."
> "And how do you arrive at that figure?"
> "I'll show you," Francis said. "Simplicity itself. Shipping space is at a premium. The Army allots as much boat space to one mule as to seven lieutenants."
> "So what!"
> "So the Army could have brought seven lieutenants over to Burma. But it didn't. It brought me."

Francis gets the wounded lieutenant out of the artillery deathtrap and back to safety at the Burma Headquarters Base Hospital. Captains and majors congratulate the lieutenant on his skill and cleverness in escaping alone through the jungle. But the lieutenant is an honest man, and insists on giving credit to the talking mule for rescuing him. This gets the lieutenant three weeks in the hospital's neuropsychiatric ward.

The lieutenant tries to insist on Francis showing his true nature to the whole Army so he can be properly rewarded ("Francis Considers OCS"), which Francis refuses to cooperate with because he does not want publicity. Francis uses the lieutenant as a figurehead to warn the Army about some enemy sabotage or mission that is about to befall Burma GHQ ("Francis Makes a Phone Call"). Francis is happy to let the lieutenant claim all the credit, which he reluctantly does because he gets tired of being sent back to the neuropsychiatric ward. But eventually the colonels and generals in G-2 (military intelligence) insist on being told where he is getting his information from. The lieutenant is not going to lie to his superior officers. The next few stories have the lieutenant sneaking out of the psycho ward to get whatever new information about Jap air raids or other impending action that Francis has just learned about, and giving it to his superiors with a "don't believe me, but has my information been wrong yet?" attitude. Eventually even his superiors are trying to catch Francis exhibiting intelligence. Stern must have planned his stories carefully to keep Francis from being "unmasked" before the war ended.

The final story ("Francis Comes to a Dubious End") wraps up Francis' and the lieutenant's wartime careers nicely. It suggests that Stern was unsure in 1946 how popular his rah!-rah!-America!! military mule would be in peacetime. Very popular, as Universal Pictures' series of seven *Francis the Talking Mule* movies from 1950 through 1957 proved. *Francis* itself went through several printings, and Stern wrote a sequel, *Francis Goes to Washington* (1948), entering the ex-lieutenant into politics with Francis as his campaign manager. It ends on a cliffhanger indicating that Stern planned at the time to write more, but in 1949 he bought a New Orleans newspaper and spent the rest of his career managing it.

Furries Among Us: Essays on Furries by the Most Prominent Members of the Fandom • edited by Thurston Howl. Illustrated.

Nashville, TN: Thurston Howl Publications, June 2015, paperback, 174 pp.

Furries Among Us 2: More Essays on Furries by Furries • edited by Thurston Howl. Illustrated by Sabretoothed Ermine.

Lansing, MI: Thurston Howl Publications, August 2017, paperback, 179 pp.

> Are they human, or are they beast? Over the past several decades, the world has seen a new phenomenon on the rise, a group of people identifying as "furries." They have appeared in the

Furries Among Us; Essays on Furries by the Most Prominent Members of the Fandom edited by Thurston Howl (Thurston Howl Publications, June 2015). One of the first serious studies of furry fandom. Cover art by Tabsley.

news and popular TV shows as adults wearing fursuits and participating in sex parties, but what are they really? This collection of essays on the furry fandom reveals furries through their own eyes [back-cover blurb].

By now furry fandom has been in existence for long enough that serious books are being written about it. And "by the Most Prominent Members of the Fandom"—in other words, by people who really know what they're talking about, rather than outsiders who have only superficially studied it. The main thing wrong with this collection of essays is that its main market is the members of furry fandom itself. It doesn't have much visibility outside of furry fandom. It's "preaching to the choir." But if any non-fan asks what furry fandom is all about, this is a very good short book to recommend to them.

The contents are:

"Introduction" by Thurston Howl. Why this book was written. Three pages.

"The Furry Fandom" by Nyareon. The difference between fictional furries like Bugs Bunny and Sonic the Hedgehog, and real human furry fans. Six pages.

"Social Furs: An Inside Look at How the Furry Fandom Socializes" by Shoji. What furry fandom is like. Five pages.

"The Furry Fandom as a Folk Group" by Hypetaph. The community of furry fandom: how united it is; fursuiters versus others; social furs versus therians, etc. Eight pages.

"Furry Erotica" by Kyell Gold. The emphasis on erotica in furry writing and publishing, in perception versus reality; furry erotica versus other forms of furry "Adult" writing. Six pages.

"The History of Furry Publishing" by Fred Patten. Furry fanzines and specialty publishers, from the beginnings of furry fandom to the present. Twelve pages.

"Yiff? Murr? Sex in the Furry Fandom" by Thurston Howl. The openness of sex in furry fandom; the reality versus the popular public stereotype of "sex orgies in fursuits"; whether fantasy hybrids among fursuiters (a wolf/tiger) indicate a predication towards sexual miscegenation. Five pages.

"My Experiences with Furry Online Dating" by Takaa. Personal experiences of realistic social relationships within furry fandom. Four pages.

"What Does Art Mean to the Furry Fandom?" by Zambuka. The emphasis in furry fandom on visual creativity; the broad range of visual media; whether fursuits are a form of art; why a fan chooses one animal species over another as a fursona. Six pages.

"The Fuzzy Notes of Furry Fingers" by Roo. Personal experiences of a furry fan becoming a furry professional musician; the history of furry music. Ten pages.

"Fursuiting and the Fandom" by Keefur. What a fursuiter is; what being a fursuiter means emotionally. Eight pages.

"First Furry Convention at Califur 2008, a Memoir" by Corvin Dallas. A personal experience of a neo-fan's first furry convention. Si pages.

"Furcons: the Ins and Outs" by Zantal Scalie. What furry conventions are like in a broader scope, by a veteran attendee. Eight pages.

"The Origins of the International Anthropomorphic Research Project" by Raphael Dogustus (Kathleen C. Gerbasi, Ph.D.). "This research was supported by the

Social Sciences and Humanities Research Council of Canada. Address correspondence to Kathleen C. Gerbasi, Department of Psychology, Niagara County Community College, Sanborn NY 14132." How the most long-running psychological-social study of furry fandom got started. Three pages.

"'By the Numbers': Comparing Furries and Related Fandoms" by Nuka (Courtney Plante, Ph.D.). Detailed results of questionnaires passed out online to numerous self-identified furry fans and at many furcons from 2011 to the present. Twenty pages.

"Social Identity Perspective of the Furry Fandom" by Doc (Stephen Reysen, Ph.D.). An academic social analysis of the IARP's questionnaires. Twenty-four pages.

"Marginalization of Anthropomorphic Identities: Public Perception, Realities, and 'Tails' of Being a Furry Researcher" by Dr. Shazzy (Sharon E. Roberts, Ph.D.). "The purpose of this chapter is to flesh out our professional views on the furry fandom, document furries' ascribed status in culture, review some of our history with the media, and discuss the implications of our research as it relates to the human interest side of the furry story." Sixteen pages.

Each of the sixteen essays is introduced with a one-page biography of the author, and his/her cartoon portrait as his/her fursona by Sabretoothed Ermine, the winner of the 2014 Ursa Major Award in the Best Anthropomorphic Published Illustration category.

So. Sixteen essays, all by experts of one sort or another. Some are humorous, or are personal anecdotes; others are dryly academic, some with footnotes and/or references. The last four should be seen as a set. (The sixteen make it clear that there is no standardization as to whether the initial f in either "furry" or "fandom" should be capitalized or not, although the majority use the lower-case.)

For the furry fans, this mostly confirms what is already known. For those who just enjoy the current furry subculture and don't know how or when it started, *Furries Among Us* and *Furries Among Us 2* will tell you. For those interested in details—what percent of furry fans just enjoy the atmosphere versus what percent adopt fursonas or wear full-body fursuits—here are statistics. For the non-fan wanting real information—such as a parent wanting to know what an adolescent son is getting involved with—these are an excellent tutorial. *Furries Among Us* won the 2015 Ursa Major Award in the Best Anthropomorphic Other Literary Work category. *Furries Among Us 2* won a 2017 Leo Literary Award and was a finalist for the 2017 Ursa Major Award in the new Best Anthropomorphic Nonfiction category. In 2017 the Library of Congress added a new subject heading for cataloging books, Furry fandom (Subculture), based on five references including this and *Furry Fandom Conventions, 1989–2015* by Fred Patten.

Furry Fandom Conventions, 1989–2015 • by Fred Patten. Furword [sic] by Kathleen C. Gerbasi. Illustrated (8 color pp.).

Jefferson, NC: McFarland, January 2017, paperback, 250 pp.

This is one of the first serious nonfiction books about the history of furry fandom; its conventions, in particular. It documents all of the furry conventions around the world from the first in 1989 to the end of 2015.

Patten, a history major in college, felt that this information should be collected and printed somewhere while all the participants (the convention organizers and attendees) were still alive to be asked. Some of it was already published online on WikiFur, the online encyclopedia of furry fandom. But much of it was not. Some of it was easily retrievable from convention chairmen and other organizers, who got it from old convention records. Other information was already lost. Some organizers said that their goals had been to have fun, not to keep records or to "engage in bureaucracy." Many conventions or organizers never replied to questions. A few boasted that they refused to cooperate. One convention threatened to sue if it was mentioned in the book (but some of its information was already public knowledge on WikiFur).

The same went for illustrations. Many convention chairmen or other staffers sent sample logos, website banners, convention souvenir book covers, T-shirt images, illustrated hotel room keys, and the like. One past chairman of a long-discontinued convention took an old souvenir book and re-scanned its cover for this book. The most cooperative were the Russian fans of RusFURence, who sent almost a dozen images when asked for one sample. Other conventions said that they hadn't kept anything. One convention chairman answered all the questions from its records, which he had, but said he had never had any artwork, which had been kept by another committee staffer who refused to send any for this book.

Furry Fandom Conventions ended up with complete or partial coverage of 116 furry conventions worldwide, 56 of which were illustrated. The book contains eight color plates, making it the first book about any aspect of furry fandom to be at least partially illustrated in color, and an index. It contains a "Furword" (the pun is deliberate) by Dr. Kathleen C. Gerbasi of the Niagara County Community College of the State University of New York, the author of the first peer-reviewed, scientifically-based study of furry fans in a scientific journal, and a member of the International Anthropomorphic Research Project. It is the first book about furry fandom from a general publisher rather than one of the furry specialty presses.

A sample entry is:

Zampacon

Zampacon, "La Prima Convention Furry Italiana," means "Pawcon." Despite its small size, it has been enthusiastically supported by all Italian furs. The same art is used for the poster, conbook cover, and T-shirt each year. The badge artist is always Aledon Rex.

Name & Date	Theme	Location	Attendance
Zampacon '12 December 29, 2012– January 1, 2013	none	Due Torri youth hostel, near Bologna	31
Zampacon '13 September 4–8, 2013	At the Beach	Maria Gabriella Hotel, Rimini	41
Zampacon '14 September 3–7, 2014	Murrs Attacks!	Hotel Morri Oceania, Bellaria-Igea Marina	54
Zampacon '15 September 2–6, 2015	Fur Ro Dah!	Hotel Morri Oceania, Bellaria-Igea Marina	60

Events

Zampacon '12: The first Zampacon was limited to 34 registrants; the limit of the hostel. 4 cancelled at the last moment, and only one new fur registered. Games were held in the lobby in the morning, and panels in the evening. Movies were shown on two nights, and there was a New Year's celebration with a mini-disco, in the lobby, games on the upper floor, a midnight fireworks show, and a toast. The poster artist was Alpha0; there was no conbook or T-shirt.

Chairmen or Organizers: Ajani, Rov, Valion

Zampacon '13: Zampacon '13 moved to the Adriatic coast in Summer, and increased from four to five days. The larger hotel permitted the removal of the attendance limit. The convention was unofficially beach-themed, with furry beach activities. Zampacon '13 added a Dealers' Den, a 20-page conbook, and a T-shirt. The poster, conbook cover, and T-shirt artist was Aledon Rex.

Chairmen or Organizers: Ajani, Rov, Valion, Maxsteel

Zampacon '14: Zampacon '14 had a new hotel but was still on the Adriatic beaches; but beach activities were cancelled due to bad weather. The 54 attendees included some from Greece, Slovenia, and the U.S. The "Murrs Attacks!" theme was a reference to the *Mars Attacks!* movie, which was shown (in English, subtitled in Italian). Six attendees joined only for the fursuit activities, including an unofficial evening Fursuit Parade through the city streets. Convention upgrades included the adoption of two cartoon mascots, an anthro white Maremma sheepdog named Dante and a lynx named Beatrice, both dressed in Italian red-white-green, designed by Aledon Rex; a glow-in-the-dark waistband, a LAN tourney, a video game tournament, a larger conbook; more con-owned equipment; and the translation of key program items into English. There were volunteers for security, the dealers' den, and spotting. The poster, conbook cover, and T-shirt artist was Black Lion. As an April fool's joke, the hotel announced that the convention had added a guest of honor: a prominent Italian politician (who was revealed at the last minute as also a notorious porn star).

Chairmen or Organizers: Ajani, Rov, Valion, Aledon Rex

Zampacon '15: "Fur Ro Dah!" was a reference to the *Skyrim* fantasy RPG game. There was a pre-convention contest for writers to submit articles for the conbook. Beach games were again possible due to fair weather. Full English translations were provided of all website and forum text to enable English speakers to join more easily. The first fursuit street parade was held, with a city permit; it was mentioned positively in two newspapers. There was a fursuit photoshoot. Zampacon '15 featured a Zampacon Mystic Quest, a convention-long treasure hunt with all attendees assigned to one of six teams, that included exploring the whole city. The poster, conbook cover, and T-shirt artist was Alpha0, and there was a Zampacon color printed lanyard. As an April Fool's joke, it was announced that the theme was being changed to My Little Zampacon to accommodate a large number of German *MLP:FIM* fans who had just joined.

Chairmen or Organizers: Ajani, Rov, Valion, Aledon Rex, Scale

Furry Fandom Conventions was a finalist for both the 2017 Ursa Major Award and a 2017 Leo Literary Award in the Best Anthropomorphic Nonfiction Work category.

Furry Fandom Conventions, 1989–2015 by Fred Patten (McFarland, January 2017). The first nonfiction book about an aspect of furry fandom from a non-furry publisher; nominated for the 2017 Ursa Major Award in the Best Other Literary Work category. Cover art by Yamavu.

The Furry Future: 19 Possible Prognostications • edited by Fred Patten.

Dallas, TX: FurPlanet Productions, January 2015, paperback, 445 pp.

The Furry Future: 19 Possible Prognostications is a good sample of one of the furry specialty publishers' theme anthologies, and how stories in furry fandom can interlock.

It is a paperback. It contains nineteen original short stories and novelettes "in which humans and/or one or more furry peoples share a future civilization." (Introduction) The stories cover a wide variety of settings: humans and bioengineered furry peoples sharing an interplanetary or interstellar civilization together; either the humans or the furries trying to make themselves an upper-class and the others a lower-class; humans making the first bioengineered furries, usually from the furries' point of view; humans having become extinct and furries having replaced them; and stories with furry aliens not related to Earth animals. The stories include action, dramas, humor, romance, and mood pieces.

One novelette is rewritten from stories in *Yarf!* in the 1990s. Another is a prequel to a forthcoming novel (since published). A third has illustrations by Roz Gibson, commissioned by its author and donated to FurPlanet; the book is otherwise not illustrated. "The Analogue Cat" by Alice Dryden, about a second-generation Bengal tiger bioengineered to be an expensive toy, who gradually degrades as later models become available, but finds a new purpose in life, won both the 2015 Ursa Major Award and the 2015 Cóyotl Award for Best Short Story:

> You're not quite a Pet any more, but not quite a Bot either; something in between, non-binary.... You don't mind so much, these days, that the breeder stole your sex years ago. You pick a new set of pronouns to go with the changes in your body, and a new name: Tozer. You're the Analogue Cat.
>
> Now you find that the firsties and the second-gens are an embarrassment the third generation hopes will die off quickly, and sometimes helps to get there.... At thirty-eight you feel used up, your striped and spotted fur losing its plushy thickness and the skin loose around your shrinking neck, but you hang on. You're not sure what for. You don't fit. These days, people want everything to be discrete and sharply defined: on/off, male/female, good/evil.
>
> You're an analogue cat in a digital world.

Three others, "Tow" by Watts Martin, "Lunar Cavity" by Mary E. Lowd, and "Thebe and the Angry Red Eye" by David Hopkins, were finalists for the 2015 Ursa Major Award for Best Anthropomorphic Short Fiction. The complete contents are: "Emergency Maintenance" by Michael H. Payne, "Tow" by Watts Martin, "Experiment Seventy" by J.F.R. Coates, "A Bedsheet for a Cape" by Nathanael Gass, "Hachimoto" by Samuel C. Conway, "Vivian" by Bryan Feir, "Family Bonding" by Yannarra Cheena, "The Future Is Yours" by MikasiWolf, "Distant Shores" by Tony Greyfox, "The Analogue Cat" by Alice "Huskyteer" Dryden, "The Sequence" by NightEyes DaySpring, "Trinka and The Robot" by Ocean Tigrox, "Lunar Cavity" by Mary E. Lowd, "The Darkness of Dead Stars" by Dwale, "Field Research" by M.C.A. Hogarth, "The Curators" by T.S. McNally, "Evolver" by Ronald W. Klemp, "Growing Fur" by Fred Patten, and "Thebe and the Angry Red Eye" by David Hopkins.

The popularity two years later of the novel *Kismet* by Watts Martin (nominated for both the 2017 Cóyotl Award and the 2017 Ursa Major Award for Best Novel) led to a surge in sales of *The Furry Future* to get Martin's prequel novelette, "Tow":

> "Gail's mouth drops open. "I'm as human as you are, you—"
>
> "You're a *rat*. You've turned your back on just being human." He sneers. "A *rat*, but you think you're better than us 'prims' now. That's what your mother called us, wasn't it?"
>
> Scowling Young Man nods approvingly at what Charles says. Linda hasn't moved yet, as far as she can tell. She's been studying Gail so raptly it's disquieting. Leon's expression is unreadable. He's been listening to this all his life, hasn't he? God, he knows better than this; he's been to Panorica, he's been around totemics.
>
> Gail shakes her head. "If you think that's what she was saying, you weren't listening at all."

The Furry Future: 19 Possible Prognostications has been a strong seller in furry fandom since it was published, mostly through FurPlanet's sales tables at furry conventions. It was a finalist for both the 2015 Cóyotl Award and the 2015 Ursa Major Award in the Best Anthology category. It was favorably reviewed on Goodreads. Cat Rambo, president of SFWA, said on *The Green Man Review* (April 15, 2018), "This book is one that scholars writing about furry fiction will want to be including on their reading lists for reasons including its focus, its authors, the snapshot of the current furry fiction scene that it provides, and the variety of approaches to anthropomorphic body modification."

Furry Nation: The True Story of America's Most Misunderstood Subculture • by Joe Strike. Illustrated.

Jersey City, NJ: Cleis Press, October 2017, paperback, 351 pp.

Joe Strike promoted the book that he was writing heavily within furry fandom, as "the first history of furry fandom," for about a year before its publication, so it was eagerly anticipated. Is it perfect? No, but it's much better than it could have been.

Joe Strike has been in furry fandom since the 1980s. He has been working on *Furry Nation* for at least fifteen years. It is full of both his own knowledge and the interviews that he conducted. He has interviewed not only all the earliest furry fans, and the current leaders of furry fandom—Mark Merlino, Rod O'Riley, Jim Groat, Mitch Marmel, Dr. Sam Conway, Boomer the Dog, leading furry artists like Heather Bruton and Kjartan Arnórsson, fursuit makers like Lance Ikegawa and Denali, academics like Dr. Kathy Gerbasi, and so on—but those outside the furry community who have impacted it. The writers of newspaper and TV news stories about furry fandom? He interviewed them. The executives of Pittsburgh's tourist bureau? He interviewed them. The directors of TV programs and theatrical animation features that have used furry themes? He interviewed them.

What *Furry Nation* covers: a definition of furry fandom, the influences that gave rise to it back to prehistoric times, the history of how it started, profiles of the earliest furry fans, how the rise of the Internet affected it, a description of furry fandom in North America today, with emphasis on its conventions and a profile of Anthrocon in depth, its artists and furry art, its fursuits, its public perception, an acknowledgment of its seedier side, and how it has grown from a tiny, unnoticed subgroup to an important influence on popular culture today. The book has 189 footnotes throughout it. There are over two dozen photographs and samples of furry illustrations from the 1980s (early fanzines and Furry Party flyers) to the present.

Some chapters: "The Many Flavors of Fur." "A Fandom Is Born." "Pretty as a Picture: Furry Art." "Together Is Just What We've Got to Get: The Convention Age Begins." "Walk a Mile in My Fursuit." "I Read the News Today, Oy Vey." "Anthrocon: The Convention That Conquered Pittsburgh."

What *Furry Nation* does *not* cover: furry fandom outside North America, and areas of furry creativity in addition to its fursuits and art. There is nothing about its literature: the furry specialty publishers, the furry novels and anthologies and collections, the furry writers' organizations, and the literary awards. This is deliberate and really nobody's fault. I can confirm personally that Strike interviewed me at length about furry literature. Allyson Fields, the Marketing Manager at Cleis Press, apologized that Strike's manuscript was so huge that whole chapters had to be edited out. A look at the attractive but small book tells why: *Furry Nation* is only 5" × 7.9" wide, almost a literal pocket book (most standard hardcovers are 6" × 9" or slightly larger) but nearly 1" thick; bulging for its size. (Joe Strike has said that if *Furry Nation* sells well, he will write a second book that contains all of the material cut from it: *Furry Planet*.)

The result unfortunately reinforces the stereotype that furry fandom is primarily a U.S. and Canadian subculture, and that most furry fans are only interested in wearing fursuits, and drawing or collecting furry artwork. There are mentions still in the book of the furry conventions outside North America, and of activities besides the furry art and fursuits; but they are so small that they are easy to miss.

A further flaw is that, as Strike alludes to in his first chapter, "And quite a few people who enjoy anthro characters no longer call themselves furry…." Specifically, a few people who were crucial or influential in starting furry fandom in the 1980s and 1990s refused to be interviewed for this book, or to answer any of Strike's questions. For potential legal reasons, they are not mentioned in *Furry Nation*. Yet they were very important furry fans twenty and thirty years ago. Any history of furry fandom that does not even mention them is badly flawed.

So what are the merits of *Furry Nation* (cover photograph of "Madelein the Lynx" fursuit head)? It's always flattering to read an entire book that presents a favorable picture of your self-adopted hobby or lifestyle; that pats ourselves on the back. (Or should that be, scritches our fur?) For the furry neofan who wonders when and how it all got started, here is the answer! For the adolescent fur whose parents want to know what furry fandom is before giving permission to go to that convention or to attend that rave, here is the book to give them.

The main physical drawback of *Furry Nation* is its small size, cheap paper, and paperback nature. Libraries tend not to get such books, so you probably can't refer anyone to it. If you want to show it to anyone, you may have to buy your copy, or show it on Kindle. Still, this is the first book about the history of furry fandom. Many furry fans—those who don't attend furry conventions only for the fursuiting and the dancing and the evening partying—are reading it. It won the 2017 Ursa Major Award for the Best Anthropomorphic Non-Fiction Work, and was a finalist for a 2017 Leo Literary Award in the corresponding category.

God of Clay by Ryan Campbell (Sofawolf Press, September 2013). The first novel of Campbell's popular *The Fire Bearers* trilogy; winner of the 2013 Cóyotl Award for Best Novel. *Forest Gods*, the second novel, was a finalist for the 2015 Cóyotl Award. Cover art by Zhivago.

God of Clay • by Ryan Campbell. Illustrated by Zhivago.

St. Paul, MN: Sofawolf Press, September 2013, paperback, 261 pp.

Forest Gods • by Ryan Campbell. Illustrated by Zhivago.

St. Paul, MN: Sofawolf Press, September 2015, paperback, 345 pp.

The series title is *The Fire Bearers*. It is packaged as a trilogy, but it is really one novel in three volumes.

In the prehistoric past, when men shared the world with anthropomorphized animal-gods, there were two very different brothers in a tribe. Clay, the older brother, respects and worships the old gods who control all men's lives, while irreverent Laughing Dog mocks the unseen gods, and swears that he controls his own destiny. The brothers love each other, in their own ways, but their differences lead both to disaster:

> Doto crouched in the forest, his clawed fingers pressing down beneath the grasses and bed of fallen leaves to touch the earth below. He went out, out, into the soil, into the trunks of the trees, the branches and leaves, the grasses and ferns. He felt the air swaying branches, the sunlight on the leaves. He felt the rodents skittering across the forest floor.… He leapt from branch to branch and winged over the canopy. He spread himself out, farther and farther. Through the keen eyes of the birds and the considering gaze of a monkey clinging to a branch above, he could see himself, crouched on the ground far below, so still that he was nearly undetectable.… All the surrounding life lived through him. But all was not right. There was an uneasiness in the forest, somewhere around the edges. Could great Atekye have risen herself up in the south of the forest, swelling her swamps to flood the forest floor once again?

Doto is a young god who usually looks like a humanoid leopard; the son of Kwaee, king of the gods, who looks like a humanoid leopard with a feathery crest. But Kwaee has become irascible and sullen to all life, mortal and the other gods alike. He has withdrawn from the forest to sulk upon his throne. Doto learns that the uneasiness is caused by the return to the forest of Ogya, the powerful god of fire and destruction, with his acolytes, the Fire Bearers. Doto races to his father to report the dread news, so that Kwaee will finally rouse himself and deal with the menace. Instead, Kwaee belittles him for bothering him with imaginary fears. He orders Doto to go and capture a Fire Bearer, if they are real.

The Fire Bearers are, of course, humans, who have migrated across the savannah and come to the forest. The presence of baboons, grey parrots, gorillas, hyenas, and elephants clearly establish this as ancient Africa. Clay and Laughing Dog's tribe has been driven to the edge of the forest by the increasing desertification of the savannah. (The development and spread of the Sahara Desert?) The tribe's ancient legends of the forbidden forest keep them from venturing into the forest. But Laughing Dog's disbelief in the gods leads him to publicly break the taboos.

As Clay is led south as Doto's captive, further into the forbidden forest-jungle, Laughing Dog becomes possessed by Ogya. Clay and Doto bond as reluctant friends, and Laughing Dog/Ogya becomes an enemy. Clay denies that humans are controlled by Ogya, the god of fire, but he has to admit that Ogya is one of gods whom the tribe worships, and humans are the only animals that have fire. Is Ogya "a benevolent trickster [or] a malevolent, world-consuming monster"? Is he manipulating humans without their awareness? And are humans just another species of animal, or something different?

The three volumes of *The Fire Bearers* do not include any anthropomorphic animals, just anthropomorphic gods. But there are several of them: Father Fam, Mother Wem, Kwaee of the forest, his son Doto, Sarmu of the savannah, Ogya of fire and the wastelands, Mpo of the ocean, and others:

He [Doto] twitched his ears backward towards the sounds of thousands of tiny feet moving over the loam. His fur lifted and stood on end with the familiar energy in the air that told him a god was nearby—a lesser god, perhaps, but a god nonetheless. Behind him, a parade of ants was approaching, winding their way around roots and fallen leaves. Carrying assorted bits of food and earth. A very large ant led them, his head half as high as Doto's knee, and he walked upright, in the manner of the gods. He was munching a pear, his mandibles clicking in a rhythmic pattern. He wore an expression of deep focus, but looked up when Doto's shadow fell over him. "Brother Doto." He grinned between bites of fruit. He did not stop marching forward, nor did his subjects stop moving behind him.

"Good day, Brother Atetea," Doto said, dipping his head. "Where are you headed today?"

The god shrugged his four shoulders. "We are building a new palace," he said around his mouthful. "This one bigger than the last. There will be so much more room for our larders! Rooms upon rooms of sticky, tasty fruit. I would invite you to come inside, but as usual, you are so terribly oversized."

"Yes," Doto agreed. "I am." He considered. Atetea might be only god of ants, but there were ants throughout the forest. "Tell me, Brother, have you noticed the stillness in the forest today?"

He [Kwaee] was a large leopard, greater in size than Doto, and across his rosettes the sun played even at night, granting him its brilliance and yet leaving him—when he wished to be—unseeable. The end of his tail twitched in impatience. He had apparently been consuming a flamingo, one gnawed pink leg clutched between his clawed fingers, and he did not look pleased at all to see Doto. The brightly colored feathers that sprouted from his brow and temples were raised high and imperious.

The Fire Bearers is not just a learning experience for Clay, Doto, and Laughing Dog. Each is subtly, physically changed, for better or ill. To say how would give away too many spoilers. Just know that, despite what each of them goes through, their unexpected journeys are life-changing. *God of Clay* won the 2013 Cóyotl Award, and *Forest Gods* was a 2015 Cóyotl Award finalist.

Gods with Fur: And Feathers, Scales, ... • edited by Fred Patten.

Dallas, TX: FurPlanet Productions, June 2016, paperback, 453 pp.

Gods with Fur, an anthology of twenty-three original short stories and novelettes by furry authors, won both the 2016 Cóyotl Award and the 2016 Ursa Major Award in the Best Anthology and the Other Literary Work categories. It contains "400 Rabbits" by Alice "Huskyteer" Dryden, which won both the 2016 Cóyotl and Ursa Major Awards in the Short Story categories. Another story, "Questor's Gambit" by Mary E, Lowd, was a 2016 Ursa Major finalist, and the book's cover by Teagan Gavet was a finalist for the 2016 Ursa Major in the Best Anthropomorphic Published Illustration category.

The theme of *Gods with Fur* is traditional gods who have taken on animal form, and gods who are animals. The complete contents are: "400 Rabbits" by Alice "Huskyteer" Dryden, "Contract Negotiations" by Field T. Mouse, "On the Run from Isofell" by M.R. Anglin, "To the Reader … by Alan Loewen, "First Chosen" by BanWynn Oakshadow, "All of You Are in Me" by Kyell Gold, "Yesterday's Trickster" by NightEyes DaySpring, "The Gods of Necessity" by Jefferson Swycaffer, "The Precession of the Equinoxes" by Michael H. Payne, "Deity Theory" by James L. Steele, "Questor's Gambit" by Mary E. Lowd, "Fenrir's Saga" by Televassi, "The Three Days of the Jackal" by Samuel C. Conroy, "A Melody in Seduction's Arsenal" by Slip-Wolf, "Adversary's Fall" by MikasiWolf, "As Below, So Above" by Mut, "Wings of Faith" by Kris Schnee, "The Going Forth of Uadjet" by Frances Pauli, "That Exclusive Zodiac Club" by Fred Patten, "Three Minutes to Midnight" by Killick, "A Day with No Tide" by Watts Martin, "Repast (A Story of Aligare)" by Heidi C. Vlach, and "Origins" by Michael D. Winkle.

The stories feature Aztec, Norse, Greek, Egyptian, and Chinese mythology. The stories by Anglin, Gold, Lowd, Schnee, and Vlach are set in their author's established series. There are comedies, dramas, detective puzzles, romances, and tragedies. There are the usual mixtures of established furry authors and first-time authors, and real names plus furry pseudonyms. There are authors in Australia, Canada, France, Singapore, Sweden, the U.K., and the U.S.

"400 Rabbits" features the Centzon Totochtin (infinite rabbits), the 400 perpetually drunken rabbits of Mesoamerican mythology; the children of Mayahuel, goddess of alcohol (pulque), and her husband Petecatl, god of medicine, healing, and sex. Together the forever-roistering Centzon Totochtin were the Mesoamerican gods of drunkenness. Dryden imagines what might happen if one of them were to sober up:

> "'Hey! Keep the noise down!' Three-Twenty-Three-Rabbit staggered into the burrow, still clutching an empty bottle which had, at some stage, contained pulque. 'What a night, huh? That was one amazing party. Wasn't it?'
>
> "Was it?" Eighty-Six-Rabbit eyeballed his brother....
>
> "What was so great about it?" Eighty-Six asked. "Tell me one thing."
>
> One of Three-Twenty-Three's ears drooped. He pushed it upright with a paw, only for the other to flop down over his eye.
>
> "Well … there was … how about…" He scratched his whiskers. "Actually, Eightsy, I can't remember the first thing about it. And that's what made it so amazing!" he finished triumphantly.
>
> "Don't you ever want to do something different with your evenings? And don't call me Eightsy."

Gods with Fur: And Feathers, Scales, … edited by Fred Patten (FurPlanet Productions, June 2016). Winner of the 2016 Cóyotl and Ursa Major Awards for Best Anthology; contains "400 Rabbits," the winner of the 2016 Cóyotl and Ursa Major Awards for Best Short Story. Cover art by Teagan Gavet.

"All of You Are in Me" by Kyell Gold is set in his world of Argaea, the locale of *Volle* and its sequels. Gold asks, in a world of equal anthropomorphic animal species, how might the Catholic Church have developed?

> I was eight, I guess, because I was holding that little plastic deer in my paw as we knelt in the pews, and I remember my ninth birthday was when Mom told me that I was too big a wolf to take toys to church…. Eight-year-old me looked down at the deer (it was a G.I. Joe, I think) in my paw and then up at the front of the church. If you've never been in a Catholic church, the altar's surrounded by the twelve Aspects of Christ. I had always looked at Jesus Dog when praying … but when I heard that line that day, I looked up at the Jesus Stag and I really understood how all the twelve species could be part of the same person. I felt the thrill when I looked at the Stag that I never had looking at the Dog…

Heidi C. Vlach's world of Aligare is original, and so are its Gods:

> Mama said there was a legend about the gods giving out names. Long ago, when the land was new and the first trees were stretching toward the dome of the Great Barrier, the mortal peoples were nameless. That was unfitting for gods' children. The Great Ones discussed and disagreed, and in the end used their vast power to poke dimples into the peoplekind's inner essence. Not enough to hurt,

only enough to make people want to prod that spot inside themselves. Smooth it over. Maybe fill it with something.

Some of the twenty-three stories in *Gods with Fur* feature well-known mythologies, others feature obscure gods from those mythologies, and still others entirely make up their own mythologies and gods. But all are imaginative, and most, even the comedies, are respectful to those gods.

Green Fairy • by Kyell Gold. Illustrated by Rukis.
St. Paul, MN: Sofawolf Press, March 2012, paperback, 271 pp.

Red Devil • by Kyell Gold. Illustrations by Rukis.
St. Paul, MN: Sofawolf Press, January 2014, paperback, 272 pp.

Black Angel • by Kyell Gold. Illustrated by Rukis.
St. Paul, MN: Sofawolf Press, March 2016, paperback, 386 pp.

In the first novel of Gold's *Dangerous Spirits* trilogy, Solomon Wrightson, a wolf senior at Midland's Richfield High, is in trouble. During his childhood and early adolescence, he was a loner but basically just one of the kids. In high school, the wolves are the jock gang, going out together on the school baseball team. The coyotes also hang together, although they are looked on as second-class wolves.

But in their senior year, it all starts to fall apart. Sol has realized that he is gay, and has joined a gay e-mail group where he formed a relationship with Carcy, an older ram. Sol thought that he had kept this a secret except from his study partner who is also his only friend, Meg Kinnick, a sardonic otter goth girl; they are two loners hanging out together. They have planned to go to Millenport together the next summer when Sol gets a car; Meg to get a job away from her parents, and Sol to move in with Carcy.

However, the emotional pressure of keeping his emerging homosexuality a secret is wearing Sol down:

> Part of it was that for the last year, Sol had been terrified that he would let something slip about being gay. It had started out innocently enough, a couple weeks over the summer reading some material online, the burst of realization, the growing wave of guilt afterwards. He'd created an anonymous e-mail account to post to a forum for gay teens, where Carcy'd been one of the people to tell him there was nothing wrong with him. E-mail had led to IM had led to texting, and Sol had gotten his head around his sexuality without having to talk to anyone in his family, or at his church. Or the team.

Also, Sol's lack of interest in girls has been noticed by his classmates who suspect he may be gay. His loss of interest in baseball, coming just when Taric, a coyote senior is trying to make the team, leads the wolf coach to take Sol off the team and give his spot to Taric. This in turn leads Sol's jock father to threaten to withhold the car unless Sol gets back onto the team:

> "Listen," his father said. "There's no reason you shouldn't be better than a coyote at baseball. They might be a little faster, sure, but baseball's a team sport and you're part of a pack. No reason you shouldn't be better."
>
> Sol squirmed in his seat. It wasn't fair. He'd made it through eleven and three-quarters years of school doing well enough to play. Why couldn't coach have waited just two months before demoting

him? Even if it had happened after his birthday, he'd have the car. He could run away to Millenport with Meg as soon as he graduated. Just having that to look forward to would make the tension in these evenings tolerable. He tried to think back to when he'd been able to have a relaxing time with his father, and the last time he could remember had been when they'd gone to Natty's [his older brother] last football game.

But this is only half of *Green Fairy*. As part of a school project, Sol has to read a 1901 book, a translation of "The Confession of Jean de Giverne," written by the teenage de Giverne from his prison cell while awaiting execution for the murder of his gay lover. Sol's reading of this, while under the influence of Meg's green absinthe, causes him to vividly "go into" the lives of the spoiled Gallian chamois dandy and his lover, a transvestite dancer in the chorus line at the infamous Moulin Rouge, the most scandalous establishment of Lutèce's notorious Montmartre district:

> To an innocent chamois, as I was just two months ago, the chaos and cacophony of Montmartre is bewitching. It is an explosion of bright colors, a flood of smells, a patchwork of language from all corners of Gallia, gathered in a honeycomb of small rooms, each of which seems to have a window giving out onto the street and a fox, a badger, a rabbit, a mouse leaning out of it shouting or singing. It gives one the air of having entered a new world, and in early April, the ragamuffins sell dewy blooms of flowers just showing cracks of color through their green shells, the bohemians pull out their paintings of blue skies and vast gardens to show under the shelter of oilcloth with the light rain hissing softly atop. Father, father, can you see why I followed Thierry there?

In a series of alternating episodes, set off by a different typeface, Gold transports the reader along with Sol into the flamboyant life of Montmartre in 1901 and of Jean and the white-furred Niki. But as Sol's RL life deteriorates—Taric and his older sister Tanny are bad winners who go out of their way to harass Sol; his father tries to imprison him in a hated summer job; his obsession with becoming a vegetarian (like Carcy) begins to undermine his health; he gets hints that Carcy's love for him is barely superficial—and he uses more and more of Meg's absinthe to go deeper into Jean's world, Sol finds himself segueing from focusing upon Jean to focusing upon Niki in the first person (in a third typeface). He becomes an invisible observer of the transvestite fox's home life. And he gradually becomes aware that he is seeing things that Jean never saw; that could not have been in Jean's manuscript.

In *Red Devil* and *Black Angel*, Gold moves on to one of Sol's and Meg's acquaintances and to Meg herself. Each has "impossible" meetings with a ghost or an imaginary character who never lived, and each begins to find evidence that this character is manifesting in reality. All involve homosexuality or lesbianism, although they are written to not be erotic. Gold's *Dangerous Spirits* trilogy tastefully presents mature themes featuring adolescent characters for an all-ages readership.

Griffin Ranger. Volume 1, Crossline Plains • by Roz Gibson. Illustrated by Amy Fennell.

Dallas, TX: FurPlanet Productions, January 2015, paperback, 369 pp.

Griffin Ranger. Volume 2, The Monster Lands • by Roz Gibson. Illustrated by Cara Mitten, Amy Fennell, and Roz Gibson.

Dallas, TX: FurPlanet Productions, August 2017, paperback, 557 pp.

Griffin Ranger is set in a totally alien alternate universe. The land masses are the same as on our Earth, but the life forms and civilization that have evolved are dominated by birds. (The reader will have fun identifying both geographical features such as the Twin Continents, the Alpha River, the Five Lakes, and the Endless Ocean, and the cities and towns like Defiance, Flatlands City, and Foggy Bay.) Since birds don't have hands, the main intelligent landbound mammals are the raccoon/lemur-like "hanz" that are their symbiotic partners, and two species of canines: the wild wolfen, and the more domestic herders that have evolved from them. This Earth's civilization is dominated by the griffins, who are the principal inhabitants of what the reader will recognize as the Americas, Europe, and Asia. But in the last few hundred years the greenies, an aggressive bird species, have erupted from the Emerald Isles (New Zealand) to spread over the world. The griffins of the Northern Continent have allowed the greenies' partial settlement there under strict supervision, but there are suspicions that the greenies are preparing to take over totally.

A Prologue in volume 1 introduces the giant thunderbirds native to the Northern Continent, and some of the greenies who have been allowed to settle there. The greenies are obviously up to something both nefarious and deadly.

Chapter 1 introduces both the protagonist and most of the main species. This provides a colorful and necessary expository lump before the action starts:

> Harrell [White-Shoulders] was the largest male griffin for hundreds of miles. Only his ex-mate, Vaniss White-Shoulders, was bigger. He stood six feet tall, with bright-yellow eyes, a massive, orange beak and white forehead. The rest of his plumage was dark brown, except for a long white tail, white forelegs and the white wing-shoulders that gave him his clan name. The scales of his forelegs were the same yellow as his eyes, tipped with black talons, five inches long. Fully spread, his wings were twenty-five feet from tip to tip, powered by a huge chest sheathed in muscle.

Griffins during their adolescence traditionally go on a continent-wide "wander" of exploration. Harrell, the Griffin Ranger in charge of an area north of Earthquake City, learns that his daughter Aera, who is on a joint wander with four companions, is a week overdue. They went missing right about where the incident with the thunderbirds occurred, near the central Northern Continental agricultural city of Crosstown Plains, populated about equally with griffins and greenies. Harrell is worried, but not enough to abandon his territory to search for the missing youths, until his ex-mate Vaniss, the Ranger in charge of Earthquake City and his organizational superior, assigns him to find them. To aid Harrell, Vaniss gets him two assistants: Kwaperramusc (Kwap), an exotic griffin from the islands north of the Dry Continent (Indonesia and Australia) and the Rangers' best Investigator, and Tirrsill, an inexperienced but willing young female hanz.

Harrell, Kwap, and Tirrsill go to Crossline Plains, despite unexpected opposition. The lower-ranking greenies are cooperative, but they don't know anything. The non-cooperation of the greenie officials is expected; what is more troubling is the unconvincing innocence or open hostility of the local griffins, especially the resident griffin ranger.

The trio learns that other griffins and their hanz have gone missing near Crossline Plains. Their investigation draws them into a series of violent attacks, attempted murders with a high body count of bystanders, and more. Someone is desperate to keep them from learning anything. What they find could destroy their whole world.

Griffin Ranger is top-notch reading, whether for its well-crafted mystery, its action, or for the exotic civilization in which it is set. *Volume 2, The Monster Lands*, was a finalist for a 2017 Leo Literary Award. The two volumes have many scenes of the griffins' culture:

Harrell didn't know what else to say, silently watching the changing landscape as the rail-runner began its long descent out of the mountains. The air grew warmer and thicker as the rail-runner entered the valley, speeding through dense orchards of citrus and nut trees, their limbs laden with flowers or unripe fruit. Greenies fluttered amid the trees, cutting branches, thinning fruit or working on irrigation lines. They may be rude, arrogant, and noisy, but no one could say greenies were not industrious.

Earthquake City seemed to go on forever, filling the valley floor, up the mountains and finally down to the coast. The sky was hazy and dotted with griffins and greenies, and in the distance, he could see the tall forms of the business and trade towers. Most of the buildings in the valley housed herders, wolfen and greenie workers, while the griffins got the prime territory up on the mountains and by the coast. The occasional fire or landslide was a small price to pay for the winds and spectacular views the high grounds provided.

Except for one area that had been developed by greenies into a major shipping port, the coastline was left fallow. It was considered too vital for the wellbeing of fish stocks and migrating birds to risk damaging. Other than griffin roosts and a few ocean-front cottages owned by well-connected hanz or greenies, there were few signs of civilization up and down the continent's western edge.

Harrell flew north along the beach until Vaniss' roost came into sight. A large, airy glass and steel structure, it was in little danger from the frequent fires that burned through the coastal chaparral.

If anyone doesn't recognize the inspiration for the greenies, they are the keas of New Zealand's mountainous areas; this world's only carnivorous parrots. They are notorious for coming out of the mountains into New Zealand's skiing lodges and upland towns to raid garbage cans and demolish automobiles, television antennas, and whatever else they can.

The Heavenly Horse from the Outermost West • by Mary Stanton. Illustrated by Judith Mitchell.

Riverdale, NY: Baen Books, June 1988, paperback, 344 pp.

Piper at the Gate • by Mary Stanton. Illustrated.

Riverdale, NY: Baen Books, May 1989, paperback, 306 pp.

Many of the reviewers of this adventure fantasy have said that it is like *Watership Down*, but with horses instead of rabbits. Not exactly. *Watership Down* tries to be as realistic as possible except for its intelligent, talking rabbits. *The Heavenly Horse* is much more fantastically complex, with its structured organization of equine herds into formal officers; the concepts of the Army of One Hundred and Five (a representative of each of the domesticated breeds of horses) who live in the horsey Heaven known as the Courts of the Outermost West; and the equine equivalents of Satan: the Dark Horse; his lieutenant, the fanged horse Anor the Destroyer; and the Soul Taker, who tempts horses into betraying themselves:

> "A new horse," said a big, clumsy-looking Thoroughbred mare. Her name was Snip, and she was unranked in the herd hierarchy. Horses, by instinct and their own Laws, are herd animals, and have a strictly observed order of precedence: Lead Mare, Second-in-Command, Story-Teller, Caretaker, and unranked. Some herds, such as Bishop Farm's, have Dreamspeakers—mares blessed with dreams from the mouth of Equus, the horse god.

The herd of brood mares at Bishop Farm—Fancy (Lead Mare), Feather (Second-in-Command), El Arat (Story-Teller and Dreamspeaker), Susie (Caretaker), and two unranked (Snip and Cissy) are all agog when Emmanuel Bishop and his son David bring a new mare to join them. The new horse, Duchess, is a buckskin to everyone else, but El Arat, the Dreamspeaker, sees her as a many-colored Appaloosa.

> "You must know, Cory, that we horses are part of the whole, just as you dogs are—one of many under the One Who Rules Us All."
>
> "Our own gods, the horse gods, are both good and evil—both kind and cruel. And, like many gods, your own, perhaps, among them, some are more one than the other. There is Equus, our good Lord, and his Army of One Hundred and Five, who live in the Courts of the Outermost West. Each stallion in the Army of One Hundred and Five is a Breedmaster; each a foundation sire for the breeds in the world of men. And the Army is ranked, as all herds are ranked—according to duty and function. The Breeds themselves are numbered: the oldest god is Equus the First. The Dancer, Breedmaster of the Appaloosa, is Second; El Hakimer, Breedmaster to the Arabians, is Third—and so on down to the youngest breed, the Palomino, One Hundred and Fifth."
>
> "With Equus in the Courts live a band of Mares. As each stallion is Breedmaster; so each mare is Breedmistress. My own Goddess-mare, Jehana, is Dreamspeaker to these mares, and indeed, to Lord Equus himself."

Duchess is the destined Breedmistress for the Appaloosa, the last true Appaloosa mare. The Appaloosa breed is dying out. If Duchess can be united with the Dancer, the breed will be saved. She is unaware of her own identity. Equus and the Dancer, watching from the Courts of the Outermost West, are aware of her, but they are helpless to intervene in her fate. The Black Horse, the equine Devil, is eager for her death which will render the Appaloosa bred extinct. The One Who Rules Us All has decreed that she must reach the Courts from the mundane world on her own, without interference from either Equus or the Black Horse. But the Black Horse has already tried to surreptitiously kill Duchess, setting his Harrier Hounds (demonic reptilian equivalents of dogs) disguised as mortal dogs against her. This allows Equus and the Dancer to secretly help her in her travels to the Courts.

Secretly? The Dancer wants to challenge the Black Horse's second in command, Anor the Destroyer, the Executioner, a carnivorous horse "whose teeth, they say, are as sharp as a lion's, who drinks blood and eats meat, whose hooves are like swords," to a fight to the death. But he can only help Duchess secretly, by journeying to the mortal world and posing as a normal horse at Bishop Farm. He will lose his divinity and have to submit to the rule of men. He will become as vulnerable as any mortal horse, and they can be sure that the Black Horse will not miss this opportunity to try to kill him, too. "'And finally,' Equus leaned close to the Dancer, his voice compelling, 'you may *not seek out* Anor. He must come to you, or the Balance will be well and truly overset.'"

What follows is an exciting and suspenseful adventure as Duchess, so mistreated in her previous life that she is feral and lashes out at everyone, is surreptitiously guided from mortal horsehood to take her rightful place in the heavenly Courts. The Dancer carries out the first part of his assignment by becoming a mortal stallion and traveling to the Bishop Farm, but he cannot resist his stallion nature by escaping into the wilderness with Duchess and Susie (a Paint) to start his own herd (joined by Cory as an honorary horse). This breaking of the Balance gives the Black Horse the power to send Anor and Scant after them. The Dancer's tiny and fragile herd must face all the powers of the equine supernatural underworld.

The Heavenly Horse has a happy ending, but Stanton followed it a year later with *Piper at the Gate* which continues the story. The Dancer and Duchess have a strong, handsome foal, Piper, who grows up and is taken by Bishop Farm owner's son David to start a new Appaloosa stud, Sweetwater Ranch, in Montana's Big Sky country. Six years later,

Piper has become Sweetwater's Dancing Piper, the prize stud and Lead Stallion of its forty-strong herd. It is at this point that the Soul Taker, the equine female personification of evil, strikes again. Duchess, Lead Mare at Bishop Farm, is tricked into killing herself, and the Dancer breaks out of his stall and disappears. *Piper at the Gate* is the story of Piper's rescue of his parents and of his saving of the Appaloosa breed.

Huntress • by Renee Carter Hall.

Dallas, TX: FurPlanet Productions, September 2015, paperback, 213 pp.

Leya is an adolescent lioness in an anthropomorphic African veld who lives in the village of Lwazi. But she doesn't want to grow up to become just another tribal wife and mother. She dreams of becoming a *karanja*, a member of the nomadic band of female expert huntresses who hunt for meat for all the villages. Becoming a *karanja* is a prestigious, almost religious goal, but it means rigorous training and the renunciation of living with men—of ever getting married, or having children:

> The first time she'd seen them, she had been very young. But she hadn't been afraid. The other cubs, male and female alike, had hidden behind their mothers, frightened by the huntresses' fierce eyes and sharp weapons. Where the villagers wore beads or stones, the *karanja* sported necklaces of bone and hoof and claw, and their loincloths were made of zebra hide in deference to Kamara's first kill, a material only they were permitted to wear.
>
> They were all mesmerizing, exotic and dangerous and beautiful, their eyeshine flashing like lightning-strikes as they took their places around the fire. But there was one Leya could not look away from.
>
> Masika, the *karanjala*, first among the *karanja*. Her headdress of fish-eagle feathers stood out from her noble face like a mane, and her loincloth was of giraffe hide, just as their first male wore. Her eyes were sharp and watchful, her every muscle toned and tensed, and like all the *karanja*, she proudly bore the twin scars on her chest where her breasts had been cut away. Leya sat silently, drinking in Masika's presence, watching everything the huntress did, every movement, every manner.

Leya follows her goal relentlessly, tirelessly as she grows up. She leaves her village to follow the *karanja* on their outskirts, and finally her perseverance impresses them enough that she is made one of their group. But this is only half the story. Goals change over the years. What someone wants to be at six years old, or at eleven, or fourteen, is not the same thing at eighteen or twenty-one or older. Leya begins to regret parting from the village playmate who had just begun to become a lover. She feels longings when the *karanja* visit a village and she sees mothers with their children:

Huntress by Renee Carter Hall (FurPlanet Productions, September 2015). Set in a fantasy Africa with anthropomorphic animals; winner of the 2014 Cóyotl Award for Best Novella, and a finalist for the 2014 Ursa Major Award for Best Short Fiction. Cover art by Sekhmet.

> Every woman in this village, Leya realized, understood Ayanna's joy. But not one of them would know what it meant to watch that zebra crumple to the ground, to hold a knife and cut its throat because it meant everything you'd ever wanted. She could tell Ayanna about it, and her friend would smile and nod in the right places, but that would be all.

No huntress has ever left the *karanja* (or have they?), but by this time the other *karanja* are all her friends, and wish her well. But Leya's hard life, her scars and her lack of breasts have marked her irrevocably. What is an ex-*karanja* to become? There is no role model for the rest of her life.

Huntress is harsh, tender, exhausting, gentle, thoughtful, and beautiful. It won the Cóyotl Award as the Best Novella of 2014, presented at the RainFurrest 2015 convention where this book went on sale. It was also a finalist for that year's Ursa Major Award.

"Huntress," the novella, was first published in the anthology *Five Fortunes* in January 2014. But if you've read it there, don't think that you've read all there is. *Huntress*, the book, contains three more, brand-new short stories set in the same world.

"The Shape of the Sky" features Mtoto, the young apprentice of Ndiri, the painted-dogs' wandering healer:

> The young dog stretched, enjoying the soft breeze on his fur and how the warmth of the sun came back when the breeze stopped. As he preferred, he wore only the clay amulet he'd had since he was born. When he went among the villages to trade his pots and cups, he tied on a loincloth to respect their customs, but here among the baobabs, there was no custom but his own.

Mtoto is now living alone when a young leopardess with her eland treks across his home. Masozi, the leopardess, is proud but desperate, and Ngoma, her more-than-a-pet who gives her milk and blood, is about to give birth. Mtoto helps them, and without knowing it, he is helped as well.

"Kamara and the Star-Beast" is a story that Leya, as an older cub, tells the still-younger cubs of Lwazi about the legendary first *karanja*:

> You know Kamara the Huntress was the greatest of all her kind. There was nothing that ran on land that she could not bring down, no bird she couldn't snare, no fish she couldn't catch. She was strong, and she was swift, and she was clever—and yes, she was proud.

One day Kamara comes across a trail of strange hoofprints that suddenly change to the tracks of other animals, even birds. Kamara follows the trail for days:

> At last she caught up with it, and if anything could have been stranger than its trail, it was the beast itself. It had the hindquarters of a zebra, the front legs of a heron, the great ears of the hare, the snout of the red pig, and the tough skin of the elephant.

The thing taunts Kamara that she can't catch it. She finally gives up, but complains to the god Yaa about it. Yaa's decision isn't exactly what Kamara wants.

"Where the Rivers Meet" tells how Ndiri, the painted-dogs' wandering healer, grew up to such a lonely profession. She was orphaned when she was too young to know her parents, and she was taken in by a grandmother who was a healer. To her village, a healer was the same thing as a magician, and everyone else feared both Ndiri's grandmother and her.

This is the story of how Ndiri discovered boys. And Mtoto. And death.

Hall says in an afterword that her fantasy Africa is based on elements from throughout the continent. (And elsewhere—*karanja* is a Hindi word.) But it feels vividly real, just as the cover by Sekhmet is so realistic that you almost believe in anthropomorphic lionesses.

Imperium Lupi • by Adam Browne. Illustrations, maps by the author.

Kent, England: Dayfly Publications, July 2017, paperback, 724 pp.

The book starts off with three complex full-page maps and several insignia. One map is of the walled city of Lupa, captioned "The capital of Wolfkind." The insignia are of such things as "Buttle Skyways," showing a dirigible, and "Lupan Laws," the seal of the Lupan Republic's government. There is also a ten-page lexicon at the rear of the book of terms used in the novel, such as:

> **Chakaa:** The hyena answer to the Howlers, they are forbidden to use white-imperium by their beliefs, but unlike wolves they cope well with the psychotic side effects of purple-imperium. Even so, Chakaa are often unstable and are sidelined by the exacting standards set by noble-born hyena society, and only tolerated at all for their great strength and usefulness in battle.
>
> **The Politzi:** Lupa's police force, consisting largely of hogs, rats, rabbits and other lesser beasts who are for the most part unable to wield imperium directly.
>
> **Queens Town:** Cat colony on the east coast, independent of Lupine Law. It was allowed to remain sovereign Felician territory as part of an ancient peace settlement between Felicia and Lupa. It is the first port of entry for any cats, or other beasts, coming to the Lupine Continent from across the Teich.

Imperium Lupi is set on the world of Erde. The first character that the reader meets in Part 1, Chapter 1, is Howler Rufus, a red-furred wolf, on a train:

> The pain subsiding, Rufus leant back into his seat, chest heaving beneath his cloak. He glanced around the dilapidated carriage; his fellow passengers diverted their curious gaze or hid behind newspapers. Little beasts mostly, mice, rats, rabbits, all the lesser races, who wouldn't dare speak to Rufus without being spoken to.
>
> The train slowed and the station panned into view, its fine marbled columns standing proud, each tarnished by the faintly spangled lustre of imperium ash. Rufus reached over and grabbed his helmet from the adjoining threadbare seat. He placed it over his brow; the padded metal hugging his sleek wolfen skull. It was black, save for the cheeks, which were white. Luminous red triangles were set beneath each eye-hole, like that found on Rufus' brooch. Made of the wonder mineral imperium, they glowed even in the muted daylight, and against the helm's white cheeks they resembled two bloodied fangs lying atop freshly fallen snow. The helm's nose was covered by a grille punctured by a dozen round holes that enabled Rufus to breathe. Only his inquisitive green eyes and perky red ears remained visible, endowing him with menacing anonymity.

The minutiae of this civilization are described in fine detail. It would be easy for a cosplayer to make the costumes, or for a model-builder to craft the vehicles and devices:

> At the bottom of the sprawling stairs, Ivan peeled away from Rufus, keys jangling in paw, and found his monobike parked by the road—and a fine machine it was, too, its large, singular wheel housed seamlessly under a chunky, polished black chassis marked on the flank with a small white spider motif.
>
> Brushing globules of rainwater from the seat, Ivan threw an armoured leg over his marvellous bike, inserted the keys, and started it up with a kick of the pedal. Amidst a loud bang and several ear-thumping pops, imperium ash exploded forth from the exhaust in grey, yet slightly glittery clouds. The inside rim of the bike's lone, broad wheel nestled between Ivan's legs lit up in a bright ring of white as the imperium-laced gyroscope came to life. The bike rose up a little and righted itself, like a metallic beetle awakening from hibernation.

It takes an age for the plot to get moving, but the richness of the buildup is exquisite. Here is an important quote:

"The imperium in our bodies is what gives us Howlers power," the imperologist went on, enjoying his role as the wellspring of knowledge, "but there's a price. Whenever it's burnt, whether it be in a car, a train, or our muscles, imperium of all colours decays into imperium ash. It's bad enough when it clogs Lupa's air, but when it fouls our bodies up it causes great pain … it's well you know."

Bruno gulped audibly.

There is also drama:

A flash of light and puff of ash burst from the pistol's end. A fraction later and a colourful spark dashed off the leading monobike's one wheel. The tyre exploded and tore itself apart in an instant.

The assassin's monobike shuddered and twisted violently to one side, before catapulting itself seat over wheel and flinging the rider in front. He sailed through the air and disappeared amidst the carnage as his machine slid along the cobbles, shedding a shower of sparks and pieces of chrome bodywork all the way, before smashing into a heap of rubbish piled against the end of the alleyway.

There are many major characters in *Imperium Lupi*, such as the wolf Howler officers Rufus Valerio and Ivan Donskoy, Troopers veteran Uther "Wild-heart" (orphan; family name unknown) and young Linus Mills (all Bloodfangs); Rufus' politically well-connected wife Janoah Valerio; the effete Felician aristocrats Montague and Penelope Buttle who keep appearing or being referred to; the Hyena terrorist Prince Noss and The Hyena Organisation for Recognition of Nationhood (THORN); and the rabbit tavern cook Casimir Claybourne.

The convoluted plot revolves around the Lupan Republic's dominance of the Lupine Continent on the world of Erde. There are schemes within Lupa's elite wolf government to turn the Republic into an Empire; there are schemes by some of the other animal peoples within Lupa for their own independent nations; there are fears around Erde that Lupa's dependence on the powerful but ultimately deadly imperium (Lupa city is perpetually under "the choking clouds of the Ashfall") is slowly poisoning the entire world, and schemes by some to get rid of imperium by ending Lupa's dominance; and there are schemes by some who just want to end wolfkind's rule.

Imperium Lupi is a rich mixture of action, comedy, mystery, tragedy, political intrigue at the highest levels, and sentient bugs, among the animal peoples of the world of Erde. The wolves dominate, but there is plenty here for the fans of rabbits, pigs, hyenas, otters, and others. *Imperium Lupi*, winner of a 2017 Leo Literary Award, is proof that not all of the best anthropomorphic literature is being produced within furry fandom.

In Wilder Lands: The Fall of Eldvar • by Jim Galford.

Seattle, WA: CreateSpace, August 2011, paperback, 452 pp.

Into the Desert Wilds • by Jim Galford.

Seattle, WA: CreateSpace, August 2012, paperback, 436 pp.

Sunset of Lantonne • by Jim Galford.

Seattle, WA: CreateSpace, August 2013, paperback, 545 pp.

The Northern Approach • by Jim Galford.

Seattle, WA: CreateSpace, August 2014, paperback, 432 pp.

Bones of the Empire • by Jim Galford.

Seattle, WA: CreateSpace, August 2015, paperback, 508 pp.

Eldvar seems like a stereotypical fantasy world, inhabited by humans, pointy-eared elves, dwarves, and orcs alike; some of whom are skilled magic-users. But they all persecute the animal peoples, the wildlings, like Estin. "While the town [the city-state of Altis] may have been run by an amalgam of races, his kind were not welcome."

What does Estin look like?

> He dragged his claws across the stones…. Thick pads covered the inner-side of his hands and his feet, giving him an incredible grip and the ability to climb out of harm's way with ease … he had long since learned that his hands and feet would scale buildings as easily as any tree…. Estin noted dryly that his own ears were no less pointed [than the elves].… He looked down and saw that one of the guards must have leapt and was hanging precariously from Estin's eight-foot long black-and-white striped tail.… He had a strong tail, capable of lifting himself off the ground, but it was not built for picking up armored humans…. "That's a good…," the man stopped and looked at the others, "what the hell is it, anyway?" … By the time he was stuffing the last bite of the third [orange] into his long mouth and realized just how much juice was matted into his fur.

The "what the hell is it, anyway?" clues the reader that Estin is unusual even for a wildling. He is the only one of his kind that he knows of … a prey animal, not a predator. (Description makes it clear that he is a ring-tailed lemur.)

The only other wildlings that Estin ever sees are slaves—and Nyess, the *de facto* boss of Altis' underworld:

> Nyess was a wildling—an animal person—just like Estin, though he bore little similarity. Slightly smaller in stature, Nyess looked just like a large rat, whereas Estin had somewhat more of a human body shape. The only non-animal thing about Nyess was his thin shirt and pants, as well as the tiny top hat he always wore to make himself appear more professional. The man really only cared about being able to manipulate other beings into projects that furthered his hoarding of coin.

Estin has grown up while hiding in the slums of Altis, a loner working for Altis' criminal underworld run by Nyess. Estin is especially unfamiliar with the wildling tribes of the mountains north of Altis, since his tribe lived in the south. It all comes to a head for Estin when he senses that he has just become expendable to Nyess, and that Altis is no longer safe for him.

Estin's escape with the fox-woman Feanne helps to emphasize Estin's wildling nature:

> As they progressed, Estin sniffed the air, trying to learn what was around them, if only to distract him from the nausea he was suffering. He recognized the pines, but a thousand other scents confused him and blurred together. Some were likely flowers, some animal, some he simply had no idea. Having not left the city in so many years, everything out here was alien to him, drowning his mind in new scents that he had no way to sort out.
>
> Struggling to make sense of all the things his nose picked up, Estin tried to center his thoughts and managed to pick out strong familiar aromas in an effort to piece things out one at a time. The rich smell of Feanne's heavily-oiled leather vest and loincloth was easy to latch onto as a singular point in the sea of scents. Once he smelled that, he separated her unique scent from that of the leather, making a note of it so that he could recognize her more easily. It was a heavy woody smell of fur, mixed with the oils of the leather that had stained her fur, along with the more bitter additions of blood and one other item that he could not quite pick out. He was sure it was animal, but it was distinct from the leather and from Feanne herself. It smelled vaguely fox-like, but could have been just another wilding, or even a different breed of fox.

That takes *In Wilder Lands* up to about page 80. The rest of the novel tells of Estin's life as a member of Feanne's wilder forest community:

Estin hurried outside, stumbling as he emerged into blazing sunlight. He stood there a moment, letting his eyes adjust, but when they did, he barely believed what they showed him.

Wildlings were everywhere. Ulra and another bear were off to one side of the forest clearing, dragging dead wood the size of small trees in from the tree line, likely for firewood. Several wolves—including Ghohar—were scattered near the wood line, patrolling the camp's edges for intruders. He spotted several other breeds running around, but they were there and gone so quickly, that he had a hard time identifying them.

"You, you, you!" exclaimed an excitable ferret, racing up on him. The young male darted in circles around Estin, prodding him with a clawed finger as though checking on his previous wounds. Like many of the others around the camp, the ferret was dressed in little more than a loincloth. "Asrahn got you all fixed up, that's great! Where are you going now? Hrm? Say something!"

Estin's ever-evolving role in the wildling community—later, among the humans as the war grows out of all sides' control—and his confused relationship with Feanne (their different breeds definitely complicate matters) makes *In Wilder Lands* and its sequels a richly convoluted, excessively long (spanning many years), surprise-filled, but very readable series. Estin and his friends are not present in *Sunset of Lantonne* and *The Northern Approach*. The action moves to Ilarra, a young elven magic student, and Raeln, her magically bonded wolf wilding "brother." But all the characters come together at the climax. The five novels of *The Fall of Eldvar* make a well-plotted, gripping, and somewhat exhausting adventure series.

Inhuman Acts: A Collection of Noir • edited by Ocean Tigrox.

Dallas, TX: FurPlanet Productions, September 2015, paperback, 316 pp.

According to the publisher, this is a horror anthology: "Explore thirteen anthropomorphic noir stories about betrayal, corruption and deceit from award-winning authors and up-and-coming writers. Pour your favourite whiskey and light up a cigarette as Stanley Rivets, PI shares with you his collection of case files from dim to dark to downright ugly" (blurb).

Stanley Rivets, the stereotypical sable P.I. who tells these stories—"A sable in a long beige trench coat sits behind the desk, dark ears perking at the entrance of the newcomer. The wide brim of his fedora raises to see what visitor would stop by this late at night." He wears his trench coat and fedora while sitting in his office? Well, maybe he's just returned, exhausted, from a case—appears only in the very brief Foreword and Afterword. Too bad. It would have been nice to get a full story with him.

Rivets tells thirteen stories; not cases of his own, but thirteen that he's heard of. Some highlights: Ocean Tigrox starts the anthology out with one of the best here, "Muskrat Blues" by Ianus Wolf. It's specifically a pastiche of *The Maltese Falcon*, with Mike Harrison, a pig P.I., investigating the murder of his best friend, another P.I.—a muskrat; two prey animals in a grim and gritty city where the prey animals are usually at the bottom of the anthro-animal social pole. But Alex Richards didn't take any guff, and neither does Harrison. Wolf packs a neat summary of Hammett's novel (or Warner Bros.'s movie; take your pick) into a taut twenty-five pages of noir, with enough originality that even if you're a fan of *The Maltese Falcon*, you're not likely to guess whodunit. And enough presence of predator and prey animal traits to make this a satisfying furry story, too.

"Danger in the Lumo-Bay" by Mary E. Lowd is a clever futuristic sf murder mystery, set in what would be a holodeck if this were *Star Trek* fiction. The defective lumo-bay in a Tri-Galactic Navy ship is being repaired. Captain Pierre Jacques (hairless sphinx cat),

Dr. Waverly Keller (Irish setter), and chief engineer Jordan LeGuin (orange tabby cat) test it with a "Murder in the Morning" scenario that casts the male captain and the female doctor as two P.I.s investigating a Maltese Falcon case with lots of dead bodies. Then something goes wrong with the lumo-bay's program. Who is the killer in "Murder in the Morning"? Are the captain and the doctor really safe? This is a mystery on two levels.

"Every Breath Closer" by Slip Wolf starts off with a grabber of a paragraph:

> I won't lie and say the ten thousand I'd lost didn't cross my mind when the police started to process the scene. Mostly, I was just numb as I watched the dead otter's limbs twisted around themselves on the wet pavement, rain driving at the tarp that kept blowing off her, all the evidence at the scene finding a drain to go down. There was broken glass around Susan Britches' body and a gaping, jagged grimace in the condo's glass side, five stories up. I suspected the broken music award by the curb was used to break the window. In that condo, where Susan had paid me my retainer just days ago and begged me to quietly and discreetly find her missing daughter, was an explanation for Susan's demise.

Owen Spenhardy, the squirrel stereotypical hard-drinking, trenchcoat-wearing P.I., expects that he's lost his client. Instead, he is hired by the daughter's former teacher to continue the search for her. This story has a real reason for the cast to be anthropomorphic animals: you can stuff and mount animals after their deaths, which you can't do with humans (unless you're a mad taxidermist as in *House of Wax*). Doctor Aiden Engelhände, a fox artistic taxidermist, wants to have Bethany found in order to honor his best student by preserving her after her eventual natural death—he says. This is another well-written story that's not too believable, but with an imaginative plot that's undoubtedly furry.

"Ghosts" by Solus Lupus, featuring Helen, a cat, and Rosa, a coyote, is very short, very sad, and very memorable. I like it very much.

"Crimson on Copper" by Tony Greyfox could be an Isaac Asimov story with anthro animal characters. Detective Faraday, a laughing hyena cop (who isn't laughing), is called to a sales room where three people have been extremely messily slaughtered, apparently by one of the automatons for sale—but automatons are made so they can't kill. Faraday has to find either why the machine acted murderously against its programming, or who the real killer is—or both. Greyfox enhances the anthro aspect nicely: "I stepped over the blood cautiously, thankful that hyenas don't have long tails like the fox who was busily trying to blot blood from his tail tip."

"Bullet Tooth Claw" by Marshall L. Moseley has a witty and believable style:

> I was at Tavern Law on 12th, the bar at which I spend so much money I get thank-you cards from the bartender's Mom. It was three in the afternoon, too early for drinking, which is why I'd started at noon. Basset hounds have an advantage that way—we look droopy and have naturally red-rimmed eyes, so we can get away with being in the bag when most dogs can't.

Archie Bellclan, an Uplifted basset P.I., investigates when Simon Tanner, his friend, is murdered. "When your human dies, you're supposed to do something about it." The investigation is suitably noirish, and the Uplifted animals' natural abilities are used intelligently. A winner.

"Brooklyn Blackie and the Unappetizing Menu" by Bill Kieffer is another animal-P.I.-investigates-a-friend's-death. And 34 other deaths. Everyone in the turtle's Harlem apartment building is dead. Blackie, a wolf/dog hybrid P.I., is sure that the police are on a false trail and conducts his own investigation. This is another story that makes clever use of the animal natures of its cast. It has my candidate for the best line in the book: "My soul craved justice, but it would take bloodshed instead."

Thirteen stories. Most are well-written but depressing; one has a surprise happy ending. I'd only rate a couple as clunkers. Overall, *Inhuman Acts* is worth the cover price for fans of dark detective fiction. It won the 2015 Cóyotl Award for Best Anthology.

The Island of Dr. Moreau: A Possibility • by H.G. Wells. Frontispiece by C.R.A. [Charles Robert Ashbee].

London: William Heinemann, April 1896, hardcover, 229 pp.

This is arguably the first "furry" adult novel, not counting the talking animals of children's literature. (Or the adult *Metamorphoses/The Golden Ass* of Lucius of Apuleius, which was caused by a magic salve and the gods.) It was intended as an anti-vivisection polemic, and it made quite a stir when it was published, although not entirely for the reason that Wells intended. According to the introduction by Alan Lightman in a later edition (Bantam Classic, 2005):

> Ranked among the classic novels of the English language and the inspiration for several unforgettable movies, this early work of H.G. Wells was greeted in 1896 by howls of protest from reviewers, who found it horrifying and blasphemous. They wanted to know more about the wondrous possibilities of science shown in his first book, *The Time Machine*, not its potential for misuse and terror.

The public focused less upon the animal-men than upon Dr. Moreau's callous vivisection experiments. In the novel, the physiologist comes across as an obsessed sociopath who cares only for his scientific research, and is oblivious to the pain he causes to his animal subjects. But to the public, he was a crazed monster. This image is clearly emphasized in the second motion picture adaptation, *Island of Lost Souls* (1932), in which Charles Laughton plays Dr. Moreau as a whip-cracking sadist who seems interested in his experiments only as a justification for his cruel tortures of his victims, and to create subjects whom he can rule as a god.

The novel is presented as the journal of Edward Prendick, an Englishman who is shipwrecked in 1887 somewhere off the west coast of South America. He is rescued by a small schooner traveling to an unidentified island to land Montgomery, a medical technician, and a cargo of caged animals. It is on the boat that Prendick encounters the first of the Animal Men:

> We left the cabin and found a man at the companion obstructing our way. He was standing on the ladder with his back to us, peering over the combing of the hatchway. He was, I could see, a misshapen man, short, broad, and clumsy, with a crooked back, a hairy neck, and a head sunk between his shoulders. He was dressed in dark-blue serge, and had peculiarly thick, coarse, black hair. I heard the unseen dogs growl furiously, and forthwith he ducked back,—coming into contact with the hand I put out to fend him off from myself. He turned with animal swiftness.
>
> In some indefinable way the black face thus flashed upon me shocked me profoundly. It was a singularly deformed one. The facial part projected, forming something dimly suggestive of a muzzle, and the huge half-open mouth showed as big white teeth as I had ever seen in a human mouth. His eyes were blood-shot at the edges, with scarcely a rim of white round the hazel pupils. There was a curious glow of excitement in his face.
>
> "Confound you!" said Montgomery. "Why the devil don't you get out of the way?"
>
> The black-faced man started aside without a word. I went on up the companion, staring at him instinctively as I did so. Montgomery stayed at the foot for a moment. 'You have no business here, you know," he said in a deliberate tone. "Your place is forward."
>
> The black-faced man cowered. "They—won't have me forward." He spoke slowly, with a queer, hoarse quality in his voice.

The schooner's drunken captain, who takes a dislike to Prendick, throws him off the boat with Montgomery at the unnamed island. There Prendick meets Montgomery's employer, the biologist Dr. Moreau. They seem to have a staff of the queer animal-like natives of the island.

Prendick comes to assume that Dr. Moreau is conducting experiments to turn men into animals. He flees the biologists' compound into the jungle, where he finds the Beast Folk's community and their bizarre religion:

> "Say the words," said the Ape-Man, repeating, and the figures in the doorway echoed this, with a threat in the tone of their voices.
>
> I realised that I had to repeat this idiotic formula; and then began the insanest ceremony. The voice in the dark began intoning a mad litany, line by line, and I and the rest to repeat it. As they did so, they swayed from side to side in the oddest way, and beat their hands upon their knees; and I followed their example. I could have imagined that I was already dead and in another world. That dark hut, these grotesque dim figures, just flecked here and there by a glimmer of light, and all of them swaying in unison and chanting,
>
> "Not to go on all-fours; that is the Law. Are we not Men?"

The Island of Dr. Moreau: A Possibility by H.G. Wells (William Heinemann, April 1896). The earliest science-fiction novel to suggest transforming animals to human form and intelligence by scientific means. Embossed cover.

But when Prendick is reunited with Moreau, the scientist tells him that the opposite is true. He is turning animals into humans—"triumphs of vivisection"! The strange religion that Prendick has seen has been created by Moreau to keep the Beast People less animal-like and more human.

Dr. Moreau explains at length, to Prendick's disgust and horror. Prendick, speaking as the surrogate for Wells, is in favor of scientific research but conducted in a moral, humane manner; while Moreau stands for "science without sentiment"—the philosophy that, forty years later, resulted in the often-fatal Nazi experiments upon concentration camp prisoners. Moreau keeps the upper hand in his own laboratories, until the puma escapes and it and Moreau kill each other. Montgomery is soon also killed, and Prendick goes to live with the humanized Beast Folk. But without Moreau's constant efforts to keep them semi-human, they gradually devolve back into feral beasts. Prendick flees the island and is rescued, but nobody believes him. When the island is revisited four years later by a British warship, they find "nothing living thereon except certain curious white moths, some hogs and rabbits, and some rather peculiar rats."—presumably the larger carnivores and omnivores have eaten each other, and then died off.

The Island of Dr. Moreau was effective as an anti-vivisection screed, but nothing more because everybody knew that no vivisection could ever really change animals into men. Today, with advances in genetics and DNA manipulation, it does not look so impossible. In any case, this novel is the forerunner of all of the science-fiction stories of futuristic evolution and/or artificial mutation, and of "uplifted" animals since then.

Jonathan Livingston Seagull—A Story • by Richard Bach. Photographs by Russell Munson.

New York: The Macmillan Company, August 1970, hardcover, 93 pp.

> It was morning, and the new sun sparkled gold across the ripples of a gentle sea.
>
> A mile from shore a fishing boat chummed the water, and the word for Breakfast Flock flashed through the air, till a crowd of a thousand seagulls came to dodge and fight for bits of food. It was another busy day beginning.
>
> But way off alone, out by himself beyond boat and shore, Jonathan Livingston Seagull was practicing. A hundred feet in the sky he lowered his webbed feet, lifted his beak, and strained to hold a painful hard twisting curve through his wings. The curve meant that he would fly slowly, and now he slowed until the wind was a whisper in his face, until the ocean stood still beneath him. He narrowed his eyes in fierce concentration, held his breath, forced one ... single ... more ... inch ... of ... curve.... Then his feathers ruffled, he stalled and fell.
>
> Seagulls, as you know, never falter, never stall. To stall in the air is for them disgrace and it is dishonor.
>
> But Jonathan Livingston Seagull, unashamed, stretching his wings again in that trembling hard curve—slowing, slowing, and stalling once more—was no ordinary bird.

So begins *Jonathan Livingston Seagull*, one of the seminal works of the Flower Power, do-your-own-thing era of the late 1960s and early '70s. Richard Bach, a pilot from before he entered college, had already written three books about the joy of flying aircraft before he penned this paean to the philosophy of abstract flight as a metaphor for existence itself.

Jonathan is a seagull who lives for flying, unlike the other gulls who consider it as just the means to get to where food is. This makes him Different, and to be Different is to be unpopular, ignored by the gang. Unlike most loners who secretly yearn to be accepted, however, Jonathan's desire to become a better flyer really is all that he is interested in. After numerous failures, Jonathan works out the aerodynamics to get past this age-old barrier:

> He closed his eyes to slits against the wind and rejoiced. A hundred forty miles per hour! And under control! If I dive from five thousand feet instead of two thousand, I wonder how fast...

Jonathan is sure that his faster and more maneuverable flying techniques will be welcomed by his fellow gulls. Instead, he is outlawed by the Breakfast Flock for reckless irresponsibility without even being allowed to demonstrate his discovery. Instead of being shattered by his ostracism, Jonathan takes advantage of his solitude to relentlessly learn to fly even faster and better. One day two ethereal gulls appear at his wingtips to take him to the next level of learning:

> "'We're from your Flock, Jonathan. We are your brothers.' The words were strong and calm. 'We've come to take you higher, to take you home.'"

"So this is heaven," Jonathan assumes, reasonably enough. He gains an aerodynamically improved body with glowing white feathers. But the truth is more complex, as he eventually learns from this Flock's Elder Gull, Chiang. Chiang teaches Jonathan that heaven is not a place, it is a state of perfection. When he has learned all about flying that there is to be learned—when he can instantly transport himself across the galaxy; when he can fly through solid mountains—then he will be nearer heaven.

When Chiang transmigrates to a higher plane, Jonathan takes his place as instructor to the newer arrivals in this place. But he becomes dissatisfied. Jonathan flies through time and space back to Earth. He meets Fletcher Lynd Seagull, a gull like himself who had devoted himself to better flying and had been Outcast for it. Instead of just becoming Fletcher's personal guru, however, Jonathan assembles a new flock of similar Outcasts and brings them back to practice on the outskirts of the Breakfast Flock where they cannot be ignored:

> "Well, sure, O.K., they're Outcast," said some of the younger gulls, "but hey, man, where did they learn to fly like that?"

The Elders may disapprove, but soon Jonathan has all of the younger gulls as his awed students:

> "He spoke of very simple things—that it is right for a gull to fly, that freedom is the very nature of his being, that whatever stands against that freedom must be set aside, be it ritual or superstition or limitation in any form.
> "Set aside," came a voice from the multitude, "even if it be the Law of the Flock?"
> "The only true law is that which leads to freedom," Jonathan said. "There is no other."

Bach's metaphysical parable of self-improvement, love, and a pop–Oriental mysticism is short; barely 9,800 words. It is a thin book, quickly read and very easy to read for its feel-good exuberance.

The Jungle Book • by Rudyard Kipling. Illustrated by J.L. Kipling, W.H. Drake, and P. Frenzeny.

London: Macmillan and Co., June 1894, hardcover, 224 pp.

The Second Jungle Book • by Rudyard Kipling. Illustrated by J. Lockwood Kipling, C.I.E.

London: Macmillan and Co., November 1895, hardcover, 244 pp.

Kipling's famous *Jungle Book* is actually two books; *The Jungle Book*, published in 1894, and *The Second Jungle Book*, published in 1895. The first contains, besides some poems, three tales of Mowgli, the feral man-cub, and the anthromorphized animals of the North Indian jungles; plus "The White Seal" with talking seals, "Rikki-Tikki-Tavi," with a talking mongoose and king cobras, "Toomai of the Elephants" with Little Toomai, a young mahout, and Kala Nag the wise old elephant (not anthropomorphic), and "Her Majesty's Servants" with the talking horses, mules, camels, bullocks, and other pack-animals of the Royal Army in India. The second book contains five more tales of Mowgli and his animal companions, plus "The Undertakers" about anthropomorphized river scavengers, and "The Miracle of Purun Bhagat" and "Quiquern," both without anthropomorphized animals.

The Mowgli tales are "Mowgli's Brothers," "Kaa's Hunting," and "Tiger! Tiger!" in *The Jungle Book,* and "How Fear Came," "Letting in the Jungle," "The King's Ankus," "Red Dog," and "The Spring Running" in *The Second Jungle Book*.

The stories about Mowgli and Bagheera the black panther, Baloo the bear, Akela (Father Wolf), Raksha (Mother Wolf), and the other wolves of the Seeonee Pack, Shere Khan the man-eating tiger, Kaa the Rock Python, the Bandar-log Monkey People and their Cold Lairs, Tabaqui the jackal, and others are what people remember most about the two *Jungle Books*. "Mowgli's Brothers," the first story in the first Book, which sets up the premise, is the best-known:

> The tiger's roar filled the cave with thunder. Mother Wolf shook herself clear of the cubs and sprang forward, her eyes, like two green moons in the darkness, facing the blazing eyes of Shere Khan.
>
> "And it is I, Raksha (the Demon), who answer. The man's cub is mine, Lungri—mine to me! He shall not be killed. He shall live to run with the Pack and to hunt with the Pack; and in the end, look you, hunter of little naked cubs—frog-eater—fish-killer, he shall hunt *thee*! Now get hence, or by the Sambhur that I killed (*I* eat no starved cattle), back thou goest to thy mother, burned beast of the jungle, lamer than ever thou camest into the world! Go!"
>
> Father Wolf looked on amazed. He had almost forgotten the days when he won Mother Wolf in fair fight from five other wolves, when she ran in the Pack and was not called the Demon for compliment's sake. Shere Khan might have faced Father Wolf, but he could not stand up against Mother Wolf, for he knew that where he was she had all the advantage of the ground, and would fight to the death. So he backed out of the cave-mouth growling, and when he was clear he shouted:
>
> "Each dog barks in his own yard! We will see what the Pack will say to this fostering of man-cubs. The cub is mine, and to my teeth he will come in the end, O bush-tailed thieves!"

For those who were raised on the Disney version of *The Jungle Book* (and *Robin Hood*), it may come as a surprise that Kaa the Rock Python is one of Mowgli's friends, not an enemy.

> Kaa, the big Rock Python, had changed his skin for perhaps the two-hundredth time since his birth; and Mowgli, who never forgot that he owed his life to Kaa for a night's work at Cold Lairs, which you may perhaps remember, went to congratulate him. Skin-changing always makes a snake moody and depressed till the new skin begins to shine and look beautiful. Kaa never made fun of Mowgli any more, but accepted him, as the other Jungle People did, for the Master of the Jungle, and brought him all the news that a python of his size would naturally hear. What Kaa did not know about the Middle Jungle, as they call it,—the life that runs close to the earth or under it, the boulder, burrow, and the tree-bole life,—might have been written upon the smallest of his scales.
>
> That afternoon Mowgli was sitting in the circle of Kaa's great coils, fingering the flaked and broken old skin that lay all looped and twisted among the rocks just as Kaa had left it. Kaa had very courteously packed himself under Mowgli's broad, bare shoulders, so that the boy was really resting in a living arm-chair.
>
> "Even to the scales of the eyes it is perfect," said Mowgli, under his breath, playing with the old skin. "Strange to see the covering of one's own head at one's own feet!"
>
> "Ay, but I lack feet," said Kaa; "and since this is the custom of all my people, I do not find it strange. Does thy skin never feel old and harsh?" ["The King's Ankus"]

The social impact of the Mowgli tales cannot be understated. The newly-formed Boy Scout movement in Great Britain and the U.S. in the 1910s used their imagery and symbolism, especially in the Cub Scouts, with "packs" and "dens," and the Akela merit badge. There were high-profile movie adaptations, especially the animated movie by Walt Disney in 1967 which produced its own novelization, *The Story of Walt Disney's Motion Picture: The Jungle Book. Adapted from the Mowgli Stories by Rudyard Kipling* by Mary Carey (Whitman Publishing Co., October 1967, 190 pp.). There was a well-received literary unauthorized sequel, *The Third Jungle Book* by Pamela Jekel (Roberts Rinehart International, November 1992, 217 pp.), with ten tales in which Mowgli grows to adulthood and fathers a child, and Baloo the bear dies of old age.

More importantly, since the copyrights on the two books by Kipling expired, there have been a bewildering number of new editions and adaptations. There have been accurate new editions of *The Jungle Book* and *The Second Jungle Book*, editions of both books combined under *The Jungle Book* title, editions of just the eight Mowgli tales of both books under *The Jungle Book* title, simplifications for young children, editions with Kipling's text but illustrations from the Disney animated movie, and more. With all this, practically all proto-furry fans have been influenced by the Mowgli ambiance from their youth, and many have read the original Kipling stories in one version or another. You should, if you haven't.

Kismet • by Watts Martin.

Dallas, TX: FurPlanet Productions, January 2017, paperback, 323 pp.; Dallas, TX: Argyll Productions, January 2017, paperback, 323 pp.

Is this a first for furry publishing? The only differences between these two editions are the publisher's name and illustrated logo on the title page, the ISBN number, and the cover by Teagan Gavet. Both covers are dark blue and feature the protagonist in a spacesuit in deep space, but the Argyll cover displays her at a distance without showing what she looks like, and the FurPlanet cover is a closeup showing that she is a rat-woman. The FurPlanet edition is marketed as furry science fiction; the Argyll edition is marketed as just science fiction, for those outside furry fandom who may buy sf but not a furry book.

Whether it is read as hard sf or as furry fiction, *Kismet* is a winner. Several hundred years in the future, mankind has settled the Asteroid Belt. Mankind has also developed advanced bioengineering that enables people to have themselves bioengineered into anthropomorphic animals. There has been the mix of social acceptance and rejection that this results in for over a century. At this present, most of Earth is human and most of the anthropomorphs have migrated to the Asteroid Belt. In the Belt, the humans are called cisforms and the anthropomorphs are totemics.

Gail Simmons is a rat-woman totemic in the Ceres Ring, with her AI spaceship *Kismet*. She's a salvage operator, a salvor, doing odd jobs of space hauling and space junk reclamation. She's basically a hermit, living inside *Kismet*. The ship smart-AI brain is her only friend.

Gail is contacted by an old childhood acquaintance whom she hasn't seen in two decades. He's a yacht charter pilot now, and he's just seen what looks like a derelict spaceship while making a chartered flight. His customer won't give him the time to check it out, so he's notifying Gail. Gail and *Kismet* find what appears to be an abandoned

Kismet by Watts Martin (FurPlanet Productions, January 2017). A strong sf novel with a strong rat-woman protagonist. Winner of the 2017 Cóyotl Award for Best Novel, and a finalist for the 2017 Ursa Major Award for Best Anthropomorphic Novel. Cover art by Teagan Gavet.

or sabotaged spaceship and two dead bodies. When Gail reports this, it leads to her being accused of theft and murder, and the missing cargo to be a handheld databox—a Macguffin—that holds information that at least one party will kill to get, that can mean "the end of the human race."

The adventure involves action, suspense, betrayal, and murder. Gail and two allies (it would be a spoiler who say who they are) travel to different parts of the Ceres Ring and discuss a lot of totemic history. Other totemics met include Ansel Santara, a red fox-man; Bright Sky, a wolf-woman; Karen Dupree, a rabbit-woman; Robert Bunten, a raccoon-man, Officer Jon Wolfe, a leopard-man (there's a joke about a leopard named Wolfe); Travis Duarte, a stag-man; Nevada Argent, a gray fox vixen; and an implied thousands of other background totemics as bank officers, mechanics, police and judiciary, waitresses, and more in the Belt. And plenty of cisforms (humans), because totemics may be the majority in the Belt, but there are lots of humans, too.

Jack Thomas, an FBI agent from the U.S. assigned to Interpol and sent to the Ceres Ring on a case that turns out to be mixed up with Gail's, is a handy character to explain the totemics to:

> Ansel sniffs. "'We don't need shoes."
> "Says the fox bitching about walking on gravel," Gail chuckles. "I think some of it's kind of aesthetic, but some of it's practical. Shoes and fur aren't a comfortable combination."
> "I'm still trying to get a sense of what animal characteristics totemics have adopted and why [Jack says]. I can read our emotions through your ears. And tails. But I'm presuming that while Ansel has better hearing and smell than I do, he has full color vision, isn't allergic to chocolate, and doesn't have any other drawbacks from canine/vulpine genetics mixed in."
> Ansel grins. "That's an advantage to being able to mix and match genes. On the flip side, cisform humans can wear clothes that fur makes impractical. And they don't get fleas, mange, or other furry problems that can't be addressed by flipping a genetic switch."

The civilization of the Asteroid Belt—Cerelia River, Ceres Ring, the Panorica Federation, the Rothbard Republic, and several independent arcologies like New Coyoacán; plus organizations like PFS (Panorica Federation Security), RJC (Ring Judicial Cooperative), and RTEA (River Totemic Equality Association)—may be confusing all at once, but Martin develops them gradually, one or two new locations or terms at a time. It's like being a tourist in an exotic foreign country. If you don't stay in your hotel room, you pick up on things fast. New Coyoacán is very tourist-friendly.

But *Kismet* also takes you places that a tourist wouldn't see:

> She'd seen pictures of Alexandria before the accident, but it's shocking how grand the entrance plaza still remains. Copper walls—from the scent, it's not paint, but a true high-copper alloy—soar behind her up into darkness overhead. High, long windows provide multi-story panoramas of space and the ships docked outside. The plaza itself forms a wide, tiled avenue running between buildings and the buildings, full of unnecessary steps and too-high rooflines supported by grand columns, drip with the opulence of wasted resources. The closest ones, she's sure, had been museums, the tourist destinations the platform's owners had expected to be the primary draw. If she remembers right it never came close to breaking even. One conspiracy theory suggests the owners sabotaged it themselves for insurance money.

Kismet is grand in scope and close in depiction of both its cisform and totemic characters. It was a winner of a 2017 Leo Literary Award and a finalist for both the 2017 Cóyotl Award and Ursa Major Award in the Best Novel category. This novel is also a sequel to Martin's 20-page "Tow" in *The Furry Future*. Gail Simmons, the rat-woman totemic, is someone that you will remember.

Koa of the Drowned Kingdom • by Ryan Campbell. Illustrated by Cooner.

Dallas, TX: FurPlanet Productions, September 2015, paperback, 146 pp.

    Koa of the Drowned Kingdom is one of FurPlanet's "cupcakes"; novellas instead of novels. It seems at one point to be a variant of the *Cinderella* legend, but that's misleading.

    The setting can be taken variously as another world, as completely imaginary with funny animals, or somewhere in Melanesia in the far future. It's a civilization of giant mangrove trees rising out of the Southern Sea, inhabited by anthropomorphic fruit bats (flying foxes), otters, wallabies, and monitor lizards. (No other Melanesian fauna like rhinoceroses or monkeys, though.) Their money is the rupiah, which in real life is the currency of Indonesia. Magic is real, though officially only practiced by the bats.

    The society is developed in rich detail. Each mangrove tree is a huge separate Kingdom with homes and shops upon its branches, with the trees all locked together by rope bridges and boat travel at the bottom. Each giant tree is divided into habitats ranging from the Crown at the top, down through the Head, the Shoulders, the Belly, the Knees, and the Toes at the bottom which are the mangrove's roots rising above and sinking beneath the ocean. The trees' branches are Arms. The habitats are also divided socially, with the Crown inhabited by the flying fox aristocracy who set great prestige on their ability to fly, down through the Shoulders relegated to the upper classes, the Belly to the merchants, and the Knees to the lowest class, the otters who are fishermen. Nobody lives on the Toes, which dip into and out of the ocean. Different Kingdoms are the Kingdom of Titan, the largest tree; the Kingdom of Beards, whose branches are covered in beardlike moss; the Kingdom of the Great Drinker, a bulbous hollow mangrove with a large pool of drinkable water collected from rain and dew in its belly; and others—including the Drowned Kingdom, Atlas, once the mightiest of all until it was uprooted by the Great Storm and toppled beneath the Southern Sea. Kingdom can also refer to the social strata, with the Crown as the elite of the Upper Kingdoms and the Knees as the least desirable of the Lower Kingdoms. The division is not just social; the flying foxes use magic to keep other animals out of the Crown and Head Kingdoms.

    Koa is a young flying fox trapped in the Knees of Titan. He cannot fly. He was orphaned and his wings shredded beyond repair in the Great Storm that destroyed his Kingdom of Atlas. The shredding of his wing membranes has made him hideously disfigured and an outcast to the other flying foxes. He was adopted by a gregarious otter family living in Titan, and he has grown up with eight foster brothers and four foster sisters. His best friend is his brother Tug. Besides fishing, Koa and Tug spend their time scouring the muddy shallow seabed beneath Titan for whatever has been dropped or thrown away by the flying foxes living in the Crown—it may still be worthwhile to the bottom-class otters.

    Koa has reached the age when he is beginning to develop amorous urges, but toward other flying foxes, not otters. Specifically toward Maiel, the son of a wizard aristocrat in the Crown of Titan. But they almost never meet socially since Maiel seldom comes down below Titan's Head, and Koa is too embarrassed by his torn wings to venture into the bats' world; especially since haughty Hayden makes a point of publicly humiliating him when he does.

    When Ruduuk, a monitor lizard merchant, offers him a temporary glamour (good only until midnight) so he can appear as a handsome, aristocratic flying fox and attend the exclusive Firefly Ball in the Crown to meet Maiel, this is when *Koa of the Drowned Kingdom* seems to turn into a disguised *Cinderella*. Don't You Believe It! There is treachery, surprises, danger, fights to the death—well, you don't want a spoiler. Just read it. You won't be disappointed.

Campbell writes excellent prose. Here is the general setting:

> The rope ladder to which he [Koa] clung shook, and he gripped it more tightly with his toes. Above him, thousands of feet tall, the mighty mangrove swayed in the ocean breeze. This was Titan, and of all the Kingdoms, it was easily the largest and mightiest. But because of its massive size, the tree caught more of the wind, and was always in motion, bowing and dancing before the endless expanse of the Southern Sea. Looking up, Koa could see its powerful arms stretching out over the water, heavy with green leaves and ripening fruit, lights twinkling in the settlements on the eastern bough where night's shadow already fell. Still higher, he could make out the Crown of Titan, where all the flying foxes lived. All but him.

Here is what Koa finds in the Crown of the Kingdom of the Beards:

> Beauty and wealth met his eyes. The branches of the great tree twined everywhere, shaped by magicians into pathways and winding pillars lined with flowers and heavy fruit. Glowlamps dangled upward from the floor on long, swaying vines that could be reeled down to illuminate something close by in light of any color. Ladders and woven staircases linked floor and ceiling to dizzying effect, with flying foxes strolling about hanging from their feet, or standing on the ceiling above with equal ease. Koa's head whirled; it was difficult to remember which direction was which. He plucked a leaf from a nearby branch and let it go, watching it twirl and dive to the ceiling above, where others of his kind played and talked. He could understand why so many objects were lost, dropped into the Nets above.

Although there are some scenes of M/M romance, they are very chaste. *Koa of the Drowned Kingdom* is colorful and imaginative; a delight for all ages. It won the 2015 Cóyotl Award for Best Novella.

The Last Unicorn • by Peter S. Beagle.

New York: The Viking Press, March 1968, hardcover, 218 pp.

For the fans of adult anthropomorphic fantasy before furry fandom existed, *The Last Unicorn*'s coming in 1968 was a real treat.

> The unicorn lived in a lilac wood, and she lived all alone. She was very old, though she did not know it, and she was no longer the careless color of sea foam, but rather the color of snow falling on a moonlit night. But her eyes were still clear and unwearied, and she still moved like a shadow on the sea.

One day she overhears two hunters saying that there are no more unicorns left in the world: "The unicorn stood still at the edge of the forest and said aloud, 'I am the only unicorn there is.' They were the first words she had spoken, even to herself, in more than a hundred years." She leaves her wood to venture into the world and learn if here are any other unicorns left. She meets many men who think she is a loose mare. Beasts recognize what she is, but do not care.

> Then one afternoon the butterfly wobbled out of a breeze and lit on the tip of her horn. He was velvet all over, dark and dusty, with golden spots on his wings, and he was as thin as a flower petal. Dancing along her horn, he saluted her with his curling feelers. "I am a roving gambler. How do you do?"
>
> The unicorn laughed for the first time in her travels. 'Butterfly, what are you doing out on such a windy day?" she asked him. "You'll take cold and die long before your time."

The butterfly says:

> "No, no, listen, don't listen to me, listen. You can find your people if you are brave. They passed down all the roads long ago, and the Red Bull ran close behind them and covered their footprints. Let nothing you dismay, but don't be half-safe." His wings brushed against the unicorn's skin.
>
> "The Red Bull?" she asked. "What is the Red Bull?"

The unicorn's search for the Red Bull takes her to the nine black wagons of Mommy Fortuna's Midnight Carnival, where she finds Schmendrick the Magician. They escape together from Celaeno the harpy, Elli (Old Age personified), and another to continue their search for the Red Bull of King Haggard. It takes them to the band of Captain Cully, where they are joined by "a thin thorn of a woman," Molly Grue.

> When she tried to get by, the magician stood in her way. "You don't talk like that," he told her, still uncertain that Molly had recognized the unicorn. "Don't you know how to behave, woman? You don't curtsy, either."
>
> But Molly pushed him aside and went up to the unicorn, scolding her as though she were a strayed milk cow. "*Where have you been?*" Before the whiteness and the shining horn, Molly shrank to a shrilling beetle, but this time it was the unicorn's old dark eyes that looked down.
>
> "I am here now," she said at last.
>
> Molly laughed with her lips flat. "And what good is it to me that you're here now? Where were you twenty years ago, ten years ago? How dare you, how dare you come to me now, when I am *this*?" With a flap of her hand she summed herself up: barren face, desert eyes, and yellowing heart. "I wish you had never come. Why do you come now?" The tears began to slide down the sides of her nose.

The three go on until they come to the town of Hagsgate and King Haggard's castle, where the Red Bull wanders free. Molly helps Schmendrick transform the unicorn into a human girl to escape the Red Bull:

> "What have you done to me?" she cried. "I will die here!" She tore at the smooth body, and blood followed her fingers. "I will die here! I will die!" Yet there was no fear in her face, though it ramped in her voice, in her hands and feet, in the white hair that fell down over her new body. Her face remained quiet and untroubled.

Schmendrick argues that he is helping her:

> "All right," he said. "It would make no difference to you if I had changed you into a rhinoceros, which is where the whole silly myth got started. But in this guise you have some chance of reaching King Haggard and finding out what has become of your people. As a unicorn, you would only suffer their fate—unless you think you could defeat the Bull if you met him a second time."

Schmendrick, Molly, and the unicorn-girl posing as the Lady Amalthea enter the castle where they meet the indifferent King Haggard and his young son, Prince Lir. What happens to them and to the Red Bull completes the novel.

The Last Unicorn has remained a favorite of furry fans ever since the fandom began. There are the unicorn and the Red Bull throughout the novel, and plenty of incidental talking or mythological animals such as the butterfly, the dragons that Prince Lir slays, and the castle's autumn-colored taking cat. The book was filmed as a popular animated feature by Rankin/Bass Productions in 1982, but many fans today still prefer the novel.

The Life and Perambulation of a Mouse • by Dorothy Kilner.

London: John Marshall, April 1784, pamphlet (two volumes).

The modern era of talking animals in literature is generally believed to start with Lewis Carroll's *Alice's Adventures in Wonderland* (July 1865). That is the oldest novel still commonly published today, and the earliest that people (both children and adults) read voluntarily for pleasure. Yet there were quite a few stories in the late 18th century with talking animals.

Before about the 1750s, popular attitudes toward animals were about the same as toward inanimate objects. Children were allowed, if not encouraged, to treat pets and other animals as breakable toys. As an aspect of the Age of Enlightenment, such tormenting of dumb beasts began to be considered as cruel. One result of this was the development of uplifting children's literature. Stories were written for parents to give to their children for their moral edification, as didactic lessons of virtue and kindness to animals. The earliest of these told from a talking animal's viewpoint was Dorothy Kilner's 1784 *The Life and Perambulation of a Mouse*, in which Nimble the mouse relates his autobiography consisting mostly of being the victim of cruel pranks by children. Children continued to tie cans to pets' tails into the 19th century, but after about 1770 they Knew It Was Wrong.

Dorothy Kilner (1755–1836) and her brother's wife Mary Ann were prolific writers of children's stories, then commonly printed as pamphlets to be given to children or read aloud to them by a mother or nursemaid. They were considered to be moral education more than a child's entertainment.

The Life and Perambulation of a Mouse is framed as being dictated to the author by Nimble, a mouse, during a winter indoor house party of young folk. A girl proposes that each guest should relate an incident of their life that will entertain them all, with two days to prepare their story. The author muses to herself aloud:

> The adventures of my life (though deeply interesting to myself) will be insipid and unentertaining to others, especially to my young hearers: I cannot, therefore, attempt it.—"Then write mine, which may be more diverting," said a little squeaking voice, which sounded as if close to me. I started with surprise not knowing any one to be near me; and looking round, could discover no object from whom it could possibly proceed, when casting my eyes upon the ground, in a little hole under the skirting-board, close by the fire, I discovered the head of a mouse peeping out. I arose with a design to stop the hole with a cork, which happened to lie on the table by me; and I was surprised to find that it did not run away, but suffered me to advance quite close, and then only retreated a little into the hole, saying in the same voice as before, "Will you write my history?" You may be sure that I was much surprised to be so addressed by such an animal; but, ashamed of discovering any appearance of astonishment, lest the mouse should suppose it had frightened me, I answered with the utmost composure, that I would write it willingly if it would dictate to me. "Oh, that I will do," replied the mouse, "if you will not hurt me."—"Not for the world," returned I, "come, therefore, and sit upon my table, that I may hear more distinctly what you have to relate." It instantly accepted my invitation, and with all the nimbleness of its species, ran up the side of my chair, and jumped upon my table; when, getting into a box of wafers, it began as follows.

Nimble begins, "Like all other newborn animals, whether of the human, or any other species, I can not pretend to remember what passed during my infant days. The first circumstance I can recollect was my mother's addressing me and my three brothers, who all lay in the same nest, in the following words:-'I have, my children, with the greatest difficulty, and at the utmost hazard of my life, provided for you all to the present moment; but the period is arrived, when I can no longer pursue that method: snares and traps are everywhere set for me, nor shall I, without infinite danger, be able to procure sustenance to support my own existence, much less can I find sufficient for you all; and, indeed, with pleasure I behold it as no longer necessary, since you are of age now to provide and shift for yourselves; and I doubt not but your agility will enable you to procure a very comfortable livelihood."

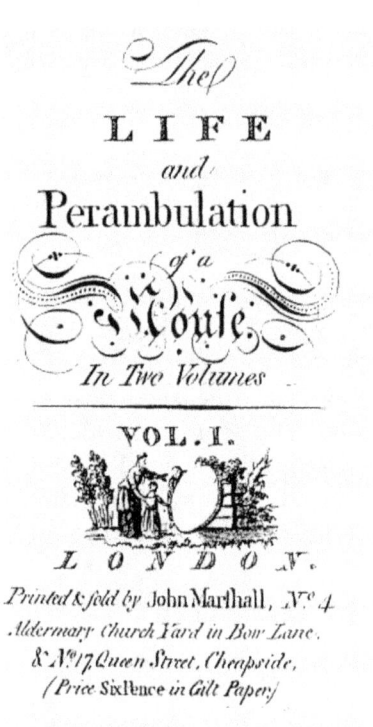

The Life and Perambulation of a Mouse by Dorothy Kilner (John Marshall, April 1784). **The earliest modern fantasy that can be called a novel with anthropomorphic animals. Typeset cover.**

Nimble and his siblings are hardly out of their nest for a week when Nimble witnesses his brother Softdown caught in a trap. He and Longtail, after seeing their brothers quickly caught and killed, agree to leave the house and separate. The rest of the story is Nimble's picaresque adventures as he goes from one location to another, escaping traps and predators such as cats and owls, and often overhearing the conversations in the households he passes through. These all involve moral lessons from parents and nursemaids to their children not to torture small animals, as well as to be kind to the poor.

The original two volumes of the story are presented as the dictation having been interrupted, and resumed several months later. The narrator finds Nimble starving to death, as he has been searching unsuccessfully for Longtail, escaping from more traps, predators, and thoughtless children, and overhearing more moral conversations illustrating kindness to animals and the lower classes. The story ends with Nimble restored to health by the narrator, and agreeing to spend the rest of his life as her pet:

> "[Y]ou will live in this large green-flowered tin canister, and run in and out when you please, and I will keep you constantly supplied with food. But I must now shut you in, for the cat has this moment entered the room."

The Life and Perambulation of a Mouse was reprinted for children to read until about 1870. It is published today as an example of early children's literature, for scholars rather than for children.

The Lion, the Witch, and the Wardrobe: A Story for Children • by C.S. Lewis. Illustrated by Pauline Baynes.

London: Geoffrey Bles Ltd., September 1950, hardcover, 172 pp.

Prince Caspian: The Return to Narnia • by C.S. Lewis. Illustrated by Pauline Baynes.

London: Geoffrey Bles Ltd., September 1951, hardcover, 194 pp.

The Voyage of the Dawn Treader • by C.S. Lewis. Illustrated by Pauline Baynes.

London: Geoffrey Bles Ltd., September 1952, hardcover, 224 pp.

The Lion, the Witch, and the Wardrobe: A Story for Children by C.S. Lewis (Geoffrey Bles Ltd., September 1950). **The first novel in Lewis' mega-popular *The Chronicles of Narnia*; named by every proto- and early furry fan as a major influence. Cover art by Pauline Baynes.**

The Lion, the Witch, and the Wardrobe 108

The Silver Chair • by C.S. Lewis. Illustrated by Pauline Baynes.
London: Geoffrey Bles Ltd., September 1953, hardcover, 220 pp.

The Horse and His Boy • by C.S. Lewis. Illustrated by Pauline Baynes.
London: Geoffrey Bles Ltd., September 1954, hardcover, 200 pp.

The Magician's Nephew • by C.S. Lewis. Illustrated by Pauline Baynes.
London: The Bodley Head, May 1955, hardcover, 184 pp.

The Last Battle • by C.S. Lewis. Illustrated by Pauline Baynes.
London: The Bodley Head, March 1956, hardcover, 184 pp.

The Complete Chronicles of Narnia • by C.S. Lewis. Illustrated by Pauline Baynes. Introduction by Brian Sibley.
London: HarperCollins, September 1998, hardcover, 523 pp.

If there is one novel—nay, series—that every early furry fan read, not once but many times, it was *The Chronicles of Narnia*, or *The Lion, the Witch, and the Wardrobe* and its sequels. They are full of magic, but what furry fans liked the most were Aslan, the talking lion; himself and the other talking animals.

The Lion, the Witch, and the Wardrobe introduces Aslan:

> But as for Aslan himself, the Beavers and the children didn't know what to do or say when they saw him. People who have not been in Narnia sometimes think that a thing cannot be good and terrible at the same time. If the children had ever thought so, they were cured of it now. For when they tried to look at Aslan's face they just caught a glimpse of the golden mane and the great, royal, solemn, overwhelming eyes; and then they found out they couldn't look at him and went all trembly.
> [...]
> "Welcome, Peter, Son of Adam," said Aslan. "Welcome, Susan and Lucy, Daughters of Eve. Welcome He-Beaver and She-Beaver."
> His voice was deep and rich and somehow took the fidgets out of them. They now felt glad and quiet and it didn't seem awkward to them to stand and say nothing.

Before they meet Aslan, they meet the Beavers:

> The first thing Lucy noticed as she went in was a burring sound, and the first thing she saw was a kind-looking old she-beaver sitting in the corner with a thread in her mouth working busily at her sewing machine and it was from it that the sound came. She stopped her work and got up as soon as the children came in.
> "So you've come at last!" she said, holding out both her wrinkled old paws. "At last! To think that ever I should live to see this day! The potatoes are on boiling and the kettle's singing and I daresay, Mr. Beaver, you'll get us some fish."

Aslan is in all seven books, of course. Reepicheep, the mouse cavalier, is in *Prince Caspian*, *The Voyage of the* Dawn Treader, and *The Last Battle*:

> "'Oh! Ugh! What on earth's that! Take it away, the horrid thing."
> He [Eustace] really had some excuse this time for feeling a little surprised. Something very curious indeed had come out of the cabin in the poop and was slowly approaching them. You might call it—and indeed it was—a Mouse. But then it was a Mouse on its hind legs and stood about two feet high.

A thin band of gold passed round its head under one ear and over the other and in this was stuck a long crimson feather. (As the Mouse's fur was very dark, almost black, the effect was bold and striking.) Its left paw rested on the hilt of a sword very nearly as long as its tail. Its balance, as it paced gravely along the swaying deck, was perfect, and its manners courtly. Lucy and Edmund recognized it at once—Reepicheep, the most valiant of all the Talking Beasts of Narnia and the Chief Mouse. It had won undying glory in the second Battle of Beruna.

[…]

"Ugh, take it away," wailed Eustace. "I hate mice. And I never could bear performing animals. They're silly and vulgar and—and sentimental."

"Am I to understand," said Reepicheep to Lucy after a long stare at Eustace, "that this singularly discourteous person is under your Majesty's protection? Because, if not—"

The Horse and His Boy has Bree and Hwin, talking horses from Narnia that were kidnapped as foals and enslaved in Calormen:

The Horse had lifted its head. Shasta stroked its smooth-as-satin nose and said, "I wish you could talk, old fellow."

And then for a second he thought he was dreaming, for quite distinctly, though in a low voice, the Horse said, "But I can."

Shasta stared into its great eyes and his own grew almost as big, with astonishment.

"How ever did you learn to talk?" he asked.

"Hush! Not so loud," replied the Horse. "Where I come from, nearly all the animals talk."

"Wherever is that?" asked Shasta.

"Narnia," answered the Horse. "The happy land of Narnia—Narnia of the heathery mountains and the thyny downs, Narnia of the many rivers, the plashing glens, the mossy caverns and the deep forests ringing with the hammers of the Dwarfs. Oh, the sweet air of Narnia! An hour's life there is better than a thousand years in Calormen." It ended with a whinny that sounded very like a sigh.

In *The Last Battle* there are Puzzle the donkey:

They were quite tired of looking for him when at last his large grey head peered cautiously out of the doorway and he said, "Has it gone away?" And when at last they had got him to come out, he was shivering the way a dog shivers before a thunderstorm.

"I see now," said Puzzle, "that I really have been a very bad donkey. I ought never to have listened to Shift [the Ape]. I never thought things like this would begin to happen."

There are also Jewel the unicorn, Ginger the cat, and seemingly hundreds or thousands of others.

The Lion, the Witch, and the Wardrobe and the following six *Chronicles of Narnia* (later rearranged so *The Magician's Nephew* comes first) are a perpetual treat for any furry fan.

Little Fuzzy • by H. Beam Piper.

New York: Avon Books, January 1962, paperback, 160 pp.

Little Fuzzy by H. Beam Piper (Avon Books, January 1962). The first novel in Piper's *Little Fuzzy* trilogy. When furry fandom started, one of its major influences was charismatic animal-like interstellar aliens, and *Little Fuzzy* was always named. Cover art by Victor Kalin.

The Other Human Race • by H. Beam Piper.
New York: Avon Books, June 1964, paperback, 190 pp.

Fuzzies and Other People • by H. Beam Piper.
New York: Ace Books, August 1984, paperback, 216 pp.

When the first furry fans gathered in 1980–81, they agreed that they had been influenced by three things: a love for cartoon animals in animation and comic books, talking animals in children's books like *Charlotte's Web* by E.B. White and *Ben and Me* by Robert Lawson, and sf stories with charismatic animal-like aliens. *Little Fuzzy* by H. Beam Piper was almost always one of the first novels cited.

Little Fuzzy was published in 1962, and was nominated for the Hugo Award for Best Novel. It is set on the newly-colonized planet Zarathustra, believed to be uninhabited. Jack Holloway, a sunstone prospector exploring in a new region, discovers a small unknown animal that he names Little Fuzzy. Others emerge from the wilderness, and they all exhibit unusual intelligence for animals:

> Jack went back to the workshop, built a fire on the hand forge and forged a pointed and rather broad blade, four inches long, on the end of a foot of quarter-inch round tool steel. It was too point-heavy when finished, so he welded a knob on the other end to balance it. Little Fuzzy knew what that was for right away; running outside, he dug a couple of practice holes with it, and then began casting about in the grass for land-prawns.
>
> Jack followed him with the camera and got movies of a couple of prawn killings, accomplished with smooth, by-the-numbers precision. Little Fuzzy hadn't learned that chop-clap-clap routine in the week since he had found the wood chisel.
>
> Going into the shed, he hunted for something without more than a general idea of what it would look like, and found it where Little Fuzzy had discarded it when he found the chisel. It was a stock of hardwood a foot long, rubbed down and polished smooth, apparently with sandstone. There was a paddle at one end, with enough of an edge to behead a prawn, and the other end had been worked to a point. He took it into the living hut and sat down at the desk to examine it with a magnifying glass. Bits of soil embedded in the sharp end—that had been used as a pick. The paddle end had been used as a shovel, beheader, and shell-cracker. Little Fuzzy had known exactly what he wanted when he'd started making that thing, he'd kept on until it was as perfect as possible, and had stopped short of spoiling it by overrefinement.

When one of the Fuzzies is slain, Holloway demands that the killer be tried for the murder of a sapient being.

The book's back-cover blurb summarizes it best:

> Friends of Little Fuzzy Vs. the Chartered Zarathustra Company
>
> The chartered Zarathustra Company had it all their way. Their charter was for a Class-III uninhabited planet, which Zarathustra was, and it meant they owned the planet, lock, stock and barrel. They exploited it, developed it, and reaped the huge profits from it without interference from the Colonial Government.
>
> Then Jack Holloway, a sunstone prospector, appeared on the scene with his family of Fuzzies and the passionate conviction that they were not cute animals but little people.
>
> The Company was aghast at this threat to their power and profits. If Holloway could prove the Fuzzies were people, Zarathustra would automatically become a Class-IV inhabited planet, the Company's charter would become void and the Colonial Government of the Federation would take over.
>
> The Company did not hesitate to resort to coercion, murder—even genocide—to prevent the Fuzzies from being declared the ninth extrasolar sapient race.

Little Fuzzy is both a courtroom and a scientific melodrama. Where is the legal dividing line between clever animals which are still "only animals," and beings intelligent enough to be considered people with all pertinent rights and obligations? Where is the scientific dividing line between sapience and non-sapience? Piper carefully works out a scenario that keeps the Fuzzies seemingly right on the borderline for most of the story, then reveals them at the climax to be fully intelligent, in a manner that seems natural and not overly manipulative.

Little Fuzzy ends with the Zarathustra Company's power broken, Fuzzies' legal rights guaranteed, and several individual Fuzzies established as popular characters. However, the ending sets up a large question as to how both humans and Fuzzies will get along together under the totally new political situation on Zarathustra. In June 1963, Avon authorized Piper to write two more Fuzzy novels, thanks to the sales of the first novel and to its Hugo nomination. The two were *The Other Human Race/Fuzzy Sapiens*, published in June 1964, and *Fuzzies and Other People*, not published until August 1984, almost twenty years after Piper's suicide. They were popular, but not as popular as the original Fuzzy novel.

Little Fuzzy is not only important for its influence in the creation of furry fandom. It has remained popular. When its copyright lapsed in 2006, almost a dozen unauthorized editions appeared within the first couple of years. New sequels continue to be written; notably *Fuzzy Ergo Sum* by Wolfgang Diehr (2011), and *Caveat Fuzzy* (2012) and *The Fuzzy Conundrum* (2016) by John F. Carr and Wolfgang Diehr.

Unfortunately, from the anthropomorphic standpoint, since the main point of *Little Fuzzy* is whether the Fuzzies are intelligent or not, there is no Fuzzy dialogue in it to quote. They are, and there is plenty of Fuzzy dialogue in the sequels.

A Marriage of Insects: A Novel of the World Tree • by Bard Bloom.

Yulan, NY: Padwolf Publishing Inc., July 2007, paperback, 193 pp.

Sythyry's Journal: A World Tree Chronicle of Transaffection, Adventure, and Doom • by Bard Bloom.

Seattle, WA: CreateSpace, April 2010, paperback, 626 pp.

> Nethry Chrestilium was not her name. She had put her real name aside when she started working among the monsters and wild folk. She knew that she would be doing things which most primes would call foolhardy or wicked, and she did not want her real name attached to them. So she had, in essence, folded it up and packed it away in a box at her parents' house, wrapped in cheap silk, to pick up again when she retired.
>
> But her retirement was a long ways off—if it ever came. She knew quite well that for every colleague of hers who retired, three died at work. She worked in the most dangerous territory on the upper branches of the World Tree, outside the heavy walls of magic around the cities.

The World Tree Role Playing Game was co-created by Bard Bloom (with Victoria Borah Bloom) in January 2001; it was a finalist in the Best Anthropomorphic Game category of the Ursa Major Awards that year. "The World Tree's branches are fifty miles wide and thousands long, and their flat upper sides are the home of civilization" (advertisement copy). Characters/players are divided among eight prime species: five mammalian, one of small dragons, one of floating cephalopods, and one insectile: "The

Herethroy (cricketfolk), peaceful and agrarian." The Herethroy are the main characters in this novel:

> Three hundred people strolled or sat, nibbled a dozen varieties of stuffed vegetables or conversed in the fashion of farmers everywhere about weather and crops and spells for storing vegetables or evicting pests. Their chitin shone like matte emeralds and sapphires in the dismal sunlight, and those that could afford it showed off inlay-work of copper or yulexion or gold. Everyone wore their best, for they were wealthy by farmers' standards: tight-fitting silk embraced arms, legs, and the middle limbs that can serve as either. The co-lovers and some males wore confectionary painted leather hats rising between their many-jointed antennae, or short capes of painted lace, or tied glittering ribbons between each pair of knobs on their tails. The women dressed less flamboyantly but no less elegantly.

The wedding—a triad, uniting three members of the three-sexed crickets—is actually an arranged affair among the minor nobility between three infants. Boragette Norrow is at the age where the only thing of importance is stripping off all of zie's clothing as fast as zie can. (Zie = a pronoun for neuters among creatures of more than two sexes.) Casamint Imbarr dashes about the wedding party crashing into the guests until his exasperated father levitates him above the crowd. Marjoram Rowns isn't sure what marriage is, but is sure that she wants no part of one; she throws a temper tantrum until she exhausts herself.

Thirty years pass.

The newlyweds have grown up separated. Marjoram has become a warrior under the name Rajel, partnered with Arrhwy the Sleeth (a not-very-anthropomorphized intelligent panther) and Oostmarine the Orren (otter), until the latter is killed fighting a monster during one of their adventures. Rajel's meeting with Oostmarine's family at his melancholy funeral makes her dwell upon her own mostly-forgotten familial obligations.

After thirty years, Boragette is a successful farmer in nearby Dorly with a new lover, Chicory, while Casamint is an aspiring scholar of drama with a lover, Skirret, among his fellow students. They are not at all happy to receive notes from Rajel calling them home to honor their all-but-forgotten married state. After several days spent awkwardly in Comblefree, where the clannish farmers treat them as "foreigners" more than as minor nobility, an offer of employment for Rajel and Arrahwy seems a solution to their problems:

> "I wish to engage your services as travel guards," writes the Rassimel (raccoon) enchanter Ilzatheinen, "from Lenkasia to a small village named Soohoon under the control of Byronny Meme, and, perhaps, to some of the cities of the Transwynt. This is not to be a dangerous trip; indeed, I am bringing my daughter…"
>
> […]
>
> Arrhwy shrugged. "Ilzatheinen brings his daughter. You bring your husband and mari."
>
> Rajel raised her antennae. "Now there's a thought. Not one of the three of us is having a good time in Comblefree … and I don't think we'd do much better in anyone else's town. Spending a bit of time together, without other Herethroy around to bully Boragette, doing something halfway intellectual to interest Casamint. Let me see if I can talk them into it."

So she can, and so they do. Naturally the nice, safe job turns out to be anything but, with surprises pleasant and unpleasant, betrayals, and deaths (but nothing permanent). Above all, this is a comedy of manners with exceedingly polite monsters, temples of hideous demon-gods that could rent themselves out to Hallowe'en amusement parks, and the most unbelievably exotic restaurants they could imagine in the most cosmopolitan city on the World Tree. Somehow everything relates to the travelers' romantic entanglements: Rajel, Boragette, and Casamint fall into and out of love with each other in varying combinations; Arrhwy is cheerfully insulting to all; Chicory joins the party; and Nethry Chrestilium (remember her?), a Rassimel, gets unexpectedly involved with Ilzatheinen's daughter Zallarilla. There are more bedroom histrionics than battles, and with all the combinations of sexes and species, it is hard to keep track of who's on top.

A Marriage of Insects is full of witty turns of phrases, and beautiful descriptions of magical landscapes. At first its frequent usage of World Tree terminology ("A nycathath can do much more with one cley than any prime can…") will continuously send the reader to the Glossary at the back of the book, but one quickly picks up the needed vocabulary; and this does make the whole setting much more original and exotic than the usual anthropomorphic novel which merely features a furry cast in a mundane setting.

At the end, as in all the best comedies of manners, true love prevails—whatever that may turn out to be in this world.

Sythyry's Journal: A World Tree Chronicle of Transaffection, Adventure, and Doom is not a sequel, but it does take place in the same *World Tree* setting, and is very enjoyable.

Memoirs of a Polar Bear • by Yoko Tawada. Translated by Susan Bernofsky.

New York: New Directions Books, November 2016, paperback, 252 pp.

This was originally published as *Etüden im Schnee* (konkursbuch Verlag, March 2014). It isn't published as furry fiction but as mainstream literature, so it is probably classed as fabulism or literary fantasy:

> I'd taken part in a congress that day [in Kiev], and afterward all the participants were invited to a sumptuous feast. When I returned to my hotel room at night, I had a bear's thirst and greedily drank water straight from the tap. But the taste of oily anchovies refused to leave me. In the mirror I saw my red-smeared lips, a masterpiece of the beets. I'd never eaten root vegetables voluntarily, but when a beet came swimming in my bowl of borsht, I immediately wanted to kiss it. Bobbing amid the lovely dots of fat floating on top—which at once awoke my appetite for meat—the beet was irresistible.
>
> The springs creak beneath my bearish weight as I sit on the hotel sofa thinking how uninteresting the conference had been yet again, but that it had unexpectedly led me back to my childhood. The topic of today's discussion was The Significance of Bicycles in the National Economy.

A "Polar Bear" is actually three polar bears over three generations; a grandmother, mother, and son. The first, never named, is captured and brought as a cub to Moscow, where she is trained to perform in a circus, apparently around the 1960s. Her part is "The Grandmother: An Evolutionary Theory":

> After hours and days spent vigorously shaking my hips, my knees were in such bad shape that I was incapable of performing acrobatics of any sort. I was unfit for circus work. Ordinarily they would have just shot me, but I got lucky and was assigned a desk job in the circus's administrative offices.
>
> I never dreamed I had a gift for office work. But the personnel office left no talents of their workers unexplored if they could be employed and exploited to the circus's advantage. I would even go so far as to say I was a born office manager. My nose could sniff out the difference between important and unimportant bills.

After learning record-keeping, she begins to write her autobiography in her spare time as a hobby, until she learns that a human supervisor has been taking it and getting it published—without telling her or sharing the money. She discovers how to manage her own sales, and finds that her autobiography is a best-seller. She's become an intellectual, and is invited to literary conferences. But a famous intellectual polar bear as a member of the intelligentsia becomes an embarrassment to the Soviet establishment. She is encouraged to move to Siberia (the climate will be so much more comfortable to polar bears), and finally to emigrate to West Germany; then to Canada where she finds too much freedom. She marries a polar bear from Denmark, has a daughter, and they re-emigrate to East Germany.

Part II, "The Kiss of Death," is about the first bear's daughter Tosca; but the narrator is a human in the East German national circus (later identified as Barbara). When the Soviet Union gives the circus nine polar bears—nine bears arrogant with Soviet labor demands, who go on strike—she incidentally learns about Tosca.

She brings in Tosca hoping that she will be an encouraging role model for the Soviet bears. When she isn't—"When her [Tosca's] vehicle passed the quarters of the nine polar bears, they immediately began to heckle her: 'Strike-breaker! Scab!'"—she works with Tosca to develop a solo act. Eventually she writes Tosca's biography, rather than Tosca writing an autobiography.

Finally Barbara and Tosca become so close that Tosca takes over writing the narrative. After the reunification of Germany, they travel around the world as a duo:

> During the performance, I took great pleasure in watching the children in the audience. They stared at us open-mouthed and wide-eyed. In Japan we received a letter that said: "it must be exhausting to put on a bear costume in this heat and perform onstage. Please accept my heartfelt thanks for your wonderful performance! Our children were ecstatic." Apparently there were audience members who were incapable of believing I was really a bear. How fortunate that no one came into the dressing room and asked me to take off my bearskin.

When they retire, Tosca is sold to the Berlin Zoo where Knut is born. Part III, "Memories of the North Pole," is Knut's story, a blend of fiction and fact. Knut was born in the Berlin Zoo, and is probably the most famous polar bear in history. There were Knut T-shirts and plush dolls. Knut's keeper Matthias became almost as popular, and when he unexpectedly died, Knut was distraught by his disappearance:

> And this news too reached me in the form of a newspaper article: Matthias is dead. He died of a heart attack. At first I didn't understand what that meant. I read it through several times. Suddenly a thought struck me like a stone: I can never see him again.

Although the protagonists are individual polar bears in a human world, there are others in supporting roles: the nine Soviet circus bears, the first bear's Danish husband Christian, and others. The first bear is briefly confused by human anthropomorphic fiction:

> The protagonist was a mouse. Her form of gainful employment: singing. Her audience: the people. On the vocabulary list I found the word *Volk*, which corresponded to the Russian *narod*.
> [...]
> As long as the mouse went on singing, the *Volk* gave her its full attention. No one aped her, no one giggled, no one disrupted her concerts by making mouse noises. This is just how my own audience behaved, too, and my heart leaped as I remembered the circus.

The bear is disappointed when she learns the story of the mouse singer is only fiction; a literary conceit.

Memoirs of a Polar Bear has a melancholy, ethereal ending that fits the book nicely. The real Knut died. The book's Knut goes on. In fiction, he can live forever. The novel was a finalist for the 2016 Cóyotl Award for Best Novel.

Monkey Wars • by Richard Kurti.
New York: Delacorte Press, January 2015, hardcover, 409 pp.

Monkey Wars has been described as "a dark fable in the tradition of"—different reviewers have compared it to several other adult talking-animal novels; but almost always including *Animal Farm* and *Watership Down*. The British edition was nominated for two literary awards. It has been translated into French, German, and Japanese.

The novel, set in India, is based on the proliferation of wild street monkeys, usually rhesus macaques, in Delhi and Kolkata. They travel in troops and attack people if they are disturbed—sometimes when not provoked. The specific event that inspired *Monkey Wars* was from *The New Delhi Times* for 21 October 2007: "In a sinister development, the deputy mayor of Delhi, S.S. Bajwa, died this morning after being attacked by a gang of rhesus macaques." But whenever the authorities try to curb the monkey problem, they are attacked by devout Hindus because all monkeys are believed to be sacred to Hanuman, the monkey god. Authorities have tried importing langur monkeys, a larger species, to scare the rhesus monkeys away, but with mixed success. The novel takes advantage of this:

> They struck at noon.
> Monkeys shrieked in confusion as langur fighters sprang down from the cemetery walls, howling in an attacking frenzy. As they stormed through the tombs, fear and panic flashed everywhere. And with the screams came the smell of blood.

A troop of rhesus monkeys that had been living peacefully for generations in an abandoned human cemetery (which in India is full of miniature Hindu temple reproductions) is suddenly ruthlessly attacked by an organized army of langur monkeys. The langurs kill all the rhesus males, drive out the females and children, and take over the cemetery for themselves.

The beginning of the novel is divided into two stories, told in mostly alternating chapters; those of Papina, a young rhesus girl, and of Mico, a young langur boy. Papina and her mother Willow are traumatized by the disappearance of their males, and by being driven into the streets of Kolkata that are already filled by as many slum monkeys as they will hold. Mico, who is too young to question what he is told, is delighted by the palatial new home that the langur Lord Ruler Gospodar announces that he has found for them.

The short chapters are full of action and tension. Papina, Willow, and the other rhesus females are harried into increasingly shabby and dangerous neighborhoods. They are finally rescued by Twitcher, a rhesus male who takes them to a temple of Hanuman where they can live in peace, if not the luxury that they had known in the cemetery.

Mico, who is more curious than most langur children, is told to not ask questions:

> "But asking questions is…" Mico frowned. "It's what monkeys do. Monkeys question."
> "The langur troop aren't like other monkeys. We were chosen," Trumble [Mico's father] replied solemnly. "Chosen to fight for peace. The langur keep the streets safe from the hordes of wild monkeys out there. If we questioned every decision Lord Gospodar made"—Trumble broke off to look around the cemetery—"we wouldn't have all this."

Mico gradually sees things that do not match what he is told. Despite the langur's advertised freedom and luxury, they are ruled by Lord Gospodar and his Ruling Council of General Pogo, Deputies Tyrell and Hani, and one ordinary monkey to represent the concerns of the common langurs. Monkeys who question the Council tend to be ostracized or to disappear. In scenes within Mico's chapters, Deputy Tyrell acts like Stalin in the first days of Soviet authority (or like Napoleon at the beginning of *Animal Farm*), constantly volunteering for minor positions that, added up, will transfer power to him.

Mico and Papina get together in Chapter 12. I have revealed several minor spoilers getting this far, so I won't continue in as much detail. Even though Mico has tried to keep a low profile among the langurs, he is noticed by Deputy Tyrell. Papina's attempts to get the cemetery back for the rhesuses get her branded as a troublemaker by the other rhesuses who are content to let well enough alone. When she meets Mico, she is forbidden to associate with him.

Papina's talents cause her to rise in the rhesuses' hierarchy, and she can see the coming battle with the langurs. Mico's fears are realized when he sees that the langurs are preparing to take their supremacy outside the cemetery—"The city is looking to us," Gospodar declared. "It needs us to eradicate the scourge of savage monkeys! The Ruling Council and I are of one mind: in the name of peace, we must mobilize for war!"—but he remains hesitant to turn against his own leaders, his own people, his own family:

> Mico shuddered as the dampness of the night crept up on him. He scrambled to the top of the wall and perched himself on the smooth coping stones.
> On one side of him was the cemetery, on the other the city stretching out into the distance. He was perched between two worlds in more ways than one. Whichever decision he made seemed to lead to unhappiness. Maybe he should just spend the rest of his life sitting up here on this wall.

Will Mico and Papina join together to prevent a bloody, fatal confrontation? Or will they remain separate for a tragic, Romeo-and-Juliet conclusion?

Or will something unexpected happen?

Kurti's writing is straightforward but gripping; *Monkey Wars* deserves the accolade of "unputdownable." Since Mico and Papina are both monkey young adolescents, *Monkey Wars* could serve as a Young Adult novel. It is published as an adult literary novel from a major publisher, and it got good reviews, so your public library may have it.

MoonDust: Falling from Grace • by Ton Inktail.

Seattle, WA: CreateSpace, December 2015, paperback, 380 pp.

This is an excellent science-fiction novel. It's also an excellent furry novel. Humanity is extinct; transgenic animal people, created for the war effort, are all that are left. The protagonist, Imogene Haartz, is a young caribou (reindeer)-human hybrid; she shaves her fur when sent by the military to a hot climate, and takes prescribed drugs to suppress her antlers' growth. Who needs antlers in the Army? Everyone is a boar or a rabbit or a ferret or an otter or a tiger or some other animal, whether the species is specified or not.

It's also an extremely bleak novel. Everyone is miserable until they die (metaphorically). Imogene has grown up in the mid–22nd century in the rubble of Helsinki. The world has evolved until there are only two super-powers left, the UNA (United Nations of America) and the Pan-Asian Federation. If they aren't in a shooting war, they're in a cold war so frigid that everyone expects it to boil over at every moment. Imogene's father was killed in the last active fighting:

> Imogene stared up at her mother's apartment building.
> Old and gray, it rose to ten stories of utilitarian serviceability. Of the four buildings that had surrounded a small park, only it survived. Two others were rubble, while the fourth clawed at the sky with broken, concrete fingers.

Most of Helsinki was like that. Twelve years after the United Nations of America "liberated" the city, the cleanup effort was far from complete. Especially away from the wealthy neighborhoods. Imogene couldn't remember what it was like before the UNA. Derelict buildings and mounds of broken concrete seemed the natural state of things.

Imogene has gotten out of the UNA Army at 18 after her mandatory military service, prepared to rejoin her fiancé, get a civilian job, and rejoin life. She finds that her boyfriend hasn't waited for her, and there are no civilian jobs for a teenager with only military training:

> She wished for the thousandth time since returning that she'd picked something other than demolitions for her military specialization. At least if she'd gone in for motor pool she'd have a chance. More people would pay you to fix a car than to blow one up.

After searching fruitlessly for months, she goes to a UNA recruiting office to re-enlist. Only this time, instead of the Army where she'll be sent to another hot-climate city that's mostly broken concrete, she picks the Luna Corps—the UNA's space program. It's the one area of service that's neat and shiny instead of depressing—and there are so few volunteers that she feels secure of getting in. (Even if it means taking more antler-suppression drugs. Who needs antlers in a spacesuit?)

The sf nature of the novel is evident:

> There, tunneled into the jagged peaks of the Atlas Mountains, lay Toubkal Spaceport. One of four major launch sites under UNA control, Toubkal's 500 kilometre-long linear induction catapult kept up a steady stream of traffic into low Earth orbit.
>
> Imogene's middle tightened. The catapult was basically a large-bore electric cannon. Was the distance she was about to put between herself and all her earthly problems really worth becoming a caribou-shaped artillery shell?

So is the furry nature:

> A dramatization of the Unification Wars, the vid focused on the valor and heroism of the transgenic soldiers, glossing over the fact they were counted as chattel and had no choice but to fight. That wasn't the only creative liberty taken, but it rankled Imogene the most. True, she hadn't known her grandparents, let alone the great-grands who'd been forced to war, but it still served the humans right their own bio-weapons got loose and their animal slaves were the only ones immune.

The novel introduces Imogene's squadmates on the Moon: Sergeant Robert Hendricks (Dalmatian), Fiona Whiting (polar bear), Ryan Sanders (ground squirrel), Victor Vidal (puma), Bruce Andersen (stag), Lauren Porter (lynx), and Alexei (white rabbit). There are several chapters showing the military in peacetime. Imogene gets to know her squadmates; she makes friends and enemies. Then the war boils over—this is not a spoiler since the cover by Katrin "LeSoldatMort" Buttig shows the spacesuited Imogene looking at nuclear detonations on Earth. The last half of the book describes Imogene's and her team's desperate fight to survive, as they hope to return to a UNA base—if there is anything to return to—and learn what has happened to Earth.

MoonDust: Falling from Grace is a harrowing, exhausting thriller:

> They rested as long as their dwindling power supplies let them dare, then struck out across the flats.
>
> Smooth, dusty terrain fled past under Imogene's loping bounds. The valley floor was easy, and even the rolling foothills hardly slowed their march. Scattered pea-size bits of rock and metal continued to drizzle, but she ignored them as much as she could. The best course of action was to hurry on to Borda.
>
> As they climbed, the drizzle turned to a ballistic hail, pelting in from the north. She kept her visor

pointed down and her legs pushing her forward. Then a wave of larger impacts broke over the landscape, and Imogene's blood turned cold.

Her gaze darted over the bleak surroundings. No cover. All they could do was sprint for the still distant mountains.

Towers of dust shot up from the larger strikes, leaving craters the size of manholes. She dodged around the holes, praying she and her friends wouldn't be hit.

It becomes a bit melodramatic at the end, but the reader is kept guessing until the last page whether Imogene or any of her team will survive. The novel's furry nature is both deep—Imogene considers a trans-species romance, and whether the inability to have children would be a serious problem—and superficial. All of the characters are clearly funny animals, who could be turned into humans with only minor rewriting.

It may be pertinent that the author's only other credits (as Ton Inktail or a.k.a. Tonin; the © is Andy Rohde) are two equally harrowing thrillers, short stories in the FurPlanet anthologies *Abandoned Places* and *Bleak Horizons*. *MoonDust: Falling from Grace* will leave you eager for Ton Inktail's next novel.

Mort(e) • by Robert Repino. Illustrated by Sam Chung.

New York: Soho Press, January 2015, hardcover, 358 pp.

Mort(e) by Robert Repino (Soho Press, January 2015). **The first novel in Repino's *The War with No Name* series, one of the most imaginative works of anthropomorphic fiction published today. Cover art by Sam Chung.**

Culdesac: A Novella from the War with No Name • by Robert Repino.

New York: Soho Press, November 2016, paperback, 121 pp. (including an 11-page preview of D'Arc).

D'Arc: A Novel from the War with No Name • by Robert Repino. Illustrated by Sam Chung and Kapo Ng.

New York: Soho Press, May 2017, hardcover, 386 pp.

Before he took his new name, before the animals rose up and overthrew their oppressors, before there was talk of prophecies and saviors, the great warrior Mort(e) was just a house cat known to his human masters as Sebastian. It was a time that now returned to him only in dreams and random moments of nostalgia that disappeared as quickly as they arose. All of it except for Sheba. The memory of her was always digging at him like a splinter under a nail.

The first dozen pages of *Mort(e)* are Sebastian's early life as a housecat, and his meeting Sheba, the large, slobbery dog of the man next door. It's not until page 14 that Sebastian first learns of the war to exterminate humans, when he observes one of "his masters" watching the TV news:

It was always the same: a river of text flowed beneath explosions, people running, buildings on fire, green trucks rolling along highways, men and women with helmets marching, building bridges, demolishing things, using flamethrowers to burn massive hills of dirt. And in between all the images were videos of creatures that Sebastian had seen crawling in the grass outside the window: ants. They were always on the television, always marching in a line, sometimes covering entire fields and picking apart dead farm animals. Sebastian saw people running away from ants the size of the Martinis' car. The monsters could walk on their hind legs, and their jaws were strong enough to lift a human at the waist.… All the channels were playing the same thing now. Nothing buts ants and fires. But this time, there was footage of a new creature. A pack of wolves, walking on their hind legs, approaching the camera. One of them carried a club in his hands the same way Daniel would hold a hammer. This was followed by a choppy clip of a group of animals marching alongside the giant ants. Sebastian could hear people screaming.

Sebastian gets out of his house and briefly becomes a feral cat, until he changes: "That night, while he sat behind the Martinis' garage, the hair on his paws fell away. He was not alarmed. He simply brushed away the remaining strands, stretched out the toes into fingers, and rubbed the paws together." Sebastian quickly begins to understand human speech, stands upright and grows to human size.

When the humans in his neighborhood are all killed or evacuate, and the changed pets are left to take over before the giant ants arrive, Sebastian leaves to search for the missing Sheba, who is probably dead.

Chapter Two focuses on the ants. The protagonist is Hymenoptera Unus, the thousands-of-years-old Queen of the Colony who launched the war to exterminate humans. Warfare between the humans and ants was practically eternal. The Colony's previous Queens—the Lost Queen and the Misfit Queen—had died because of the humans. Hymenoptera Unus was smarter and able to plan a longer-term conquest:

> From that moment on, she developed a plan for vengeance that would take millennia to execute. The Colony would acquire knowledge the way humans gobbled up resources and land. The ants would create an army with warriors who were larger, stronger, and more vicious than even the most bloodthirsty human. They would study and exploit all aspects of mankind's existence: language, community, physiology, history, and science, as well as religion, that anti-science that animated the humans, driving them to either greatness or destruction. They would exert dominion over the other ant clans and make contact with other species who viewed the humans as a mutual enemy. The Colony now had a goal beyond mere survival. Its subjects had purpose. They observed history in linear rather than circular terms. Like their enemy, they had an apocalypse to anticipate.

The true history of the unnamed war of human extinction, from the ants' viewpoint, is related. The reason for the other animals' expansion is explained.

Chapter Three, and the rest of the novel, is the cat's story. Sebastian survives. He reads human books and he learns. He encounters other intelligent cats who insist on examining him for EMSAH, a human anti-animal bioweapon.

The smart animals are involuntary allies of the Colony. The male cat explains, "The Queen started the war. We're the soldiers who are helping to end it. In return, we will be in charge of the surface." Sebastian joins the other cats, a military unit named the Red Sphinx. He takes the name Mort(e). But he never truly becomes one of the others. And he continues to search for Sheba.

Mort(e) is unusual. It's a real puzzle. Unlike most fiction, where the reader can guess what the ending will be and the real question is how the story will get there, you don't know until the end whether the animal world will succeed, or whether Mort(e) will personally survive. Repino's writing is skillful. Whether his explanation for how the animals grow hands, stand up, and grow to human size is entirely believable, at least he tries to create a reason. The setting is not the usual furry civilization, but there are plenty of scenes of the animals' society:

> "Get up, soldier," Wawa [Lieut. Wawa, a half-breed pit bull dog] said.
> "This isn't boot camp," Rigel [a bear doctor] said. "You have to—"
> "Quiet. We've got enough problems around here without you running your mouth."
> Rigel threw her hands up and headed for the door. "See you at the processing station, Lieutenant," she said.
> Bonaparte [Specialist Bonaparte, a pig] propped himself up and sat on the bed, facing Wawa through the bars. His hooves rested on his chubby knees. "The humans are watching us," he said."

Read *Mort(e)* and the rest of the *War with No Name* series. You may not like the dramatic and sometimes grisly way that things happen, but you won't want to miss them.

Mrs. Frisby and the Rats of NIMH • by Robert C. O'Brien. Illustrated by Zena Bernstein.

New York: Atheneum, April 1971, hardcover, 233 pp.

Racso and the Rats of NIMH • by Jane Leslie Conly. Illustrated by Leonard Lubin.

New York: Harper & Row, May 1986, hardcover, 278 pp.

R-T, Margaret, and the Rats of NIMH • by Jane Leslie Conly. Illustrated by Leonard Lubin.

New York: HarperCollins, June 1990, hardcover, 260 pp.

Mrs. Frisby and the Rats of NIMH was almost always cited by the earliest furry fans as one of their favorite children's books. A 1972 Newbery Medal winner for "the most distinguished contribution [of the preceding year] to American literature for children," it has always been in print. Its fans often debate whether it is pure fantasy, or fantasy mixed with science-fiction.

Mrs. Frisby is a field mouse widow living with her four children in a cinder block in a vegetable garden on the farm of Mr. Fitzgibbon. One spring Farmer Fitzgibbon begins his plowing, but Mrs. Frisby cannot move her family as usual because Timmy, her youngest son, has pneumonia. Jeremy, a crow, suggests she seek help from an ancient owl. The owl offers little help, until she tells him her name:

> But at the mention of her name an extraordinary change had come over the owl. He turned back to face her again and stared at her most intently. Indeed, he gave an agitated flutter of his wings and half flew, half hopped closer to her, bending forward until his great sharp beak was only a few inches from her face. Mrs. Frisby shrank back in fear. What had she done wrong?
> "Did you say Mrs. Frisby?"
> "Yes. You asked my name."
> "Related to Jonathan Frisby?"
> "Yes. He was my husband. He died last summer. He was Timothy's father. But how did you know about him?"
> "That is not important," said the owl, drawing back a little and looking at her in a new way—almost

as if with deference. "I will say this. His name was not unknown in these woods. And if you are his widow, that puts the matter in a different light."

The owl recommends that she go to the strange, reclusive rats who live under a thorny rosebush on the farm. The rats take her into their underground home:

> Ahead of her stretched a long, well-lit hallway. Its ceiling and walls were a smoothly curved arch, its floor hard and flat, with a soft layer of carpet down the middle. The light came from the walls, where every foot or so on both sides a tiny light bulb had been recessed and the hole in which it stood, like a small window, had been covered with a square of colored glass—blue, green or yellow. The effect was that of stained-glass windows in sunlight.
>
> Justin was watching her and smiling. "Do you like it? The carpet and the colored glass we don't really need. Some of the wives did that on their own, just for looks. They cut the glass. Believe it or not, from old bottles. The carpet was a piece of trim they found somewhere."
> "It's beautiful," Mrs. Frisby said. "But how …"
> "We've had electricity for four years now."
> "Five," said Mr. Ages.
> "Five," said Justin agreeably. "The lights"—they were the very small, very bright twinkling kind—"we found on trees. Not until after Christmas, of course—about New Year's. The big light bulbs we have trouble handling."

Mrs. Frisby arrives in the midst of a meeting about the Plan. As she (and the reader) gradually learn, the rats are escapees from NIMH—the National Institute of Mental Health in Maryland. Twenty rats, and eight mice, were part of an experiment to increase their intelligence. (It may have also given them immortality; at any rate, they didn't age.) The experiment worked so well that they figured out how to escape, though six of the mice were lost. Over the years they built their home under the Fitzgibbon farm. But Justin worries that they have to steal their food from Fitzgibbon's crops, and their electricity from his power lines. Sooner or later they may be discovered. Justin's plan, which becomes the Plan, is to all move to remote, humanless Thorn Valley; to learn to grow their own food and live without electricity or running water. Jenner leads a small opposition that wants to stay where they are and continue to live off the humans. When he is outvoted, Jenner and his followers leave to start a new colony to continue living off the humans.

Through the rats' plan to move Mrs. Frisby's cinder-block home, she overhears the Fitzgibbon family discussing at dinner that six or seven rats got electrocuted around a motor in a nearby power store, that the local newspaper wrote a humorous story calling them "mechanized rats," and that the federal government has sent out an extermination team—which Mr. Fitzgibbon has invited to come to his farm the next day to exterminate his "rat problem." Are the dead rats Jenner and his faction? Is the "federal government" really NIMH? Mrs. Frisby must warn the rats before they are fully ready to evacuate their civilization under the Fitzgibbons' rosebush.

The novel is significantly different than *The Secret of NIMH*, the animated feature film produced by Don Bluth in 1982 (which itself was a very large topic of discussion among the earliest furry fans). In the book, the rats scurry on all fours, are unclothed, generally take only what they need from humans by technological and mechanical means, and are governed by Nicodemus, a wise leader. In the movie, the rats walk upright, wear medieval-style clothes, have created an ornate underground city by magic, and Nicodemus is a traditional mighty wizard. New furry fans today who are familiar with only the movie are often surprised to learn that the book has much less magic and has a science-fiction frame,

Robert C. O'Brien was the pseudonym of Robert Conly. After his death, his daughter Jane Leslie Conly wrote two sequels, *Racso and the Rats of NIMH* (1986) and *R-T, Margaret, and the Rats of NIMH* (1990). Both are forgettable.

Mus of Kerbridge • by Paul Kidd. Map by Diesel.

Lake Geneva, WI: TSR Books, April 1995, paperback, 314 pp.

This novel reads like a cross between Brian Jacques, Georgette Heyer, and Rafael Sabatini. If you can imagine a rough parallel of the European wars of the 17th century being fought between intermixed armies of humans and the creatures of faerie, you've got the general idea. But there are no anthropomorphic animals—until the creation of Mus, a common mouse sorcerously bioengineered to become a tiny, furry Cavalier knight.

The date is specified as 1641 and 1642, although the geopolitical situation is closer to the 1670s. The names and monarchs are different, but Duncruigh, Nantierre, and Welfland are obviously Britain, France and the United Provinces. When Welfland collapses into violent civil war, the progressive revolutionaries gain support from Duncruigh. This is all that Nantierre's aggressive young ruler needs to "come to the rescue" of Welfland. As the novel begins, Nantierre is completing the defeat of Duncruigh's expeditionary army and Welfland's last revolutionary troops, and the repressive occupation of Welfland in the name of a new puppet king who is no more than a Nantierran viceroy; and is turning Welfland's large merchant fleet into an armada for the invasion of Duncruigh itself.

Mus of Kerbridge by Paul Kidd (TSR Books, April 1995). The first sale from within furry fandom to a mainstream publisher. Cover art by Paul Jaquays.

But this is a world shared equally by humans, centaurs, satyrs, pixies, and similar creatures of mythology. All are social equals, in a human-based civilization. Some species gravitate toward roles suited to their specialties—the harpies make good aerial scouts and "air couriers," while the centaurs excel as cavalry shock troops—but there appear to be no interspecies prejudices. There are humans, centaurs, etc., etc., among both the nobility and commoners of all nations.

There is also magic. Kerbridge is an old Duncruighan river and university town (Oxford?) whose centaur "baron served as commander of the royal armies on the continent." Nantierre tries to strike at him through his family at Kerbridge Castle. A spy hires Pin-William, an inept satyr sorcerer, to magically get into the castle. He tries to use a mouse as his remote-controlled agent. The brain and body of the natural mouse are too crude, so its mind must be enhanced and its body anthropomorphized to understand and carry out their orders.

> "Mus, you were a common house mouse but you can claim to be such no longer. Your homoncule—the pattern that controls your body and your mind—has been irrevocably changed. Were you to have children, they would breed true to your own type; that is the nature of the spell." The magician idly took Mus into his hand. "The changes that have been made to you are based upon the pattern of a man. You will age in much the speed and way as a man. The interesting point is the shaping of your intellect. Your mind has been pre-furnished with a number of concepts (by no means comprehensive) which have helped fill out the void left by the expansion of your facilities. The creation of a being such as yourself has been essayed in the past, but it is not a popular experiment. The mana—the magical aptitude as it were—is sucked out of the creator and drawn into the creature." The Sorcerer suddenly stopped and tapped his nose. "No, not a good explanation. Let us say that in creating a being such as yourself a magician would commence the slow wane of his own powers. On the other hand, your own powers will slowly increase."

But the brave mouse, Mus, is strong-willed enough to throw off Pin-William's control. He saves the baron's daughter, young Lady Miriam, and the two become firm friends who turn the Nantierrans' trick back on themselves, using Mus as a tiny spy to uncover enemy agents within the Duncruighan Parliament.

Mus is a delightfully anthropomorphized character. Readers will be amused and enchanted by his adjustment to his altered body and mind, his efforts to fit into the "human" society that is now his, and his exasperated attempts to get people to take him seriously as a wanna-be knight in the king's service. And Mus finds that he is not the only 'morph, after Pin-William attempts to create new animal puppet-slaves without Mus' "flaws" of independence. Mus frees one of them to become Lyssa, his female field-mouse lady fair.

What about the half-animals? Virtually all other major characters are centaurs or satyrs, with humans, harpies, and others playing only minor roles. Kidd deftly spins a Cavalier-era melodrama full of elegant court intrigue, romance, duels, and knowledgeable 17th-century military action. However, aside from providing colorful decor, there is little need for any characters to be centaurs or satyrs dressed in ruffles and lace. At least Kidd avoids the inconsistencies of less-skilled writers who put half-animals into architecture and clothing designed for humans. The most satisfying scene to take practical note of their physical differences is the Channel naval battle which presages the Nantierran invasion of Duncruigh:

> A huge black figure staggered out onto the deck, its hooves skittering for purchase on the wooden planks. Torscha Retter hunched his huge shoulders against a fresh onslaught of spray. A ship is not a natural environment for half-horses, and Torscha's hooves were hard put to keep purchase on the slippery, rolling deck. He watched in silence as human sailors swarmed nimbly up into the rigging.

Kidd makes you believe that centaurs can participate in stormy, deck-tossing naval action without falling all over themselves. *Mus of Kerbridge* is not a comedy, but it certainly blends a sense of humor with its melodrama. It is full of impish, tongue-in-cheek action, led by little Mus who is determined to out-swashbuckle every other knight in Duncruigh.

If one defines a literary classic as "a story that stays in print," then there are very few anthropomorphic classics. Many excellent novels have been published once, and are only available after they go out of print if you can find a used copy. *Mus of Kerbridge* is currently in print in a new edition.

New Coyote • by Michael Bergey.

Waterville, ME: Five Star/Thomson Gale, August 2005, hardcover, 376 pp.

Coyote Season • by Michael Bergey.

Waterville, ME: Five Star/Thomson Gale, November 2007, hardcover, 307 pp.

"Deer and elk seasons come and go, but to a human with a rifle in his hands, it's always coyote season."

Congratulations to Bergey for his smooth blend of technology and Native American mysticism. *New Coyote*, narrated by Coyote himself, covers two years in his modern life among humans in the Pacific Northwest. A normal coyote's lifespan is not comparable to a human's, but thanks to Coyote's supernatural nature, his is close enough. The story is that of his growth from little more than a talking puppy on a commune/farm to his awakening of his magical nature and his discovery of Sex:

> I was not a normal pup. Mooney's friends told each other it was something done to me in the research lab where I was born. I was healthy enough, certainly. I've always been healthy and full of energy. It's just that I didn't grow very fast, and I didn't stop growing when I should have, and I wasn't ... normal.... When I was nine years old, I was almost a hundred pounds and still growing—still long-legged and gangling like a puppy, but no longer clumsy like one. My puppy teeth had worn out years before, and no new ones had come in. I lived with Mooney and her goats and chickens and raspberry fields and pot plants in a commune called Sunbow Farms.... Mostly it was just Mooney and me. And the goats. I herded Mooney's goats for her, which is also not a natural sort of thing for a coyote to do.

Mooney is Monica Sklarsen, an aging ex-hippie who owns a large land tract on the Olympic Peninsula inherited from her grandfather, bordered by Weyerhaeuser's large commercial timber farms. Coyote, alias Sin-Ka-Lip ("The Imitator"), alias Stinkylips, is the only holdover besides Mooney on the former commune. Mooney is the only person who knows that he can talk, more or less ("'I have troupffle with the pffes and pffes,' I answered irritably. 'Those sounds don't fit into a pffropffpffer mouth. They were invented pffy creatures with tight, round little lipffs, like I have under my tail.'"), although their friend John Cultee suspects it. Dr. John is a bit of a *deus ex machina*; he is a modern shaman who teaches Mooney and Coyote Native American folklore; he was the Research Director who took advantage of a project to bioengineer more intelligent dogs to inject human DNA into a coyote pup and give it to Mooney; and he is now a respected member of the local community who helps train/disguise Coyote as a Seeing Eye dog for Mouse, a blind girl to enable her to attend sixth-grade at Central Park School, and not coincidentally so Coyote himself can start getting a basic education into "Science," the humans' new magic.

That is getting ahead of the story, however, which begins dramatically as Mooney's marijuana farm is raided by the law. Coyote's sharp nose enables Mooney to avoid getting personally caught, but the pot patch is lost. Their attempts over the next couple of years to keep Sunbow Farms and its adjoining Mooney's Wood (which she is determined to keep in its wild state as a private nature preserve) from being seized for unpaid property taxes, coincide with Coyote's maturing from an ignorant pup to an intelligent yet feral animal who is at home among both humans and the wild coyotes and semi-domesticated wolves in the area. More and more humans have to be let into the secret of Coyote's talking to protect both Mooney and Mouse, who becomes the target of do-gooders determined to protect her classmates from her "vicious" guide dog.

Coyote soon learns that he is more than just a scientific experiment. As one of the supernatural Animal People, Coyote-Spirit voluntarily allowed himself to be "reborn without memories so that he can grow up within our contemporary culture, and fully understand our way of thinking" (dust-jacket blurb). Mooney and Dr. John are the trusted Human Guides who were selected by Coyote-Spirit (a.k.a. Old-Coyote) and his Brother, Fox, to accomplish this. This has mixed results at first, thanks to Coyote's initial exposure to more popular culture than education:

> The concept of DNA detection at crime sites was confusing to me, but I had watched enough cartoons to know all about super heroes with altered DNA structures. If that wasn't magic, it was just as good. The exact meaning of John's words had escaped me, but the reference to "greater intelligence" seemed relevant enough. I already knew I was the smartest thing on four legs. I thought John was saying I didn't have Medicine Powers, but did have Cartoon Super Hero Powers. Would I begin to develop other special capabilities? Invisible would be nice, for starters.

Coyote needs all the powers he can get. Not only are there continued troubles with humans and nature (Mooney's back taxes, a school board order banning him as a Guide Dog, sharpshooting farmers protecting their livestock, a major flood), but unexpected supernatural menaces materialize. A European werewolf invades the scene, and Coyote accidentally lets loose a deadly Native American monster among his human friends. The more Coyote learns about both human "Science" and his own Medicine Powers, the more reckless he becomes (especially after he learns how to release his five exuberant Spirit Pups to "help"); until Fox exasperatedly decides that the experiment is not working and Coyote should be killed so they can start over—a decision he frantically opposes when it may be too late.

Bergey is identified as a veterinarian living in Washington's Wynoochee Valley, the location of the tale. His vivid, lyrical descriptions of both the land and wild animal behavior are scattered through the book.

New Coyote is sometimes humorous, sometimes dramatic, often beautifully pastoral, and always highly imaginative. There is solid education here, for those who are interested in the natural life of coyotes (including a graphic description of canid mating behavior). Coyote comes across as a genuine blend of human intelligence and animal instincts, participating fully in human conversations at one moment and asking for a belly rub or an ear scratch the next.

This is a Different anthropomorphic novel in the best sense. Read it, and *Coyote Season*, the sequel. Both were finalists for the Ursa Major Award for Best Novel in 2005 and 2007.

Northern Lights • by Philip Pullman.
London: Scholastic Childrens' Books, July 1995, hardcover, 399 pp.

The Golden Compass • by Philip Pullman. Illustrated by Eric Rohmann.
New York: Alfred A. Knopf, March 1996, hardcover, 399 pp.

The Golden Compass (the better-known U.S. title of *Northern Lights*) is the first volume of a trilogy *(His Dark Materials: Northern Lights, The Subtle Knife, The Amber Spyglass)*, but it is the only one of the three in which anthropomorphized animals appear prominently. They are downplayed in the other two. Readers will want to read them nevertheless to find out what happens to Lyra and her dæmon Pan, but be aware that they barely qualify as 'morphic novels because of Pan's reduced presence.

Pullman's imagination has fashioned a unique world of anthropomorphism. Lyra Belacqua is an eleven-year-old girl in a pseudo–Victorian Oxford, England. In her world, all humans have their souls manifest as talking animal companions, or dæmons. Humans and their dæmons are gender-reversed; men have female dæmons and women have male dæmons. Childrens' dæmons are able to shift into different animals; a sign of adulthood is that one's dæmon becomes fixed as a particular animal for the rest of its life. No human is supposed to touch another person's dæmon, although dæmons may touch (and fight) each other.

The book and Lyra's adventure begin when her usually-absent explorer uncle Lord Asriel returns briefly to Jordan College in Oxford. Lyra sneaks into the college's private Retiring Room to secretly watch a meeting between Lord Asriel and the college's Master. She is shocked to witness the Master try to poison Lord Asriel. As a reward for her warning, Asriel allows her to secretly watch his presentation on his research into the mysterious elementary particles that he calls Dust. He soon leaves to continue his research on Dust in the far North.

There are several introductions of dæmons in this opening:

> Lyra stopped beside the Master's chair and flicked the biggest glass gently with a fingernail. The sound rang clearly through the hall.
> "You're not taking this seriously," whispered her dæmon. "Behave yourself."
> Her dæmon's name was Pantalaimon, and he was currently in the form of a moth, a dark brown one so as to not to show up in the darkness of the hall.
> As Lyra held her breath, she saw the servant's dæmon (a dog, like all servants' dæmons) trot in and sit quietly at his feet, and then the Master's feet became visible too, in the shabby black shoes he always wore.
> [...]
> The Master's dæmon had the form of a raven, and as soon as his robe was on, she jumped down from the wardrobe and settled in her accustomed place on his right shoulder.
> Lord Asriel's dæmon, a snow leopard, stood behind him.
> "Are you going to show the projections in here?" she said quietly.
> "Yes. It'll create less fuss than moving to the lecture theater. They'll want to see the specimens too; I'll send for the Porter in a minute. This is a bad time, Stelmaria."
> Back and forth the arguments ranged, and Lyra felt her eyes closing. Soon she was fast asleep, with Pantalaimon curled around her neck in his favorite sleeping form as an ermine.

Lyra is ignorant of the politics of this world, which seem to revolve around a powerful Church dominated by Calvinism that has abolished the Papacy and grown into a larger worldwide faith known as the Magisterium. A powerful secretive agency of this Magisterium is known by the vague title of the General Oblation Board, which opposes Lord Asriel's Dust research as heresy. A compass-like device that can predict the future, an alethiometer, has predicted tragedy for Oxford if Lord Asriel's research continues and the Oblation Board connects the colleges with his heresy. The alethiometer also predicts that Lyra must be allowed to play a crucial role in what is to happen.

Much happens. The important anthropomorphic developments are that Lyra becomes suspicious of Mrs. Coulter when her dæmon Ozymandias, a golden monkey, tries to steal the alethiometer. Lyra escapes and, after various adventures, reaches the far North where she helps the missing children escape from the Gobblers with the help of Iorek Byrnison, one of the talking armored polar bears of the bear Kingdom of Svalbard; and a Texan cowboy in a hot air balloon, Lee Scoresby, and his dæmon hare Hester:

> [Iorek] dropped the reindeer leg in the dirt and slumped on all fours to the gate. Then he reared up massively, ten feet or more high, as if to show how mighty he was, to remind them how useless the gate would be as a barrier, and he spoke to them from that height.
> "Well? Who are you?"
> His voice was so deep it seemed to shake the earth. The rank smell that came from his body was almost overpowering.
> "I'm Farder Coram, from the gyptian people of Eastern Anglia. And this little girl is Lyra Belacqua."
> "What do you want?"
> "We want to offer you employment, Iorek Byrnison."
> "I am employed."
> The bear dropped on all fours again. It was very hard to detect any expressive tones in his voice, whether of irony or anger, because it was so deep and so flat.

There is an extended scene where Lyra and her human friends help Iorek Byrnison to recapture the kingship among the *panserbjørne* from the usurper Iofur Raknison. And there are many other dæmons seen in passing. But the principal talking animal in *The Golden Compass* is Pantalaimon, as a wolverine, a goldfinch, a sparrow, a monkey, a seagull, and numerous other forms.

At the end of *The Golden Compass*, Lyra and Pan are transported to a parallel world where people's souls are within their bodies, so *The Subtle Knife* is not anthropomorphic at all except for Pan. *The Amber Spyglass* is little better, although readers do find out what form Pan is fixed into when Lyra reaches adulthood. Read *The Golden Compass* and see if you can pass up the other two—bet you can't!

Off Leash • by Daniel Potter. Illustrated by Sabertooth Ermine.

El Cerrito, CA: Fallen Kitten Productions, October 2015, paperback, 295 pp.

Marking Territory • by Daniel Potter. Illustrated by Johanna T.

El Cerrito, CA: Fallen Kitten Productions, November 2017, paperback, 381 pp.

High Steaks • by Daniel Potter.

El Cerrito, CA: Fallen Kitten Productions, January 2018, paperback, 373 pp.

> It had started as a good day. Objectively that was a lie, but after six months of unemployment self-delusion becomes a survival trait. I was two days from getting booted off unemployment, with my girlfriend AWOL for the last week. By "good day" I mean I had wrestled a small drop of hope out of my heart that one of the half dozen jobs I had applied to while guzzling down iced coffees might result in an interview.

Thomas Khatt, an unemployed librarian in Grantsville, Pennsylvania, has been practically living in his local coffee shop for the last six months as he applies for job after job. Over the weeks he has noticed his reclusive neighbor as another regular customer; an old man, presumably retired, reading books with a pet cat. One day Thomas and the old man happen to leave the shop at the same time. The old man is immediately struck by a hit-and-run car. As he dies, Thomas blacks out and awakens in his own home as a cougar.

While he is trying to figure out what has happened to him, his door unlocks itself and an elderly hippie witch, Mistress Sabrina, comes in to welcome him to "the Real World." She demonstrates enough magical power to convince him that objecting would be a bad idea, so he follows her and Rudy, a talking squirrel, to her home where he meets her familiar, a sable named Cornealius. They magically restore his power of speech. While this is going on, Thomas is barraged with a confusing flood of information about how the Real World works:

> "TAU?" I paced below him [Rudy], eyes crossing, trying to look at my muzzle, the spell wire looked to thread in and out of it.
>   Rudy responded with the tone of voice of a phone employee reading the company boilerplate. "Talking Animal Union. We represent all animals with the gift of speech or capable of speech within the domain of the council of Merlins. An animal being defined as a being possessing corporeal form but lacking hands and viewed as nonhuman by those on the other side of the Veil. The TAU endeavors to insure familiars are well treated and allows no bonding to take place without its blessing."

Thomas is overwhelmed by what he learns, but generally doesn't like the sound of it:

> I watched the squirrel warily; every question I asked generated at least a half dozen more. Yet one thing had become crystal clear; I wanted no part of this world. Losing my thumbs, my house and my girlfriend in exchange for the chance to be sold off to some pimple-faced apprentice did not sound like a fair deal to me.

He especially doesn't like it when he starts to wonder how and why it applies to him in particular:

> My thoughts drifted out, back into the world. How had this happened to me? My mind probed into the last day, looking for things I had overlooked. It all went back to the old man, who had to be another magus. O'Meara had said that a magus named Archibald had been murdered. What had the baristas called the old man? Archie? Archie the Archmagus, poor guy. And that horrible car accident—surely nothing about it had been accidental.

Thomas decides to take charge of his own life, even if he is not familiar with the Real World yet. He faces the dangers of our "world beyond the Veil," of being a cougar loose in a residential neighborhood, and of the Real World, refusing to join the TAU or to become bound to a magus—or to an apprentice—as a familiar.

> To stay off the leash, he'll have to take advantage of the chaos caused by the local Archmagus' death and help the Inquisition solve his murder. A pyromaniac squirrel, religious werewolves, and cat-hating cops all add to the pandemonium as Thomas attempts to become the first Freelance Familiar [blurb].

Yes, this is Book 1 of a series, *Freelance Familiars*, and judging by *Off Leash*, it's a winner. All of the characters are intelligent, with many in the Real World hiding secrets. Potter's writing is wry and full of detail: "The cat, who looked like the sort of thing a Chihuahua could beat up for lunch money" … "For a moment I feared I had fallen into a Disney film and the kitchen appliances were about to burst into song. I gave the toaster a withering look just in case." … "No need to sweat, or in my case, pant, however." … "'It's bigger on the inside,' voices from *Doctor Who* exclaimed in my head. They were right." … "The white cat rolled her eyes. 'I'm so glad I was never human. The thumb fetish you all have is so undignified.'" Thomas, in looking out for himself as a cougar in two worlds, becomes enmeshed in the deadly magical politics of the Real World.

Stories of one individual taking on The System are always enjoyable, and are doubly so when it's a partially furry system. *Off Leash* does not feature just animal-headed humans. The animal natures of the talking but otherwise unmodified cougar, the squirrel, the owl, the housecat, the redneck werewolves, and others are important plot elements. In *Marking Territory* (*Freelance Familiars* #2), Thomas gets involved in a power struggle between the magic factions that affects all Grantsville:

> You might mistake him for a giant raven, but the beak had a wicked curve to it, his talons vicious hooks. This was no scavenger. He was a black eagle, feathers darker than the others, given almost no shine by the glare of their lamppost perch. He hopped forward, gliding down toward us. A single crow followed his lead, her body bursting into a blue light and form blurring as she swooped beneath the eagle, landing as an elegant woman in a white dress. She wore a falconry glove, which the eagle alighted upon as the last of the blue light faded from a ring she wore.

Freelance Familiars arguably features magical animals rather than anthropomorphic animals, but who cares as long as they are talking animals?

Off the Beaten Path • by Rukis. Illustrated by the author.

Dallas, TX: FurPlanet Productions, July 2014, paperback, 385 pp.

Lost on Dark Trails • by Rukis. Illustrated by the author.

Dallas, TX: FurPlanet Productions, January 2015, paperback, 312 pp.

The Long Road Home • by Rukis. Illustrated by the author.

Dallas, TX: FurPlanet Productions, July 2015, hardcover, 403 pp.

Off the Beaten Path by Rukis (FurPlanet Productions, July 2014). **The first volume of Rukis' *The Long Road Home* trilogy, set in her *Red Lantern* world. Winner of the 2014 Cóyotl Award and 2014 Ursa Major Award for Best Novel. Rukis does the covers and interior illustrations for her own books.**

> When I turned thirteen years of age, the village elder told me I had become a woman. When I had turned fourteen years of age, my mother told me I had become a burden. When I had turned fifteen years of age, my father told me I had become a wife. He had been paid [by] a man from the Anukshen to take me away from everything I knew and every person I cared for, to become his third wife.

This is one of those trilogies that is almost impossible to review without giving away spoilers. Basically, except for the anthropomorphic-animal and fantasy-world aspects, the setting is North America shortly after the British colonies along the Eastern Coast have won their independence. In *Off the Beaten Path* Shivah, the narrator (bobcat), is a young woman of a native tribe in a valley beyond the "Otherwolf" lands. She has only known two tribes, her own Katoshen and the neighboring Anukshen. They barely tolerate each other, grudgingly trading together. Both are extremely patriarchal, treating women as little more than slaves and baby-making machines. Shivah is married against her will to Methoa'nuk, an arrogant and brutal Anukshen Honored Warrior for two horses and a brick of salt. Despite her attempts to be a "good wife," she disgraces him (or maybe he just blames his disgrace on her). Methoa kills their year-old son, and encourages the Anukshen to stone her to death. She recovers consciousness weeks later, having been nursed back to health by two wandering trappers from far-off differing tribes, Ransom, a tall coyote, and Puck (Puquanath Roatok), a blind white fox medicine man who "sees" with his ears:

> His ears twitched more than most people's I'd seen, picking up sounds around us I certainly wasn't hearing. His nose flared as he looked my way, taking in my scent ... which I was beginning to realize was as bad, if not worse, than the coyote's.

Shivah learns from them that, after her "death," Methoa had led the Anukshen to war with the Katoshen, and the two tribes had wiped each other out; so she could not go back to either even if she had wanted to. Ransom and Puck had not planned for her to stay with them beyond their nursing her back to health, but she obviously has no place to go and cannot survive on her own, so they allow her to join them as they journey toward the fabled (to her) Otherwolf lands.

This takes the story to about page 50. What Shivah learns and does in the Otherwolf lands (they call it Amuresca), besides look for revenge against Methoa'nuk, is the rest of the novel—and more.

Ransom and Puck remain important characters throughout the first book. They are an Odd Couple. Ransom is a "civilized native" despite his contempt and distrust of the Otherwolves. He dresses like one of their backwoodsmen, carries a rifle, and smokes hand-rolled cigarettes. Puck is more of a traditional tribal healer and shaman. Shivah learns about the Otherwolves from them:

> "'Are there different tribes?'"
> "Different Nations." Ransom snorted, spitting. "Y'don't often meet the desert-dwellers though; they actually keep to their own land most o'the time. Most of the settlers are from Amuresca. Dogs. Rats. Cats here an'there."
> "I thought they were all wolves." I blinked, surprised.
> "Even the dogs ain't 'wolves.'" Ransom laughed. "Wait 'til you see 'em someday. Some of 'em's not recognizable as much o' anything. Got their faces all mushed in. There's a few wolves, I guess ... but most of 'em don't look like real wolves. Not tribal wolves."
> "The Wolves of the Northlands think they are cursed," Puquanath said, stopping on a rocky outcropping and sniffing the wind, his tail prickling on end for a moment. "That the Spirits changed their bodies so as to show us they were apart from us ... that they could not be trusted. They vehemently opposed the Alliance with the Otherwolves, even went to war with several of the tribes that agreed to it. It was bloody..."
> "Bloody stupid." Ransom snorted. "I don't trust an Otherwolf—any Otherwolf—but killin' ourselves off faster is just makin' it easier for them to move on in. If the tribes had allied at the start, they'd never've gotten a foothold. Then we could've taken their shit, and kept our land. But the leadership just wasn't there, an' there were too many old grudges."

Rukis makes it obvious that her furries are thinly-disguised humans. Shivah, a bobcat, suspects at first that Ransom, a coyote, intends to rape her. But Rukis does a good job of making this a superficially furry world. There are otter, mountain lion, rat, and husky characters, plus a Crow who may be an imaginary animal spirit, and even a rumored saber-toothed tiger. Rukis has drawn her own wraparound covers and interior illustrations.

The NC-17 rating is deserved. There are scenes of brutal violence, gore, and graphic romance, both heterosexual and homosexual. But the violence is justified, and the eroticism is brief and pertinent to the story. The worst criticism that I can make is that the anthropomorphization is too superficial, resulting in such scenes as a sentient furry trapper loading non-sentient pelts onto a non-sentient mule. *Off the Beaten Path* and its sequels are fine adult novels with three well-developed protagonists, including a strong woman. Recommended, especially to those who like fiction about the 18th-century North American continent beyond the Eastern seaboard. *Off the Beaten Path* won both the 2014 Cóyotl and Ursa Major Awards for Best Novel, while *The Long Road Home* was a 2015 Cóyotl Award finalist.

Otters in Space: The Search for Cat Havana • by Mary E. Lowd.

Seattle, WA: CreateSpace, August 2010, paperback, 185 pp.

Otters in Space II: Jupiter, Deadly • by Mary E. Lowd.

Dallas, TX: FurPlanet Productions, July 2013, paperback, 227 pp.

In a Dog's World • by Mary E. Lowd.

Dallas, TX: FurPlanet Productions, July 2015, paperback, 181 pp.

Otters in Space III: Octopus Ascending • by Mary E. Lowd.

Dallas, TX: FurPlanet Productions, July 2017, paperback, 227 pp.

Despite the title, the protagonist of *Otters in Space*, Kipper Brighton, is a tabby cat:

> The bus stop sign and shelter were in front of a giant, white church. The Church of the First Race was an historical building, preserved from the time when humans still walked the Earth. It dwarfed the taller but smaller-scale high-rises around it. It was the oldest building in New LA. Kipper had been inside once and sat on the monstrous pews, but, like most cats, she didn't feel comfortable with First Race doctrine. It was a dog religion—they preached that humans, the First Race, had left Earth as emissaries to the stars and would return to bring all the peoples of Earth into a confederation of interstellar sentience. Someday.

Otters in Space: The Search for Cat Havana by Mary E. Lowd (CreateSpace, August 2010). The first volume of a popular trilogy, which was nominated for the 2010 Ursa Major Award for Best Novel. Cover art by Mary E. Lowd.

Kipper's sister, the always-hyper Petra, is running for district representative on an it's-time-we-put-more-cats-into-the-government platform. Cats outnumber dogs by four to one in the population, but only one of the forty-six representatives is a cat. And that's one cat too many, as far as the dogs are concerned, especially those who are antagonistic toward Petra's in-your-face style of campaigning.

Kipper, as a temp, gets a lot of short-lived jobs, but many lately have been with Luna Tech, the cat/dog company that deals with the otters' Moon-based colony:

> "What happened to the cat I'm replacing?" Kipper asked.
> "Violet?" Cheryl [a white miniature poodle] shrugged. "No one knows. She didn't show up for work on Monday, and we haven't heard from her since. Is there anything else you need?"
> "No..." Kippur answered, setting down a pawful of Petra's fliers on the desk. It was strange, but this was the fifth cat she'd temped for at Luna Tech in the last year. If they had quit or called in sick, that would be one thing, but each of these five cats had simply stopped showing up. She wondered what kept happening to them. Why wasn't anyone worried about all these disappearing cats?

Kipper finds cryptic scraps in Violet's desk that could hint that she and the other missing cats have snuck away to a secret cat haven. It seems far-fetched, but Petra enthusiastically accepts it. So when a black dog comes to kill Kipper (apparently hired by her own cat boss for Finding Out Too Much), and Petra disappears leaving a GONE TO ECUADOR! BACK SOON note, it seems perfectly logical. Kipper persuades the ditzy but basically friendly would-be assassin, Trudith—"Black lab mutts weren't always the brightest."—to drive her through Mexico and Central America to Ecuador to follow after Petra:

> The ten lanes of concrete were dead in the dark of night, and Trudith's headlights were the only light around. It was rumored that the freeways in the area had remained unchanged since the time of humans, except for normal maintenance and repainting the white, yellow, and dotted lines. It was also rumored that the freeway was only six lanes wide, total, back then.
> Corroded, rust orange skeletons of human cars had been found in junkyards and among the ruined human cities. The dinosaur cars were monsters compared to today's vehicles. Just like human buildings. Just like humans themselves. Kipper couldn't understand why dogs worshipped them, waiting for them to return. If humans had been so great, they wouldn't have left cats—that is, THE WORLD—in the condition it was in. They wouldn't have taken off into space and just ABANDONED everyone. Kipper could feel the darkness making her thoughts morbid.

Ecuador may or may not be the home of a secret "Cat Havana," but it is certainly the well-known terminal of the Space Elevator leading to the otter-run Moonville Funpark and the otter-designed Deep Sky Anchor space station. Kipper can believe more easily in a hidden cat paradise in space than in Ecuador, so she doesn't waste any time searching in Guayaquil; she heads right for the space elevator.

The last 100+ pages tell what Kipper finds in "otter space." It is a fast-paced blend of hard-astronautical tech run by anthropomorphic animals, and a more complex political situation than she had expected between the cats, dogs, and otters. It's much more dazzling than she had guessed. All three species have both friendly and unfriendly members. There are other species, too. The space station has an immigrant-squirrel-run restaurant. One of the otters' space tugs has a giant octopus cook! The otter-run space station and spaceships are so convincingly and appealingly described, even for humans, that you will want to go there!

The basic plot—find the missing sister and the secret cat sanctuary—is simplistic, but the details of Kipper's world are intriguing. The intelligent animals are not imitation humans of conveniently equal size, as in most furry fiction: "While the Chow groped for another bottle, Kipper made her escape. She pivoted around, dropped to all fours, and hastily loped away." "After a quick roadside lesson in handling Trudith's vehicle, Kipper adjusted the seat to accommodate her smaller stature. She had to slide the chair almost all the way forward for her feet to reach the pedals. Nonetheless, it was a nice car. A VERY nice car." "The furry peoples of the world could never be as deeply attached to clothing as all the history books suggested that humans had once been. It's just not practical to get too attached to a coat of cotton when you're already wearing a coat of the finest fur." *Otters in Space* gets off to a fairly pedestrian start, but it quickly picks up speed.

The first edition of *Otters in Space* was published by CreateSpace in August 2010. It sold so well, and was a finalist for the Ursa Major Award for Best Anthropomorphic Novel of 2010, that FurPlanet picked it up in January 2012 for the current paperback edition. *Otters in Space II: Jupiter, Deadly* was a finalist for both the 2013 Cóyotl Award and the 2013 Ursa Major Award, and *Otters in Space III: Octopus Ascending* was a 2017 Ursa Major and Leo Literary Award finalist. Lowd's *In a Dog's World*, in the same setting, was a 2015 Ursa Major finalist.

Out of Position • by Kyell Gold. Illustrated by Blotch.

St. Paul, MN: Sofawolf Press, January 2009, paperback, 324 pp.

Isolation Play • by Kyell Gold. Illustrated by Blotch.

St. Paul, MN: Sofawolf Press, January 2011, paperback, 420 pp.

Divisions • by Kyell Gold. Illustrated by Blotch.

St. Paul, MN: Sofawolf Press, January 2013, hardcover, 385 pp., paperback, 383 pp.

Uncovered • by Kyell Gold. Illustrated by Blotch.

St. Paul, MN: Sofawolf Press, July 2014, hardcover, 451 pp., paperback, 427 pp.

Over Time • by Kyell Gold. Illustrated by Rukis and Kenket.

St. Paul, MN: Sofawolf Press, January 2016, hardcover, 432 pp., paperback, 381 pp.

Out of Position by Kyell Gold (Sofawolf Press, January 2009). The first of five volumes of Gold's *Out of Position* series, also known as the "Dev and Lee" series for the two main characters. Winner of the 2009 Ursa Major Award for Best Novel. Cover art by Blotch (Tess Garman and Teagan Gavet).

Tales of the Firebirds • by Kyell Gold. Illustrated by Tess Garman.

Mountain View, CA: 24 Carat Words, June 2018, paperback, 167 pp.

The *Dev and Lee* series, featuring the tiger Devlin Miski and the fox Wiley Farrel, late-adolescent homosexual lovers, and the theme of college and professional football, in Gold's *Forester University* universe (*Waterways, Winter Games,* the *Dangerous Spirits* trilogy, etc.), has proven immensely popular with furry readers. Gold has ended it after five novels, but followed it immediately with his current *Love Match* trilogy, featuring the young African sports star Rochi "Rocky" N'guwe and his developing homosexuality, and the theme of college and professional tennis, in the Forester U. universe.

Dev and Lee are introduced in *Out of Position* as seniors at Forester University. Dev is a star on the college football team, and Lee is a student and gay rights activist. A gay prank that Lee pulls on Dev results in Dev's realizing his homosexual nature, and to him and Lee becoming male lovers.

The series is told in mostly alternating chapters narrated by Dev and Lee. Dev's chapters contain long, detailed scenes of his football games. Gold does an excellent job of making them exciting even to readers who know and care nothing about the sport.

Dev and Lee are secret lovers in *Out of Position* until the climax, when Dev comes "out of the closet" at a football press conference. The other four novels each cover a year, beginning in 2006. *Isolation Play* starts immediately after *Out of Position* and deals with the aftermath of Dev's and Lee's revelation: Dev's hostile teammates, the shocked parents of both, a reporter determined to use them in a sensationalistic story, and facing life after graduation. In *Divisions*, Dev and Lee pursue equally their professional careers, their personal lives, and the results of their open homosexuality. Dev becomes a professional football player for the Chevali Firebirds, and Lee becomes a professional football talent scout to share his interests. Dev's parents and siblings support his choice, while Lee's open homosexuality leads to his parents' divorce and his mother's becoming involved in Families United, a militantly anti-gay religious group.

In *Uncovered*, Dev and Lee's different interests are pulling them apart. Dev is almost monomaniacal about improving his playing and helping the Firebirds win their first championship, while Lee resumes his true interest as a gay right activist, especially after his mother's Families United group pressures another young gay football player into committing suicide. In *Over Time*, Dev and Lee decide whether their interest in each other is serious and long-term enough that they should buy a house together.

There is no fantasy in the *Dev and Lee* series except for the characters being anthropomorphized animals in an alternate world. They are excellent realistic novels about two young homosexual lovers beginning life after college. Here, a group of Dev's teammates ask him to have Lee show them what the gay community is like:

> (Dev) We grab a big table at the Unicorn and their cocktails do look pretty fabulous, in a couple senses of the word. I get something called a Cinnamon Swish, and Lee orders a Tangerine Sparkle. The other guys order cocktails, except for Kodi, who orders a beer, and then they sit around and watch the rest of the patrons, who are also watching us.
>
> "Six big guys sitting in a gay bar," Lee says. "Of course you attract attention."
>
> But nobody really comes up to us. When our drinks come, served by a slender, attractive cheetah in shorts and an open short-sleeved collared shirt, Ty takes a sip of his and then says, "It looks so normal in here."
>
> "Except that it's all guys," Vonni says.
>
> "Yeah, but they're not doing anything."

Lee licks the rim of his glass. "If you want to see that, there are a couple other places…"

"No, no." Vonni laughs.

"Well, gay guys are just people, you know? We like to drink in a safe place and hang out together. We don't whip out our cocks at the least provocation."

"See, Pike?" Ty elbows him. "You ain't gay."

"Har har." Pike drinks from something cloudy and creamy. "Jury's still out on you, right?"

Ty grins. "I got no worries."

Here is a scene of one of Dev's games:

(Dev) But Hellentown is playing pretty inspired defense, too. They double-cover Strike on pretty much every play. Jaws runs well, but when we get down to their twenty, Aston underthrows Strike in the end zone. The cheetah lunges forward, not in time to stop one of their cornerbacks from grabbing the ball out of the air. Strike tackles him immediately, but it deflates us. We were so close and now we have nothing to show for it.

I go back out onto the field with more determination, and as Pike breaks up one of their run formations, Gerrard and I bring down their running back, a big elk, for a two-yard loss. On the next play, Carson tackles the tight end at the line. We rush the lion on third down, and he has to throw the ball away. So they don't get any points off the turnover, and we feel good.

Out of Position and *Isolation Play* won the 2009 and 2011 Ursa Major Awards for Best Novel, and *Divisions* was a finalist for the 2013 Cóyotl Award in that category. *Tales of the Firebirds* is a postscript, a collection of a dozen short stories about Dev, Lee, and many of the supporting characters in the series to flesh out their personalities. Read these wherever there is any interest in serious gay fiction, fantasy or not.

The Pride of Chanur • by C.J. Cherryh.

New York: DAW Books, January 1982, paperback, 224 pp.

Chanur's Venture • by C.J. Cherryh. Map by David A. Cherry.

West Bloomfield, MI: Phantasia Press, October 1984, hardcover, 201 pp.

The Kif Strike Back • by C.J. Cherryh. Map by David A. Cherry.

West Bloomfield, MI: Phantasia Press, May 1985, hardcover, 294 pp.

Chanur's Homecoming • by C.J. Cherryh. Map by David A. Cherry.

West Bloomfield, MI: Phantasia Press, August 1986, hardcover, 312 pp.

Chanur's Legacy: A Novel of Compact Space • by C.J. Cherryh. Map by David A. Cherry.

New York: DAW Books, August 1992, hardcover, 396 pp.

The five *Chanur Saga* novels started coming out just as furry fandom was coalescing in 1982. It was a major "have you read?" topic of discussion of early furry fans. First there was a single sf novel in 1982, then a sequel trilogy in 1984-'86, then after nobody expected it, a final ending six years later. The five novels were a perfect example of the charismatic animal-like alien sf story that was one of the three founding influences of furry fandom. They were read at the time, and they have continued to be read ever since.

The Pride of Chanur appeared as a DAW Books original space-opera paperback novel in January 1982; part of C.J. Cherryh's ongoing interstellar series, and a follow-up to her mega-popular *Downbelow Station* that had won the Hugo Award the previous year. *Downbelow Station* had been set in the human-explored area of galactic civilization. *The Pride of Chanur* went beyond that.

> There had been something loose about the station dock all morning, skulking in amongst the gantries and the lines and the canisters which were waiting to be moved, lurking wherever shadows fell among the rampway access of the many ships at dock at Meetpoint. It was pale, naked, starved-looking in what fleeting glimpse anyone on *The Pride of Chanur* had had of it. Evidently no one had reported it to station authorities, nor did *The Pride*. Involving oneself in others' concerns at Meetpoint Station, where several species came to trade and provision, was ill-advised—at least until one was personally bothered. Whatever it was, it was bipedal, brachiate, and quick at making itself unseen. It had surely gotten away from someone, and likeliest were the kif, who had a thieving finger in everything, and who were not above kidnapping. Or it might be some large, bizarre animal; the mahendo'sat were inclined to the keeping and trade of strange pets, and Station had been displeased with them in that respect on more than one occasion. So far it had done nothing. Stolen nothing. No one wanted to get involved in question and answer between original owners and station authorities; and so far no official statement had come down from those station authorities and no notice of its loss had been posted by any ship, which itself argued that a wise person should not ask questions. The crew reported it only to the captain and chased it, twice, from *The Pride*'s loading area. Then the crew got to work on necessary duties, having settled the annoyance to their satisfaction.
>
> It was the last matter on the mind of the noble, the distinguished captain Pyanfar Chanur, who was setting out down her own rampway for the docks. She was hani, this captain, splendidly maned and bearded in red-gold, which reached in silken curls to the middle of her bare, sleek-pelted chest, and she was dressed as befitted a hani of captain's rank, blousing scarlet breeches tucked up at her waist with a broad gold belt, with silk cords.

The main characters of *The Pride of Chanur* are Captain Pyanfar Chanur and the crew of *The Pride* (especially her young niece Hilfy), all lion-like hani of the planet Anuurn. The first novel, and the series, is set in Compact Space, an interstellar civilization beyond human space. The seven species that mix through Meetpoint Station are the mahendo'sat, kif, hani, tc'a, stsho, knnn, and chi; but the *Chanur Saga* focuses on the hani. *The Pride of Chanur* comes to Meetpoint Station, opens up, and an unknown lifeform escaping from the kif races aboard. The hani and the kif are not friends, and Pyanfar refuses to give the Outsider up, which leads to warfare. Nobody likes the kif, but the others don't appreciate the hani of *The Pride* for giving them a reason for starting a shooting war, either. Nobody else realizes that the reason is an alien who represents a new stargoing species that, so far, only the kif know about. The alien, who learns quickly to communicate, says his name is Tully. He won't reveal his species' location, but he wants to join the crew of *The Pride* to stay free from the kif. The events give a picture of the social structure of the female-dominant hani.

The Pride of Chanur ends with the kif defeated, Tully restored to the humans, and *The Pride* resuming its career as a merchant ship. *Chanur's Venture* begins with Tully returning to Meetpoint Station as a human representative. The humans will join Compact Space, but only if Pyanfar and *The Pride* will speak for them.

> She was hani, Pyanfar Chanur, maned and bearded in curling red-gold, sleek of pelt. Her left ear bore the gold rings of successful voyages along its rim, and the bottommost ring had a monstrous gaudy

teardrop pearl. Her red blousing breeches were silk, with the faintest striping of orange; and wrapped about the waist was a belt whose dangling ties were finished in precious stones and gold and bronze.

Chanur's Venture, *The Kif Strike Back*, and *Chanur's Homecoming* put Pyanfar and *The Pride* into new adventures. *Chanur's Legacy* is set ten years later with Hilfy Chanur, now the captain of *Chanur's Legacy*, a new ship, as the protagonist. Pyanfar has become the President of Compact Space, so Hilfy, in addition to the responsibilities of captaincy, is smothered by requests for favors from her important aunt. Hilfy's attempt to prove that she can accomplish something on her own leads to this adventure.

Whether they are called the *Compact Space* series or the *Chanur Saga*, *The Pride of Chanur* and its sequels continue to be read as furry fiction as well as science-fiction. *The Pride of Chanur* was a finalist for the Hugo Award for Best Novel.

Redwall • by Brian Jacques. Illustrated by Gary Chalk.

London: Hutchinson Children's Books, October 1986, hardcover, 352 pp.

Mossflower • by Brian Jacques. Illustrated by Gary Chalk.

London: Hutchinson Children's Books, July 1988, hardcover, 431 pp.

Mattimeo • by Brian Jacques. Illustrated by Gary Chalk.

London: Hutchinson Children's Books, October 1989, hardcover, 446 pp.

Mariel of Redwall • by Brian Jacques. Illustrated by Gary Chalk.

London: Hutchinson Children's Books, October 1991, hardcover, 387 pp.

Salamandastron • by Brian Jacques. Illustrated by Gary Chalk.

London: Hutchinson Children's Books, August 1992, hardcover, 391 pp.

Martin the Warrior • by Brian Jacques. Illustrated by Gary Chalk.

London: Hutchinson Children's Books, October 1993, hardcover, 375 pp.

The Bellmaker • by Brian Jacques. Illustrated by Allan Curless.

London: Hutchinson Children's Books, June 1994, hardcover, 336 pp.

Outcast of Redwall • by Brian Jacques. Illustrated by Allan Curless.

London: Hutchinson Children's Books, July 1995, hardcover, 360 pp.

This is the only series title to which all the sequels are not listed, because there are twenty-two *Redwall* novels. Brian Jacques wrote approximately one a year from 1986 to his death in 2011. But they are almost all the same.

The basic plot is a classic of anthropomorphic literature. Redwall is an ancient, high-walled abbey in Mossflower Wood, inhabited by British small woodland herbivores and omnivores. Mice, hedgehogs, squirrels, and otters. The abbey is always besieged by evil predators; foxes, rats, weasels, wildcats, stoats, and the like, with a horde of followers; would-be conquering armies, or pirates. Their leaders have names like Cluny the Scourge, Slagar the Cruel, and Badrang the Tyrant. Nearby in the forest are the badger fortress of Salamandastron, with its hare troops of the Long Patrol, and the wandering shrew tribe of Guosim (Guerrilla Union of Shrews in Mossflower) led by their Log-a-Log, who can be counted upon to come to the rescue.

The *Redwall* books are also known for: the comic exaggerated accents and speech patterns of some of the species, notably the mole yeomen's broad Yorkshire drawl ("Cumm yurr quickly, gennelmice, asten ee."), and the hares' aristocratic British ("I say, Buck, here comes the jolly old shrew fleet, wot.") The riddles that have to be solved to save the Abbey. The sumptuous feasts of the Redwallers. And in the later books, the cute Dibbums, the infants and very young children of the Redwallers. The series becomes slightly more dramatic in the later books, often with the tragic death of one of the sympathetic supporting cast.

The first three novels (*Redwall*, *Mossflower*, and *Mattimeo*) are a mini-trilogy. The hero of *Redwall* is the young mouse Matthias, who saves Redwall Abbey from the sadistic Cluny the Scourge (rat) and his army of five hundred rats by finding the lost sword of Martin the Warrior (mouse). *Mossflower* jumps back in time to tell how Martin saves the animals of Mossflower Wood, including Loamhedge Abbey, from evil wildcat Queen Tsarmina, and brings help from the badgers and hares of Salamandastron. *Mattimeo* takes place when Matthias is a skilled adult warrior, and sinister Slagar the Cruel (fox) plots to defeat the Abbey inhabitants by capturing their children for blackmail, including Matthias' rash young son Mattimeo.

After that, the *Redwall* novels skip about in time and location, focusing on Redwall Abbey, Salamandastron, the Long Patrol, the Guosim, or an individual from them. But almost all involve a threat to Redwall Abbey by a horde of cruel predators; their defeat by, in part, the solving of an ancient riddle; and a great celebratory feast somewhere during the events. Reading any one of the twenty-two novels is great. Reading four or five of them shows how repetitious they become.

Redwall begins with the abbey at peace. All dangers are thought to be in the past:

> Once more the Abbot's heart softened towards the little mouse. "Poor Matthias, alas for your ambitions. The day of the warrior is gone, my son. We live in peaceful times, thank heaven, and you need only think of obeying me, your Abbot, and doing as you are bidden. In time to come, when I am long gone to my rest, you will think back to this day and bless my memory, for then you will be a true member of Redwall."

The army of Cluny the Scourge approaches:

> At lightning speed the big rat's claws shot out, and grabbed them both cruelly by the ears. The stupid henchrats yowled piteously as they were lifted bodily from the floor and swung to and fro. In a fit of rage, Cluny bashed their heads together. Half senseless, they were hurled towards the doorway, with his angry words ringing in their skulls. "Beetles, worms, rotten sparrows! Get me meat. Tender, young, red meat! Next time you bring m rubbish like this, I'll spit the pair of you and have you roasted in your own juice. Is that clear?"

The Redwallers do not believe the warning at first:

> The silence was broken by scornful snorts and derisive laughter. Furry elbows nudged downy ribs. Mice were beginning to smile from sheer relief. Cluny the Scourge, indeed!
>
> Feeling slightly abashed, Matthias and Constance [badger] looked pleadingly towards the Abbot for support. Abbot Mortimer's old face was stern as he shook the bell vigorously for silence.
>
> "Mice of Redwall, I see there are those among you who doubt the word of your Abbot."
>
> The quiet but authoritative words caused an embarrassed shuffling from the Council of Elders. Brother Joseph stood up and cleared his throat. "Ahem, er, good Father Abbot, we all respect your word and look to you for guidance, but really…. I mean …"
>
> Sister Clemence stood up smiling. She spread her paws wide. "Perhaps Cluny is coming to get us for staying up late."
>
> A roar of laughter greeted the ironic words.
>
> [...]
>
> "Oh my whiskers, what a mess."
>
> "Hadn't we better pack up and move?"
>
> "Maybe Cluny will spare us."
>
> "Oh dear, oh dear, what shall we do?"
>
> Matthias sprang to the middle of the floor brandishing his staff in a way that surprised even him. "Do?" he cried. "I'll tell you what we'll do. We'll be ready."
>
> The Abbot could not help shaking his head in admiration. It seemed that young Matthias had hidden depths.
>
> "Why, thank you, Matthias," he said. "I could not have put it better myself. That's exactly what we will do. We'll be ready."

Read the first three *Redwall* novels, then as many more as you can stand.

Sandeagozu • by Janann V. Jenner. Illustrated by Robert Crawford.

New York: Harper & Row, October 1986, hardcover, 442 pp.

This unique and imaginative animal fantasy, set during 1932, features five cagemates from a large New York City pet shop specializing in exotic animals, who plan to escape and set out across Depression-era America for that legendary animals' paradise, Sandeagozu— the San Diego Zoo. Led by Sherahi ("tiger killer"), the giant pythoness, the band of odd fellows consists of her, Manu the langur, Dervish the coatimundi, Duchess the scarlet macaw, and Junior the venomous cascabel (a South American rattlesnake).

Virtually all the reviews summarize the plot as that: five exotic animals escape from a New York City pet shop to journey across America to the San Diego Zoo. Yet *Sandeagozu* is not exactly that, and very much more than that. That event, the meeting of the animals in the pet shop and their decision to escape together, does not begin until a quarter of the way through the novel. Jenner first builds a leisurely but fascinating backstory, rich in detail and characterization. The reader barely notices, and does not care, that the main story has yet to begin.

Sandeagozu is primarily Sherahi's novel. It begins in 1915, with her mother's search for a safe birthing place in the Burmese jungles. The mixture of animal fact and fantasy begins here:

> The mother remembered those nervous days and was glad that they were over. "Now," she thought, "for the Blessing." Python custom dictated that each brooding female could bestow a single blessing in her lifetime. This blessing would enable the chosen hatchling to develop the unique mental powers possessed by many members of the Elder Race, but most often reserved for those that the pythons called the Leather Skins: crocodiles and their kin. Bestowing her blessing was a heavy responsibility

and the pythoness had already scryed the embryonic minds of most of her children. "There must be one unusual one in this clutch," she thought. "I can't waste the gift on an ordinary child. I must find the right one. They'll begin to hatch very soon and then it'll be too late."

The opening pages describe Sherahi's early life in the wild. Again a mixture of nature lore and fantasy, they establish all animals' telepathy:

> She saw the old serpent [U Vayu] crawl beneath the altar of the glinting statue of the Buddha and form a compact coil. He settled his wide head on the topmost curve of his neck and then suddenly glared at her. "Go away, Sherahi," he ordered in a voice that she had to obey and she felt him abruptly shut his mind to her intrusive probe. It was like the slamming of a heavy, metal-studded door. She heard his sibilant hiss and he repeated, "Go away, Sherahi. The rituals are serious. Not play for babies."

And also the "snake tongue" which describes their reptilian biological traits: "Sherahi's thoughts were interrupted by the faint quopping of her labial pits and she fnasted the trail of a mother rat." More importantly, the telepathy enables all animals to communicate with each other. Sherahi converses with other snakes, bats, and the Great Serpent Nats who are the ophidian gods such as Quetzalcoatl, the Feathered Serpent, the Great Worm Ouroboros, Jormungand the Midgard Serpent, and Lachesis who was a great serpent but is now a caterpillar. These are throwaway scenes, but they establish how later the animals in the pet shop are able to plan their mutual escape and trek across America.

In 1921 Sherahi is captured and brought to America, where she spends years as a living prop in Naruda, Exotique Dancer and Snake Charmeuse's burlesque routine. Jenner also tells Naruda's, née Ruthie Notar's, life story in colorful detail. The street-smart Ruthie and Sherahi love each other, but by 1932 Sherahi has grown so large that Ruthie has increasing trouble caring for her in the urban U.S. Add that Ruthie has just been offered a movie contract, and Ruthie's boyfriend Bernie is finally able to convince her to trade Sherahi in for $75 and several smaller boa constrictors. The story switches to that of Ira Leftrack, proprietor of Leftrack's Pet Emporium and Animals International Ltd. of New York City. We learn all about Ira, his meek wife Irma, his spoiled, fat son Ehrich, his underappreciated assistant Birger Sorensen; and Jenner makes it so interesting that we would hardly care if she spent the whole book just talking about them.

Leftrack has built up an active business in both regular pets and importing exotic animals for sale to zoos. Yet every so often he gets stuck with "Culls"; animals that are unsaleable for one reason or another. At this time they include Manu the langur monkey, badly scarred in a savage beating by a bigger monkey; Duchess the neurotic macaw who has plucked out all her feathers; Dervish the young coatimundi who is always getting loose and causing trouble; Junior the dangerous rattlesnake—and, after a three-month hunger strike from the disappointment of being abandoned by Ruthie, plus untreated mouth rot, the emaciated and listless Sherahi.

But Sherahi, who has had enough of being "betrayed" and mistreated by humans, plans a breakout of the Culls:

> Manu turned to the Duchess and Dervish and said, "Sherahi wants to take us to Sandeagozu. It's a wonderful place. I've heard Sorensen and Leftrack talk about it many times. Only the luckiest, most beautiful animals get to go there. It's always warm in Sandeagozu and there's lots of food and sunshine, and…" he added, looking at Dervish, "lots of playmates and mates."

Sherahi and Manu have to struggle to convince the other three to trust them (the Duchess is sure it's all a plot for one of the snakes to eat her); then, once they are out, to stay together for their mutual benefit. They face many dangers, not only from humans but from other animals, starting with those hidden beneath them; the rat nations of the subway tunnels, and the crocodiles of the sewers who prove much less trustworthy than expected.

The novel is not halfway through, and the surprises are just starting. Can they successfully cross the United States together? Why, for the longest time, it seems like they will never get out of New York City! What ultimately happens to the five is neither what they nor the reader expect, but the ending is fitting and should not disappoint. *Sandeagozu* stands apart from anything else that you have ever read.

The Seventh Chakra • by Kevin Frane.

St. Paul, MN: Sofawolf Press, January 2010, paperback, 328 pp.

The Seventh Chakra has one of the more intriguing plots in anthropomorphic literature. The setting is a multispecies world whose civilization goes back about four thousand years. Sophisticated ruins show that a powerful "pre-civilization" existed before that. One of the more pervasive organizations of this world is the Iolite League, an omnipresent religion:

> The Iolite League was an international entity, with membership in the millions. For most of those people, the League represented a spiritual and philosophical ideal: that all people were God's creatures, and that God had made people as different as they were as a means to ensure that they had to embrace what things made them so similar. Life was a sort of test, and it was only in being able to see past the superficial that true peace and harmony could be achieved for the world. The Iolite League strove to help guide people toward that lofty goal, on the individual level and on the group level. It was an uphill battle, but matters of spirituality were not meant to be simple.

One of the missions of the Iolite League is to gather as many of the "pre-civ" artifacts that it can, and study them at its headquarters, the Château Sainte-Mireille on a large island in the Deepwater Archipelago. The Château is a cross between a religious center and a vast museum. *Some*thing annihilated that unknown pre-civilization, and the Iolite League determines to make sure that its accidental rediscovery does not destroy the current world.

> The goal of the project [Project Scheherazade] was for the Iolite League to gather up as much information on the pre-civ world as possible—to recapture the world's lost stories and make sure that they would never again be lost to time. Here and there, ancient tomes, assorted artefacts, and even fragments of computer data from that period would crop up, and the Iolite League made an open show of wanting to catalog all such material for its archives.
>
> Given the extreme value that such mysterious antiquities held on the black market for wealthy collectors and eccentric aficionados of history, however, it was sometimes necessary for the Iolite League to send in members of Sahasrara to make sure that such lost effects made their way safely back to the library of Château Sainte-Mireille, where they might be used for the benefit of all instead of fueling the greed or the whims of an individual. Besides, some of this lost, ancient information might well be dangerous, and was best kept out of public domain for now, until any risks were properly assessed.

Sahasrara, the "sword" of the Iolite League, is one of the League's seven secret operations groups. One of the benefits to its agents is the anti-aging gene therapy augmentation that enables them to serve for decades in the prime of youth.

Arkady Ryswife (ferret) is the leader of a four-man Sahasrara team that is sent to infiltrate Shambhala, a prestigious gambling club in Seizo, the capital of Tomosabaki. His teammates are Kentian McEvoy (wolf), Il-Hyeong Quinn (fox), and Ming-Jun Devra (rabbit). Shambhala had come into possession of unusually impressive pre-civ relicts and had agreed to sell them to the League, but had reneged to sell them for a larger sum to the Octavians, a shadowy organization that specialized in obtaining pre-civ artifacts for sale to the highest bidder. Arkady's team, in disguise, is assigned to get the artifacts before they can be delivered to the Octavians:

> This mouse certainly seemed the meek sort, if no less professional for it. "Sir," he said to Arkady. "Mr. Cibola [raccoon] would like to invite you to join him at his private table upstairs."
>
> Arkady picked up the flute of wine and took a sip. This was the good stuff; his host-to-be was making quite the gesture. "I would be delighted," he replied. When he turned back to face his fellow gamblers at his current table, more than a few [of] them were looking back at him with wide eyes, clearly recognizing the name that the mouse had just dropped. "Pardon me, friends," the ferret said to them as he reached out to take in his remaining chips.

Arkady's team is successful, but with much more violence than was hoped for, and the death of Kentian. These things happen in missions of this sort, but Arkady blames himself for not having managed things better. Worse, he wonders if his other two teammates have lost their faith in him. This is compounded when their next mission is a mysterious rush covert ops assignment without replacing Kentian or even allowing time to attend his funeral:

> "Tomorrow? You've got to be kidding me!"
>
> Dr. Mayflower shook her head. The kangaroo maintained her composure, but she was clearly unnerved by the news that she was delivering. "I've got my team preparing for it now," she said. "Believe me, this is last-minute news to us, as well."
>
> [...]
>
> Arkady clutched at the back of his neck, wringing at his fur and scruff as he stared down at the blank table and tried to make sense of this asinine decision. "We're about to leave on a mission," he said. "A mission that we were just given, one which is apparently of the utmost importance, since they're wanting to brief us in the middle of the night. Why is the augmentation—which isn't even supposed to be happening now—suddenly taking precedence?"

Their mission is to the unfriendly Democratic Republic of Ridgecrescent, and it involves the all-important, ultra-elusive Pyxis Sequence. Not only does the mission go wrong in more ways than Arkady can imagine possible, he is horrified when the other members of his team appear to not listen to him at all:

> "Come on," Arkady said. "We can't just kill him."
>
> Il-Hyeong, still facing Arkady, nonchalantly lifted his gun again and fired sideways, twice, both bullets striking the cougar in the chest. The feline slumped and then toppled over onto his side, blood forming a dark pool in front of him, his paws still bound behind his back.

The Seventh Chakra is a complex secret-agent thriller. It was a finalist for the 2010 Ursa Major Award for Best Novel. Frane has written other works in the setting, including the novel *Thousand Leaves* (2008) and the short stories "Shadows of Novoprypiatsk" and "False Doctrine."

The Silver Tide • by Michael Tod. Map by Barbara Anne Knight.

London: Orion Books, January 1993, hardcover, 226 pp.

The Second Wave • by Michael Tod. Map by Barbara Anne Knight.

London: Orion Books, November 1994, hardcover, 255 pp.

The Golden Flight • by Michael Tod. Map by Barbara Anne Knight.
London: Orion Books, October 1995, hardcover, 239 pp.

The Dorset Squirrels • by Michael Tod. Maps by Barbara Anne Knight.
Abergavenny, Wales: Cadno Books, December 1999, paperback, 690 pp.
   Stephen Jones and Jo Fletcher reported in *Science Fiction Chronicle,* December 1993:

> Publishing mogul Anthony Cheetham just happened to be a guest of BBC Radio Wales' book programme *And Now Read On* at the same time as frustrated first-time novelist Michael Tod. Mr. Tod spent some time regaling listeners with his all-too-familiar tale of woe: he'd written a novel, *The Silver Tide,* a sort of squirrel version of *Watership Down,* but couldn't find anyone to publish it. As his conservatory-designing business had been hit by the recession and he was stony broke, he raised capital by selling shares in the book to family and friends and published the volume himself. The financial constraints were such that, picking up the last consignment from the printers, he ran out of petrol and had to stop at a friend's house and sell him copies of the book so he could get home. Local booksellers were duly impressed with his talent and took more than 1,000 copies. Mr. Cheetham was also impressed, and bought the book itself, as well as two sequels. So who says publishers never listen? Look out for *The Silver Tide* in mass-market format in January.

   Watership Down is a hard act to follow, but Tod's trilogy (called both *The Woodstock Saga* and *The Dorset Squirrels*) comes close enough to put him solidly in the ranks of the better British "nature novelists," along with Richard Adams, William Horwood, and Garry Kilworth.
   In *The Silver Tide,* a community of native red squirrels in Purbeck, in Dorset on the Channel coast, is confronted by a wave of larger, aggressive American grey squirrels spreading throughout Britain, or "New America" as they call it. The peaceful red squirrels do not know how to react to the arrogant grey squirrels, whose attitude seems similar to the stereotype of the American settlers who considered the native Americans a "decrepit bunch of savages" who did not deserve the land that they lived upon. After one of the Reds of Blue Pool is killed, the others regretfully abandon their ancestral land and begin a trek to find a new home—if there is anyplace in Britain where Reds can live which the Greys will not eventually take over.
   But the story is much more complex than this. The Greys do not fight only with their teeth and claws; they have Stones of Power:

> His queasiness increased and he had some difficulty in focusing his eyes. When his vision cleared he saw that the Greys were arranging a square of stones at the base of his tree. There were "lots" of stones, certainly more than eight. He tried to count again. For some reason, it seemed to be important to know how many stones there were.
>   […]
>   The Grey, Quartz, came forward and put his forepaw on one of the corner stones. Juniper's whiskers instantly buzzed and tingled, much worse than before, and his body started to shake uncontrollably.
>   The Grey lifted his paw and the buzzing and shaking stopped. Juniper hung limply out of the drey coughing and retching, his head aching intolerably.

The Greys have learned how to manipulate Earth power; the primal force controlled through Leylines, pyramidology, and similar metaphysical practices. The Reds have their own power through their worship of the "life-giving Sun." The Greys' Stone Power is more immediate and obvious, but the Reds' prayers to the Sun are also answered in a more subtle way.

As with *Watership Down*, *The Woodstock Saga* builds up colorful cultures for the squirrels. The Reds have plant names: trees for the males (Oak, Rowan, Larch, Chestnut) and flowers for the females (Burdock, Bluebell, Meadowsweet). The Greys all have harsh mineral names (Flint, Marble, Granite, Chert). But the cultures are not uniform within each species. One refuge which the Blue Pool Reds find is already settled by a tribe of Reds who have a monarchical caste system, and the two Red societies clash.

In *The Second Wave*, a group of Greys who are willing to embrace the Sun faith unfortunately fall under the influence of Crag, the Temple Master, a Red fanatic who has perverted their gentle nature religion. He turns the Greys into a Crusading army to slay all Red "degenerates" who do not agree with his decrees of harsh penance for their "sins." So what at first seems to be a conflict between two colors of otherwise-identical squirrels turns out to be much more interestingly complex. Both groups are menaced when Blood the pine marten comes to Ourland (Brownsea Island).

The Golden Flight has a final Reds versus Greys confrontation, combined with problems of peace creating unexpected difficulties, and the potential of squirrel overpopulation on Ourland:

> Marguerite knew that things were now seriously wrong on Ourland. Instead of peace and prosperity bringing pleasure and happiness to the island, the virtually unlimited leisure time was undermining, if not destroying, the whole culture of the squirrels.

The biggest annoyance about Tod's writing is an overuse of coincidence and divine intervention. The Reds' young intellectual, Bright Marguerite, "invents" counting *just* in time to figure out a defense against the Stone Power. Why do prayers to the Sun work so well for the Reds of Blue Pool, but apparently not for other Reds? If prayer were as efficacious as it seems here, the divinity of the Sun and the "right way" to worship ought to have become obvious to all squirrels long since. However, the novels have enough merit to overcome this minor flaw. *The Silver Tide* and its sequels are fine reading for all fans of *Watership Down*; similar to it but with enough differences to be refreshingly original.

Sirius: A Fantasy of Love and Discord • by Olaf Stapledon.

London: Secker & Warburg, June 1944, hardcover, 200 pp.

Sirius is the biography of Sirius the dog, as written by Robert, the fiancé of Plaxy Trelone, Sirius' human sister-lover. Robert is the only human to be told the full story of Sirius, and to enter into it towards its end as the third part of a romantic triangle so unusual as to bewilder all three of them. Robert, a RAF fighter-pilot during World War II, does not claim to be a writer, but he has to become Sirius' biographer by default.

Robert is drafted into this role when he uses his leave to track down Plaxy, his temporarily-missing lover, to a lonely shepherd's cottage:

> I rose to meet her, but something strange arrested me. Interspersed with Plaxy's remarks was no other human voice but a quite different sound, articulate but inhuman. Just before she came round the corner of the house she said, "But my dear, don't dwell on your handlessness so! You have triumphed over it superbly." There followed a strange trickle of speech from her companion; then through the gate into the garden came Plaxy and a large dog.
>
> He was certainly no ordinary dog. In the main he was an Alsatian, perhaps with a dash of Great Dane or Mastiff, for he was a huge beast. His general build was wolf-like, but he was slimmer than a wolf, because of his height. His coat, though the hair was short, was superbly thick and silky, particularly

round the neck, where it was a close turbulent ruff. Its silkiness missed effeminacy by a hint of stubborn harshness. Silk wire, Plaxy once called it. On back and crown it was black, but on flanks and legs and the under surface of his body it paled to an austere greyish fawn. There were also two large patches of fawn above the eyes, giving his face a strangely mask-like look, or the appearance of a Greek statue with blank-eyed helmet pushed back from the face. What distinguished Sirius from all other dogs was his huge cranium. It was not, as a matter of fact, quite as large as one would have expected in a creature of human intelligence, since, as I shall explain later, Trelone's technique not only increased the brain's bulk but also produced a refinement of the nerve fibres themselves. Nevertheless, Sirius's head was far loftier than any normal dog's. His high brow combined with the silkiness of his coat to give him a look of the famous Border Collie, the outstanding type of sheep-dog. I learned later that this brilliant race had, indeed, contributed to his make-up. But his cranium was far bigger than the Border Collie's. The dome reached almost up to the tips of his large, pointed Alsatian ears. To hold up this weight of head, the muscles of his neck and shoulders were strongly developed. At the moment of our encounter he was positively leonine, because the hair was bristling along his spine.

Sirius: A Fantasy of Love and Discord by Olaf Stapledon (Secker & Warburg, June 1944). **An early sf novel about an animal raised to human intelligence through selective breeding, and the social results that follow. Cover art uncredited.**

Sirius is the only successful result of Plaxy's father's attempts to create a dog with human intelligence and, hopefully, a human lifespan. None of the others have been more than "smart dogs," not really dogs of human intelligence as Sirius shows himself to be:

> Plaxy's father, Thomas Trelone, … work on the stimulation of cortical growth in the brains of mammals was begun while he was merely a brilliant young research worker, and it was subsequently carried on in strict secrecy.… Thus it was that for many years his experiments were known only to a few of his most intimate professional colleagues in Cambridge, and to his wife, who had a part to play in them.

After experimenting for many years on different animals, Trelone settles upon dogs because, "Nevertheless, from Trelone's point of view dogs had one overwhelming advantage. They were capable of a much greater freedom of movement in our society." Trelone's experiments are henceforth disguised as attempts to breed more intelligent sheep-dogs. He and his wife Elizabeth move to an old farmhouse in sheep-raising country near Trawsfynydd in North Wales to do this. Sirius' littermates are indeed no more than the "super-sheep-dogs" that Trelone publicly breeds, but Sirius is special. Trelone pretends to keep him as a pet, but within their home he and his family raise Sirius to be as human as they can. Baby Plaxy is born at the same time as Sirius, and an especially close bond grows between them. "But what he [Trelone] did want was that Sirius should be brought up to feel himself the social equal of little Plaxy."

The novel is Sirius' life story as dictated by him and Plaxy to Robert: Sirius' infancy within their farm-home, his youth around Trawsfynydd learning the social differences between dogs and humans, his apprenticeship with a local shepherd as a very smart but still-disguised super-sheep-dog, his emotionally confused adolescence as he and Plaxy are separated by their maturing physical instincts, his rebellious rejection of humanity and embracing of his "wolf instincts," his successful introduction to Trelone's colleagues at Cambridge until he tires of being a show-piece, his shock upon discovering the worst side of human society in London's slums, and the trauma of World War II. It is the war that destroys them all. The older children are all drafted for war work. Thomas Trelone is killed in a German air-raid, and elderly Elizabeth dies soon after. Only Plaxy and Sirius are left, and without the larger human family to disguise themselves within, Sirius' super-canine efforts to keep the farm running and the unnatural relationship between him and Plaxy become the gossip of the North Wales district. Sirius is accused of being Satanic or a Nazi spy, which are too extreme for any but the most credulous to listen to; but the close emotional relationship between the adolescent girl and the dog are too obvious and scandalous to ignore.

The novel focuses upon two principal themes; Sirius' intellectual and emotional attempts to understand his existence as a "missing link" between human and animal society, and the relationship between himself and Plaxy.

At the time of *Sirius'* publication in 1944, there were some critical comparisons with Philip Wylie's *Gladiator* (1930), the novel that was an acknowledged inspiration for the *Superman* comic book. Both novels are fantasies about super-beings whose strengths make them misfits among their own kind, and ultimately lead to tragic fates. *Sirius* was the first realistic sf novel about breeding an animal to human-level intelligence. It is still good reading today.

Skeleton Crew • by Gre7g Luterman. Illustrated by various.

Seattle, WA: CreateSpace, August 2014, paperback, $8.95 (259 pp.)

Skeleton Crew by Gre7g Luterman (CreateSpace, August 2014). One of the self-published furry novels that was so popular it has been reprinted by a furry fandom specialty publisher. Cover art by H. Kyoht Luterman (the author's wife).

Small World • by Gre7g Luterman. Illustrated by Rick Griffin.

Lansing, MI, Thurston Howl Publications, April 2018, paperback, $11.99 (301 [+ 1] pp.)

Skeleton Crew may be the first hard science-fiction novel with absolutely no humans in it. The cover by H. Kyoht Luterman (the author's wife) shows two of the main characters; Commissioner Sarsuk, a kraken, holding Kanti, a geroo. All of the other characters in the novel are geroo. There are over a dozen full-page illustrations showing such geroo characters as Kanti, Saina, Tish, Captain Ateri, Chendra, and more.

The geroo are unclothed, with thick tails and fur. There are frequent mentions in the text of twitching ears, tail rings, and the like. Kanti is called Shaggy for his unruly fur.

Skeleton Crew is set entirely within the huge generation exploratory starship *White Flower II* in interstellar space. There is a two-page cutaway diagram of the *White Flower II* by Brandon Kruse. Four centuries earlier, the krakun came to the primitive planet Gerootec and offered to hire thousands of the overpopulated geroo as their starship crews. The geroo who went into space and their descendants would never see Gerootec again, but they would live in luxury compared to the backward geroo on their homeworld. Technically, the *White Flower II* belongs to the krakuns' Planetary Acquisitions, Incorporated, with a mission of finding new planets that can be colonized.

New planets for the krakun. Never for the geroo.

After 400 years, some geroo are asking if the krakun are their employers or their slavemasters. Commissioner Sarsuk is Planetary Acquisitions' representative to the *White Flower II*. He is the novel's villain.

> The richest geroo lived at the top of the ship, with the fanciest apartments and nicest shops. Kanti had never seen the insides of any of those apartments, but he had heard the rumors of their enormous size and luxurious amenities. Could those rumors really be true? Was it even possible that only a few, privileged geroo claimed entire decks of the ship?
>
> The poor lived in crowded conditions at the bottom of the ship—level twenty-five. The extra-tall deck housed a general mess hall and a barracks-style dormitory. No one paid to use either, so they acted as a safety net for hapless geroo. No matter how far down on their luck, the crew could always count on a hot meal and a dry place to sleep in the belly of the White Flower II.
>
> Strictly speaking, all krakun vessels prohibited alcohol. But enforcement of that law was half-hearted at best. Showing up to work drunk might land a crewman before a judge, but only the krakun really cared if anyone drank during their down-time.
>
> If a krakun caught someone drinking, he'd probably toss that geroo in the recycler. But that's how the monstrous creatures handled most problems they encountered. Fortunately, the White Flower II seldom hosted anyone from Krakuntec. The commissioner visited periodically to check on the ship, but he wasn't liable to stroll down any of the decks—not any of the ones with a three-meter clearance, at least.
>
> Kanti headed off to the gravity down-wells and hopped back to deck twenty-four. The wells were essentially stairwells without the stairs—simple platforms that geroo could jump off to reach the level below. The artificial gravity in the wells was turned down to a tiny fraction of normal, so each hop was slow and gentle.
>
> Each platform shadowed the opening down to the next level; so to travel multiple levels, one simply hopped, turned around, and hopped again until reaching the desired deck. The overlapping structure ensured that a geroo could not fall multiple levels accidentally.

The *White Flower II* has a crew of ten thousand geroo. Exactly. 10,001 would be overpopulation, and the krakun's policy for overpopulation is—messy. And that's one "law" that Commissioner Sarsuk enforces ruthlessly.

Both the tech-talk and the plot are fascinating. This review is heavy on the novel's technology, and reveals almost nothing about its plot, because the plot is full of twists and surprises. Even revealing this much of the technology probably gives away some major spoilers. But *Skeleton Crew* is a real page-turner. You can hardly put it down for wanting to find out what will happen to Kanti and his friends next.

> A well-placed kick into Kanti's stomach dropped him back to the deck, grasping his gut and gasping for breath.
>
> Ateri knelt before the shaggy geroo and whispered in his ear. "Listen very closely to me, kerrati. You will not discuss what was said here today—ever. You will never, ever, say the words, 'skeleton crew' again. Is that understood?"
>
> Kanti nodded. Tears streamed down his muzzle.
>
> "If you do, I promise that I will find out," Ateri said calmly. "And when I do, I will rip chunks of you out with my bare paws … and toss them into the recycler one by one … until all that remains of you … is your blood in my fur … and your screams in my ears."

Skeleton Crew is set in the same universe as Rick Griffin's short story "Ten Thousand Miles Up." The book ends with a three-page "Epilogue: One Year Later" by Griffin.

This CreateSpace edition is dated and first published in August 2014, but later printings have added artwork dated 2015 and the Epilogue by Rick Griffin dated October 17, 2016. This edition has been withdrawn from sale and replaced by a new September 2017 edition from Thurston Howl Publications with a series title, *The Kanti Cycle*, added; plus a new cover and interior art by Rick Griffin. A sequel, *Small World*, followed in April 2018, with a third, *Fair Trade*, to come.

The Stray Lamb • by Thorne Smith.

New York: Cosmopolitan Book Corporation, November 1929, hardcover, 309 pp.

Thorne Smith was the author of several mega-popular humorous fantasies during the late 1920s and early '30s. His one anthro classic was *The Stray Lamb*. This bawdy fantasy was published probably less than a month after the "Black Thursday" stock market crash that set off the Great Depression. This makes *The Stray Lamb* the only anthropomorphic novel written during and set in the Roaring Twenties, the era of wild Prohibition parties, of sheiks and flappers and bootleggers and bathtub gin. How would anthropomorphized animals fit into this? Very comedically, as Smith tells it.

T. Lawrence Lamb, a forty-year-old investment banker, is bored with life. It has become a monotonous routine of daily commutes to Wall Street to make money, then back at the end of the day to spend the evening getting mildly drunk alone in his study. He and his wife have grown to despise each other. She has social pretensions (she likes to be called Sapho), which she indulges by encouraging her artistic hangers-on to attend literary soirees at their home, financed by his money while ridiculing him for making it.

Mr. Lamb's best friend is his twentyish daughter Hebe, a flapper whose wild and free spirit he appreciates. The two have been forced together by Sapho's disapproval of their lifestyles; of his refusal to approve and participate in her pretentious social activities, and of Hebe's refusal to act "like a lady." Hebe is currently being abetted by her equally uninhibited friends. Mr. Lamb subconsciously yearns to join them, but he is too inhibited by their age difference and his lifetime of respectability.

This is the situation when the little russet man appears. He is obviously a god, seemingly a cross between Pan and Budai, the Chinese god of humor. He is aware of the growing desolation in Mr. Lamb's spirit:

> "'What would you prefer to be?' asked the plump caller, carefully placing his umbrella on the floor beside his chair. 'What would you like to do?'
>
> […]

"I don't know," [Lamb] said rather helplessly. "Haven't the vaguest idea when you put it to me straight. One thing I do know, I'm tired of being a human being. I think I'd like to be things if I could—animals, birds, beasts, fish, any old sort of a thing, just to get another point of view, to keep from thinking and acting always as a man, always as a civilized being, an economic unit with a barrel full of obligations constantly threatening to run up against something and smash."

The next morning, Mr. Lamb wakes up as a horse. Sapho is horrified—she is sure he has done it deliberately to embarrass her, and that the servants will all quit—while Hebe is incredulous but delighted:

> The horse was listening intently, ears pitched forward, and at this last remark he winked slowly and deliberately at Hebe. The girl was amazed. It was her father all over. At that moment she accepted the fact that something strange had occurred.
>
> Then after a few minutes of thoughtful consideration, looking this way and that as if to determine the best way of procedure, Mr. Lamb cautiously got himself out of bed, but not without considerable clattering and convolutions. Hebe watched him with amused interest. She knew it was her father.
>
> [...]
>
> Bending an eloquent glance upon his daughter, he pointed with his hoof to the mirror. Obediently the girl went over to the mirror and after much shaking and nodding of her father's head, she adjusted it to his satisfaction.
>
> "That's something like," thought Lamb, surveying his reflection with no little satisfaction.
>
> He was a fine body of a horse—a sleek, strapping stallion. Black as night with a star on his forehead. He turned slowly, taking himself in from all angles.
>
> "Rather indecent, though," he thought. "Wish I had a blanket, a long one. Oh, hell! I'm a horse, now. Horses don't mind. Still it doesn't seem quite—well, I just never did it before, that's all."

The Stray Lamb by Thorne Smith (Cosmopolitan Book Corporation, November 1929). **A bawdy humorous fantasy about a staid businessman who turns into various animals when drunken. The only popular anthropomorphic animal fantasy written during the Flapper Era of the 1920s. Cover art uncredited.**

Mr. Lamb spends a week as a horse, impishly playing practical jokes on Sapho's snooty friends and on his stuffy upper-class neighbors. After that he is a seagull, taking advantage of his aerial abilities to make several drunkards believe that they have developed *delirium tremens*. Unfortunately, his later transformations are not discretely at home in the night—or when he is sober:

> At a late hour that night he was still drinking highballs and running up a commendable check at a night club for the benefit of Sandra, his daughter, and Melville Long. Mr. Lamb had danced with more diligence than grace. Now, however, he was past dancing. In fact, if the truth must be known, Mr. Lamb was rapidly disappearing, the top of his head being level with the table cloth, and in a few minutes even the little of him with which he saw fit to grace the table was withdrawn from public view.

[...]
The party looked down and saw what the waiter saw—a long, large, tawny tail protruding from under the table.
[...]
At this moment Mr. Lamb decided to relieve the tension of the situation. A long, sleek head with a pointed snout appeared above the table, slid onto the rumpled cloth and looked moistly at the three young people. In the due course of time the head was followed by a body, which slumped back awkwardly in its chair.

"I don't want to be hasty," said Hebe, "but roughly speaking, I think my father and our host leans toward kangaroo. What will we use for money now that he has gone?"

The drunken kangaroo causes a brawl that results in a wild car chase and the first of several courtroom scenes with sarcastically frustrated judges. Later transformations, which Mr. Lamb grows increasingly distressed with (they are not all "nice" animals), include a goldfish, a dog, a cat, and a lion, the last of which becomes handy to protect Hebe and Melville Long from gangsters when they decide to become bootleggers. Meanwhile, Sapho, who wants to keep Mr. Lamb's fortune while ridding herself of a husband who is an uncontrollable menagerie, begins considering that it is not murder to kill an animal...

The Stray Lamb has been in and out of print many times since 1929. The transformations do not begin until fifty pages into the story, but they are witty and hilarious after that.

Summerhill • by Kevin Frane.

Dallas, TX: Argyll Productions, January 2013, hardcover, 285 pp.

Summerhill, probably a dog, is introduced at an interdimensional cruise ship's dinner gathering. The others at his table try to guess what he is:

> "I tell you," the ankylosauromorphic cyborg said in its fluid, polished, robotic voice, "he's got to be some sort of wolf. Just on two legs, is all."
>
> Summerhill kept his ears perked and his mouth shut. He lifted his own glass of golden, bubbling something-or-other to his lips and took a sip, his eyes meeting the little girl's for a moment of grateful acknowledgment.
>
> "Oh, please. Have you ever SEEN a wolf?" asked the Crown Prince of the Akashic Realm, lines of disapproval appearing on his otherwise smooth, pale blue face. He and Summerhill had met earlier in the evening; the two shared a taste for fizzy beverages. "He's far too small, and the colors are all wrong."
>
> The girl quietly begged pardon and broke away from the group. As she left, she offered Summerhill a tiny wave with her slender fingers, along with one final smile of sympathy and encouragement.
>
> A being that looked like a pinkish cloud of gas with a self-contained thunderstorm rumbling all through itself chimed in. "No, I saw a wolf here aboard the ship just this morning." Blue tendrils of electricity crackled over its wispy form as it somehow created the sounds of speech. "He didn't look anything like this."

Warning: Your copy of *Summerhill* is not defective. It really does begin with Chapter 2. Chapter 1 appears after that.

Summerhill, who may be a dog, is aboard the interdimensional luxury liner S.S. *Nusquam*. He is:

> a colorful fellow, at least by the standards he'd known before coming aboard. He looked much like a dog, a wolf-like dog that was on the small side or perhaps a coyote-like dog that was on the large side; or maybe something in between. His fur had hues of yellow and red, though in most places those colors blended to form a more appropriately canine brown, or cream, or cinnamon or deep reddish-

black. The gray of his eyes matched the gray of the sky of the world from which he'd come, which he'd lately taken to thinking may not have been a coincidence.

Summerhill had been the only inhabitant for all of his life of the World of the Pale Gray Sky, although its being filled with empty skyscrapers and empty supermarkets filled with food that never spoiled hinted that there had once been other inhabitants. He eventually got bored of being all alone, so he set off to explore it. Just before walking off it into space, he met a duplicate of himself who warned him, "'Find Katharine. Make sure you stick with her and everything will be fine." So he walks off into interstellar space, where he runs into and sneaks aboard the S.S. *Nusquam* with its bizarre passengers and crew, and finds Katharine, a human woman from New Zealand who promptly has him arrested by two robots. So much for sticking with her!

By this time it is clear that *Summerhill* is not your usual anthropomorphic sf novel. It is strongly reminiscent of Robert A. Heinlein's short stories "By His Bootstraps" and "—All You Zombies—," two complex time-travel/paradox tales in which all of the characters turn out to be the same character, time-traveling back and forth and meeting himself at different ages:

> Bringing the bowl to his muzzle, he opened his mouth and extended his tongue—
> —and then spotted a small note left sitting on the platter.
> It had been hidden underneath the bowl of stew, the paper having curled and warped due to the heat. There was writing on it, and before he even tried to read it, Summerhill recognized the handwriting as his own.
> He didn't know when he'd ever seen himself write anything, but he recognized his handwriting all the same. The words appeared to have been hastily scribbled, too.

Summerhill is also reminiscent of another sf thriller where, at one point, the hero shouts frustratedly to anyone who will listen, "I DON'T UNDERSTAND ANYTHING THAT'S GOING ON!" Summerhill is much more blasé about it. He metaphorically just relaxes and enjoys the scenery while he and Katharine are running from the ominous Consortium, from robots with rayguns, and from whatever else is chasing them. And the scenery is very exotic:

> The lifeboat had crashed onto what appeared to be the surface of an enormous coral reef. Giant polyps sported a rainbow of tentacles of varying sizes. Conical sponges formed miniature forests, anchored to the reef's calcium exoskeleton at narrow points that looked like they might break off with even the slightest nudge. Blazing red tendrils fanned out like massive antlers that belonged on the head of a great hoofed animal.
> […]
> "Okay," Summerhill said, drawing a deep breath to calm himself, "if we just crashed, then WHERE did we crash?"
> Katharine stared out the window for a while longer, transfixed by the view outside… she turned to look at him and said, "I think we've struck a nevereef,"
> Summerhill raised an eyebrow. "Should I know what that is?"
> "I'm sketchy on most of the details myself," Katharine said. "I mean, some of the sailors mention them from time to time. They're some kind of navigational hazard that the ship has to avoid when sailing the gulf between realities, but I don't know much about them beyond that." She nodded toward the viewing port. "I'm actually kind of surprised that it even looks like a reef, to be honest."

From reef to forest to swamp, the landscape keeps changing. Katharine grows increasingly worried and despondent as they go on but do not seem to make any progress; but Summerhill remains serene.

Summerhill is a colorful, fast-moving romp that keeps the reader guessing what's going on. It was a finalist for the 2013 Cóyotl Award for Best Novel.

Sundiver • by David Brin.
New York: Bantam Books, February 1980, paperback, 340 pp.

Startide Rising • by David Brin.
New York: Bantam Books, September 1983, paperback, 474 pp.

The Uplift War • by Davin Brin. Maps.
West Bloomfield, MI: Phantasia Press, April 1987, hardcover, 513 pp.

Brightness Reef • by David Brin. Introduction by James Gunn. Illustrations by Alan M. Clark.
Norwalk, CT: The Easton Press, September 1995, hardcover, 526 pp.

Infinity's Shore • by David Brin.
New York: Bantam Spectra, December 1996, hardcover536 pp.

Heaven's Reach • by David Brin.
New York: Bantam Spectra, June 1998, hardcover, 458 pp.

Many authors of stories with animals who have been bioengineered to an anthropomorphic intelligence refer to them as having been "uplifted." Here are the books that created that term.

In David Brin's six *Uplift Universe* novels, the Five Galaxies (a civilization of "Galactics") contains many intelligent species, not all friendly to each other. The senior species are believed to have been uplifted to sapience by a mysterious unknown Progenitor. The humans are "wolflings" that have evolved to intelligence, and achieved space travel and joined the Five Galaxies without having been uplifted. Many of the species have become patrons to their own client species that they are uplifting through gene manipulation and controlled mutation. This is an expensive process, so the client species are divided into those that have reached independence, and indentured clients that are still working off their debt to their patrons.

The first three novels constitute the Uplift Trilogy. The last three, written ten years later, are the Uplift Storm Trilogy.

Sundiver is about an expedition into a sun's chromosphere to investigate a supposed lifeform living there. The scientists besides Jacob Denwa, the protagonist, include several alien patrons and their indentured client assistants. The villain turns out to be Culla, a Pring assistant to Bubbacub, a Pila patron. Culla was trying to free the Prings from their indentured client status. But the novel begins with Jacob and other humans uplifting dolphins:

"Makakai ... are you ready?"

[...]

"Yesss ... let'sss do it!" came the warbling, squeaky voice at last. The words sounded breathless, as if spoken grudgingly, in lieu of inhalation.

A nice long speech for Makakai. He could see the young dolphin's training machine next to his, its image reflected in the mirrors that rimmed his faceplate. Its gray metal flukes lifted and fell slightly with the swell. Feebly, without their power, her artificial fins moved sluggishly under the transient, serrated surface of the water.

[...]

"I think we have the brainwave information we need now, Jacob. I don't know how you did it, but Makakai's attention span in English was at least twice normal. Manfred thinks he's found enough associated synaptic clusters to give him a boost in his next set of experimental mutations. There are a couple of nodes that he wants to expand in the left cerebral lobe of Makakai's offspring."

Startide Rising, which won both the Hugo and Nebula Award for the Best Novel of 1983, is set two hundred years later, around the exploratory Terran spaceship *Streaker* with a crew of 150 uplifted dolphins (including the captain), seven humans, and one uplifted chimpanzee. The *Streaker* discovers a vast graveyard of 50,000 ancient spaceships of the unknown Progenitors. This sets off a battle between several Galactic species to seize the *Streaker* and its coordinates for the derelict Progenitor fleet, or to prevent their own enemies from gaining them, and other Galactics to help the Terrans. The point-of-view keeps shifting among many characters: humans, neo-dolphins, the neo-chimpanzee, the various Galactics, and the Galactics' own client species.

Fins had been making wisecracks about human beings for thousands of years. They had *always* found men terribly funny. The fact that humanity had recently meddled with their genes, and taught them engineering, hadn't done much to change their attitude.

Fins were still smart-alecks.

Protocols my left eye! Those rules were set up so humans and chimps and fins will act in just the right way when Galactics are around. If the *Streak* gets stopped by a Soro patrol, or has to ask a Pilan Librarian for data somewhere, *then* Dr. Metz or Mr. Orley—or even you or I—might have to pretend we're in charge ... because none of those stuffed-shirt Eatees would give the time of day to a race as young as fins. But the rest of the time we take our orders from Captain Creideki.

Hell, that'd be hard enough—taking brown from a Soro and pretending you like it because the damned ET is nice enough to admit that *humans*, at least, are a bit above the level of fruit flies. Can you imagine how hard it would be if we actually had to *run* this ship? What if we had tried to make dolphins into a nice, well-behaved, slavey client race? Would you have liked that?

Yet, there were moments like the present, when Toshio wished there were compensations for being the only human boy on a starship crewed mostly by adult dolphins.

Brookida switched to Anglic. Though somewhat shrill and stuttered, it was still better than Toshio's Trinary. Dolphins, after all, had been modified by generations of genetic engineering to take up human styles, not the other way around.

In *The Uplift War*, winner of the 1988 Hugo Award for Best Novel, the Earth colony planet Garth, inhabited by humans and neo-chimpanzees, is seized by the avian Gubru who hold it to force Earth to reveal the location of the Progenitor derelict fleet.

It was ironic. The furry, canny Synthians were among Earth's few "allies" in the political and military quagmire of the Five Galaxies. But they were also fantastically self-centered and famous cowards. Swoio's departure as much as guaranteed there would be no armadas of fat, furry warriors coming to Garth's aid in her hour of need.

Just like there won't be any help from Earth, nor Tymbrim, them having enough problems of their own right now.

Athaclena found the situation bitterly ironic. Once again, the races of Earth were in the spotlight, as they had been ever since the notorious "Sundiver" affair, two centuries ago. This time an interstellar crisis had been sparked by the first starship ever put under command of *neo-dolphins*.

Brin's six *Uplift Universe* novels are full of colorful alien species as well as uplifted neo-chimpanzee and neo-dolphin characters from Earth. They had a strong impact on furry fans of the 1980s and 1990s, and they are still popular anthropomorphic literature today.

Sunset of Furmankind • by Ted R. Blasingame.
Raleigh, NC: Lulu, September 2011, paperback, 510 pp.

Second Chance: Furmankind II • by Ted R. Blasingame.
Raleigh, NC: Lulu, May 2015, paperback, 460 pp.

Sunset of Furmankind tackles a tough premise. The main character hates bioengineered Furs, and on the first page he murders one. He is sentenced to be either executed or made into one against his will. The reader can guess that he will eventually change his mind about them, but can the author make him a sympathetic-enough character to keep a readership of furry fans interested in what happens to him until this occurs?

The background: in the late 21st century, six extrasolar planets are discovered, at the same time that faster-than-light travel is developed enabling mankind to reach them:

> Initial colonies to each of them suffered high mortality rates due to accidents and sometimes harsh living conditions. While humans are highly adaptable, they were just not physically hardy enough to endure some of the conditions they faced.
>
> Then a breakthrough happened in another field of research that would forever change humanity. Genetic scientists working on a cure for cancer could take a single damaged cell from a patient and correct the aberrations in its DNA, but the trick was getting the healthy cell to replicate its new code in through the millions of other cells in the body....
>
> Years later, genetic scientists from the Terran Colonization Coalition soon began tinkering with condemned prisoners in secret and used the McEwen process to combine human DNA sequences with data from other Terran life forms, primarily canine (dogs), feline (cats), ursine (bear) and vulpine (foxes). It was their hope to *improve* humanity in such a way to give settling colonists an edge on their survival.
>
> The genetic mutations were successful and brought about the development of four new races, the *Canis*, the *Felis*, the *Ursis*, and the *Vulps*. These new races were able to stand upright as bipeds due to enlarged digitigrade back leg muscles and bone structure. The forepaws had fingers and opposable thumbs for using tools, yet were padded for running on all-fours. The tongues and vocal cords were altered for human-type speech and they retained their human intelligence while also maintaining animal instincts specific to each species.
>
> [...]
>
> With the success of genetic manipulation, the Anthro Human Colonization Program was formed, and these new races were sent to the untamed colonies of Earth in an effort to see if the changes would give them an edge on survival in the wild environments. The *Canis* were sent as a starter colony to planet Khepri, the *Felis* to Bastien, the *Ursis* to Diamanta, and the *Vulps* to Javan.
>
> If the test subjects failed, the condemned would be considered an acceptable loss, but if they succeeded in surviving, it would provide new avenues for the overgrowing human population to spread out into the stars, even if no longer completely human.

The experiment is successful, and a call is publicized throughout Earth for volunteers to be transformed into furmen to become settlers in "anthro-human starter colonies."

Twenty-five years later, furmen have become reasonably common on Earth between their transformation and their permanent departure as extrasolar colonists on more newly-discovered worlds:

> As will happen, there has become a movement on Earth promoting "pure" humans as the dominant race, but the legislation that was passed at the start of the project continues to protect the rights of all Furs when possible. Despite this, some countries on Earth have outlawed Furs altogether.

Brian Barrett is one of these furman-haters. When he kills a Feli, a humanoid mountain lion, his only chance to avoid execution for murder is to agree to become the Feli's replacement and spend the rest of his life as an interstellar cougar colonist.

Blasingame makes Barrett as sympathetic as possible. Although branded as one of the human-only religious fanatics, he actually killed for a strong personal motive: his ex-fiancée left him for a Feli lover, who was the furman he murdered. It was months of brooding on his betrayal that caused him to develop a prejudice against all furmen. Like most humans, Barrett has had little personal experience with the furmen. So after he agrees to accept transformation, Barrett is forced to live among furmen while awaiting his fate.

Blasingame describes the North American facility of the Furmankind Institute and its Felis Wing, and the nine-month transformation and orientation period to get used to their new bodies, and learn about the planet to which they will be sent, in extreme—not to say excruciating—detail. The human volunteers (Barrett is posing as a volunteer) are assigned to dorms in groups of four. All in Barrett's dorm are to become Felis, but the Institute is for all four furmans, so they encounter wolfmen, bearmen, and foxmen:

> Kristen and Jenni tried not to stare, but they were both fascinated at the sight of the Furs that occupied tables throughout the cafeteria. The common chairs with the horizontal slots in the seat backs near the bottom cushion now made sense to them, as it allowed the furman patrons to occupy a chair without having to sit on their own tails.

Barrett's sentence requires him to take a new name and false history, so early in the novel he becomes Jonathan Sunset. The detailed narrative fills pages and pages, describing Barrett's story as a murderer in prison; the Institute and Barrett/Jon's developing relationship with Kristen, Dante, and Jenni, and their slow nine-month transformations into furmen in clinical detail.

Sunset of Furmankind is much more than a study of the volunteers' physical changes. The novel builds a social picture of the Institute, gradually pulling back from Jon to focus on all four of the Felis Wing dorm-mates; later expanding to include all sixteen of the transformees (four each of the four species) plus the Institute's administrative staff. The cast experience personal dramas, social bonding, deaths, and more, leading to their "graduation" as full Furmen and assignment to a new extrasolar colony.

Second Chance, the sequel, describes Jon's and the other Furs' first year as pioneers on an extrasolar planet. The two books are recommended to those who want the details of how humans might transform into anthropomorphic animals. Blasingame has combined all of his *Furmankind* novels in 2018 into *Furmankind*, a Kindle electronic 2499-page edited edition.

Tailchaser's Song • by Tad Williams. Map by the author.

New York: DAW Books, November 1985, hardcover, 348 pp.

Tailchaser's Song

When *Tailchaser's Song* was first published, about half its reviews called it "a *Lord of the Rings* with cats," and the other half called it "a *Watership Down* with cats." It does mix the realistic-animal-species fantasy featuring a detailed religion/folklore and language, with the adventure quest into a realm of supernatural evil. It has some aspects of an Orpheus and Eurydice with cats, although Tailchaser and Pouncequick do not realize when they set out that their search for Tailchaser's fiancée Hushpad will take them to the feline Hell and back.

Tailchaser's Song was arguably the first realistic-animal adventure fantasy to feature cats. *Solo's Journey*—*In the Long Dark*—*Cat House*—the *Windrusher* books—the *Wild Roads* trilogy—all the *Warriors* novels—these and all other dramas featuring "realistic" taking cats with their own language and folklore may owe a debt to *Watership Down*, but they were also all published after *Tailchaser's Song* proved the huge market that exists for feline adventure fantasies of that type.

Fritti Tailchaser is a young orange tom just eight months old, of the Meeting Wall clan of about sixty cats, both feral and domestic, of the Folk of Behind-Edge-Copse. The reader is dropped into the midst of a detailed feline society dense with cat-language and mythology. Williams deftly makes it easy to understand these terms and legends as they appear in the narrative.

Tailchaser is enjoying the carefree life of a young hunter on the edges of this complacent clan, dominated by the lazy Elders at the monthly Meeting Nights where the cats gather to socialize and listen to the Master Old-singers tell ancient oral tales of cat-gods and tricksters.

Tailchaser is excited because he has recently danced his first Dance of Acceptance with a young fella, the demure Hushpad. But she has disappeared—the M'an-dwelling where she lived is empty of life and furniture. When he frantically reports this at the next Meeting, others complain that an alarming number of the Folk have recently gone missing. The Elders decide to send a delegation to Firsthome, the legendary Courts of Harar, to inform the Queen of Cats and ask her help in stopping the disappearances. Tailchaser is too young to be picked as one of the delegation. Miffed and worrying that the delegation is not concerned about Hushpad individually, Tailchaser vows to set out on his own quest to find her—trailed by his friend, the eager kitten Pouncequick, who cannot be discouraged from accompanying him.

Tailchaser's Song by Tad Williams (DAW Books, November 1985). This "*Watership Down* with cats" was the first anthropomorphic fantasy to feature cats. It was a major influence with early furry fans, and is still popular. Cover art by Michael Embden.

Up to this point, *Tailchaser's Song* is reminiscent of *Watership Down*, although the cats are more anthropomorphized in their intelligence and their formal government. Once the quest begins, the similarities switch to Tolkien. During a grueling months-long trek through fields and woods, the two meet other animal folk like the rikchikchik (squirrels) and visl (foxes) who have also been experiencing losses, although these have been openly slaughtered by ominous creatures like giant snakelike cats with glowing yellow eyes and scarlet claws. Eatbugs, an elderly, clearly mad cat all muddy with tangled fur and wild eyes, joins them for awhile. When Tailchaser and Pouncequick eventually arrive at the feline–Edenic forest Firsthome, it is almost impossible to avoid thinking of Frodo and the Fellowship's arrival in the Elf-home of Lothlorien.

From there, along with the new quester Roofshadow who is seeking the destroyers of her clan, the three track the monsters north to the Vastnir mound in Ratleaf Forest:

> As they walked, Fritti became aware of a slight feeling of irritation, something very unsettling at the very rim of his consciousness. He felt a faint buzzing, or humming—but it was as thin and insubstantial as the noise of a brzz-hive a hundred leagues away. But it was there—and very subtly, it was getting stronger.
>
> When they stopped to rest in the wind-dampening shelter of a standing stone, he asked his companions if they had sensed it, too.
>
> "Not yet," said Roofshadow, "but I expected you would first. It's a good thing you can."
>
> "What do you mean?" asked Fritti, mystified.
>
> "You heard Squeakerbane. You heard Fencewalker. There's something happening in these wilds, and that's why we're here. Better that we sense it before it senses us."
>
> "What kind of something?" Pouncequick's eyes were bright and curious.
>
> "I don't know," said Roofshadow, "but it is bad. It is *os* in a way that I have not sensed before."

Bad is an understatement. They descend underground into a literal feline Hell, very similar to the horrific landscape of Mordor that Frodo and Sam experience:

> Before them sprawled a vast cavern, the roof as high above as the treetops of Rootwood. It was lit by the luminescent earth they had seen in the tunnel, and also by the faint blue glow of stones that protruded down through the ceiling rock. The phantom light rendered all in the cavern into spirits and vaulting shadows.
>
> Below, on the cavern floor, countless cats moved back and forth like termites in rotten wood. Most of them appeared to be normal Folk, although their faces were so full of despair and pain that they seemed almost a different race. Among them moved the Clawguard, lumpish and huge, directing the streaming, insectlike hordes as they crept to and fro.
>
> It's like some horrible dream of Firsthome, Fritti thought.

Tailchaser, Pouncequick, and later Roofshadow are enslaved as laborers digging tunnels underneath the whole world for Lord Hearteater, the bloated feline Satan who dares not go aboveground. Practically the last half of the novel takes place in the fascinatingly disgusting underground world, which includes many striking locales such as the cavern of the Scalding Flume, a ruddy-glowing river of boiling water. Lord Hearteater rules this world through three feuding, rival corps of demonic cats: the Clawguard, the brutal, reptilian-like red-clawed giants who have been kidnapping cats for slave labor; the Toothguard, and the Boneguard, who seem to be little more than dry, dust-filled bags of skin over living skeletons. So much of the adventure is spent in these Hellish caverns that the brief climactic escape, the destruction of Lord Hearteater's realm, and the happy ending seem like little more than afterthoughts.

The novel is a satisfying adventure quest that creates a whole world of "realistic" talking cats. It has remained popular for over forty years.

Tails of the City • by R.S. Pylman. Illustrated by D.C. "Rain" Simpson.
Raleigh, NC: Lulu, September 2006, hardcover, 212 pp.

    Tails of the City was one of the great "lost furry classics of the Internet" of the 1990s, until the new print-on-demand technology of the 2000s made it available once more. As Regan Pylman explains in her foreword, she was going to college in mid–1997 when she was inspired by the BBC dramatization of Armistead Maupin's *Tales of the City* to begin this furry pastiche for serialization on the Internet. Every Friday for about a year, she posted a new chapter on her website until there were fifty of them. It received considerable favorable attention at the time. Another college student, D.C. Simpson (who was just beginning his *Ozy and Millie* campus comic strip) drew sketches of the main cast. Other furry artists asked permission to draw it as a comic book, and an early furry publisher talked about collecting it into a novel. It became one of the most read furry Internet stories of the 1990s. But years passed, none of the interest developed into anything, and the serial eventually disappeared from the Internet and was forgotten,

> Until I discovered Lulu.com. Now I have a chance to present the book to those individuals who would like to have a copy. Going through, I've rediscovered what I already knew… there are continuity errors that can't be reconciled without major rewrites.… I've resisted the temptation to fix the problems, because they would require presenting *Tails of the City* in a significantly different way than it was originally presented. As you read it, I ask your indulgence. I ask you to remember that it was written an episode a week, over a period of about a year [v].

    "Write what you know" is basic advice to every beginning writer. For a college student, a "slice of life" human-interest story about college students and their neighbors can't go wrong. Avalon is a furry college town where Michelle Singer (coyote) and Stacie Hansen (mountain lion) meet in a market. Michelle invites Stacie to a Saturday morning gathering of TV cartoon and anime fans at a local student commune, and the soap opera is off and running.
    The reader is quickly introduced to the other cartoon fans who live in the neighborhood and gather at the old house at 13 Encinal Street. David Hunter, another coyote who is renting the house, is a young ex-commando who has just lost his job when his computer programming company goes out of business. He is forced to take a lowly stock clerk job to pay the rent. Tim Kern is a portly red wolf photo-artist who is always trying to talk the girls into posing for him. Stephanie, David's lover, is a gregarious lop-eared rabbit girl with three other boy friends. Mirrium Dare, one of the roomers at 13 Encinal, is an insecure hyena girl who works nights as a security guard in a modern yet creepy office building, where she daydreams of being as brave as such pop-fictional heroes as Green Lantern or her favorite, Biker Vixen.
    The cast expands further through Michelle's job as a clerk at Pale Moon Books, a New Age/Wiccan shop owned by her cousin Azrael Coyotesdaughter whose female (and mostly lesbian) clientele is heavily into Earth Mother paganism with a cheerful mother-and-daughter Samhain ritual on Halloween night. (The coven includes such members as Lumiere Drakonulf, a teenaged wolf, and Seven, "a tall, handsome pantheress.") Several of them are foster parents for young orphans as well as their own children. These include a red fox kit orphan, Millicent Mudd, and a young gray wolf, Ozymandias (showing the influence of Pylman's 1997 novel and D.C. Simpson's just-starting comic strip on each other). Some incidental characters are minor, while others became very important.
    Tails of the City covers a year in the lives and relationships of these people. There

is love, both hetero- and homosexual, of different kinds among them—true love, selfish love, and love that cannot surmount fear. There is violence and murder. The novel ends as it begins, with Michelle and Stacie together in a market. Much has changed during this year, for the better for some and for the worse for others. Some are drawn closer together while others drift away from their friends. But this is what real life is like among a college group.

As a believable slice-of-life novel featuring mostly likeable personalities, *Tails of the City* is an admirable success. It is easy to understand why it won such a large following when it was being serialized during 1997–1998. As an anthropomorphic story, there is no real reason for the cast to be talking animals rather than humans. Contrariwise, 'morphism is omnipresent in Avalon's cityscape and in background details. There are several references to different species being non-fertile, so if a couple from differing species marry and want children, they must adopt orphans or the wife must have sex with someone of her species. Melissa, a skunk member of the coven, dyes her fur blue. Mirrium, the girl hyena (in which species the genders look almost identical), is insultingly called a she-male. Characters comment on the similarities between themselves and the non-intelligent members of their species.

Extras at the back of the book include Pylman's original 1998 Internet Afterword, a review by Watts Martin from the Funny Animal Liberation Front e.zine while the serial was in progress, and an 'outtake" sequence that many readers complained about. The lives of Michelle, Stacie, David, Mirrium, Steph, Azrael, and most of the others will go on, but *Tails of the City* is finally finished. If you missed it in 1997–98, be sure to read it now. It was a finalist for the 2005 Ursa Major Award in the Best Novel category.

Theta • by Sasya Fox.
Mountain View, CA: Snowfox Press, August 2013, paperback, 395 pp.

Theta is a rip-roaring space opera. The titular protagonist is Jale Bercammon, the 36-year-old chief steward(ess) of the OCS *Freeta*, a luxury space liner in an interstellar civilization. She has served aboard the *Freeta* for almost twenty years, rising to the chief steward position and coming to think of her staff and the crew of the *Freeta* as her family. The first sign of trouble on this trip is their landing on the planet Brynton, in the midst of a violent civil war. Practically all Brynti civilians are desperate to book passage off-planet, and the *Freeta* is rapidly over-packed with upper-class refugees. One of them is the mysterious Miss Theta, an apparent almost-comatose adolescent who is brought aboard as a medical patient and booked into the finest stateroom on the ship. Captain Erin is personally instructed in Theta's care, which includes giving her a prepared injection every four hours and: "Do NOT attempt to engage Theta in conversation." Fine, until Jale learns that Theta is an almost-castrated male, and he is being given not medicine but Banerethin, which ship's Doctor Jrmnia freaks out over because it is a drug so illegal that he could be executed for allowing it to be brought on board. Strangely, as the days pass, Theta becomes more rather than less coherent and amnesiac. He makes it impossible for Jale and her crewmates to ignore the order not to talk to him, but refuses to discuss who he is or what is happening to him.

Then the *Freeta* is captured by pirates. Their actions make it clear that they have chosen the *Freeta* because they learned on Brynton that it is carrying an incredibly valuable treasure, which none of the *Freeta*'s crew knows anything about. When the frustrated pirates cannot find any treasure, they kill a few passengers and crew, impress a few more as slaves—including Theta—and leave. When the crippled *Freeta* finally reaches its destination, several days overdue, it is besieged by authorities who investigate what happened in detail. Jale is given the job of telling what happened to Theta to his assigned recipient. His reaction is not anything that she expects:

> "Theta?" The [red] fox frowned, reaching up to wipe the sleep from his eyes. "No, I don't think so. I only lived on Brynton briefly," his voice dropped, hints of bitterness creeping in, "but it's something I'd rather forget. I left nothing and nobody."
>
> Jale paused, momentarily unsure how to continue. She tried a different tack.
>
> "Sorry, let me start all over again. My name is Jale Bercammon, and I'm the chief steward of the OCS *Freeta*. On Brynton, we were given a passenger with instructions to deliver him to you; he's a white fox, purple hair—"
>
> "Myshel," Carson whispered. His eyes had widened, and his face had become very slack. All hints of politeness were abruptly gone from his manner.
>
> "So you do know this fox. Myshel?"
>
> "Yes! No," he muttered, then leaned forward. "I don't want to have this conversation. Never, ever call me again," he hissed in an urgent undertone, ears flat in what appeared to her to be either rage or panic. He glanced back over his shoulder, bared his teeth, then cut the comm.
>
> Jale sat back in surprise.
>
> "My goodness."

Who Theta/Myshel is; what Jale learns about him and the ultra-mysterious Lord Knoskali who "owned" him on Brynton; what Theta learns on the pirate ship; and what they do next, in parallel adventures, leads to the rest of the novel.

Jale is a ferret. Theta is an arctic fox. Doctor Jrmnia is a pangolin. The captain of the *Freeta* is a wolf. Other characters are a collie, a snow leopard, a coyote, a weasel, a deer, a skunk, a hyena, a raccoon, an ocelot, an opossum. All mammals. No reason is given (at first) for them to be anthropomorphic, clothes-wearing animals; they just are.

Here, Jale is depressed about being too ineffectual to fight the pirates:

> Not even to save her junior steward, or Theta, or the friendly young family of pronghorns in C-3, all of whom had been taken as slaves, nor the old jackal in D-12 who had been executed, nor any of the brave engineers who had lost their lives attempting to rig a system to jettison the pirate ship that had lamprey-docked to the ventral hull.

Theta is a taut adventure full of surprises, leading to an unexpected conclusion. It comes to a definite ending, though it is followed by a brief excerpt from a sequel-in-progress.

Theta is not illustrated, but the omnipresent mammal nouns skillfully worked into the narrative never let the reader forget that this is a funny-animal novel. One that, despite its threatened and actual violence, is surprisingly sybaritic:

> "'Your room, ma'am.'
>
> Jale froze, aghast.
>
> "This ... this is where I'm staying?"
>
> "Yes, Miss Bercammon." The pink-nosed husky frowned, brow creasing in worry. "It is not to your liking?"
>
> "This is ridiculous," Jale muttered.
>
> She stared across the open room. It was, by her account, one of the largest single rooms she'd ever seen. It was built into three levels, with a massive kitchen at the top, a den and eating area below, and an entertainment level that wrapped around. One side had a pool with water running into it from the wall; steam rose vigorously. There were five tiers, each a different color than the last, and each progressively cooler, judging by the rising steam. The bottom tier had ice floating in it. From that last

> pool, the water ran as a little creek encircling the room before vanishing out of sight around the corner, where the living space appeared to be.
>   The room itself was built on a mezzanine, a little corner tier on the side of a great fortress high above Fenna City. The persistent lower cloud layer […]

Theta feels so comfortable that the reader is almost tempted to want to be captured by space pirates. Especially furry ones.

This is the first book of its author. It's a high-class act. It's primarily a space opera with furry costuming rather than a furry novel, but it is an excellent furry space opera.

Thousand Tales: How We Won the Game • by Kris Schnee.

Seattle, WA: CreateSpace, June 2015, paperback, 245 pp.

2040: Reconnection: A "Thousand Tales" Story • by Kris Schnee. Illustrated.

Seattle, WA: CreateSpace, December 2015, paperback, 86 pp.

The Digital Coyote • by Kris Schnee.

Seattle, WA: CreateSpace, July 2016, paperback, 238 pp.

Thousand Tales: Learning to Fly • by Kris Schnee.

Seattle, WA: CreateSpace, May 2017, paperback, 304 pp.

Crafter's Passion • by Kris Schnee.

Seattle, WA: CreateSpace, March 2018, paperback, 247 pp.

Liberation Game • by Kris Schnee.

Seattle, WA: CreateSpace, May 2018, paperback, 307 pp.

The chapters in *Thousand Tales; How We Won the Game* are the years during which this takes place; from "2036: The Early Adopters" to "2040: Thousand Tales." Its blurb is helpful. "The mad AI Ludo is taking over the Earth … but she just wants everyone to have fun." But it's not that simple.

Paul Kostakis is a high-school graduate who wants to go to college. However, in this regimented 2036, all youths are required to serve a government-approved social service to qualify for admission to higher education. Paul is assigned to a Green Communities Youth Initiative work camp across the country in Arizona, a shelter for the homeless and unemployable. Its coordinator is a friendly-appearing sadist who obviously intends to fail Paul. When he stops a madman with a gun from killing anyone in the cafeteria, she records Paul's actions as "excessively violent." When he tries to study for his college's entrance exams, she wastes his time by ordering that he play an endless video game, supposedly to relax and socialize better.

Paul does so very reluctantly, but the Thousand Tales game turns out to be brand-new, controlled by an equally new Artificial Intelligence, Ludo. Ludo, appearing as a fantasy beautiful woman, intrigues Paul by tailoring an imaginary world to his specifications. "She" gradually reveals to him that she intends to follow her programming to help her players enjoy themselves, by immersing them in increasingly-complex fantasy worlds tailored to their desires; and she wants Paul to help recruit new players who need her aid. "In return for a few little favors, she's offering "brain uploading." She can fatally dice your brain, scan it, and recreate you in a virtual-reality heaven she controls. You can do anything in there: become a griffin, upgrade your mind, fall in love, or go mad" (back-cover blurb).

Ludo offers Paul the opportunity to become Horizon, a handsome, powerful griffin mated to Nocturne, a beautiful female griffin, in the fantasy world of his dreams. Ludo creates Nocturne, but the AI has given her an independent mind and personality—she's "real," not just another avatar of Ludo. Paul hesitates because he has plans for a human future, including a life with Linda Decatur, a slightly older MIT student whom he loves. "Bring her along!" says Ludo, creating an anthro otter-man, Typhoon's Eye, for Linda. Paul/Horizon and Nocturne, and Linda and Typhoon become best friends, exploring Ludo's world as a foursome. Horizon and Nocturne are griffins; Linda is a human pirate captain and Typhoon is her otter-man first mate.

But this is only a computer simulation, and Paul and Linda are temporary visitors. They hesitate to let Ludo dice their brains and become permanent residents of her world—dead as humans outside it. Nocturne urges Paul strongly to accept. She loves him, and the human world is a dangerous place with muggers and warmongering politicians and the privations of an overpopulated society running out of resources that may at any moment take him from her. Why not live in Ludo's increasingly powerful world where he will be always safe, as the AI surreptitiously links more computers together?

Paul is tempted, but what will happen to the real world if Ludo makes all humans in it her players? How permanent will it be if human governments, fearing for the future of humanity, dismantle the AI? But do some of the governments (or other groups that may really be powerful corporations or organized crime) truly want to protect humanity, or to take it over for themselves?

There are also parts of Ludo's world that are more than distasteful. Paul/Horizon finds that one of the humans that Ludo accepts as a player is a pederast who has Ludo creating cute young children for the pederast to sexually molest and worse. But as Ludo and the pederast (who "can't help his urges") point out, the little children are all the most simple computer constructs. The pederast isn't really hurting anyone, as he would be in the real world. He's happy; nobody is being hurt; he's removed from the real world where either he would hurt someone or he would be imprisoned as a drain on society, and Ludo has gained a new player. Everyone benefits—don't they? Paul can't fault their logic, but he can't help feeling nauseated for accepting it.

Ultimately, should Paul and/or Linda accept the AI's world or oppose it? Schnee presents compelling arguments both ways. The novel goes from philosophical debates to tense and often violent action, and the reader is kept guessing until the last moment.

Thousand Tales is science-fiction, not furry fantasy, but there are numerous furry characters within Ludo's fantasy worlds. At first these are obvious constructs. Later characters, as Ludo learns and becomes more complex, may be independent players like Paul who becomes a flying griffin.

Schnee's further *Thousand Tales* stories feature other humans who become players.

In *2040: Reconnection* it's an old man who becomes a young squirrel-girl. In *The Digital Coyote*, winner of the 2016 Cóyotl Award for Best Novel, it's a senator's aide with psychological problems who becomes the titular coyote-man. In *Learning to Fly*, a finalist for a 2017 Leo Literary Award, it's an elderly airplane pilot nearing mandatory retirement who becomes a Pegasus.

After that, the series features protagonists who do not become furries. *Crafter's Passion* is about Stan Cooper, an adolescent farmer who remains human while becoming skilled at wood- and metal-working. In *Liberation Game*, Robin MacAdam uses the game and Lumina, a deer-human centauroid robot, to create a new violence-free country in corrupt and war-torn Central America. Both novels contain furry incidental characters. On the whole, Schnee's *Thousand Tales* series is science-fiction that is also rewardingly imaginative anthropomorphic literature.

Three Bags Full: A Sheep Detective Story • by Leonie Swann. Translated by Anthea Bell.

London: Doubleday, June 2006, hardcover, 344 pp.

This unusual murder mystery, originally published in Germany (*Glennkill. Ein Schafskrimi*, Munich: Wilhelm Goldmann Verlag, August 2005), begins with a "Dramatis Oves" of the nineteen sheep who will solve the murder of their shepherd, George Glenn. "Miss Maple (3), the cleverest sheep in the flock, maybe the cleverest sheep in Glennkill, quite possibly the cleverest sheep in the whole world" (p. i), is the commander of these wooly detectives, and the one who patiently keeps their wooly wits concentrated on avenging their more-or-less beloved human companion.

The novel is told strictly from the sheep's point of view. The reader observes what they do when they do; although the viewpoint does sometimes shift from that of the whole flock to that of one or a group of the sheep who are investigating separate clues:

> There ensued a discussion of some length between Heather, Cloud, and Mopple the Whale. Mopple the Whale insisted that you judged a shepherd's merits by the quantity and quality of the fodder he provided, and in this respect there was nothing, nothing whatsoever, to be said against George Glenn. Finally they agreed that a good shepherd was one who never docked the lambs' tails; didn't keep a sheepdog; provided good fodder and plenty of it, particularly bread and sugar but healthy things too like green stuff, concentrated feed, and mangel-wurzels (for they were all very sensible sheep); and who clothed himself entirely in the products of his own flock, for instance an all-in-one suit made of spun sheep's wool, which would look really good, almost as if he were a sheep himself. Of course it was obvious to them all that no such perfect being was to be found anywhere in the world, but it was a nice idea all the same. They sighed a little, and were about to scatter, pleased to think that they had cleaned up all outstanding questions.
>
> So far, however, Miss Maple had taken no part in the discussion. Now she said, "Don't you want to know what he died of?"
>
> Sir Ritchfield looked at her in surprise. "He died of that spade. You wouldn't have survived it either, a heavy iron thing like that driven right through you. No wonder he's dead." Sir Ritchfield shuddered slightly.
>
> "And where did the spade come from?"
>
> "Someone stuck it in him." As far as Sir Ritchfield was concerned, that was the end of the matter, but Othello, the only black sheep in the flock, suddenly began taking an interest in the problem.
>
> "It can only have been a human who did it—or a very large monkey." Othello had spent his youth in Dublin Zoo and never missed an opportunity to mention it.

George's death, and the villagers' lack of interest in his sheep, enables them to wander freely and investigate. Who in the tiny Irish seacoast village of Glennkill could have wanted to kill old George? Abraham Rackham, the butcher? (The herbivorous sheep believe that a slaughterer of animals could be capable of any crime.) Bible-thumping Beth, the local do-gooder? Gabriel O'Rourke, a rival shepherd? Father Will, the parish priest who is weaker than many of his parishioners? The suspiciously-acting tourist in the blood-red dress? As the sheep eavesdrop on the humans, they learn that George was considered an unfriendly hermit, living alone in his mobile caravan with his sheep and seldom going into the village, and that the hostility (George sarcastically mocked the villagers' plans to turn Glennkill into a tourist center) cut both ways. Some believe that George could not have supported himself with such a small flock, and that he must have had another, secret source of income. The humans conveniently come up to George's field to look around, openly in daylight or sneakily after dark.

> At this moment Maude squeezed her way in under the dolmen with the others, and seconds later a beam of light swept past them. Three people followed it closely. The beam of light came to rest on George's caravan and swept up the walls. It was looking for somewhere to hide.
> […]
> "Now what?" asked Tom.
> "We need that grass," said Harry. "So we break the door down."
> "Are you crazy?" said Josh. "I'm not doing that. That's a crime, that is."
> "So disposing of evidence is legal, is it?" said Harry scornfully. "If they find the dope here it's all over. No Faerie Dolmen. No pony rides. No Celtic Cultural Center. No whiskey specialties. And you can stuff your seaside hotel!"
> "Maybe there isn't any dope," said Josh.
> "What else would be in there? How did old George keep his head above water all this time? With his few pathetic sheep? You must be jokin'! Did he ever want to sell up? Laughed in your face when you come along with your money, so he did. Here was this grand view just wasted on his sheep, and now he's dead at last, do we want Glennkill getting itself in the papers as a mecca for the drugs trade?"
> The sheep's knees were shaking with indignation.

The sheep are disconcerted to discover that Glennkill's humans are not the only ones who have been acting suspiciously. There are clues that someone in their own flock knows more than he or she is telling. Some surprises are learned by listening in on human conversations, such as that George's death may be related to an unsolved murder seven years earlier. Others are revealed by the sheep's natural instincts:

> "'The red woman isn't stupid either,' said Othello, almost a touch too proudly.
> "Oh no." Miss Maple nodded. "The red woman isn't a bit stupid."
> "I'd never have expected George to have a child," said Maude. "You did smell it, didn't you?" Several sheep had now joined the interesting conversation between Maple, Othello, and Maude. They nodded. The family scent. Sweat and skin and hair. Unmistakably George's daughter."

The final problem, once the sheep are sure they know who killed George, is how to bring the killer to justice? The village's main tourist attraction, the annual "Smartest Sheep in Glennkill" contest, provides the occasion.

Three Bags Full has gotten favorable reviews for its cleverness. A sequel, *Garou: Ein Schaf-Thriller*, was published in Germany in June 2010, but it has not yet been translated into English.

The Time He Desires • by Kyell Gold. Illustrated by Kamui.

Dallas, TX: FurPlanet Productions, December 2016, paperback, 113 pp.

Kyell Gold's novella *The Time He Desires* and novel *Love Match* have been written simultaneously, so neither one is a spinoff of the other. Aziz Alhazhari, the cheetah protagonist in *The Time He Desires*, is the father of Marquize Alhazhari, the protagonist's best friend in *Love Match*.

Both are set in Gold's anthropomorphic Forester University universe. Aziz is a 45-year-old Muslim from the nation of Madiyah who immigrated to the Union of the States with his wife Halifa and his young son Marquize two decades ago. He settled in Upper Devos (read: Brooklyn), bought a pawnshop that grows to a chain of four pawnshops, joined a mosque, became active in the community, and has been living more-or-less happily ever after.

Now he is confronted with a major cultural change combined with a midlife crisis. His son, now a teenager, has declared his homosexuality and walked out. He and his wife have been drifting apart; they are still friends but are no longer in love, and have developed separate interests. Aziz is interested in his pawnshops and his mosque—he goes there for evening prayers every day—while Halifa has gotten active in local charities.

Most importantly, and what brings the crisis to the present, is that the Vorvarts group, a huge developer, has been moving into the community. Vorvarts had previously bought two whole blocks for an Upper Devos Homeporium super-mall, "a six-story blue glass and chrome monster" that clashes with the old brownstone apartment buildings and small shops of the neighborhood. Vorvarts had to get approval from the Upper Devos Business Council, the local homeowners' association, which had been easy. Vorvarts had promised that the fancy Homeporium would bring lots of new shoppers and trade to the community.

The Time He Desires by Kyell Gold (FurPlanet Productions, December 2016). Gold's novella about Muslim attitudes toward homosexuality in America, with furry characters, was widely reviewed outside furry fandom, as well as being a finalist for the 2016 Cóyotl Award. Cover art by Kamui.

> But that had been five years ago, and as it happened, the people ... who'd been forced to find somewhere else to live when their buildings had been bought, they had been part of the neighborhood not easily replaced. The people who lived and shopped at the Homeporium generally stayed there, not venturing outside to quaint old Upper Devos, and when they did come into the pawnshop, distinctive in their clean, crisply cut clothes, they gawked about with the air of tourists visiting a historical monument. Aziz's business had fallen off; few of those people were hard up enough to have to pawn their possessions, or interested in buying someone else's memories.

Now Vorvarts wants to expand into the blocks where the remaining Business Council lives and has their shops. Vorvarts is offering a generous price, but the destruction of the neighborhood would mean the end of the community. Aziz wants to stay, and so does Tanska, a Siberian tigress who has a small bakery, but he feels that it's a losing battle.

> He looked back into her [Tanska's] eyes. "I want us to stay," he said. "But I can't see any way to make anyone else stay. We spent thousands of dollars researching the community laws to see if we had legal grounds to prevent it. Fighting it in court would take hundreds of thousands, more than you and I have, and if we did that it would destroy the community anyway; the rest of the Association would hate us for delaying their payments."

Aziz's best friend Doug, an elderly Prevost's squirrel who runs a bookshop, is ready to take Vorvart's money and retire to the sunny beaches of Coronado on the other coast of the States. Aziz's wife is also ready to sell out and move. She can find charities to become active in anywhere. "You know that the smart business decision is to sell. The money we would make by staying open in this location for another year or two, as people move out, would not come close to the price they've offered us." Their disagreement, although peaceful, brings their marriage to its end.

But this looming decision, while important, is not the major plot of *The Time He Desires*. A frantic red fox, Benjamin Tonnen, comes into Aziz's pawnshop looking for a video camera that his husband Gerald DeRoot, a cougar, pawned a year ago with their honeymoon film still in it. Aziz is polite, finds the camera, and sells it back to Tonnen. But this gets him thinking about homosexuality; the States' changing social attitudes towards it, Islam's teachings about it, how it took their son from them, and what Halifa really thinks about it (as opposed to just agreeing with her husband like a good Muslim wife). Aziz wonders why Tonnen's cougar husband sold the video and their honeymoon footage if their gay marriage is still secure, so he finds DeRoot and hesitantly asks him. What he learns from Gerald, and how he and Gerald—a homosexual, who is supposed to be shunned by Muslims (but Muslims are also supposed to abstain from alcohol, and most Muslims, especially those in the States, don't worry about that restriction)—come to feel about each other, helps Aziz to make his decision about how to react to the changing community.

The Time He Desires is another high-quality story by Kyell Gold. It differs from his others by looking at homosexuality from a Muslim rather than a Christian attitude. It was a finalist for the 2016 Cóyotl Award in the Best Novella category. There is an "About This Book and Islam" afterword for those who want to learn more.

To Journey in the Year of the Tiger • by H. Leighton Dickson.

Seattle, WA: CreateSpace, September 2012, paperback, 344 pp.

To Walk in the Way of Lions • by H. Leighton Dickson.

Seattle, WA: CreateSpace, October 2012 paperback, 348 pp.

Songs in the Year of the Cat • by H. Leighton Dickson.

Seattle, WA: CreateSpace, July 2013, paperback, 313 pp.

Swallowtail & Sword: The Scholar's Book of Story and Song • by H. Leighton Dickson.

Seattle, WA: CreateSpace, April 2015, paperback, 255 pp.

Snow in the Year of the Dragon • by H. Leighton Dickson.

Seattle, WA: CreateSpace, May 2018, paperback, 336 pp.

> It was hard to believe that a man could see twenty-three winters before he began to live. It is harder even to believe that his life began all at once, on one night, with the occurring of three obscure and apparently random things; the death of a bird, the flash of golden eyes and the first of One Hundred Steps. But for Kirin Wynegarde-Grey, it did happen, just this way. His life began, as all great and terrible things do, in the Year of the Tiger.

It is the reader's option whether to take Dickson's *The Rise of the Upper Kingdom* series as science-fiction, set about 5,000 years in the future, or as high fantasy. "This is a powerful, post-apocalyptic story of lions and tigers, wolves and dragons, embracing and blending the cultures of Dynastic China, Ancient India and Feudal Japan. Half feline, half human, this genetically altered world has evolved in the wake of the fall of human civilization" (blurb). Kirin Wynegarde-Grey is a genetic lion-man, and there are plenty of other half-feline men and women—leopards, tigers, ocelots, cheetahs, jaguars, lynx—in these five books to please the reader.

> His boots echoed as he trotted down a winding staircase made of polished teak, raising his tail slightly so that the tuft would not sweep the wooden steps. They had servants for that sort of thing and he despised getting dirty, even if it was only his tail. Soon, he was in the Hall of Warriors.

Kirin is Captain of the Empress' personal guard. While the rest of the great Palace is preparing to mark the turning of the Year of the Ox into the Year of the Tiger, he is assigned to leave on a long mission. The Upper Kingdom is guided by a Council of Seven, revered Seers whose visions have infallibly led the Empire in wisdom and peace for centuries. Now someone is killing the Seers by unknown means:

> "You four," bids the Empress, "with the addition of Kerris Wynegarde-Grey, will journey to *Sha'Hadin*, to discover who or what is killing my Seers. You will use any, and all, means at your disposal, all of your venerable skills to see that it is stopped, and stopped soon. Without the Gifts of Farsight and Vision, *Pol'Lhasa, DharamShallah*, and all of the Upper Kingdom will be vulnerable, and once vulnerable, shall surely fall."

The four are Kirin Wynegarde-Grey (lion), the Captain of her guard; his adjutant Major Ursa Laenskaya (female, snow leopard), an obsessed militant; Fallon Waterford (tigress), the Empire's Scholar, very knowledgeable but very young and naïve; and Sherah al Shiva (cheetah), the Empire's Alchemist, an older *femme fatale* of complex personality, dubious reliability, and an unguessable personal agenda. Kerris, Kirin's twin but silver-grey where Kirin is golden, is the Empire's Geomancer; a talented Geomancer, for all that he seems to be an unreliable drunken ladies' man.

Their goal is *Sha'Hadin*, the mountainous monastery that is the home of the Council of Seven. The party meets high suspense before it even reaches *Sha'Hadin*:

> *This* was *the perfect place for an ambush*, Kerris agreed silently. The mountain rose up steeply on one side, and the narrow ledge that had been their trail now flattened out, in a wide, almost level plateau. Below them, the gradient was less sharp, but deadly still, for to start a fall would surely see it to its

stony end. Giant rocks dotted this section of trail like spikes on the back of a sleeping dragon. The mountains were full of such stories, of creatures much larger than cats, and to his credit Kerris believed them. He had seen too much not to.

He scanned those giant stones with narrowed eyes.

He heard the moan of hollow wind, the drum of Imperial hooves fading away.

He studied the elderly man, who suddenly seemed not nearly so desperate for help, nor nearly as elderly, as he too watched the trio attempting to pick their way around the cart and get to wider ground.

[…]

As if reading those very thoughts, the jaguar turned back, fixing the grey lion with a glare that could freeze his blood. There was a flash and something metallic slid out from a sleeve.

To quote the blurb from *To Walk in the Way of Lions*, it

picks up where "Journey" leaves off, in the harsh deserts of Khanistan. The team is running under a very set of different dynamics than before, for not only will they be forced to confront enemies tracking from the North and a hostile force from the Palace following from the South, but they must face their own demons that are plaguing them from within. It's man against man, cat against cat, Seer against Alchemist,… And soon, against all reason, they take the first steps beyond the Empire's borders into the realm of the Ancestors, of carnivorous horses, of Dogs, Bear and Rats, and Kirin Wynegarde-Grey will find out what it means to follow the code of Bushido to the gates of death and beyond…

These two volumes—really a single novel—are the first in Dickson's *The Rise of the Upper Kingdom* series. *Songs in the Year of the Cat* continues the characters' stories; *Swallowtail & Sword* is an "interlude" of eight stories plus poems featuring each character before they begin their journey; and *Snow in the Year of the Dragon* continues the series.

Dickson's melodrama is sometimes over-the-top. She makes the adolescent Fallon Waterford too brainless at the beginning, to allow for her character development into a more realistic adult through the course of the adventure; and Fallon's slangy babble is too far removed from the formal speech of the other characters to be convincing. But there is a wonder and a glory, and many surprises, that rises above all the little flaws in her epic saga. This is an excellent example of anthropomorphic literature.

Transformations: A Forest Tales Story • by Bernard Doove. Illustrated by Stephie Stone [and others].

Milpitas, CA: Fauxpaw Publications, July 2005, plastic comb bound, 75 pp.

Life's Dream: The Journal of Pandora and Karl • by Bernard Doove. Illustrated by Kacey Miyagami and others.

Seattle, WA: CreateSpace, December 2007, paperback, 250 pp.

More Terrible Than Chains: A.K.A. Leeana's Story • by Bernard Doove. Illustrated.

Seattle, WA: CreateSpace, November 2008, paperback, 360 pp.

Forest Tales: A Chakat Family Journal • by Bernard Doove. Illustrated.

Seattle, WA: CreateSpace, May 2010, paperback, 466 pp.

Other Trails Taken: A Chakat Family Journal, Book II • by Bernard Doove. Illustrated.

Seattle, WA: CreateSpace, May 2011, paperback, 499 pp.

Tales from the Chakat Universe • by Bernard Doove. Illustrated.

Seattle, WA: CreateSpace, May 2012, paperback, 321 pp.

Flight of the Star Phoenix • by Bernard Doove. Illustrated.

Seattle, WA: CreateSpace, November 2012, paperback, 388 pp.

Bernard Doove created his sf series about chakats, bioengineered hermaphroditic centauroid felines in a 24th Century interstellar society, for his Chakat's Den website in the 1990s. He and numerous guest writers have written over a hundred stories set in the Chakat Universe. Most of these were first published on the Internet, and in the long out-of-print *Fur Plus* fanzine. *Transformations,* one of the longest and most self-contained stories, was the first to be published as a stand-alone book. The first edition has been replaced with a more conventional CreateSpace edition today.

A matter transporter accident (actually sabotage; read the story for details) destroys the transporter while a human, Dale Perkins, is being beamed down to Chakona, the chakats' main planet. His body pattern is lost, and the only way to save his mind/identity is to embody it in a duplicate of the previous lifeform beamed down, whose body pattern is still in the transporter. This is Star Corps technician Chakat Goldfur, returning to her homeworld. Forestwalker, Goldfur's sibling, arrives at the spaceport to find two Goldfurs waiting, physically identical but one inhabited by the mind of a very confused human male. The chakats agree to take care of Dale at their home while the technicians experiment to get his human body out of the transmitter.

Compared to most science fiction, there is little action or drama in *Transformations*. It is designed as a "slice-of-life" introduction to the physiology and culture of the chakats by throwing an outsider into their midst, in the most intimate way possible. It is "bad" writing in that the author and/or characters regularly start scenes by describing their background in excessive detail. However, for a story that is meant to be an introduction to the Chakat Universe, this may be forgivable; and it does demonstrate the depth of the background that the writers have created.

The second paragraph begins, "I had come here to pick up Goldfur from the spaceport. Hir foxtaur lifemate, Garrek, was away at his home village and I had volunteered to drive hir back and forth. Shi was currently working on the Corps' geosynchronous space station and was beaming there and back from the transporter facilities at the spaceport. Shi had taken on the long overdue work of major maintenance and upgrades because…" (etc., at considerably more length). When the chakat sisters are ready to drive Dale home from the spaceport, "Dale seemed fascinated by the taur-adapted vehicle. These Personal Transport Vehicles had only a single large door on either side, as well as a hatchback. These allowed us to easily step inside and settle ourselves on the moulded couches in front and beside the doors. Swing-away backrests…" again etc. The explanation of how the matter transporter works—"After the creation of the body pattern, a matrix of the subject's mind is made, preserving their personality and experiences, and is transmitted to the destination. Only then…"—goes on and on. The descriptions work much better, fortunately, once they are put into dialogue form after the characters arrive at the siblings' home, and Forestwalker, Goldfur, and Dale start talking to each other.

Doove, with the help of his guest writers, has developed an intriguing non-human, quadrupedal civilization. The above spelling of "hir," which occurs in the first paragraph, is a good example. Since chakats are hermaphroditic, both male and female, human gender pronouns such as "him" and "her" do not apply to them. Dale (and the reader) must get used to "hir," "shi," "shir" and other terms in a gender-neutral vocabulary. Dale is bombarded with culture-shock situations from both outside and inside his new body. These including learning to walk on four legs instead of two; dealing with a body with both male and female equipment and emotions (Goldfur has been breast-feeding babies, so Dale also has lactating breasts); going about in a society without human modesty taboos (nobody has designed practical pants for a quadrupedal body yet, so chakats are nude below the waist with their genitalia exposed); and living in extended, free-loving families.

The chakats' pre–*Transformations* history goes back to the Gene Wars of the mid–21st Century, and a spate of bioengineering in the 22nd Century. In addition to the centauroid felines that are Chakona's main population, Dale meets more immigrant wolftaurs, foxtaurs, and skunktaurs, besides lots of anthropomorphized two-legged wolves and foxes, than other humans. Thus, it is unsurprising that some critics of the series have accused Doove of being overly fixated on intelligent furry mammals in both two-legged and four-legged forms. Another criticism is that some writers have concentrated on the more sexual aspects of this society in their stories. Doove has downplayed the sexuality in *Transformations* and tried to keep what there is in good taste to make it an introduction suitable for as many readers as possible.

There are twenty-two illustrations in *Transformations* by twelve artists. The front cover, by Stephanie "Cybercat" Stone, won the 2005 Ursa Major Award in the Best Anthropomorphic Published Illustration category.

Over the next seven years, Doove reprinted his own serialized chakat stories rewritten into six more CreateSpace novels, most with the original online illustrations by many artists. They feature the chakats, foxtaurs, other 'taurs, regular morphs, humans, and every species in Doove's Chakat Universe. They expand out from the planet Chakona throughout Doove's 24th-century galaxy. *Life's Dream* won the 2007 Ursa Major Award in the Best Anthropomorphic Novel category. Doove's seven chakat fixup novels are fine examples of furry sf fiction.

Transmutation NOW! • by Phil Geusz.

Ridgecrest, CA: The Raccoon's Bookshelf, August 2007, paperback, 344 pp.

Transmutation NOW! is one of the earliest anthro specialty-press novels. Phil Geusz wrote the original draft during 1997–8. It was first published electronically by Starfire Publishing around 2001 and then by Infinite Imagination about a year later, each time as a downloadable electronic book with minor revisions. The last eBook edition went out of print in 2005. This paperback from The Raccoon's Bookshelf, which debuted at Mephit Furmeet 2007, is its first "hard" edition with more touch-ups. It is an example of one of the first furry specialty publishers that disappeared almost immediately (the novel has been reprinted), and of a futuristic plot that has been outdated by actual technology, but is still excellent reading.

Unlike most anthro novels which feature a large society of anthropomorphic animal-people, *Transmutation NOW!* is about (at first) only two animal-people in the human world. When transmutation becomes possible (but fantastically expensive), a movie studio wants to turn aging actor Jack Strafford into a genuine humanoid white rabbit for a megaspectacular remake of *Alice in Wonderland*. Jack agrees because the studio promises to regress his human body to its mid-twenties prime when he is restored at the end of the production. Unfortunately, he has barely begun the months-long transmutation process when terrorists nuke Tokyo, and a couple of brief Short Wars ruin the American economy. When revived, Jack finds that his movie studio is bankrupt and out of business, and that, due to lack of funding, the scientists at Trans-Tech Genetics had to leave him much more lapine than had been planned:

> It took a terribly long time to wean me off of all the drugs, as my new body initiated a rabbit's panic reaction whenever I became frightened. A lot of things frightened me at first, like fire, smoke, predator scent and loud noises. Eventually I developed some control over the reflex, but the process took time and I never really mastered it entirely. All rabbits are naturally of a rather high-strung nature compared to normal humans, and it seemed that I was to be no exception. Learning to walk again was a major psychological step forward for me, as well. Until this art was re-mastered, I had been forced to hop about my suite on all fours. It took days of physical therapy to get me back upright. Even more time passed while I became accustomed to having thumbless forepaws. My movie role required carrying and manipulating things, but Dr. Franken told me not to worry, that my part had been rewritten. Hands had simply gotten too expensive, he explained. I was "way over budget."

Strafford finds that the rabbit's instinctual panic reaction to anything frightening (such as large dogs) is now hardwired into his brain, which makes living in normal human society impossible. Dr. Jacob Franken teams him up with Rupert, a scientist who turned chimpanzee to study chimps in the wild and could not be turned back after Trans-Tech shuts down. The two move to an isolated house built to their needs near a small Alabama town of sympathetic people, where they expect to live for the rest of their lives.

But the world will not let them withdraw. First they are attacked by a cult, the Holy Congregation, Sword and Army of the Lord, that brands them AN ABOMINATION BEFORE GOD. Jack and Rupert escape in a commando battle—and add another transmutee whom they rescue from the cult, Jocko, a capuchin monkey, to their household—but the publicity, plus the expenses of adding anti-terrorist security to their hideaway, forces Jack back into show business. He quickly becomes very popular making celebrity endorsements:

> I was wearing one of my new hats, a shared invention of Mary Allen (my groomer/makeup specialist) and I. It was very similar to a baseball cap made of shiny soft satin. The headgear was designed to be worn backwards, and had two large ear holes cut in the top that allowed my aural appendages free play. On what should have been the front, over the bill, was a stylized carrot on a green background. Above the carrot was printed, 'This Rabbit Powered By Fresh Vegetables." Below was the logo of the North American Produce Grower's Association. Every department store in the country was selling a commercial version with fake adjustable ears and it seemed that they simply couldn't get enough of the things.

Then Jack is attacked by a pair of transmutated 35-foot-long intelligent poisonous snakes. This raises the threats to an unknown new level:

> My friend had spoken very frankly to me, even more so than to Jocko and Rupert, about the consternation that the snakes were causing in Washington. In fact he spoke perhaps even more freely than he really should have, but he understood my personal interest in the filthy things. The more that was learned about them, the more new questions were raised.

[...]
Also, why was someone with such incredible resources behind them interested in small potatoes like Jocko, Rupert and me? We were of no conceivable threat to an organization possessed of such massive power. For that matter, what was the role of the Congregation, Sword and Army of the Lord in all of this? There was no doubt that they had been behind the first attack on the Island, even if we couldn't prove it in a court of law. But how could they get their hands on the kind of technology that it took to make the second attempt? Things weren't fitting together at all.

Transmutation NOW! alternates between scenes of Jack's growing prominence as America's most beloved bunny rabbit—magazine and TV stardom, and naturally he is featured in a live-action Bugs Bunny movie—and his escapes from increasingly impossible-to-survive deathtraps by his known and unknown enemies, which soon take on international political dimensions. Then things get really metaphysical…

The action sequences are well-plotted and very suspenseful, and Jack's successes as an incredibly popular rabbit-man in a human world will vicariously satisfy 'morph-fan readers.

Transmutation NOW! is also an example of how a well-written novel can remain fine reading despite becoming technologically outdated. If a movie studio today wants to make a live-action *Alice in Wonderland*—or *The Lion, the Witch, and the Wardrobe*, or any other film featuring seemingly live animal people (which they have by now)—it can easily do so via computer graphic imagery. The medical transmutation of humans for this purpose has become unnecessary.

Trick or Treat • edited by Ianus J. Wolf.

Las Vegas, NV: Rabbit Valley, September 2013, paperback, 313 pp.

Trick or Treat, Volume 2: Historical Halloween • edited by Ianus J. Wolf.

Las Vegas, NV: Rabbit Valley Books, October 2014, paperback, 373 pp.

Rabbit Valley's Halloween 2013 theme anthology offers "something for the adults to enjoy." It presents eleven new stories; five scary horror "tricks" and six "delectable romantic and erotic" "treats."

Ianus J. Wolf says in his Introduction that this is the first of Rabbit Valley's planned annual Halloween anthologies, to mix furry horror and adult erotica, so there will be more to come for those who like it. "Halloween just isn't Halloween without both the scary and the sweet."

The two sections are each introduced by the two EC Comics–style 'horror hosts" shown on the cover, Trick the wolf and Treat the cat. The "tricks" all come first, to leave you with an erotic pleasant taste. They are "Hellhound" by Renee Carter Hall, "Son of the Blood Moon" by Bill "Hafoc" Rogers, "Slough" by Ray "Stormcatcher" Curtone, "Unrealty" by Rechan, and "Wild Night" by Tarl "Voice" Hoch.

All five are well-written. The blurb describes these as "fun horror stories," and their mood is mostly eerie, not really scary. Except for "Hellhound," which was a finalist for the 2013 Cóyotl Award for Best Short Story. A confused puppy in a pound is adopted as a pet dog by Laura, who has just separated from an abusive husband. As the puppy grows, he remembers that he is really a Hellhound, banished by his sadistic supernatural Master to be reborn as a natural dog, to bond with his loving human owner, and then to savagely tear that human apart when the Master orders it. Will Chance, the dog, bond so thoroughly with Laura that he can resist the power of the Master?

"Slough" is unique, a furry story featuring Carter, a snakeman who morphs into a different kind of snake every time he sheds his skin. Black racer, water moccasin, garden snake, rattlesnake—he can never know whether he will be a harmless variety or a poisonous snake with a really bad temper next. Lexine, his mink girlfriend, tries to help him stabilize into a safe snake permanently. The Halloween connection seems slight, but it is definitely supernatural, and has a successful surprise ending for the reader.

"Unrealty" is funny-animal furry, but it does feature a truly eerie setting. Jake Blake is a recently-divorced realtor (hence the pun in the title) who has moved (his ex-wife got their house) into the only-completed show-model house in his new housing subdivision under construction. On a dark Halloween night, he is taking his six-year-old daughter out trick-or-treating when he realizes that he has forgotten his cell phone back home. So he makes a side trip there to get it, and is dumbfounded to find all of the other half-built homes under construction are suddenly finished and wired for electricity, with— WHAT?—living in them, all ready for Halloween night. There is no real reason (other than that this is a furry anthology) for Jake and his daughter to be anthropomorphic otters rather than humans, and while "Unrealty" avoids the stereotypical built-upon-an-abandoned-graveyard explanation, it doesn't give ANY explanation! The unfinished housing subdivision is just suddenly finished and full of spooks.

"Treats" presents six stories: "The Witch Doctor" by Huskyteer, "The Pharaoh's Throne" by NightEyes DaySpring, "The Things We Do for Love" by Naomi Bellina, "Phobophilia" by White Yoté, "The Magic of Desire" by Roland Jovaik, and "Once a Year" by Ianus J. Wolf.

These are all funny-animal stories where the characters are just animal-headed humans. There are two winners here; "The Witch Doctor" and "Phobophilia." The first is the sweetest story in the anthology, and I mean that in a good way. Lots of tender loving and no sex. Marty Doubleclaw (Shiba Inu dog) is a divorced young father whose only interest is in making sure that his young son Luke enjoys himself when it's his turn to take custody of the boy. Marty has a slight accident on Halloween that sends him and Luke to the hospital, and a sympathetic young wolf nurse persuades them to spend the evening serving in the children's ward's Halloween party. Marty learns to stop holding himself in and get on with life to be a proper father for Luke, and for his own good.

"Phobophilia" is the most imaginative story here. It is definitely not set on human-inhabited Earth, but on another planet of anthropomorphized animals, in this story mostly wolves. The main characters are an ethereal galactic being that feeds on fear, and a teenage wolf superhero fan. White Yoté has some clever names for his furry world's comic book characters: Hugh Mann, the Justice Pack, El Super Lobo, Lead Dog, Malamute Marvel, Poison Dapple (a pony), and FabulOso ("a gigantic brown bear in a luchador costume"). The action is all M/M erotica, but the setting is convincingly a furry world even if it is really just Earth with funny animals.

The other four stories are mostly just stories about adult funny animals having lots of graphic sex at mixed-species all-adult Halloween parties.

Rabbit Valley Books only produced two annual Halloween anthologies, but the first was a finalist for the 2013 Cóyotl Award in the Best Anthology category. Both are good examples of furry publishers' theme anthologies featuring furry fandom's usual authors.

The Ursa Major Awards Anthology: A Tenth Anniversary Celebration
• edited by Fred Patten. Illustrated.

Dallas, TX: FurPlanet Productions, June 2012, paperback, 349 pp.

The Ursa Major Awards Anthology contains eight of the ten award-winning stories in the award's Best Anthropomorphic Short Fiction category from 2001 to 2010. It omits the 2008 winner, "In Between" by Kyell Gold, and the 2010 winner, "Bridges" by Gold, both of which are R-rated stories. In their place it includes three of the finalists from those ten years.

The eleven stories are "Beneath the Crystal Sea" by Brock Hoagland (2001 winner), "Familiars" by Michael H. Payne (2002 winner), "In the Line of Duty" by M.C.A. Hogarth (2003 winner), "Felicia and the Tailcutter's Curse" by Charles P.A. Melville (2004 winner), "In His Own Country" by Kristin Fontaine (2005 winner), "Jacks to Open" by Kyell Gold (2006 winner), "Don't Blink" by Kyell Gold (2007 winner), "Six" by Samuel C. Conway (2002 finalist), "Drifting" by Kyell Gold (2009 winner), "Ailoura" by Paul DiFilippo (2002 finalist), and "St. Ailbe's Hall" by Naomi Kritzer (2004 finalist). In addition, the five-page Introduction gives the complete history of the Ursa Major Awards to 2012.

The stories include sword-and-sorcery, fantasy, space opera, gambling, superheroes, science-fiction, slice-of-life, and religion. They are all high-quality representatives of those themes. *The Ursa Major Awards Anthology* was a finalist for the 2012 Ursa Major Award in the Best Anthropomorphic Other Literary Work category.

"Beneath the Crystal Sea": Perissa (leopardess bravo), Captan Connal (fox), and Yoran (otter seaman) are jumping off Connal's ship after a sunken treasure:

> She [Perissa] quickly sank the fifty or so feet, coming to rest on the tower's flat roof where Connal and Yoran awaited. The infamous rogue grinned at her, apparently breathing with ease, the otter grimly holding his breath. She wanted none of that. Should the spell be worthless, she wanted as much time as she could manage to get the weights off. She took a slight, cautious inhalation. There was no sudden, strangling sensation followed by a surge of panic. Connal's grin grew even wider. She breathed out, then in, deeply. There was a feeling of heaviness in her chest, but other than that it was identical to air. After that she ignored the medium and breathed normally.

"Familiars": Cluny, a squirrel who wants to learn magic, finds herself bound as the familiar of Crocker, an inept novice sorcerer:

> "Oh, come on." She glared up at him. "You do healings and make light and work doubling magic, so don't tell me—"
>
> "Sure, small stuff." He waved an arm, drops spattering Cluny's fur. "But I can't even evoke a chapter one fireball, and with finals next week…" He sighed, his chubby face lost in the evening shadows coming through the dorm room curtains. "The magisters are gonna kick me outta Huxley for sure. You'd better request a transfer to another novice."
>
> Stomach tightening, Cluny turned away. "I have. Every week all semester."

"In the Line of Duty": Alysha Forrest, a 25th-century cat-human woman, is a junior officer in the United Alliance Vessel *Scattersky*. They get a distress call:

> For once, cheerful Captain Maurberry wasn't laughing. She couldn't blame him.
>
> "This is where the distress call led us."
>
> "We don't appear to have much time, sir."
>
> The Tam-illee man rubbed his chin, his much larger brown ears straining forward. He didn't look as much like a fox as Alysha looked like a cat, but they shared their humanoid faces and ancestry in common. "No. They were planning to use the giant to aerobrake, but their navigation computer malfunctioned and they don't have the power to get off their current course."

"Jacks to Open": In a world superficially our own but furry, the Persian is a Las Vegas casino designed for a canid clientele:

> There was no haze of smoke in the Persian, even by the bar where Sean was sitting. As far as he could see and smell, the patrons of the Persian were entirely canid: wolves, coyotes, foxes, dingos, and dholes. No other red wolves, but that was okay. He was used to being mistaken for a coyote, and used to being the only red wolf in the room. It was illegal, of course, to restrict entry based on species, and the Persian did no such thing.... There are no shortages of casinos in Las Vegas, and if one doesn't exactly suit, then it's easy enough to go elsewhere and leave the Persian to the canids.

"St. Ailbe's Hall": Jasper, an enhanced dog (Siberian husky), wants to be baptized into the Roman Catholic church. Father Andrew must decide what to do about it:

> "'I didn't know that they were allowed in churches,'" one of the men said as Lisa and Jasper disappeared around the corner. He was looking at Father Andrew.
> Father Andrew had been staring after Lisa and Jasper, but now he turned back. "I don't believe there's a rule against it," he said, and ducked his head to shake hands with a child.
> [...]
> Leo—"This is really becoming the controversy du jour, amigo. Two phone calls so far; it'll be ringing off the wall once everyone's had lunch and a chance to think things over. Everyone seems to want a 'No Dogs Allowed' sign on the door. So far I've just been noncommittal and as soothing as possible, but it's clear I' going to have to make some sort of decision here. What do you think?"

The Ursa Major Awards Anthology: A Tenth Anniversary Celebration is a sampler of the best in anthropomorphic literature.

Volle • by Kyell Gold. Illustrated by Sara Palmer.

St. Paul, MN: Sofawolf Press, January 2005, paperback, 325 pp.

Top: The Ursa Major Awards Anthology: A Tenth Anniversary Celebration **edited by Fred Patten (Fur-Planet Productions, June 2012). An anthology of the Ursa Major Award winners in the Best Short Fiction category from 2001 to 2010. Cover art by Blotch (Tess Garman and Teagan Gavet).** *Bottom: Volle* **by Kyell Gold (Sofawolf Press, January 2005). Winner of the first Ursa Major Award for Best Novel by a book from a furry specialty press, and the first of Gold's popular** *Argaea* **series. Cover art by Sara Palmer, itself a finalist for the 2005 Ursa Major Award for Best Published Illustration.**

Pendant of Fortune • by Kyell Gold. Illustrated by Sara Palmer.
St. Paul, MN: Sofawolf Press, January 2006, paperback, 314 pp.

The Prisoner's Release and Other Stories • by Kyell Gold. Illustrated by Vince Suzukawa, Taurin Fox, Adam Wan, and Arthur Husky.
St. Paul, MN: Sofawolf Press, January 2007, paperback, 299 pp.

Shadow of the Father • by Kyell Gold. Illustrated by Sara Palmer.
St. Paul, MN: Sofawolf Press, January 2010, paperback, 322 pp.

Weasel Presents: Tales from Argaea • by Kyell Gold.
Dallas, TX: FurPlanet Productions, June 2011, paperback, 169 pp.

Kyell Gold explicitly describes *Volle*, the first novel in his *Argaea* series, in his Author's Note as "anthropomorphic gay erotica." It, *Pendant of Fortune*, and *The Prisoner's Release and Other Stories* were also arguably the best anthropomorphic novels yet written at the time. The writing is of high quality; literary yet naturalistic, never becoming esoteric or pedantic. The setting is a well-thought-out, detailed anthropomorphic civilization in which species characteristics such as scenting are major plot elements. The homoerotic subplot in *Volle* (which ranges from lyrical to unpleasantly brutal) becomes the key to the murder mystery in *Pendant of Fortune*, where its anthropomorphic nature is especially important. Readers must decide for themselves whether the very strong homoerotic theme is to their tastes; but these novels are too well-written to be simply ignored.

Volle (rhymes with "wall") is a young red fox in a multispecies early 19th-century civilization dominated by the neighboring unfriendly kingdoms of Ferrenis and Tephos. Born on the border but raised in Ferrenis, he is trained as a spy due to his intelligence and aptitude, despite doubts caused by his casual attitude toward authority and his blatant homosexual nature. When Intelligence picks up rumors of a plot against Ferrenis, Volle is reluctantly sent into Tephos as the only spy capable of passing as the lost heir of a long-dead red fox nobleman, which (it is hoped) will gain him entry to its royal palace and enable him to socialize among its top ministers.

Here are some examples of Gold's detailed descriptions. Volle and fellow spies Reese (hare) and Seir (mouse) are on their way to Tephos' capital city, Divalia:

> As they emerged from the woods late in the third day, they saw the land rise up ahead of them, and got their first view of the land of Tephos. The mountains rolled gently across the landscape, lower, softer, and greener than the Red Mountains of Ferrenis. This was the northern edge of the range; to their left, the mountains stretched away southward. To the north, they subsided into rolling hills and then flatter farmland.
>
> The open area the carriage was now entering sloped down to a river valley across a grassy plain. The river wound in tight curves through the plain, but to the north, where it fed the farmland, it widened and ran straighter. Volle studied the river with indifference. He could see a building where the road met the river, and supposed that would be the inn where they were staying, and the border post into Tephos.
>
> "The Otrine," Seir said, leaning past him to look at the river.
>
> "I know. And those are the Ancient Hundred." He indicated the mountains with his muzzle. "How closely guarded is the border?"
>
> "Here? Not much. We're still going to use the disguise for you, though."

A detail from Volle's first royal banquet at the palace in Divalia:

> There were, by his quick count, about a hundred place settings at the table. They were filling in rapidly, as each guest entered, paid his or her respects to the royal couple, and were seated. He looked curiously to see whether the herbivores had their own section. At the Academy, they'd been seated at a separate table, because the smell of meat made some of them ill. Here, he noticed deer and goats sitting beside bobcats and wolves. Either it didn't bother the nobles here, or they had gotten used to it.

Volle later prepares for a private dinner party:

> After the brushing, Welcis [Volle's personal attendant, a skunk] brought out a scented powder, more expensive than the common powder used in the baths, and brushed Volle lightly with it. It smelled of lavender, but the scent was so light that even Volle's sensitive nose had trouble detecting it further than a few inches away. The powder absorbed some of the moisture from his fur and neutralized most of the strong smell it gave off. It was considered impolite to conceal your scent, but foxes, mustelids, and other strong-smelling animals often muted theirs at formal occasions, out of consideration for others.

Gardens, churches, inns, and other establishments are all described in great depth, with frequent comments on the richness (and importance) of the scents as well as the sights to the animal populace. The first half of *Volle*, describing Volle's settling into the social life of Tephos' nobility, has the lush indolence of a furry Regency romance. The second half swings over into politics and espionage. Volle makes a mistake with shockingly fatal consequences to his friends. While he tries to redeem himself, a personal enemy accuses him of treason at the Tephosian court, threatening both his mission and his life.

Pendant of Fortune is a murder mystery set six years later. It, *Volle*, and *The Prisoner's Release* are closely connected. *Shadow of the Father* takes place a generation later and features Volle's teenage son, Yilon. *Weasel Presents* is a collection of five Argaean short stories, most featuring Volle's gay weasel best friend, Lord Helfer.

Volle, *Pendant of Fortune*, and *Shadow of the Father* were the winners of the 2005, 2006, and 2010 Ursa Major Awards for Best Anthropomorphic Novel of the year. The awards are deserved, but readers should not be misled by this G-rated review into forgetting that these are both adult-only graphically homoerotic novels.

Waiting for Gertrude: A Graveyard Gothic • by Bill Richardson. Illustrated by Bill Pechet.

Vancouver, BC: Canada, Douglas & McIntyre, October 2001, hardcover, 184 pp.

If a list is ever compiled of The Ten Weirdest Furry Novels, *Waiting for Gertrude* is sure to place high on it; a literary erotic fantasy about the high-society social posturing among some of the last two centuries' most famous writers, composers and actors, reincarnated as the lusty tomcats and queens who prowl through Paris' tourist-attraction Père-Lachaise Cemetery.

Père-Lachaise was created in 1804 at the start of the French Empire, reportedly because Napoleon wanted Paris to have a prestigious burial place comparable to London's Westminster Abbey. It was inaugurated by the removal there of the remains of the poet La Fontaine and playwright Molière. Many of the celebrities of the past two-plus centuries who have lived and died in Paris are interred there, including such composers as Chopin, Rossini, Bizet, Poulenc and Dukas; such writers as Balzac, Daudet, Proust and Oscar Wilde; such artists as Delacroix, Modigliani, Corot, Seurat and Daumier; and such performers as actress Sarah Bernhardt, dancer Isadora Duncan, and singers Edith Piaf and Jim Morrison. (There are also scientists, financiers, politicians, military heroes, and filmmakers among others, but they do not appear in this novel. Parisian tourist-information websites provide more complete information.) Like Los Angeles' Forest Lawn Memorial Park, it is a spacious cemetery where hundreds of tourists come daily to visit the final resting places of the famous, or more likely to gawk at the more imposing memorials that their families or admirers have placed there. Père-Lachaise has a particularly high concentration of 19th-century marble cenotaphs and mini-mausoleums in exaggerated florid bad taste.

In recent decades, Père-Lachaise has also become notoriously infested by feral cats, who have made themselves so much at home among the various tombs that they stare haughtily at the tourists as though they are intruders. The cemetery is closed to the public at night, but anyone standing outside after dark can tell by the caterwauling all night long that when the humans are away, the cats lead an active social life.

Canadian popular author and radio host Bill Richardson's postulate is that the cemetery's cats are actually the reincarnations of the humans buried there. They have updated their talents to create a modern society that blends their human intellects with their new feline instincts. As the leaders of literature and art of their day, the most famous also strive to set the styles among the upper classes of the cats—in a very catty manner, of course. The singers put each other down in posturing to become the premier *prima donna* with feline vocal chords.

> Q: Madame Callas, what was your reaction when you discovered that you had been reborn as a cat?
> A: Initially, surprise, of course.... However, astonishment soon gives way to willing acquiescence. And why would it not? If there's one thing one learns from a life in the opera, it's that destiny will not be denied.... You merely accede to the fact that this life, like any other, is nothing more or less than a costume party: un ballo in maschera, as Verdi would have it. Did you ever see my Amalia, by the way? I can recommend my 1957 La Scala performance, Gianandrea Gavazzeni conducting.

Gioacchino Rossini continues to relax "in retirement" (while implying that he could out-compose anyone else if he felt like it), while others busily adapt their former works for cats. For instance, Georges Bizet's new version of his Toreadors' chorus from *Carmen*:

> Tom cats of Paris,
> Strong and stiff and proud,
> Out on the prowl,
> Ready to howl;
> We're at your service ma'am we'll waste no time,
> All our cannons are primed.
> We're eager and we're preened,
> We're fairly clean;
> We're here to serve our queen. [etc.]

La Fontaine adapts his rollicking 18th century versifying to 20th century travel guides for the feline tourists visiting the cemetery:

> It always seems to happen, friends,
> As past these tombs one slowly wends,
> A certain gravitas descends:
> A mood of melancholy.
> Inevitably, graveyards spawn
> The fear that when we're dead and gone
> We'll never see another dawn.

> But that's the food of folly,
> Snack not thereon! Instead, be wise,
> Just look around, believe your eyes.
> The buried do not claim the prize
> Of lulled, sepulchral boredom.
> One lapses, then one goes to seed,
> But soon one howls, and soon one breeds.
> In other words, the life one leads
> Is full, not dull, post mortem. [etc.]

Famous males court famous females (and notoriously homosexual Oscar Wilde chases after "Lizard King" Jim Morrison) in the uninhibited manner of randy cats. But one of Père-Lachaise's more famous foreign residents is conspicuously missing. Mid-20th century American writer/poet Gertrude Stein has not been reincarnated yet. And after a few decades of waiting impatiently, Stein's inseparable companion Alice B. Toklas (the novel's narrator) decides to take matters into her own paws. Toklas, who was usually the organizer/hostess of Stein's literary salons, has become one of the cemetery's leading caterers at their top social events. She plots to spike the refreshments at the Annual Renaissance Revue with an aphrodisiac that will put all the females instantly onto heat, and cause an orgy that will result in so many new kittens that Gertrude will surely be among them—won't she? Unfortunately, Toklas does not take into account the mysterious cat-thief who has recently arisen among the felines, stealing such priceless *objets d'art* as Bernhardt's wooden leg, Rossini's glass eye, and the exaggerated genitalia from the nude marble statue of Wilde over his tomb. This thief has their own agenda, and the conflict between the two has a bizarre result.

Richardson's witty novel is by turns spritely, pretentious, and almost impenetrably esoteric as he mimics the writing styles and known personality traits of Parisian celebrity authors, entertainers, philosophers, and society leaders from 1806 to the present. Fortunately, he minimizes the "quotations" from those celebrities who were notoriously boring, and emphasizes the sophisticated but lively social infighting among the toms and queens which is the prominent background to Alice B. Toklas' ongoing search (including resorting to black magic) for the super-aphrodisiac that she needs.

Watchers • by Dean R. Koontz.
New York: G.P. Putnam's Sons, February 1987, hardcover, 352 pp.

Watchers, Koontz's most popular novel, is both science-fiction and "realistic" suspense fiction involving genetic engineering. In a detailed analysis in *Critical Companions to Popular Contemporary Writers* (1996), Joan G. Kotker argues that it is a successful combination of science-fiction, suspense, a technothriller, a love story, a police procedural, gangster fiction, "and overriding all of this, an inspiring dog story whose suspense is based on a series of threats to a very special dog."

Travis Cornell is a loner who is going hiking with a gun, mostly to protect himself against rattlesnakes, but maybe to commit suicide. He has lost any will to live. He has come to think of himself as a jinx; anybody whom he cares for dies.

> As Travis was about to step out of the sun and continue, a dog burst from the dry brush on his right and ran straight to him, panting and chuffing. It was a golden retriever, pure of breed by the look of it. A male. He figured it was little more than a year old, for though it had attained the better part of its full growth, it retained some of the sprightliness of a puppy. Its thick coat was damp, dirty, tangled,

> snarled, full of burrs and broken bits of weeds and leaves. It stopped in front of him, sat, cocked its head, and looked up at him with an undeniably friendly expression.

The dog appears friendly, but it does everything to keep Travis from continuing down a deer trail into the forest. Travis eventually realizes that the dog is trying to protect him. The first scene of suspense follows as Travis slowly retreats with the unseen thing in the forest following him and the dog protecting him.

> The unknown adversary's raspy breathing was so creepy—whether because of the echo effect of the forest and canyon, or because it was just creepy to begin with—that Travis quickly took off his backpack, unsnapped the flap, and withdrew the loaded .38.
>
> The dog stared at the gun. Travis had the weird feeling that the animal knew what the revolver was—and approved of the weapon.

The novel cuts to Vincent Nasco, a hired killer who is carrying out a hit. The beginning of *Watchers* alternates several apparently unconnected scenes with those of Travis and the dog. Travis almost immediately realizes that the dog possesses human-level intelligence.

Dying of curiosity, he keeps the dog. A new digression introduces Nora Devon, a paranoid woman as soul-dead as Travis was. She is terrified of her TV repairman. For the next few dozen pages, Koontz switches between scenes of Travis conducting intelligence tests on the dog, whom he names Einstein; Nora Devon being toyed with by the sexual predator, Vince Nasco being asked by his anonymous employer to murder more people, and the unseen menace killing people. After killing three doctors in a row, Nasco performs the unpardonable sin of torturing his final victim into telling him what connection the doctors had. They all worked at Banodyne Laboratories on a top secret project to increase animals' intelligence—a research laboratory from which two experimental animals have just escaped.

Koontz draws Travis' and Nora's stories together, with Einstein acting as a canine chaperone/Cupid to develop a romance between them. But Nasco has decided that the escaped dog is worth a fortune to him, if he can find it. The novel also starts to play up the savage slaughters that the other escaped animal, called The Outsider, is committing around Southern California.

So: Travis and Nora slowly fall in love, with Einstein's approval. They do not know that Nasco is looking for Einstein to sell to the highest bidder, and that the killer plans to leave no human witnesses behind. Nasco's anonymous hirers, presumably Soviet agents out to destroy the U.S. government's research project, will want to kill Einstein and also his new human friends if they learn about them. The Outsider, a bioengineered killing animal derived from a baboon, has a telepathic affinity to Einstein and is searching to slaughter him and anyone with him. Once Einstein, Travis, and Nora figure out how to genuinely communicate with each other, and the dog tells them his secret, Travis and Nora vow to keep anyone from taking Einstein away from them.

What makes *Watchers* of interest to anthropomorphic fans is, of course, Einstein. He is not just a human mind in a doggy body. He is an intelligent canine with a canine's instincts. First they figure out a code of wagging his tail for yes and barking for no; then Nora teaches him to read.

> Einstein was on the floor, on his belly, reading a novel. Since graduating with startling swiftness from picture books to children's literature like *The Wind in the Willows*, he had been reading eight and ten hours a day, every day. He couldn't get *enough* books. He'd become a prose junkie. Ten days ago, when

the dog's obsession with reading had finally outstripped Nora's patience for holding books and turning pages, they had tried to puzzle out an arrangement that would make it possible for Einstein to keep a volume open in front of him and turn the pages himself. At a hospital-supply company, they had found a device designed for patients who had the use of neither arms nor legs. It was a metal stand onto which the boards of the book were clamped; electrically powered mechanical arms, controlled by three push buttons, turned the pages and held them in place. A quadriplegic could operate it with a stylus held in his teeth; Einstein used his nose. The dog seemed immensely pleased by the arrangement. Now, he whimpered softly about something he had just read, pushed one of the buttons, and turned another page.

Finally, Travis gets a Scrabble game so Einstein can spell out words, a letter at a time, with the tiles.

This is in Part One of the novel. In Part Two, the three go on the offensive against their pursuers. They elaborate upon the one Scrabble game, and upon human-canine communication, until Einstein is able and comfortable having long conversations with them.

Koontz is a virtuoso at playing the reader's emotions, making alternately Travis, Nora, Einstein, or one of their very few human friends seem in deadly danger. Even though Einstein is the only intelligent animal in the novel, Koontz makes him so charismatic that *Watchers* is a thriller that every furry fan just *has* to read.

Watership Down • by Richard Adams. Fold-out map.

London: Rex Collings Ltd., November 1972, hardcover, 421 pp.

Tales from Watership Down • by Richard Adams. Illustrated by John Lawrence.

London: Hutchinson, September 1996, hardcover, 198 pp.

Watership Down is a literary classic, and like most literary classics, it is recommended reading in many high schools. Teachers have reported that it is a hard sell to some adolescents who feel that they are too old to be reading "fuzzy bunny" books.

How many "fuzzy bunny" books open with a first-chapter quote from Aeschylus' *Agamemnon*?

> CHORUS: Why do you cry out thus, unless at some vision of horror?
>
> CASSANDRA: The house reeks of death and dripping blood....

It is hard for fans of anthropomorphic literature today to imagine a time before *Watership Down* existed. The con-

Watership Down by Richard Adams (Rex Collings Ltd., November 1972). An anthropomorphic animal classic and a seminal influence on the creation of furry fandom. This established the fantasy concept of an animal species having its own language and religion. Cover art uncredited.

cept of featuring talking, intelligent "realistic" animals in an adult novel, a dramatic adventure rather than an intellectual political or moral allegory—creating a detailed language and a religion for an animal species—those were invented for *Watership Down*. How many talking-animal books for adults were there between *Animal Farm* (1945) and *Watership Down* (1972)? Hardly any. How many have there been since *Watership Down*? Lots! How many of those have not been adventure quests featuring a particular animal species with its language and religion? Very few!

Watership Down begins in the English countryside, at the long-established Sandleford Warren. In just a few words Adams establishes the natural society of a rabbit warren, dominated by an alpha buck (the Chief Rabbit) and a clique of the mature bucks (the Owsla) who boss the younger rabbits around. Some of the younger rabbits take this, waiting until they become old enough to join the Owsla, while others leave to become a lone wandering rabbit (Hlessi) without a warren.

Hazel and his brother Fiver are younger rabbits in the Sandleford warren. Fiver is small, neurotic, and notorious for seeing danger everywhere. In fact, he is a genuine lapine Cassandra, with the major difference that there is someone who believes him. Hazel has seen his forecasts come true too often to ignore him when he suddenly predicts doom for the whole warren:

> The two rabbits went up to the board at a hopping run and crouched in a patch of nettles on the far side, wrinkling their noses at the smell of a dead cigarette end somewhere in the grass. Suddenly Fiver shivered and cowered down.
>
> "Oh, Hazel! This is where it comes from! I know now—something very bad! Some terrible thing—coming closer and closer."
>
> He began to whimper with fear.
>
> "What sort of thing—what do you mean? I thought you said there was no danger?"
>
> "I don't know what it is," answered Fiver wretchedly. "There isn't any danger here, at this moment. But it's coming—it's coming. Oh, Hazel, look! The field! It's covered with blood!"
>
> "Don't be silly, it's only the light of the sunset. Fiver, come on, don't talk like this, you're frightening me."
>
> Fiver sat trembling and crying among the nettles as Hazel tried to reassure him and to find out what it could be that had suddenly driven him beside himself. If he was terrified, why did he not run for safety, as any sensible rabbit would? But Fiver could not explain and only grew more and more distressed. At last Hazel said,
>
> "Fiver, you can't sit crying here. Anyway, it's getting dark. We'd better go back to the burrow."
>
> "Back to the burrow?" whimpered Fiver. "It'll come there—don't think it won't! I tell you, the field's full of blood—"

When Sandleford's Chief Rabbit ignores Fiver's insistence that the whole warren must flee, Hazel determines that they will go alone if they have to. They end up leading a group of eleven wanderers searching for the site that Fiver has foreseen as their new home. In this first quarter of the novel, they encounter the dangers that homeless rabbits aboveground naturally face; predators such as foxes, hawks, and men with shotguns who treat all wild rabbits as garden-destroying vermin. Individual rabbits begin to stand out: Blackberry, who comes up with clever ideas; Bigwig, the massive former Owsla member who becomes Hazel's second-in-command; Dandelion, the storyteller. It is Dandelion's stories in the tradition of primitive creation myths that establish the rabbits' sun-god Frith and the first rabbit, the trickster El-ahrairah (Elil-Hrair-Rah).

The wanderers' almost-fatal stop at Cowslip's treacherous warren teaches them to distrust rabbits who do not believe in Frith and El-ahrairah. Their hardships—including learning the horrifying fate of the Sandleford Warren—mold them from nervous loners into a tight-knit warren in all except a physical home, who accept Hazel as their Chief Rabbit—Hazel-rah.

Most authors would have made their successful arrival at their goal the conclusion. The arrival of Hazel's warren at Watership Down comes barely a quarter through the novel. The new warren needs females to successfully establish itself. One of Hazel's insights of genius is to befriend other animals besides rabbits in their new neighborhood. They nurse an injured black-headed gull, Kehaar, back to health and he gives them aerial information about the countryside. This includes a human farm with domestic rabbits in a hutch, and another warren a couple of miles away.

The Watership Downers have adventures at both places, especially with the overcrowded super-warren, Efrafa, from which they need to help a group of discontented does to escape. Efrafa turns out to be organized as a military dictatorship under General Woundwort, who sets out to conquer and destroy all other warrens almost as soon as he learns of them. Woundwort is a terrifyingly intelligent leader who seems invincible. The Downers' scheme to aid the unhappy does to flee to their warren is immediately thrown into chaos by the General's realizing what is happening. Woundwort's relentless pursuit and the dramatic siege of Watership Down by the Efrafans fills the last quarter of the novel.

Watership Down is one of those famous novels that was rejected by over a dozen publishers when it was first submitted. The first edition, only 2,000 copies, got immediate rave reviews and won two literary awards. A British mass-market edition was published by Puffin Books in January 1974, and it has not been out of print since then. The animated motion picture was nominated for the Hugo Award for Best Dramatic Presentation in 1979. Both are recommended, but the novel is a must-read if there ever was one.

Waterways • by Kyell Gold. Illustrated by John Nunnemacher.

St. Paul, MN: Sofawolf Press, January 2008, paperback, 315 pp.

Kyell Gold first posted "Aquifers" on the Internet in 2005, and its sequel, "Streams," in 2007. He added the third story, "Oceans," turning the trilogy into a novel, *Waterways*, in 2008.

> My idea for the series [Gold states in his Foreword] was to show the different stages of a young man coming to grips with his sexuality in a potentially hostile world. An aquifer is an underground stream, and in "Aquifers," Kory wrestles mostly with himself. In the second part, "Streams," his hidden, underground secret has been exposed, leading to repercussions from family and friends. And as all streams flow to the ocean, so do all of us live in part of a larger society, and as we explore and shape our own identity, we push out against those who share the world we live in. "Oceans," the last part, chronicles the effect Kory's decisions have on his world.

Kory Hedley, a seventeen-year-old otter senior in Hilltown's Carter High School, is going through adolescence. In his case, the changes are more confusing than usual. Kory has noticed that all of his gaming pals of the last few years are developing obsessions around girls and sports, which he has no interest in. A poem he writes in English class wins praise from his teacher but ridicule as "girly stuff" from the budding jocks. He cannot work up any real feeling for his girlfriend Jenny, who drifts away from him. When Kory feels the emotional thrill that has been described as "love" upon meeting another boy, Samaki Roden, a black fox at the municipal swimming pool who is semi-openly homosexual, he begins to wonder if he, too, could be gay?

Kory's emotional conflicts are both the usual ones that result when all his teen peers including his best friend, Sal (otter), start going out with girls and invite him to double-date with them, and having a rigidly intolerant Catholic parent, his mother, who insists on micromanaging his social life. Kory has already learned to lie to her to have any personal freedom such as going to movies he wants to see instead of those she selects for him. Now he has a much more important secret to hide. Kory, conflicted, goes to his parish priest for advice, but to his surprise Father Joe (a Dall sheep) encourages him to not suppress himself:

> "Kory," Father Joe said gently. "This is a confusing time of life for you, and a confusing issue to be dealing with."
> "I don't want to deal with it," he snapped. "I want to fight it. I know what the Church says."
> The sheep's horns bobbed again. "I know what the Church's official position is. I also know how I want to minister to my flock." He reached into his desk and pushed a small card across the desk. "I happen to hold out hope that the Church will moderate its views. In the meantime, these people can help you out. It's a Catholic group. I know David." He tapped the card. "He used to be a priest. He felt he could better serve by leaving the Church. He's a good wolf."
> Kory stared at the card. He could read the words Dignity/USA on it, but nothing else from his position on the chair. He made no move to pick it up. "You're supposed to tell me I'm going to hell if I give in."
> "Yes, I suppose, but if you knew that, you wouldn't have needed to come see me."

As Gold says, in "Aquifers" Kory comes to accept his own homosexuality and his feelings for Samaki. In "Streams" their relationship is strained when Kory wants to continue to keep it secret while Samaki doesn't mind being open about it; and when its revelation forces Kory to choose between his homosexuality and remaining at home. In "Oceans," Kory's lifestyle is shown affecting the relationships among his mother and brother, his school pals, his religion, and his chances of going to college.

Waterways is a sensitive, excellently-written novel about adolescent homosexuality. But it is also a better-thought-out depiction of a multi-species anthropomorphic community than most writers devise. Kory's home is designed for an otter family:

> He walked across the living room, skirting the edge of the central pool that joined all the rooms of the ranch-style house, and walked across the bridge and down the short hall that led to his and his brother's rooms, opening the door on the left wall and closing it behind him.
> Through the window to his right, he saw his brother walking up from the back yard. He dropped his stuff on the bed under the window and flopped down on it. Just lying in his own bed in his cozy room made his head feel a little better.
> Outside, he heard the splash as his brother dove into the pool from the back yard, and a moment later the younger otter's head bobbed up in the small corner in his room that was open to the pool.

A center for gay adolescent homeless youths is made as multi-species as possible:

> In places like the school or public library, the interiors were deliberately minimalist so as not to favor any one species over another. Even though the Rainbow Center received some public funding, the equal-access laws known as the Orwell Act only applied to the common areas of the building, and then only to specify that the area be equally welcoming to all. Margo interpreted that to mean "as welcoming as possible to all," a passion which showed in the ceiling rungs, for squirrels and other climbers, the hard salt licks in the walls, the shallow trough of water running along one side of each of the ground-floor rooms, the sheltered corner with the thick triangular shade stretched over it to block out the light, and dozens of other small touches.

There are small touches throughout of multi-species design, such as laminated college brochures for aquatic applicants, or the foxes' *Pounce Pounce Revolution* video game. Whether you read *Waterways* for its plot of adolescent acceptance of homosexuality or for its richly-detailed anthropomorphic setting, it is a novel that should not be missed. It won the 2008 Ursa Major Award for Best Novel. In 2018 a 10th anniversary hardcover edition was published, with an updated text and two sequel short stories.

We the Underpeople • by Cordwainer Smith. Edited by Hank Davis.

Riverdale, NY: Baen Books, December 2006, paperback, 476 pp.

This is a new collection, but every furry fan should have read these sf stories long ago. Humans have bioengineered animals into intelligent anthropomorphic underpeople to be their new labor/slave class, and the underpeople fight for equality and freedom. It's one of the oldest clichés in furry literature, but every cliché had to start somewhere. This is it.

Cordwainer Smith (Dr. Paul Myron Anthony Linebarger, 1913–1966) wrote his stories of the underpeople, the bioengineered animal servants of mankind in the distant future, over fifty years ago. They have been published in a variety of editions; most, sadly, after his death. *We the Underpeople* contains *all* the stories related to the underpeople in a single volume; the novel *Norstrilia* and the five short stories that precede it. There is also a new six-page Introduction by Robert Silverberg. We could not ask for these classic stories in a handier format.

In the really far future, the planets of the whole galaxy share a civilization loosely known as the Instrumentality of Mankind, unofficially ruled by the benevolent yet ruthless Lords of the Instrumentality. The Lords created the underpeople so that all men would never have to work again.

Most of Smith's sf was set in his interstellar Instrumentality, but the majority of his stories did not involve the underpeople. This collection, edited by Hank Davis, may stretch the point by calling all six "underpeople stories," but they do present every one of Smith's works in which the underpeople are present, even if offstage.

"The Dead Lady of Clown Town," the first story of the underpeople in chronological order, tells how the Dead Lady, Lady Panc Ashash, once a real human and now only a recorded memory pattern in a robotic body on Fomalhaut III, encourages the first underpeople revolution by introducing the misplaced human witch Elaine to the dog-girl D'joan and her followers in the forgotten Old City under the new soaring human city of Kalma. This is the story of Elaine and of D'joan and the tragic first underpeople rebellion, but it forecasts the conclusion of their whole saga in its now-famous opening sentence: "You already know the end—the immense drama of the Lord Jestocost, seventh of his line, and how the cat-girl C'mell initiated the vast conspiracy."

The next two stories are marginal underpeople tales, important for their background. "Under Old Earth," set just before the Rediscovery of Man, establishes that the perfection imposed upon humanity by the Lords of the Instrumentality is sterile and lifeless. Lord Sto Odin, almost a thousand years old, ventures into the Gebiet ghetto under Earth's human cities and discovers that the shorter-lived underpeople, despite their flaws—*because* of their flaws—have a more vital culture. Although the underpeople are mostly unseen, Smith's writing style evokes their passions:

> The beat and the heat and the neat repeat of the notes which poured from the congohelium—metal never made for music, matter and antimatter locked in a fine magnetic grid to ward off the outermost perils of space. Now a piece of it was deep in the body of Old Earth, counting out strange cadences. The churn and the burn and the hot return of music riding the living rock, accompanying itself in an air-carried echo. The surge and the urge of an erotic dirge which moaned, groaned through the heavy stone.

"Mother Hitton's Littul Kittons," the mysteriously deadly orbital defenders of Norstrilia, shows that the underpeople are not the only animal bioengineering that humanity has done. It also presents the first clear picture of Old North Australia, the richest and most powerful world of the Instrumentality (hinted at in "The Dead Lady of Clown Town"), which will become so important at the climax of the underpeople's story.

"Alpha Ralpha Boulevard" takes place during the first days of the Rediscovery of Man, when mankind gives up its stifling, boring safeness to make life interesting once again. Two true men, Paul and Virginia, venture from their comfortable surface city into the top underground level. This is the story that introduces C'mell, the cat-girl who was "as beautiful and as bright as a flame. Her skin was clear, the color of cream, and her hair—finer than any human hair could possibly be—was the wild golden orange of a Persian cat." The story does not have much to do with the underpeople, but it does introduce C'mell.

The final two titles are the short story "The Ballad of Lost C'mell" (20 pages) and the novel *Norstrilia* (261 pp. You could read the former alone and skip the novel, for "The Ballad of Lost C'mell" tells in outline form all that really happens. But the details—ah, the details:

> The story is simple. There was a boy who bought the planet Earth. We know that, to our cost. It only happened once, and we have taken pains that it will never happen again. He came to Earth, got what he wanted, and got away alive, in a series of very remarkable adventures. That's the story.

How can anyone not read the details with chapter titles so alluring as "At the Gate of the Garden of Death," "Anger of the Onseck," "The Palace of the Governor of Night," "FOE Money, SAD Money," "The Road to the Catmaster," "The Department Store of Hearts' Desires," "Birds, Far Underground," and "Counsels, Councils, Consoles and Consuls"? The first half of *Norstrilia* is not about the underpeople at all; it is the story of Rod McBan—Roderick Frederick Ronald Arnold William McArthur McBan the 151st, the richest boy on the richest world in the Instrumentality. But rich people collect enemies, and Rod tries to escape by fleeing to Earth and disguising himself as an underpeople. It is at this point that he meets C'mell and becomes involved with the underground rebellion.

Ah, C'mell. The other characters are almost as memorable.

> C'mell, the most beautiful of the girlygirls of Earth. Jean-Jacques Vomact, whose family must have preceded the human race. The wild old man at Adaminaby. The trained spiders of Earthport. The Subcommissioner Teadrinker. The Lord Jestocost, whose name is a page in history. The friends of the Ee-telly-kelly, and a queer tankful of friends they were. B'dank, of the cattle-police. The Catmaster. Tostig Amaral, about whom the less said the better. Ruth, in pursuit. C'mell, in flight. The Lady Johanna, laughing.

C'mell is mentioned twice? Well, she is worth it. So is this book.

Where the Blue Begins • by Christopher Morley.

Garden City, NY: Doubleday, Page & Co., October 1922, hardcover, 225 pp.

Each in turn may call this a fairy story, a dog story, an allegory or a satire, but all will be moved by the beauty and the meaning—a beauty and a meaning that seems to live within the realm of those books that go on and on making friends and spreading enchantment. Gissing, its hero, is a dog who searches the world for an ideal, and then finds in the smoke of his own furnace fire a hint of the heavenly blue that he had been seeking [blurb, slightly edited].

Mr. Gissing, a gentledog of leisure contentedly residing in Canine Estates with Fuji, his butler (a Japanese pug), on an income of 1,000 bones a year, becomes dissatisfied and leaves home to search for where the blue begins (a purpose to life).

Gissing becomes an eerily canine predecessor of the notorious Frank Abignale, Jr., who during the 1960s successfully impersonated an airline pilot, a college teaching assistant, a doctor, an attorney, a federal bureaucrat, and more. Gissing adopts some orphaned puppies to experiment with parenthood; he becomes a floorwalker at the Beagle and Company department store and is quickly promoted to General Manager; he takes up theology and is invited to become a lay reader and preach a sermon (he is disappointed that he is not allowed to wear priestly garb), until he shocks Bishop Borzoi and the congregation with the heresy that God may be a biped; he stows away on the steamship *Pomerania* and soon becomes second officer to Captain Scottie. Ultimately, he returns home exhausted with intellectual riddling, satisfied to resume his mundane life.

Morley admirably creates a canine world through names alone. There are Mike Terrier, the curate Mr. J. Rover Poodle, the upper-class and working-class neighbors Mrs. Airedale and Mrs. Collie, the nursemaid Mrs. Spaniel and little Shaggy, her puppy, Gissing's adopted puppies Groups, Bunks, and Yelpers, haughty Mr. and Mrs. Chow and their "intolerably spotless" little Sandy, the landlady Mrs. Purps, the salesclerk Miss Whippet, the matronly Mrs. Mastiff, the compulsive shopper Mrs. Dachshund, the parishioners Mr. Dobermann-Pinscher, Mrs. Griffon, and Mrs. Retriever. There are the place names like Dalmatian Heights and the little shrine of St. Spitz. These are intermixed with humanless real locales like Paris and Atlantic City, Murray Hill and Fifth Avenue and Broadway and Wall Street, Delmonico's Restaurant and Trinity Church, and real historical personages like the Grimm brothers, Hans Christian Andersen, and Masefield; to make this our real world only inhabited by dogs, rather than some imaginary planet of dogs.

Gissing succeeds temporarily in his assumed positions through a confident manner and allowing his would-be superiors to project their own preferences upon him:

> Gissing calmly swallowed his tea, and ate the meringue. He would have enjoyed another, but the capable secretary had already removed them. He poured himself a second cup of tea. Mr. Beagle junior showed signs of eagerness to leave, but Gissing detained him.
> "One moment," he said suavely. "There is a little matter that we have not discussed. The question of salary."

But each time Gissing becomes dissatisfied. He has not "found the blue" yet. He flees, looking for he knows not what, until he finds himself alone on an unknown coast.

> Suddenly, where the hill arched against pearly sky, he saw a narrow thread of smoke rising. He halted in alarm. Who might this be, friend or foe? But eager agitation pushed him on. Burning to know, he hurried up to the brow of the hill.
> The smoke mounted from a small bonfire of sticks in a sheltered thicket, where a miraculous being—who was, as a matter of fact, a rather ragged and dingy vagabond—was cooking a tin of stew over the blaze.
> Gissing stood, quivering with emotion. Joy such as he had never known darted through all the cords of his body. He ran, shouting, in mirth and terror. In fear, in a passion of love and knowledge and understanding, he abased himself and yearned before this marvel. Impossible to have conceived,

yet, once seen, utterly satisfying and the fulfillment of all needs. He laughed and leaped and worshipped. When the first transport was over, he laid his head against this being's knee, he nestled there and was content. This was the inscrutable perfect answer.

"Cripes!" said the puzzled tramp, as he caressed the nuzzling head. "The purp's loco. Maybe he's been lost. You might think he'd never seen a man before."

He was right.

And Gissing sat quietly, his throat resting upon the soiled knee of a very old and spicy trouser.

"I have found God," he said.

This is not quite the end of the book. Gissing suddenly finds himself back at home in Canine Estates with his adoptive family. Was it all a dream? He resolves not to worry about it.

Ah, he said to himself, it is all very well to wear a crown of thorns, and indeed every sensitive creature carries one in secret. But there are times when it ought to be worn cocked over one ear.

He opened the furnace door. A bright glow filled the fire-box: he could hear a stir and singing in the boiler, and the rustle of warm pipes that chuckled quietly through winter nights of storm. Over the coals hovered a magic evasive flicker, the very soul of fire. It was a pentecostal flame, perfect and heavenly in tint, the essence of pure colour, a clear immortal blue.

It would be easy to quibble about logical fallacies in *Where the Blue Begins*. Was it all a dream, or not? Where did the lone human tramp come from in an otherwise human-less world? Does Mr. Gissing find himself too easily accepted in his make-believe roles? But this is an enchanted story, meant for the emotions rather than for logical analysis. Does this make the reader feel good? Yes. (At least the 1920s reader. A scholarly dissertation should be written on the 1850s–1950s assumption that all animals really were in awe of humans and wished they could be owned by humans and become humans themselves.) It was a literary success at the time, and is now slightly dated but still enjoyable today.

A Whisper of Wings • by Paul Kidd. Illustrated by Terrie Smith.

Flushing, NY: Vision Novels, October 1999, paperback, 354 pp. (pp. 349–352 are advertisements)

A Whisper of Wings is set in a world of butterfly-winged and -sized foxes living in tribal societies roughly analogous to Australian aboriginal cultures, though the land is more forested than Australia's Outback desert. But although these Kashran live close to nature, they are neither socially primitive nor cute picture-book woodland pixies. Their society is thousands of years old, and rigidly locked into stratified castes and unchangeable traditions. The Kashran possess a psychic force or aura, the Ka, which is more vital than their wing-muscles in enabling them to fly. Individuals with particularly powerful auras, and the mental strength to control them, can focus them into deadly weapons. Their planet also has a world-spirit, an ecological "Mother Nature" flow, which some Kashran can tap into.

These background details are gradually introduced, described, and woven together to become important elements of the story of the mountain forest Katakanii tribe. Shadarii and Zhukora are very dissimilar sisters, daughters of the Lord of one of the tribe's many male-dominated clans. Zhukora is a young huntress, impatient and hot-tempered, already resentful of her socially predetermined future as the subservient wife of some strutting male. Shadarii is a dreamy, "useless" girl with a habit of wandering away from tasks to spend hours contemplating the beauties of nature. She is also mute, and her lack of speech plus her disinterest in the clan's normal life have gotten her a reputation as simple-minded.

As these and other characters are introduced and linked together, a picture forms of a world approaching catastrophe. For a thousand years, the Katakanii and neighboring tribes have lived in a complex society in a close balance with nature. The common hunters and artisans support an aristocracy of a priesthood and chieftains, who display their social status by conspicuous consumption, notably by hosting the most lavish feasts at ceremonial clan and tribal gatherings and sponsoring clan sports events. Decades of a moist climate are ending, and the mountain area is entering a dry spell. The lush environment which had permitted a Kashran population expansion is fading, but the aristocracy refuses to scale back its luxurious lifestyle.

> Prakucha was a noble like herself, and so Zhukora addressed the intruder with his formal title. She fixed him with her glorious eyes and speared him with her scorn.
> Her enemy felt her power and gave a cool, delighted smile.
> "Oh Zhukora-Ki! Always so full of fight. Must you be so absurd? Anyone can see that the kill belongs to me."
> Prakucha used the 'Ki" endearment reserved for little children. Zhukora remained utterly unmoved. Long hair spilled down across one eye, shading the dangerous glint of female fury.
> "I say my spear took the beast."
> Prakucha shook his head, as though explaining simplicities to a child.
> "And I say that mine was the weapon that struck first."
> "Then that is a lie."
> The male hunter clucked his tongue.
> "But I cannot lie. I am your superior. Are you challenging me? Me, a hunter of the upper tier? Oh Zhukora, do be reasonable."

The ominous situation is, as with many social problems, first openly addressed by malcontents and dissatisfied youth who use it as an opportunity to rebel against tradition. Tribal leaders try to ignore complaints and to silence insistent doomcasters as troublemakers. Intertribal friendly rivalry turns into brutal competition for hunting grounds. Zhukora, who is already unhappy about many elements of the Kashran stagnant society, begins to rally her friends among the young hunters into a sports team that disguises a budding terrorist group. There is practically a separate novel in the sections describing the Kashran jiteng sport, a form of aerial soccer which evolves from ceremonial to deadly as Zhukora and her Skull-Wing team play it. Meanwhile, Shadarii's growing affinity to the world's lifeforce opens an unimagined psychic potential, but her low status and her disinterest in Kashran society draw her away from the growing conflict.

When Zhukora tries to use her sister as a pawn in her plotting, a double tragedy results. One is immediate. The other is more subtle and slowly developing. The Ka is not only a psychic force for physical use, it permeates and influences the personality. The more that Zhukora concentrates on using violence to shatter the aristocracy's rigid control before starvation overwhelms her tribe, the more she becomes determined upon the slaughter of the entire ruling structure and the conquest of the whole world to force her bloody new society upon all Kashran. The more that Shadarii withdraws from her increasingly alienated peers to commune with nature, the more she transforms into a genuine Nature Goddess and attracts a cult of worshippers who prefer to live outside of the Kashran society rather than reform it. Two sisters evolve into rival primordial forces, each powerful enough to save or to destroy a world.

Shadarii sat in meditation beside a broken rock. Her eyes were closed, her fur dulled, her lips were parched and dry. Even so, the girl sat utterly oblivious to the world.

She let her mind wander with the desert breeze. She felt the sands and scorching heat—the careful patterns that the flies wove above her ears. A gecko's eggs lay buried in the dust beneath her tail. Sun and sand, earth and air…. Shadarii reached out and let herself merge with her world.

Even here there was beauty; amongst the dust, Shadarii she [sic.] had found wonder. A desert sunset, the desert moon—dead twigs etched against an endless sky. Shadarii had learned to understand this place, and in so doing, she had discovered love.

Shadarii shivered as she felt the power flow. She was the Chosen One, and all her sufferings were to a purpose; Kotaru, the hunger, the loss, the guilt, the pain. She must suffer and scourge herself. When the answers finally came, she must be pure enough to see.

Why? Why do people need to fight and kill?

A Whisper of Wings was one of the earliest furry specialty press novels. The 1999 Vision Novels edition is long gone, but a 2015 Kitsune Press edition, hardcover or paperback, is still in print.

Who Censored Roger Rabbit? • by Gary Wolf.

New York: St. Martin's Press, October 1981, hardcover, 214 pp.

Who P-P-P-Plugged Roger Rabbit? • by Gary K. Wolf,

New York: Villard Books, August 1991, hardcover, 255 pp.

Who Wacked Roger Rabbit? • by Gary K. Wolf.

Colorado Springs, CO: Musa Publishing, December 2014, paperback, 306 pp.

One of the most difficult works to create, and one of the most enjoyable to read when it's done successfully, is that which is both a straight example and a parody of a genre. Gary Wolf has brought off this trick in *Who Censored Roger Rabbit?*, a whodunit in the Raymond Chandler tradition which sets his hard-boiled hero in a world where 'toon (cartoon) characters are as real as humans.

The narrator is Eddie Valiant, a stereotypical cheap private eye whose cynicism masks a basic idealism. He operates in Los Angeles, the stereotypical Tinseltown whose glittering stars have empty heads and rotten hearts. Except that it's not as stereotypical as all that. Wolf has done much more than simply postulate live Mickey Mouse–type characters mingling with humans. He's changed the basic laws of physics to integrate the common attributes of cartoon characters into normal existence. 'Toons don't speak vocally; word balloons float over their heads for a few moments before dissolving to dust. Or symbol balloons with the familiar light bulb to denote a bright idea, and so on. 'Toons can also create mental duplicates of themselves, usually in dream-fulfillment roles. One of the hallmarks of a 'toon actor is that he or she can create a mental duplicate realistic enough to serve as a double—a doppelganger—in difficult movie shots, eliminating the need for a stunt actor.

These distinctions aren't just tossed off to make Eddie Valiant's world seem amusingly wacky. They're integral to the plot. When Eddie finds his client murdered, the rabbit's body has collapsed over his final words, preventing the speech balloon from its normal disintegration, enabling Eddie to find out what they were. How much is an alibi worth when half the suspects could have set up doubles of themselves? In this world newspaper comic strips aren't drawn, they're photographed with 'toon star actors, and an important subplot involves the salaries and royalties that a 'toon star should get from his syndicate. All of these elements are handled with comedic overtones, but with a basic seriousness that makes the novel a legitimate murder mystery rather than a comedy dressed up as a mystery.

Who Censored Roger Rabbit? has an intricately tangled plot in which a varied cast of suspects is gradually discovered to have disreputable secrets. Eddie is hired by Roger Rabbit, a moderately successful Hollywood comic-strip star who feels he's being screwed by his syndicate.

> "About a year ago, the DeGreasy brothers, the cartoon syndicate, told me that if I signed with them they would give me my own strip." He laid his half-eaten carrot on an end table beside a display of framed and autographed photos, some human, some 'toon. They included Snoopy, Joe Namath, Beetle Bailey, John F. Kennedy, and, in a group shot, Dick Tracy, Secret Agent X-9, and J. Edgar Hoover. "Instead they made me a second banana to a dopey, obese, thumb-sucking sniveler named Baby Herman."
>
> "So find yourself another syndicate."
>
> "I can't." The rabbit's face collapsed. "My contract binds me to the DeGreasys for another twenty years. When I asked them to release me so I could look for work elsewhere, they refused."
>
> "They give you any reason?"
>
> "None. Being somewhat an amateur private eye myself, I did some legwork." He displayed a hind limb that would have looked exceptionally good dangling from the end of a keychain. "I nosed around the industry and uncovered a rumor that someone wants to buy out my contract and give me a starring role, but the DeGreasys refuse to sell. I want you to find out what's going on. If the DeGreasys won't star me, why won't they deal me away?"
>
> Sounded horribly boring, but one more look at his check convinced me to at least go through the motions. I hauled out my notebook and pen.

Eddie learns that Roger has a reputation for being paranoid, and that Roger's wife Jessica, a knockout humanoid 'toon beauty, has just moved in with syndicate head Rocco DeGreasy. Eddie figures that Roger is just trying to make trouble for DeGreasy, and he is about to drop the case when Roger is murdered. Then DeGreasy is also found slain. Minor inconsistencies that Eddie had ignored when he hadn't taken Roger seriously now look very suspicious to him. To cap it all, Roger returns!—or his doppelganger, which the real Roger had created to send on a shopping errand just before his murder.

So Eddie, who feels he owes the 'toon star for not believing him in time to prevent his murder, sets out with Roger's doppelganger to find who really censored Roger Rabbit, in time for Roger's doppelganger to feel avenged before he fades away. Naturally this involves finding out who really murdered Rocco DeGreasy as well. Everybody has a plausible story, but Eddie automatically assumes that anything he's told may be a lie until it can be checked out. The case builds up slowly, with dozens of clues being matched against each other until they start forming a picture. Wolf plays fair, but the story is tricky—it's told through Eddie's thoughts, which are constantly considering possibilities to be checked out, weighing ways in which a literally-true statement might be deliberately misleading, wondering if he's being overly suspicious. You're unlikely to guess which of the many choices presented is the right one until Wolf is ready to tell you.

Finally, Wolf's writing is just plain fun to read. It's lively and colorful, full of vivid images. There seem to be two or three to each page, and many are so good that you'll be tempted to start compiling a list of your favorites.

If you like unusual murder mysteries, offbeat humor, or fiction about the comic-art industry, then you should find *Who Censored Roger Rabbit?* to your taste.

Wolf wrote two sequels, but by then he had already sold the rights to the Walt Disney Studios, and he was required to adhere to its plot changes for its 1988 movie. They read more like Disney merchandising than genuine literature. For example, *Who P-P-P-Plugged Roger Rabbit?* emphasizes Roger's exaggerated stutter in the movie, which is not in the original novel. They are unfortunately forgettable.

Why Coyotes Howl • by Watts Martin.

St. Paul, MN: Sofawolf Press, January 2005, paperback, 212 pp.

It's said that nobody recognizes a Golden Age until it is over. That seems to be the case with furry-fandom magazines. For roughly a dozen years from 1987 to 2002, there was a flood of short stories in many furry magazines like *Yarf!, PawPrints Fanzine, Furry-Phile, Mythagoras, Morphic Tales, Zoomorphica*, and many others. During the latter half of this Golden Age, hundreds of stories were published on the Internet instead of in magazines. Alas, all of them have long since ceased publication, and most of the online stories have disappeared from the Internet.

Watts Martin was one of the most prolific and popular authors during this Golden Age of furry-fandom magazines. Now some of his best stories are available again, plus some new ones, in this collection of fourteen of his works. The earliest, "Only with Thine Eyes," dates back to *FurVersion* #14 in 1987. Five are printed here for the first time. Most of the reprints have been revised for this collection, so to an extent all the stories are new.

"Why Coyotes Howl," which opens the collection, and "Traveling Music," the last in the book, are both romances about young men driving on isolated roads who meet exotic women; but they are developed quite differently. Tom Hartley in "Coyotes" picks up a young Native American girl hitchhiking to a tribal reunion. The story's title will tip off the reader to the secret of Lara's clan before Tom guesses. How he reacts, and how the tribe of werecoyotes respond to his discovery of their secret, is the story. In "Traveling Music," Spencer in rural Florida encounters a girl whose car has broken down—but it's obvious from the start that she is not from our Earth:

> She didn't have golden skin at all. She had golden *fur*.
> And a golden muzzle, with a little black nose on the end of it, big almond-shaped dark eyes framed by her brown hair—mane? Even a long, fluffy tail perfectly matching her hair color. She might have stepped off the stage of *Cats*, but Andrew Lloyd-Webber would have killed for make-up that perfect.
> And something told me it wasn't make-up.
> The tail flicked wildly as the expression on her feline face changed from relief to terror. She screamed—I wasn't sure which was more unnerving, the almost-human quality of it or the faint growling undertone—and spun on one heel, fleeing into the darkness.
> […]
> Cats didn't stand on their hind legs and wear clothes… did they?
> "You spoke English," a voice said faintly from behind me. I almost fell out of the car, spinning around again.

"Traveling Music" is a sf mystery (what world is Reli from, and how did she get to Earth?) and a romance. Whether it will be a successful romance or a tragedy—whether a human person and a feline person can develop a meaningful relationship, especially on a world where one is a unique freak—is for the reader to find out.

"Only with Thine Eyes" also presents a human-cat romance, but in the context of traditional interstellar sf about the first diplomatic mission between space-going humans and a star-traveling feline species.

Eight others—"Dreams Are for Vixens," "The Fence," "Beast," "The Fox Maiden," "Vertical Blanking," "Daughter of Shadows," "Without Evidence," and "Going to the Dogs"—are an anthropomorphic mixed bag. Three of the stories are non-'morphic: "Seeing Things," a vampire tale; "The Moon in Water," in which a literary fantasy fan seeks real magic; and "Still Life, with Espresso," in which a decaying Tampa neighborhood is revitalized. These three are well worth reading; they just aren't anthropomorphic. (So is it a problem that Martin can write outside the furry-fandom borders?)

Whether about a furry world or a lone furry in a human world, most of these stories are prime examples of great anthropomorphic fiction, featuring genuine animal-humans rather than mere "humans with animal heads." From "Daughter of Shadows":

> Once more, she looked down, now at herself. Instead of seeing skin where breeches and vest did not cover her, she saw fur—plush, grey fur that shimmered in the moonlight. "Oh," she whispered, raising one of her own hands and studying it in wonder. The grey fur turned black and thinned out as it approached her wrist; her nails were short claws, and the palm and bottoms of her fingers had become light grey pads. She made a movement she could not have before, and her tail curled around her hips. It was most definitely a fox's, at least as long as one of her legs, tipped with the same black as her … paws? No, still hands, she decided.

Or from "Without Evidence":

> I had finished the bourbon and was well on my way to the end of a dark Garanelt ale when a wolf walked in. He stood well over six feet tall, with a scar running the length of his muzzle and fur that managed to match the black leather outfit he wore. The bartender glanced at me and nodded slightly. I made my way back to the bar, sitting down at the wolf's right.

It's too bad that none of Martin's more popular Ranea stories are in the book, but he explains in his Afterword that most of those were published in *Yarf!* and were still available at the time in back issues. *Why Coyotes Howl* contains only stories that were out of print or were never published before. If you are familiar with Martin's writing, you have probably already bought this book. If not, don't miss this opportunity to discover it now.

A Wilder West • by Ted R. Blasingame.
Raleigh, NC: Lulu, August 2014, paperback, 258 pp.

> The range of low granite mountains baked in the prairie's summer sun, heat waves shimmering into water mirages wherever there were flat places. A ghostly dust devil stirred up dirt in a dancing pirouette while heat-loving cicadas chirred across the plain, filling the air with their rolling song of mating.

If you think that this sounds like the opening of a Western, you'd be right—except that this is a Western with a Fur, a nude half-human, half-cheetah woman named Citra Kayah. No human has ever seen anything like her before, until she saves the life of Jacob Harrison, a middle-aged showman who is attacked by a mountain lion while out riding in Oklahoma. Jake is dumbfounded, but grateful and in her debt, so he can't turn Citra down when she asks to join his small traveling Wild West show.

> "I am far from my home," she replied, "and I am in constant danger from others like you who would not hesitate to kill me for my pelt. Until I can find a way to return to where I belong, I will need your protection."

> "How can I protect *you*?" he asked, wiping the sweat from his brow.
> "Take me in as a curiosity for your show. It would allow me to hide in plain sight."

Jake's only objection is that he has always billed his show as featuring the authentic Old West, without the stuffed artificial marvels that most other carny exhibits in 1892 boast. Citra is certainly not a traditional Wild West creature. But she obviously is not a stuffed marvel like a jackalope, either. All that she'll reveal to Jake at the time is that her present alias is taken from the Sanskrit word for cheetah, which is a clue that she has or had something to do with India.

A Wilder West is billed as "A Furmankind Tale." Readers of Ted Blasingame's other *Furmankind* novels like *Sunset of Furmankind* and *Second Chance* may have an idea of what is going on. *A Wilder West* is a standalone novel, told from the viewpoint of the late 19th-century Midwesterners who have never seen a Fur before, so having read Blasingame's earlier novels is not necessary.

At first Citra is content to be shown in a cage like a rare wild animal. "Even if I have to live in a cage and let others stare at me through the bars, I will be safe and *alive*!" Her immediate danger is in posing as a big feline in a country where most men carry guns and are used to shooting any large feral animals on sight to protect their livestock. It's only by staying in a cage that she's safe.

To say what happens to Citra would give away too many spoilers, but she goes from posing as a naked animal in a cage to a featured star in Jake Harrison's Wild West Show. After she "comes out," the cat-woman becomes a figure of considerable controversy. Most who do not see her in person dismiss the stories about her as obvious typical Western Tall Tales. Those who do see her range from treating her as a social equal, to wanting to "own" her as a non-human, with a few religious fanatics denouncing her as some kind of demon. Citra's backstory is revealed about halfway through the novel, but that doesn't affect the fact that, as a non-human, some argue that she should be legally owned by someone; or that some religious fanatic with a gun may try to kill "the demon" despite her acceptance by local religious leaders. Or a more deliberate enemy may try to eliminate her, as when her cage is shot up while a rival, Longhorn Tom Johnson's Wild West Extravaganza, is in the neighborhood.

Above all is the question of how a late 22nd-century Fur comes to be in the Old West, and what is going to happen to Citra as a lone Fur in a human world. 1892 society doesn't believe in her, accepting her as at best an apparently intelligent and civilized dangerous carnivore who may turn feral at any moment. At worst, she may be declared legally property, or killed—stuffed and mounted as a freak, or just slain as a demon. She has only a few friends at first—Jake Harrison, then a couple of others. Can she live long enough to make more? And what about colleagues from the future who should be searching for her? *A Wilder West* is "different" in presenting a single Fur in a human world, rather than the usual human-vs.-furry social conflict.

And then, about ninety pages from the end, the whole plot goes in a completely different direction.

Blasingame's main fault, if it is that, may be in setting up, not exactly red herrings, but situations that are suddenly cut short. Extreme surprises do happen in real life, wiping out planned futures and setting people's lives on completely new paths. The bottom line is that readers will feel that *A Wilder West* comes to a satisfactory conclusion.

It's a good mixture of a Western and futuristic science fiction, too. Some of the technological marvels that Jake Harrison has never heard of were actually in production by 1892, but only in Europe and American East Coast metropolises like New York City and Philadelphia. So it's not unreasonable that a 19th-century Midwesterner would be unfamiliar with them. (Remember that song from Rodgers' and Hammerstein's *Oklahoma!*, "Kansas City"?) Anyhow, if you want to read a real Western with a Fur, instead of just a funny-animal Western like the animated movie *Rango*, don't miss Blasingame's *A Wilder West*.

The Wind in the Willows • by Kenneth Grahame. Frontispiece by Graham Robertson.

London: Methuen & Company, October 1908, hardcover, 308 pp.

The Wind in the Willows is world-famous today. It was almost immediately world-famous. Yet until Grahame died in 1932, he did not think that the entire book could be illustrated. The reason is because the narrative segues so often between Mole, Rat, Otter, Badger, the weasels and field-mice and hedgehogs and rabbits as natural English woodland animals; and their being imitation humans—not just Toad in stately Toad Hall, but each having a small, furnished home—sometimes tiny, sometimes of human size; rowing a boat, presumably wearing clothes (Toad certainly wears clothes and is of human size when he disguises himself as a washerwoman, yet is of toad size when he enters Rat's riverbank hole), capable of driving a motor-car and of being tried in court. Because Grahame's writing was so lyrical, everyone was willing to gloss over the disparity.

Natural woodland animals? The book begins with a blending of the animal and human worlds:

> The Mole had been working very hard all the morning, spring-cleaning his little home. First with brooms, then with dusters, then on ladders and steps and chairs, with a brush and a pail of whitewash; till he had dust in his throat and eyes, and splashes of whitewash all over his black fur, and an aching back and weary arms. Spring was moving in the air above and in the earth below and around him, penetrating even his dark and lowly little house with its spirit of divine discontent and longing. It was small wonder, then, that he suddenly flung down his brush on the floor, said "Bother!" and "O blow!" and also "Hang spring-cleaning!" and bolted out of the house without even waiting to put on his coat. Something up above was calling him imperiously, and he made for the steep little tunnel which answered in his case to the gravelled carriage-drive owned by animals whose residences are nearer to the sun and air. So he scraped and scratched and scrabbled and scrooged, and then he scrooged again and scrabbled and scratched and scraped, working busily with his little paws and muttering to himself, "Up we go! Up we go!" till at last, pop! his snout came out into the sunlight, and he found himself rolling in the warm grass of a great meadow.

The Wind in the Willows was a new kind of children's book, and people did not know what to make of it. Lewis Carroll's two *Alice* fantasies were set in what was clearly a dreamland, so it seemed natural being bizarre and shifting and, well, dreamlike. Subsequent children's fantasies such as E. Nesbit's brought one fantastic talking animal such as a Psammead into the real world, or sent a realistic human child into a magic world, as L. Frank Baum's American Dorothy Gale to Oz. But *The Wind in the Willows* was supposed to take place in the real England, but with the wild animals having little houses and being able to talk, and where the government (at least the police and the courts) treated the animals as people:

> "To my mind," observed the Chairman of the Bench of Magistrates cheerfully, "the *only* difficulty that presents itself in this otherwise very clear case is, how can we possibly make it sufficiently hot for the

incorrigible rogue and hardened ruffian whom we see cowering in the dock before us. Let me see: he has been found guilty, on the clearest evidence, first, of stealing a valuable motor-car; secondly, of driving to the public danger; and, thirdly, of gross impertinence to the rural police. Mr. Clerk, will you tell us, please, what is the very stiffest penalty we can impose for each of these offenses? Without, of course, giving the prisoner the benefit of any doubt, because there isn't any."

But the public speedily adjusted to this, and ever since, talking animals and humans have very comfortably mixed in children's fantasy—and, with Orwell's *Animal Farm* and Adams' *Watership Down*, in adult fantasy as well.

The Wind in the Willows is neatly divided into two parts. The first five chapters paint a lovely, peaceful word-portrait of the wondrous English countryside, and lazing along the river (by implication, all English rivers) during spring, summer, and autumn; but also during the depths of winter:

> The Mole came and crouched beside him [the Rat], and, looking out, saw the wood that had been so dreadful to him in quite a changed aspect. Holes, hollows, pools, pitfalls, and other black menaces to the wayfarer were vanishing fast, and a gleaming carpet of faery was springing up everywhere, that looked too delicate to be trodden upon by rough feet. A fine powder filled the air and caressed the cheek with a tingle in its touch, and the black boles of the trees showed up in a light that seemed to come from below.

Chapters 6 and 8 through 12 shift to what Disney calls "Mr. Toad's Wild Ride": Badger, Rat, and Mole's attempt to reform Toad by locking him in his bedroom, his escape and stealing a motor-car, his being sentenced to twenty years in a dungeon, his escape disguised as a washerwoman, his dashing recklessly in a railroad locomotive and barge and by horseback and the same motor-car while singing a rollicking boast:

> The world has held great Heroes,
> As history-books have showed;
> But never a name to go down to fame
> Compared with that of Toad!

…until rescued by Rat, his learning that Toad Hall has been occupied by the Wild Wood weasels and ferrets and stoats during his absence, and Rat, Mole, and Badger's reconquest of Toad Hall with him. There is a setup for Toad's adventures in the "peaceful" first half, and Rat's almost being lyrically seduced into seeking sea wanderings in the "action" last half; and somehow it all seems to fit together. The 1908 idyllic portrait of the unspoiled English countryside has been growing increasingly outdated during the years since *The Wind in the Willows* was written, yet its story seems timeless and ever-fresh.

If you have missed the delight of reading *The Wind in the Willows*, read it now. In the 110 years since its publication, there have been many authorized and unauthorized sequels. William Horwood's four 1990s *Tales of the Willows* novels (*The Willows in Winter, Toad Triumphant, The Willows and Beyond,* and *The Willows at Christmas*), and *Wild Wood* by Jan Needle (Andre Deutsch, June 1981), are recommended.

Windfall • by Tempe O'Kun. Illustrated by Slate.

Dallas, TX: FurPlanet Productions, July 2015, paperback, 325 pp.

It has been six months since the popular TV series *Strangeville* was cancelled after five seasons. The cast has split up and gone their own ways. For Max Saber (husky) and Kylie Bevy (otter), teenage supporting actors who played a high-school boy and girl on the series, this has meant returning to their homes across America. Yet they have remained in touch through texting, and after six months, both are wondering whether their TV romance might have been more serious than they realized. When Max, on his parents' Montana ranch, gets an invitation from Kylie to spend a three-week vacation in her old New England town of Windfall—the town that the creepy, surrealistic *Strangeville* was modeled upon—he takes it. Yep, their romance is real. So is the horror of Windfall.

The characters in *Windfall* are really humans with superficial animal features. But *Windfall* presents them in depth. There are constant mentions of fur, wagging tails, perked or drooping ears, the female otters' whiskers and webbed paws. A teen rhino fan asks Max to autograph his horn. "The otter threaded her tail through the hole in the [car] seat and popped the key into the ignition." Max calls Kylie "rudderbutt." Some of it is occasionally anthro-specific, as when Kylie finds a deer's skull while she and Max are camping in the woods:

> She knew that [the deer had been feral]. The eyes were too far to the sides and the neck attached at the wrong angle, leaving little room for the brain. Still it looked enough like a sapient deer's skull to give her the creeps.

But there are also human features. A sultry cocker spaniel has prominent "boobs." Readers can take these as they will, but there is probably enough "animalicity" to satisfy most furry readers. The almost-two-dozen half-toned illustrations by Slate help a lot.

Strangeville is clearly inspired by the 1990–91 *Twin Peaks* TV series co-created, co-written, and co-directed by David Lynch. *Windfall* is divided into twenty chapters, each of which begins with a TV-guide summary of a *Strangeville* episode.

> STRANGEVILLE (WED/9p) S04E04 "Inside": After her grueling battle with the army of alien ghost dragons, Sandy finally returns home to Strangeville, but not everything is how she left it.
> STRANGEVILLE (TUE/9p) S02E03 "The Nine Portals, Part 1": The Tribunal opens the Nine Portals, flooding the world with dangerous creatures. The gang must stem the tide before these monsters overwhelm them.
> STRANGEVILLE (MON/9p) S01E12 "Slugfest": Cassie learns in a vision that her dentist is secretly a slug monster. She must convince the others before her upcoming check-up makes her a perfect target for being eaten and replaced by a slug-clone.
> STRANGEVILLE (WED/9p) S04E12 "Chocolate Heart": An unknown person is causing havoc with a shipment of love-potion chocolates. Cassie, already coping with being in heat, unknowingly tries one.

Kylie's mother, Laura Bevy, was the executive producer and lead writer of *Strangeville*, and she modeled it "upon what she knew," including making the ancient Queen Anne mansion that she and Kylie inherited (and haven't fully explored yet) the creepy "haunted house" that turns out to be a gateway to the monsters' dimension. Their small town of Windfall has been taking advantage of it, as Kylie explains to Max:

> The mustelid chattered on. "These days, the town's cashing in on 'supernatural' tourism. Basically, Internet weirdos have heard we've got a bunch of ghosts and goblins, so they drive up here to be separated from their disposable income." She couldn't suppress a smirk. "Having a TV show based on the town may have helped a little."

Windfall is a combination of funny and sweet for the first seventy pages. There's a hilarious description of a video that Kylie plays for Max: "Turkish film translated into Italian, now with bootleg subtitles by a non-native English speaker" about a zombie wife returned from the dead, or maybe she's a cyborg, who gets topless and fires lasers from her nipples. Since *Windfall* is an anthro novel, the cyborg/zombie wife is feline, but YouTube has very many foreign movies with humans very like this.

Then around page 70 it starts getting into why the old Bourn Holt mansion that Kylie's mom inherited had been deserted for thirty years, and why Windfall town is getting so many tourists interested in the supernatural. Max and Kylie investigate the town's past. The novel is not quite halfway through when the first real monster appears.

Max and Kylie explore Windfall's adjoining forests and such establishments as the sea-otter-run Thomas Creel Seaweed Farm and Brewery (seaweed beer?), a two-hour drive away. As they travel together for long stretches, and they are now healthy twenty-year-olds, nature takes its course in pauses for explicit mature sex. *Windfall* is NC-17 for a reason, although the eroticism in *Windfall* is very consensual. What the two learn about the truth behind two hundred years of madness, and the reality of fighting interdimensional monsters, is almost an anticlimax.

> "And now you're supposed to pick up where you left off? Start slinging hay bales or whatever? Do they need another pair of hands that badly?"
>
> "No, it's a dog thing." He swirled his fingers at the complexity in an effort to distill it. "Mom's the alpha, and she wants me back because I'm part of her pack."
>
> The otter perked. "So are we a pack now?"
>
> "Hello again." Max gave a polite nod.
>
> Kylie followed with the requisite smile.
>
> A look of brief horror crossed the rabbit's face as she recognized them. She froze except for her twitchy pink nose.

Windfall is for readers who like lots of surreality, consensual graphic sex, and furry anthros. It was a finalist for both the 2015 Cóyotl Award and Ursa Major Award for Best Novel.

The Wrath of Trees • by Bard Bloom. Illustrated, maps by Tod Wills.

Seattle, WA: CreateSpace, December 2011, paperback, 268 pp.

> The lakku philosopher wagged her tails as she hammered nails into my trunk. Not pleasant, companionable wagging, but wagging them so that they cross each other: the gloating of a victorious predator. I was small at the time, and three of the nails poked out of my bark on the opposite side. They ached, of course, but a plant does not feel her body as acutely as an animal would. Nothing had eaten my fruit, so I had no way to resist her, or even complain.

Thus the opening paragraph of the story. If anyone wonders why the story begins as late as it does, the preceding pages are filled with three maps of the world of Kono and the island of Naoth, and a seven-page "prependix" of the characters, language and vocabulary to be encountered.

How to summarize the summary? The lakku, the main characters of Kono, "are generally humanoid, but with some aspects of dogs and birds" with two tails and fur, so they're furry. Naoth has several social/political factions. Pyzot, the nail-driving philosopher in the opening paragraph, is a member of the Rorojro faction which has recently lost its Great Faction status. She intends to use questionable and illegal methods to regain that status, which will also advance herself in Rorojro's hierarchy. She has obtained two offworld maraleni trees, which look like regular Kono trees but are sentient and can mentally control weak minds that eat their berries. Bringing any offworld plants to Kono is a capital offense, so Pyzot, her husband Saet, and Rorojro's kotanay (leader) Utsusei are playing a risky game. Pyzot is brutal, as shown by hammering the nails into Melylunnu (Melyl), the tree, who is the book's narrator. Melyl hates Pyzot, but what can a speechless tree do? especially when, if she is discovered by anyone else, she will be uprooted and burnt?

> "The method is this [Pyzot said]. Maraleni are intelligent trees. Whatever eats their berries is thereafter subject to the maraleni's observation and influence, through subtle currents.... By 'influence' I include mental control—of small animals of only minor intellect and will."
>
> [...]
>
> Saet continued for her, wagging his tails in parallel. "In short words, we feed our enemies some maraleni berries. Then the maraleni can look and listen in on our enemies from afar."
>
> [...]
>
> "I see [Utsusei said] the traditional Pyzot cleverness at work here! Or perhaps the traditional Pyzot insidiousness. How do we get reports, though? Can the trees talk?"
>
> "Again, there are many variations. A bird can be compelled to peck at a board of letters and words to spell out a message. Or I shall eat a berry myself, and endure direct mental contact with the maraleni."

It is clear that Pyzot, Saet, and Utsusei do not consider Melyl as an individual but as a tool to be used. This is their first mistake. They decide that it is too risky for Pyzot to eat a berry to get into mental contact with Melyl; who knows where the division between a weak mind and a strong mind is? Instead they need a fourth lakku, but one whom they can be sure is under their control. They pick Ffip, a young olpi (lakku slave) who is used to being ordered around:

> Ffip was not particularly impressive—not that I had seen more than a half-dozen lakku men. He was no more than five and a half feet tall, and a bit chubby. He was still a foot and a half taller than most women, and not nearly as plump, but he did look distinctly effeminate. Most men are at least six feet, and wiry. He had only two crests, which is not a rare thing of itself; Utsusei also has only two. But one was trimmed short and the other trimmed shorter yet, and he looked lopsided and perpetually confused. His fur, at least, was a respectable reddish-purple, with thin purple stripes on his shoulders and legs, just like Saet's patterns.

Ffip is extremely nervous about being put in mental contact with Melyl:

> His tails were flat in dread; he clearly had a very good idea what was going to be asked of him.
>
> "I need someone to serve as my liaison to Melyl," said Pyzot. "I can't be running out to Letse [where Melyl is planted for spying] every time I want something investigated, and I can't carry on a decent conversation with someone who talks only by commanding a bird to scribble in the sand."
>
> I suppose I could have seized that moment to volunteer that I had other ways of talking. I can create illusions of sound at an immara [something in mental communication with a maraleni], and I was sure that with some practice I could make spoken words.... In any case, I chose to keep my powers secret.

Melyl is already planning to escape Pyzot's control. She slowly enlarges her knowledge of Letse, and of Naoth, as songbirds and mice eat her berries, become her immara, and she sends them out to explore for her. When Pyzot's adolescent daughter Etefi and her best friend Nyzhi become immara, Melyl doesn't dare try to compel them to do anything; she uses them to eavesdrop only and learn about lakku social life.

The Wrath of Trees gradually turns into a picture of lakku society, its politics and religion, and finally of Naothian warfare against the rival island of Kepez. Melyl at first merely observes:

> "The maraleni experiment runs the risk of getting us all lynched if it is discovered. What risks do the others run?" asked Saet.

"Various risks, all small. Ffip might end up mindless if one of them works badly. Another might turn our fur into ice needles. The other experiments are all fairly noticeable though: anyone with a Pesamimaan Butterfly will know that *something* is up. The thing that pleases me most about the maraleni is that she's unnoticeable." I unnoticeably worried that Pyzot would realize that I was listening to her as she decided whether or not to kill me. At least, Ffip didn't notice it.

Then she tries to silently influence things. Things get complicated, on Naoth and beyond. *The Wrath of Trees* is truly unique in its planet, the physiology of its furries, and its rooted, thorny heroine; but the reader is drawn smoothly into it all. It's a very Different but nevertheless enjoyable read.

Appendix 1: Nonfiction Works

Although anthropomorphic literature consists almost entirely of fiction, there are a few nonfiction works, including an increasing number about furry fandom. It is too soon to call any of these classics, but here are five that furry fans are reading.

The Animal Fable in Science Fiction and Fantasy, by Bruce Shaw; foreword by Van Ikin. Jefferson, NC: McFarland, 2010, paperback, 268 pp.

Animal Land: The Creatures of Children's Fiction, by Margaret Blount. Illustrated. London: Hutchinson, 1974, hardcover, 336 pp.

Furries Among Us; Essays on Furries by the Most Prominent Members of the Fandom, edited by Thurston Howl. Illustrated. Nashville, TN: Thurston Howl Publications, 2015, paperback, 174 pp.

Furry Fandom Conventions, 1989–2015. by Fred Patten; furword by Kathleen C. Gerbasi. Illustrated (8 color pp.). Jefferson, NC: McFarland, 2017, paperback, 250pp.

Furry Nation: The True Story of America's Most Misunderstood Subculture, by Joe Strike. Illustrated. Jersey City, NJ: Cleis Press, 2017, paperback, 351 pp.

Appendix 2:
Author and Chronological Lists

Since the arrangement of the main part of the book is alphabetical by title, here the titles of the books are organized, first, alphabetically by the authors' last names, then second (next page) by date of publication.

Titles by Author Name

Watership Down, Richard Adams
Albert of Adelaide, Howard L. Anderson
Earthman's Burden, Poul Anderson
Claw the Way to Victory, AnthroAquatic
Jonathan Livingston Seagull, Richard Bach
The Last Unicorn, Peter S. Beagle
New Coyote, Michael Bergey
Sunset of Furmankind, Ted Blasingame
A Wilder West, Ted Blasingame
A Marriage of Insects, Bard Bloom
The Wrath of Trees, Bard Bloom
Animal Land; The Creatures of Children's Fiction, Margaret Blount
Sundiver, David Brin
Imperium Lupi, Adam Browne
God of Clay, Ryan Campbell
Koa of the Drowned Kingdom, Ryan Campbell
Alice's Adventures in Wonderland, Lewis Carroll
The Pride of Chanur, C.J. Cherryh
To Journey in the Year of the Tiger, H. Leighton Dickson
Transformations, Bernard Doove
The Fox of Richmond Park, Kate Dreyer
Theta, Sasya Fox
The Seventh Chakra, Kevin Frane
Summerhill, Kevin Frane
In Wilder Lands, Jim Galford
The Alien Dark, Diana Gallagher
The Abandoned, Paul Gallico

Anonymous Rex, Eric Garcia
The Book of Lapism, Phil Geusz
Transmutation NOW!, Phil Geusz
Griffin Ranger, Roz Gibson
Green Fairy, Kyell Gold
Out of Position, Kyell Gold
The Time He Desires, Kyell Gold
Volle, Kyell Gold
Waterways, Kyell Gold
The Wind in the Willows, Kenneth Grahame
Huntress, Renee Carter Hall
Foxhunt!, Rich Hanes
Flight of the Godkin Griffin, M.C.A. Hogarth
Duncton Wood, William Horwood
Furries Among Us, Thurston Howl, ed.
MoonDust; Falling from Grace, Ton Inktail
Redwall, Brian Jacques
Sandeagozu, Janann Jenner
Fangs of K'aath, Paul Kidd
Mus of Kerbridge, Paul Kidd
A Whisper of Wings, Paul Kidd
The Life and Perambulation of a Mouse, Dorothy Kilner
The Jungle Book, Rudyard Kipling
Watchers, Dean Koontz
Monkey Wars, Richard Kurti
The Lion, the Witch, and the Wardrobe, by C.S. Lewis
Otters in Space, Mary Lowd
Skeleton Crew, Gre7g Luterman
archy and mehitabel, Don Marquis

Kismet, Watts Martin
Why Coyotes Howl, Watts Martin
Decision at Doona, Anne McCaffrey
Felicia: The Night of the Basquot, Chas P.A. Melville
Where the Blue Begins, Christopher Morley
Mrs. Frisby and the Rats of NIMH, Robert C. O'Brien
Windfall, Tempe O'Kun
Animal Farm, George Orwell
Already Among Us, Fred Patten, ed.
Best in Show, Fred Patten, ed.
The Cóyotl Awards Anthology, Fred Patten, ed.
Dogs of War, Fred Patten, ed.
Furry Fandom Conventions, 1989–2015, Fred Patten
The Furry Future, Fred Patten, ed.
Gods with Fur, Fred Patten, ed.
The Ursa Major Awards Anthology, Fred Patten, ed.
The Bees, Lalane Paull
The Blood Jaguar, Michael H. Payne
Little Fuzzy, H. Beam Piper
Felidae, Akif Pirinçci
Off Leash, Daniel Potter
Northern Lights, Philip Pullman
Tails of the City, R.S. Pylman
Mort(e), Robert Repino
Waiting for Gertrude; A Graveyard Gothic, Bill Richardson
Bête, Adam Roberts
Off the Beaten Path, Rukis
Bambi; A Life in the Woods, Felix Salten
Thousand Tales, Kris Schnee
Barsk; The Elephants' Graveyard, Lawrence M. Schoen
Black Beauty, Anna Sewall
We the Underpeople, Cordwainer Smith
The Stray Lamb, Thorne Smith
The Heavenly Horse from the Outermost West, Mary Stanton
Sirius, Olaf Stapledon
Francis, David Stern
Furry Nation, Joe Strike
Three Bags Full; A Sheep Detective Story, Leonie Swann
Memoirs of a Polar Bear, Yoko Tawada
Inhuman Acts; A Collection of Noir, Ocean Tigrox, ed.
The Silver Tide, Michael Tod
Fabulous Histories, Mrs. Trimmer
The Island of Dr. Moreau, H.G. Wells
Charlotte's Web, E.B. White
Tailchaser's Song, Tad Williams
Who Censored Roger Rabbit?, Gary K. Wolf
Trick or Treat, Ianus J. Wolf, ed.

*FANG and *ROAR* (multiple editors)

Titles by Publication Date

The Life and Perambulation of a Mouse, April 1784
Fabulous Histories, 1786
Alice's Adventures in Wonderland, November 1865
Black Beauty, December 1877
The Jungle Book, June 1894
The Island of Dr. Moreau, April 1896
The Wind in the Willows, October 1908
Where the Blue Begins, October 1922
archy and mehitabel, December 1927
Bambi; A Life in the Woods, July 1928
The Stray Lamb, November 1929
Sirius, June 1944
Animal Farm, August 1945
Francis, October 1946
The Abandoned, September 1950
The Lion, the Witch, and the Wardrobe, September 1950
Charlotte's Web, October 1952
Earthman's Burden, July 1957
Little Fuzzy, January 1962
The Last Unicorn, March 1968
Decision at Doona, April 1969
Jonathan Livingston Seagull, August 1970
Mrs. Frisby and the Rats of NIMH, April 1971
Watership Down, November 1972
Animal Land; The Creatures of Children's Fiction, October 1974
Sundiver, February 1980
Duncton Wood, September 1980
Who Censored Roger Rabbit?, October 1981
The Pride of Chanur, January 1982
Tailchaser's Song, November 1985
Sandeagozu, October 1986
Redwall, November 1986
Watchers, February 1987
The Heavenly Horse from the Outermost West, June 1988
The Alien Dark, December 1990
Felidae, February 1993
The Silver Tide, May 1993
Mus of Kerbridge, April 1995
Northern Lights, July 1995
The Blood Jaguar, December 1998

Appendix 2

Anonymous Rex, August 1999
A Whisper of Wings, October 1999
Fangs of K'aath, April 2000
Alysha's Fall, September 2000
Waiting for Gertrude: A Graveyard Gothic, October 2001
Best in Show, July 2003
Volle, January 2005
Why Coyotes Howl, January 2005
Transformations, July 2005
New Coyote, August 2005
FANG volume 1, September 2005
Tails of the City, November 2005
Three Bags Full: A Sheep Detective Story, June 2006
We the Underpeople, December 2006
A Marriage of Insects, July 2007
Transmutation NOW!, August 2007
Waterways, January 2008
Out of Position, January 2009
Foxhunt!, June 2009
The Seventh Chakra, January 2010
Otters in Space, August 2010
In Wilder Lands, August 2011
Sunset of Furmankind, September 2011
The Wrath of Trees, December 2011
Green Fairy, March 2012
Flight of the Godkin Griffin, June 2012
The Ursa Major Awards Anthology, June 2012
Albert of Adelaide, July 2012
To Journey in the Year of the Tiger, September 2012
Summerhill, January 2013
Theta, August 2013
God of Clay, September 2013
Trick or Treat, September 2013
The Bees, May 2014
Off the Beaten Path, July 2014
Skeleton Crew, August 2014
A Wilder West, August 2014
Bête, September 2014
The Book of Lapism, January 2015
The Furry Future, January 2015
Griffin Ranger, January 2015
Monkey Wars, January 2015
Mort(e), January 2015
Furries Among Us, June 2015
Thousand Tales, June 2015
Windfall, July 2015
Huntress, September 2015
Inhuman Acts, September 2015
Koa of the Drowned Kingdom, September 2015
Off Leash, October 2015
Barsk; The Elephants' Graveyard, December 2015
MoonDust; Falling from Grace, December 2015
Claw the Way to Victory, January 2016
Gods with Fur, June 2016
Memoirs of a Polar Bear, November 2016
The Time He Desires, December 2016
Dogs of War, January 2017
Furry Fandom Conventions, 1989–2015, January 2017
Kismet, January 2017
The Fox of Richmond Park, July 2017
Imperium Lupi, July 2017
Felicia: The Night of the Basquot, September 2017
Furry Nation, October 2017
The Cóyotl Awards Anthology, November 2018

Appendix 3: Awards

The Ursa Major Awards

The Ursa Major Awards are administered by the Anthropomorphic Literature and Arts Association (ALAA), a furry fandom organization. They are presented for the best anthropomorphic work in currently twelve categories during the previous calendar year. The Ursa Major Awards were first presented in 2002, for works first published or shown during January–December 2001.

The current twelve categories are: 1. Best Anthropomorphic Motion Picture. 2. Best Anthropomorphic Dramatic Short or Series. 3. Best Anthropomorphic Novel. 4. Best Anthropomorphic Short Fiction. 5. Best Anthropomorphic Other Literary Work (usually for anthologies or collections). 6. Best Anthropomorphic Non-Fiction Work (added in 2016). 7. Best Anthropomorphic Graphic Story. 8. Best Anthropomorphic Comic Strip. 9. Best Anthropomorphic Magazine. 10. Best Anthropomorphic Published Illustration. 11. Best Anthropomorphic Game. 12. Best Anthropomorphic Website.

The UMAs are a popular vote award. Anyone who requests an electronic ballot, with up to five nominees in each category, from the ALAA may vote. The ALAA tabulates the results, and presents the Award to the artist/author/director/editor of the work getting the most votes. The results are announced at a presentation ceremony at a different furry fandom convention the next year; the 2016 Awards at Anthrocon 2017, and the 2017 Awards at FurDU 2018.

The UMA trophy from 2001 to 2014 was a framed certificate with the category and winner's name, and the UMA illustrated logo by Heather Bruton. Beginning in 2015, the trophy has been a transparent acrylic plaque engraved with the category, winner's name, and UMA logo by Heather Bruton.

The winners in the Best Anthropomorphic Novel category have been:

2001—*Casual Rex* by Eric Garcia (Villard Books)
2002—*Rescue Ferrets at Sea* by Richard Bach (Scribner/Ferret House Press)
2003—*Between Darkness and Light* by Lisanne Norman (DAW Books).
2004—*Never Again a Man* by Charles Matthias (electronic edition only)
2005—*Volle* by Kyell Gold (Sofawolf Press)
2006—*Pendant of Fortune* by Kyell Gold (Sofawolf Press)
2007—*Life's Dream* by Bernard Doove (CreateSpace)
2008—*Waterways* by Kyell Gold (Sofawolf Press)
2009—*Out of Position* by Kyell Gold (Sofawolf Press)
2010—*Shadow of the Father* by Kyell Gold (Sofawolf Press)

Appendix 3

2011—*Isolation Play* by Kyell Gold (Sofawolf Press)
2012—*Flight of the Star Phoenix* by Bernard Doove (CreateSpace)
2013—*Skyfire* by Jess E. Owen (Five Elements Press)
2014—*Off the Beaten Path* by Rukis (FurPlanet Productions)
2015—*Tiger's Eye* by Alexander Shaw (electronic edition only)
2016—*My Diary, by Fredrick Usiku Kruger, Lieutenant of the Rackenroon Hyena Brigade* by Kathy Garrison (electronic edition only)
2017—*The Wayward Astronomer* by Geoffrey Thomas (Corvus Publishing)

The winners in the Best Anthropomorphic Short Fiction category have been:

2001—*Beneath the Crystal Sea* by Brock Hoagland
2002—*Familiars* by Michael H. Payne
2003—*In the Line of Duty* by M.C.A. Hogarth
2004—*Felicia and the Tailcutter's Curse* by Chaz P.A. Melville
2005—*In His Own Country* by Kristin Fontaine
2006—*Jacks to Open* by Kyell Gold
2007—*Don't Blink* by Kyell Gold
2008—*In Between* by Kyell Gold
2009—*Drifting* by Kyell Gold
2010—*Bridges* by Kyell Gold
2011—*How to Get Through the Day* by Kyell Gold
2012—*Dangerous Jade* by Malcolm Cross
2013—*The Monkeytown Raid* by Roz Gibson
2014—*When a Cat Loves a Dog* by Mary E. Lowd
2015—*The Analogue Cat* by Alice "Huskyteer" Dryden
2016–*400 Rabbits* by Alice "Huskyteer" Dryden
2017—*Lieutenant Kruger and the Mistress Jade Trophy Game* by Kathy Garrison

---

The winners in the Best Anthropomorphic Other Literary Work category have been:

2001—*The Sound & the Furry: The Complete Hoka Stories* by Poul Anderson and Gordon R. Dickson (Science Fiction Book Club)
2002—*Ozy and Millie IV: Authentic Banana Dye* by David Simpson (Plan Nine Publishing)
2003—*Best in Show: Fifteen Years of Outstanding Furry Fiction* edited by Fred Patten (Sofawolf Press)
2004—*The Art of Usagi Yojimbo* by Stan Sakai (Dark Horse Books)
2005—*Tales of the Questor*, volume 1 by Ralph E. Hayes, Jr. (Lulu.com)
2006—*A Doemain of Our Own* by Susan Rankin (Plan Nine Publishing)
2007—*All the Newshounds Fit to Print* by Thomas K. Dye (Lulu.com)
2008—*Dog's Days of Summer* by Blotch (Sofawolf Press)
2009—*Draw Furries: How to Create Anthropo-

Left: **The Ursa Major Award trophy. Photograph by Bernard Doove.** ***Right:*** **The Ursa Major Award logo, by Foxenawolf.**

morphic and Fantasy Animals by Lindsay Cibos and Jared Hodges (Impact)
2010—*Fur-Piled #4* by Leo Magna (Sofawolf Press)
2011—*Nordguard, Book One: Across Thin Ice* by Tess Garman and Teagan Gavet (Sofawolf Press)
2012—*Slightly Damned, Book One* by Sarah "Chu" Wilson (IndyPlanet)
2013—*Slightly Damned, Book Two* by Sarah "Chu" Wilson (IndyPlanet)
2014—*Blacksad: Amarillo* by Juan Díaz Canales and Juanjo Guarnido (Dark Horse Press)
2015—*Furries Among Us; Essays on Furries by the Most Prominent Members of the Fandom* edited by Thurston Howl (Thurston Howl Publications)
2016—*Gods with Fur* edited by Fred Patten (FurPlanet Productions)
2017—*Dogs of War* edited by Fred Patten (FurPlanet Productions)

The winners in the Best Anthropomorphic Nonfiction Work category have been:

2016—*The Art of Zootopia* by Jessica Julius (Chronicle Books)
2017—*Furry Nation* by Joe Strike (Cleis Press)

The Cóyotl Awards

The Cóyotl Awards have been presented annually by the Furry Writers' Guild, an organization of writers of anthropomorphic fiction. The FWG was founded in 2010, and presently has almost 200 members.

The Cóyotl Awards are voted upon a ballot with up to five nominees by the membership of the FWG, in the categories of Best Novel, Best Novella, Best Short Story, and Best Anthology. In their first year, 2012 (for 2011 works), there were two divisions within each category; General and Mature. These were merged the following year. The Best Anthology category was added in 2013. The Cóyotl Awards are announced at a presentation ceremony at a furry fandom convention the next year; currently Furlandia in Portland, OR.

The Cóyotl Award trophy is a certificate illustrated with the Cóyotl logo, and a small coyote pup plush doll wearing a red bandana with the Cóyotl logo and category sewn on it. The plush dolls with bandanas are store-bought, with the Cóyotl logos and category name sewn on the bandana. The coyote dolls for the four categories are unofficially named Neve for Best Novel, Ella for Best Novella, Shorty for Best Short Story, and Anthony for Best Anthology.

The winners in the Best Novel category have been:

2011—General: *Inchoate Carillon, Inconstant Cucold* by Charles Mathias (electronic edition only)
2011—Mature: *Sixes Wild: Manifest Destiny* by Tempe O'Kun (Sofawolf Press)
2012—*By Sword and Star* by Renee Carter Hall (Anthropomorphic Dreams Publishing)
2013—*God of Clay* by Ryan Campbell (Sofawolf Press)
2014—*Off the Beaten Path* by Rukis (FurPlanet Productions)

The Cóyotl Award trophies. Photograph by Mary E. Lowd.

Appendix 3

2015—*Barsk: The Elephant's Graveyard* by Lawrence M. Schoen (Tor Books)
2016—*The Digital Coyote* by Kris Schnee (CreateSpace)
2017—*Kismet* by Watts Martin (Argyll/FurPlanet Productions)

The winners in the Best Novella category have been:

2011—General, *Real Dragons Don't Wear Sweaters* by Renee Carter Hall
2011—Mature, *Science Friction* by Kyell Gold
2012—*Reach for the Sky (The Battle of Britain—A Novel of Lt. Corn, Book 1)* by Vixyy Fox
2013—*Indigo Rain* by Watts Martin
2014—*Huntress* by Renee Carter Hall
2015—*Koa of the Drowned Kingdom* by Ryan Campbell
2016—*The Goat: Building the Perfect Victim* by Bill Kieffer
2017—*Dragon Fried Cheese* by Madison Keller

The winners in the Best Short Story category have been:

2011—General, *The Canoe Race* by Daniel and Mary Lowd
2011—Mature, *Best of Breed* by Renee Carter Hall
2012—*Chasing the Spotlight* by Tim Susman
2013—*Fox in the Hen House* by Mary E. Lowd
2014—*Jackalope Wives* by Ursula Vernon
2015—*The Analogue Cat* by Alice "Huskyteer" Dryden
2016–*400 Rabbits* by Alice "Huskyteer" Dryden
2017—*Behesht* by Dwale

The winners in the Best Anthology category have been:

2013—*Hot Dish 1* edited by Alopex (Sofawolf Press)
2014—*Abandoned Places* edited by Tarl Hoch (FurPlanet Productions)
2015—*Inhuman Acts: An Anthology of Noir* edited by Ocean Tigrox (FurPlanet Productions)
2016—*Gods with Fur* edited by Fred Patten (FurPlanet Productions)
2017—*Arcana: A Tarot Anthology* edited by Madison Scott-Clary (Thurston Howl Publications)

The Cóyotl Award logo, by Jessie "Electric Keet" Tracer.

The Leo Literary Awards

The Leo Literary Awards (as distinct from other non-furry Leo Awards) were created in 2017 by the Furry Book Review committee of Thurston Howl Publications. They are presented to works first published during the previous calendar year in the categories of Novels, Novellas, Anthologies, Short Stories, Poems, and Nonfiction. Authors must confirm that they identify as being part of furry fandom.

Nominators are limited to those who have had published an anthropomorphic novel, two stories, or three poems during the past five years, or edited an anthology. (There are other restrictions.) Each nominee is examined by a panel of five to ten judges who have had anthropomorphic works published during the last two years. Eligibility is dependent upon the author or publisher providing review copies directly or through the FBR to each judge. The judges will vote on each nominee, and a nominee must be approved by ⅔ of the judges.

The Leo Literary Awards are meant to call attention to anthropomorphic works of exceptional merit, by authors within furry fandom. This means that there will not be one single "best" work each year. For example, there were fifteen novels nominated for 2017 Leo Literary Awards, and four winners.

The 2017 Leo Literary Awards were announced at Anthrocon 2018. The Leo Literary Award trophy is a lion plushie designed and made by T. Thomas Abernathy.

The Leo Literary Awards presentation, on 7 July 2018 at the Anthrocon 2018 convention, Pittsburgh, PA, showing both the award certificates and the awards' plushie trophy. *Front row, left to right:* Roz Gibson, Rechan, Thurston Howl, Tim Susman. Rear row, left to right: K.C. Alpinus, Ocean Tigrox. Photograph by T.J. Minde.

Novels (including collections) judged as worthy of the Award are:

Jackalope Wives and Other Stories by T. Kingfisher (Ursula Vernon)
Imperium Lupi by Adam Browne
rewritten by Jako Malan
Kismet by Watts Martin

Novellas judged as worthy of the Award are:

The Earth Tigers by Frances Pauli
Dragon Fried Cheese by Madison Keller
Matriarch: Elephant vs. T-Rex by Roz Gibson
Jazz at the End of the Night by Weasel

Anthologies judged as worthy of the Award are:

Bleak Horizons edited by Tarl Hoch
Passing Through: Tails from the Road edited by Weasel

Short Stories judged as worthy of the Award are:

Crossroads the Namib by Jako Malan
When the Paint Dries by Rechan

The Leo Literary Award logo.

Appendix 3

The Lion of the Low Countries by Alice "Huskyteer" Dryden
Personal History by Tim Susman
To the Victor the Spoils by Ocean Tigrox

Poetry judged as worthy of the Award are:

A Deafening Dirge by BanWynn Oakshadow

Top to Bottom by Mog Moogle
Unbroken by Televassi

Nonfiction works judged as worthy of the award are:

Furries Among Us 2: More Essays on Furries by Furries edited by Thurston Howl (Jonathan Thurston)

Appendix 4:
Furry Specialty Publishers

Beginning in 1999, several specialty publishers have been created for anthropomorphic literature and (beginning in the 2010s) nonfiction books about furry fandom itself. Some companies only published a few books before going out of business, or still exist but no longer publish books. Ten publishers or imprints have lasted to the present, and most of them are growing.

This list does not include several authors who have their own imprints but only publish their own anthropomorphic novels, such as Fallen Kitten Productions (Daniel Potter), Furry Logic Productions (Gary Akins), Kitsune Press (Paul Kidd), Rockhopper Books (Steven Hammond), and Studio MCAH (M.C.A. Hogarth).

Armoured Fox Press

Armoured Fox Press, "A Publisher & Distributor of Furry & Anime Literature," is the newest furry specialty publisher and the first Canadian one. It was started by Tarl Hoch in Calgary, Alberta in October 2016, to import furry and anime fiction books and to sell them at Canadian furry conventions (which U.S. publishers do not sell at because of regulations affecting foreign businesses and import duties), and to publish its own books. Their first book was a combination of furry and anime, *Purrfect Tails* edited by Tarl Hoch, an anthology of nine short stories featuring "nekos," anime-style cat-women and -men with cat ears and tails but otherwise human, published in February 2018. They have three books by the end of 2018. The first convention that AFP exhibited and sold at was Fur-Eh! 2018 in June 2018 in Edmonton, Alberta.

Hoch is the editor of two previous furry horror anthologies for FurPlanet Productions; *Abandoned Places* (December 2014) and *Bleak Horizons* (March 2017).

Armoured Fox Press logo.

Bad Dog Books

Bad Dog Books began in September 2005 when Alex Vance, living in the Netherlands, started his small press with *FANG*, subtitled "The Little Black Book of Furry Fiction." Vance specialized in literate furry homosexual erotic fantasy. *FANG* was blurbed as "the beginning of a new era in furry publishing, and this first issue was dedicated to bringing the finest modern homoerotica to the anthropomorphic reading public."

ROAR was intended at first to be *FANG* volume 4, but Bad Dog Books began getting so much non-erotic fiction that it was decided to publish it as an all-ages companion volume, subtitled "The Little White Book of Furry Fiction." Both *FANG* and *ROAR* are magazines in a paperback book format. They initially appeared erratically. In 2018 *CLAW* was added, for feminine erotic fantasy.

Bad Dog Books have been marketed in the U.S. by FurPlanet Productions since 2007. BDB published three volumes each of *FANG* and *ROAR*, plus a half-dozen novels, to 2011, when Vance's poor health plus the fact that most sales were in the U.S. caused him to sell it completely to FurPlanet. The December 14, 2011, sale included a requirement that FurPlanet continue to publish volumes of *FANG* and *ROAR* annually under the BDB imprint. There are currently nine volumes of each, and one of *CLAW*. In June 2013, FurPlanet made Bad Dog Books its regular imprint for e-book editions. Bad Dog Books currently publishes over 200 e-book editions of titles of the other furry small presses, including the inactive Anthropomorphic Dreams Publishing (2007–2012).

Bad Dog Books logo.

FurPlanet Productions

FurPlanet Productions, in Dallas, Texas, is the largest anthropomorphic specialty publisher. It dates from March 1, 2008, when Fuzz-Wolf bought it from FurNation's furry website founder, Nexxus (James Robertson). Nexxus started FurNation Multimedia in November 1996, and slowly expanded it into a major furry online community. FurPlanet was added in 2004 as FurNation's online store, and the publisher of the existing (since July 2000) *FurNation Magazine,* plus some erotic furry comic books and novels. During 2006 Fuzz-Wolf got involved with FurPlanet's publishing activities. His responsibilities grew, and he became the editor of *FurNation Magazine* with #8, January 2007. During February 2008 he bought the FurPlanet name and its publishing activities, removing them from FurNation. (The magazine was returned to FurNation.)

FurPlanet Productions logo.

FurPlanet sells through an Internet mail-order catalogue, and sales tables at furry fandom conventions throughout the U.S. In 2016 it traveled to seven conventions. It published 22 new items—novels, comic books, art folios, music CDs, and card decks. It publishes the program book for the annual Furry Fiesta in Dallas.

FurPlanet is a hobbyist operation. Its two owners, FuzzWolf and Teiran, both have regular day jobs. They and their two long-term employees Buck Turner and Zia McCorgi run FurPlanet in their spare time. All four appear at almost every convention that FurPlanet displays at. They are sometimes joined by their friends Ajax B. Coriander and Andres Cyanni Halden, who have edited anthologies for FurPlanet in the past.

Goal Publications

Goal Publications is the almost sole venture of AnthroAquatic (Sean Gerace), in Plainfield, Connecticut. He began by editing the first volume of the Furry Writers' Guild's literary anthology, *Tales from the Guild: Music to Your Ears*, for publication in September 2014 by Rabbit Valley. In 2015 and early 2016 he edited and published three issues of *A Glimpse of Anthropomorphic Literature* as e-magazines. His first book as Goal Publications was a compendium of all three issues of *A Glimpse of Anthropomorphic Literature* in November 2016.

Technically, Goal Publications is the publishing imprint of AnthroAquatic's Ottercorrect Literature Services. He also operates AnthroAquatic Literary Editing as an Ottercorrect subsidiary. In June 2018 Goal added a second imprint, Fanged Fiction, for 18+ (adult) titles.

Goal Publications has published seven books and three T-shirts, under both imprints, to date. It also represents Jaffa Books, Australia's only furry publisher (so far), in the U.S. and has gotten its books listed on Amazon. AnthroAquatic has edited one of Jaffa Books' titles, the anthro sports anthology *Claw the Way to Victory*.

Goal Publications logo.

Jaffa Books

Jaffa Books, Australia's first furry specialty press, was founded in Brisbane, Queensland as a bookstore by Jacob F.R. Coates in March 2011 to import, publish and distribute both furry titles and authors with little to no publication history, especially in fantasy fiction. Its first books went on sale that October. JB as an importer has become the official Australian retailer for most U.S. furry specialty publishers, and all titles by Kyell Gold.

Jaffa Books has had Dealers' Den sales tables at Queensland's furry conventions (RivFur in Brisbane and FurDU in Gold Coast City) since 2013, and expanded to Western Australia (FurWAG in Perth) in 2015 and Victoria (ConFurgence in

Jaffa Books logo.

Melbourne) in 2016. JB's first original titles (only arguably furry) were the dragon fantasies *Axinstone* (December 2013) and *Impossible Magic* (August 2014); both by J.F.R. Coates in his *The Destiny of Dragons* series. It published its first "regular" furry novel, *Reborn* by J.F.R. Coates, in May 2015. By now JB has a dozen titles of its own.

Jarlidium Press

Jarlidium Press is a furry specialty publisher, but not really for text books. It was started by two Seattle furry fans, James "Tibo" Birdsall and Dan "Flinthoof" Canaan, in 1998 when they leased a commercial photocopier to publish fanzines, comic books, flyers, the convention books of Seattle's annual Conifur Northwest convention, and similar "ephemera," usually furry art-related. Its first book was the *Dela the Hooda Treasury*, Volume 1, by Style Wager and Greg Older (June 2000), a collection of the Internet comic strip. Over the years it has published several other collections of Internet furry comic strips, notably several volumes of Aaron Neathery's sf *Endtown*.

Beginning in December 2010, Jarlidium Press has begun a series of reprint collections of all 69 issues of the furry fanzine *Yarf!*, *The Complete Yarf!*, at five issues per volume. But it seems to have stalled; so far there have been only three volumes: Volume 1, issues #0–#5, November 2010, 248 pages; Volume 2, #6–#10, November 2012, 248 pages; and Volume 3, #11–#15, December 2013, 290 pages. Jarlidium Press also took over publication of the semi-annual magazine *North American Fur* with issue #4, Spring 1999; the current issue is #38, Summer 2018.

Jarlidium Press logo.

The Jarlidium Press publications are usually available only by mail-order sale from its own website catalogue, Rabbit Valley's, and the Second Ed Anthropomorphics online mail-order bookshop of Ed Zolna (since July 2003), and the few furry conventions at which Birdsall & Canaan have a sales table.

Rabbit Valley Publishing

Rabbit Valley Publishing—a.k.a. Rabbit Valley Books, Rabbit Valley Comics, or just Rabbit Valley—was started by Sean Rabbitt (two T's) in North Kingstown, Rhode Island in 1997, moving to Waltham, Massachusetts in 2001, and to Las Vegas, Nevada in 2009. He was joined by his partner (later husband) Andrew Rabbitt in 1999. Over the next decade, the Rabbit Valley Comic Shop expanded to add more staff and to offer mail-order sales of practically every furry publication that there was, including all books, comic books, and art folios.

RV's first totally original paperback was *The Prince of Knaves*, by Alflor Aalto (March 2012). Rabbit Valley has rapidly increased production until today it publishes roughly 18 new titles a year; four novels, three anthologies, six comic books, and five art collections or folios. All Rabbit Valley titles are still in print. RV added a digital furry book distribution service in February 2013 that today has over a hundred titles available. RV also does DVD and CD manufacturing for a half-dozen furry musicians.

RV is the leader among furry specialty publishers with dealer tables, attending over two dozen conventions annually. In addition to selling its own titles, RV regularly stocks those of all other furry publishers, and a host of other paperbacks published by CreateSpace ("Rabbit Valley" is a registered trademark of Heavy Amalgamated Rabbit Valley Industries LLC).

Sofawolf Press

Sofawolf Press was the first successful furry publishing company. It became official in October 1999, with its first publication, the magazine *Anthrolations* #1, in January 2000 (to #8, November 2006). It was founded by Tim Susman and Jeff Eddy, and incorporated in March 2010 when its team had grown to four regulars, with Jeff Eddy as President and Treasurer, Alopex as Vice President and Secretary, and Tim Susman and Mark Brown as members of the Board of Directors. It is currently run by Jeff Eddy from a warehouse in St. Paul, Minnesota.

Rabbit Valley Publishing logo.

Sofawolf's first book was the anthology *Breaking the Ice*, edited by Tim Susman (January 2002). It was with the publication of Kyell Gold's first novel, the Ursa Major Award-winning *Volle*, that the publisher really became prominent in the furry community. At the same time, Sofawolf was establishing itself as a publisher of high-quality furry short fiction. The mostly-annual *Heat* series, an erotic magazine in perfect-bound booklet format, began in January 2004 but quickly moved to every June–July. There are fifteen yearly issues to date. *New Fables*, Sofawolf's title for non-erotic furry literature, is published less often, but there have been five volumes since Summer 2007.

Sofawolf can be counted upon to show up at several furry conventions a year, with at least one table of furry books, calendars, T-shirts, the Artistic Visions artists' sketchbooks, and more. In Europe, it is represented by Black-Paw Productions of Germany and other furry specialty bookshops.

Sofawolf Press logo.

Thurston Howl Publications

Thurston Howl Publications, run by Jonathan Thurston, started with his anthropomorphic wolf novel *Farmost Star I See Tonight* (March 2013). It picked up speed with the charity anthology *Wolf Warriors* in October 2014. Thurston was then going to college and living in Nashville, Tennessee. He returned home to Lansing, Michigan, when he graduated and moved THP with him.

THP has grown into a company with over a dozen staff, the most visible of whom is Tabsley Abernathy, its graphic design director who has painted several of its covers. It was the first to publish a serious nonfiction book about furry fandom, *Furries Among Us* (2015), which won an Ursa Major Award. It has published over three dozen books in both paperback and electronic editions, plus two tarot card decks. THP is not a furry-exclusive publishing house, but about 90 percent of its titles are furry Young Adult, all-ages, or 18+ fantasy, horror, or sf books, both novels and anthologies. THP itself sells mostly through its mail-order catalogue, but its titles are on sale at most U.S. furry conventions through Rabbit Valley's tables, and at Germany's EuroFurence through Fusselschwarm.

Thurston Howl Publications logo.

THP runs the Furry Book Review service, "a review outlet for anthropomorphic-animal books," with a dozen reviewers (so far) posting over two dozen reviews on the Internet. The FBR administers the new Leo Literary Awards, the first juried furry literary award.

Weasel Press

Weasel Press emphasizes that it is a beat press, not a furry press. That said, it is eager to expand its furry line and actively solicits new submissions.

WP was founded by Weasel Patterson in Manvel, TX. Its first book was a re-release, *Ribbon and Leviathan* by Manna Plourde (April 2014). Today it has books of fiction and nonfiction, including poetry and plays; plus the imprints Red Ferret Press for erotica, and Sinister Stoat Press for horror. Most titles are available on Amazon in paper and Kindle editions. WP publishes a furry magazine, *Typewriter Emergencies: A Journal of Furry Lit*; and the only books of furry poetry, the *Civilized Beasts* anthologies (three volumes so far).

Weasel Patterson says that Weasel Press is not without turbulence, but overall it's doing just fine. It publishes 15 to 20 titles a year, about 1 or 2 of them furry. About 3 or 4 of these are anthologies; the rest are novels and poetry collections. Only a few titles have gone out of print. Sales are almost all of paper editions, since readers who prefer e-books can get Amazon's Kindle editions. WP has a close relationship with Thurston Howl Publications, with Jonathan Thurston on its staff as editor/consultant, and several of its covers by Tabsley Abernathy or Joseph Chou.

Weasel Press logo.

Index

The Abandoned 13–14
Abandoned Places 118
Abernathy, T. Thomas 208
Abignale, Frank, Jr. 187
academics 12, 26
activism 134
Adams, Richard 10, 143, *181–183*, 196
adaptation 100
adolescence 42, 75, 80, 84–85, 89, 116, 134–135, 146, 159, 165, 168, 173, 181, 183–185, 199
adulthood 1, 10, 11, 57, 96–97, 104, 115, 126, 131, 172–173, 177, 182, 195
adventure 3–4, 9, 36, 62–63, 68–69, 87–88, 94, 102, 126, 135–137, 156, 160, 182, 186
The Adventure of the Misplaced Hound 56
The Adventures of Huckleberry Finn 16
Adversary's Fall 82
Aeschylus 181
Aesop 3
Aesop's Fables 9, 26
Africa 26, 89–90, 134
After the Last Bells Rung 48
After Their Kind 52
Agamemnon 181
Age of Enlightenment 9, 105
Ailoura 174
Albert of Adelaide 14–16, *15*
Alice's Adventures in Wonderland 1, 10, 16–18, 22, 26, 27, 43, 57, 105, 171–172, 195
alien 10, 20, 49–51, 56–57, 86, 93, 109–110, 135–137, 152–154
The Alien Dark 18–20
All of You Are in Me 82
All the Pigs' Houses 20
All You Zombies 151
allegory 23, 25, 187
Alpha Ralpha Boulevard 186
Alpinus, K.C. 52, 59, 209
Already Among Us 20–22, *21*

Alter Ego 7
Alternate Realms 37
Amateur Press Association (APA) 1–4, 8, 10, 36
Amazon 4, 11, 16, 38, 51, 55
The Amber Spyglass 125–126
American Book of the Month Club 25
American culture 3
AmoXcalli 8
The Analogue Cat 78
analysis 22, 23, 25–26, 179
Anarchist Farm 26
Andersen, Hans Christian 26, 187
Anderson, Howard L. 14–16, *15*
Anderson, Poul 20, 23, 55–57
Anger of the Onseck 186
Anglin, M.R. 52, 82
anglocentric 27
The Animal Fable in Science Fiction and Fantasy 22–24, *23*, 201
Animal Farm: A Fairy Story 10, 24–26, *25*, 115–116, 182, 196
animal-headed 3, 27, 128, 173
Animal Land: The Creatures of Childrens Fiction 26–27, 201
The Animals' Conference 25–26
The Animals of Farthing Wood 68
animation 8, 10, 66, 79, 100–101, 105, 110, 121, 183, 195
Animation World Network (AWN) 8
anime (Japanese animation) 1, 7, 158–159
Anonymous Rex: A Detective Story 27–29
anthology 2, 5, 7–8, 11, 20–22, 36–38, 47–49, 51–53, 77–79, 82–84, 90, 94–96, 118, 172–173
ANTHRO Press 43
AnthroAquatic *47–49*
Anthrocon 60, 79, 208–209
Anthrolations 10, 37

anthropomorphic 9, 12, 13, 17, 24–25, 32–34, 37–38, 43, 89–90, 92, 95, 105–107, 111, 118–120, 138–139, 141–142, 149, 152–154, 155–157, 160, 165, 168, 171, 174–176, 180, 181–185, 193
An Anthropomorphic Century: Stories from 1909 to 2008 21–22
Anthropomorphic Dreams Publishing 11
Anthropomorphic Literature and Arts Association (ALAA) 8, 205–207
anthropomorphism 2, 3, 17, 35, 81, 99–101, 123, 125–126, 131, 134, 170, 173
Antoine, Brian W. 37
apocalypse 36, 166–168
Apuleius (Lucius Apuleius Madaurensis) 9, 96
Aquifers 183
Arabian Nights 62
The Architect of Sleep 1
archy and mehitabel vi, 29–31
archy does his part 29–31
archys life of mehitabel 29–31
Argaea 175
Argyll Productions *101–102*, 150–152
Argyron 52
Arizona 161
Arkham Bridge Publishing 69–71
Armoured Fox Press 211; logo *211*
army 9, 66–67, 69–71, 116–117, 122, 138, 144
Arnórsson, Kjartan 79
Around About Ottersgate 42
art show 8, 11, 79
artificial intelligence (AI) 39, 52, 60, 101
As Below, So Above 82
Ashbee, Charles Robert (C.R.A.) *96–97*

217

Index

Asia 86, 116
Asimov, Isaac 95
Assignment in Eternity 21
At the Gate of the Garden of Death 186
Atlantic City 187
Australia 8, 14–15, 20, 47, 51–52, 83, 86, 186, 188
AuthorHouse 11
autobiography 40, 106, 113
automatons 95
Avon Books **109–111**
awards 3, 5, 7, 12, 29, 34, 35–36, 37, 40, 49, 52–53, 60, 63, 68, 74–77, 78–80, 82, 86, 89, 92, 94–96, 101–102, 104, 110, 111, 114, 115, 120–122, 125, 129–131, 133–135, 137, 142, 152–153, 159, 165–166, 170, 172–175, 177, 183–185, 198, 205–210
Axis 10
Aztec 82

Babar the Elephant 27
Bach, Richard 98–99
Bad Dog Books (BDB) 59, 212; logo **212**
Baen Books 21, 87–89, 185–186
Baird, Rob 52
Baker, Adam 52
Bakhtin, Mikhail 22
Bakis, Kirsten 23
The Ballad of Lost C'mell 186
Bambi: A Life in the Woods 31–33, 40
Bambi: Eine Lebensgeschichte aus dem Walde 31–33
Bambi's Children: The Story of a Forest Family 31–33
Barking Mad 12
Barsk: The Elephants' Graveyard 33–35
Batrachomyomachia (*The Battle of Frogs and Mice*) 9
Batteiger, John vi
Baum, L. Frank 195
Baynes, Pauline 27, **107**
BBC 158–159
BBC Radio Wales 143
Beagle, Peter S. 104–105
Beast 193
A Bedsheet for a Cape 78
The Bees **35–36**
Behesht 60
Bell, Anthea 64–66
Bellina, Naomi 173
The Bellmaker 137–139
Ben and Me 110
Beneath the Crystal Sea 38, 174
Bergey, Michael 124–125
Bernofsky, Susan 113–114
Bernstein, Zena 120–122
The Best and Worst of Worlds 52

Best in Show: 15 Years of Outstanding Furry Fiction 2, 8, 36–38, **37**, 42–43
Best Novel Award 29, 34, 36, 40, 43, 68, 78, 80, 101–102, 110, 114, 125, 129, 131, 133, 135–137, 142, 152–153, 158–159, 183–185, 198, 207
Bête 38–40
bibliography 23–24, 27, 36
bioengineered 21, 43, 52–53, 69–71, 78, 101, 122, 124, 152, 154–155, 168–170, 180, 185–186
biology 67
bipeds 154
The Birds 26
Birds, Far Underground 186
birthplace 1
Black Angel 84–85
Black Beauty: His Grooms and Companions: The Autobiography of a Horse. Translated from the Original Equine 26, 40–42
Blair, Eric 24–26
Blasingame, Ted R. 154–155, 193–195
blasphemous 96
Bleak Horizons 118
The Blood Jaguar 42
Bloom, Bard 111–113, 198–200
Bloom, Victoria Borah 111–112
Blotch **133**, **175**
Blount, Margaret 26–27
Bluth, Don 121
The Boar Goes North 38
Bond, Michael 27
Bones of the Empire 92–94
The Book of Lapism 43–45, **44**
The Book of Silence 54
Boomer the Dog 79
Boston, Massachusetts 8
Bottom of the Ninth 47
Boy Scout 100
Bradfield, Scott 20
Brain Wave 23
Brandenburg, Jim 3
Breashears, Gene 37
Br'er Rabbit 3, 26
Bretnor, Reginald 20
Bridges 174
Brightness Reef 152–154
Brin, David 22, 152–154
Britain 11, 25, 26–27, 52, 55, 61, 68, 97, 100, 115, 122, 127, 138, 143, 182–183, 195–196
British Science Fiction Association (BSFA) 40
Broadway 187
Brooklyn Blackie and the Unappetizing Menu 95
Brooks, Walter R. 11, 71
Brown, Frederic 20

Brown, Howard V. **23**
Browne, Adam 91–92
Bruton, Heather 79
Bryant, Dave 38
Buddhist monk 9
Buffy the Vampire Slayer 20
Bugs Bunny 3, 74, 172
Bulgakov, Mikhail 23
Bullet Tooth Claw 95
Burckhardt, Marc **15**
burlesque 57, 140
Burma 72, 139
Buttig, Katrin "LeSoldatMort" 117
By His Bootstraps 151

CaféPress 63
Cairyn 52
Caldwell, Clive 18
California 1, 180
Califur 74
The Call 52
The Call of the Wild 3, 40
Cambridge 144–146
Campbell, John W. 40
Campbell, Ryan **80–82**, 103–104
Canada 7, 11, 52, 80, 83, 114, 178
Canis Major 37
Čapek, Karel 22, 23, 26
capitalism 26
Carey, Mary 100
carnivalization 22, 23
Carr, John F. 111
Carroll, Lewis 10, 16, 22, 27, 57, 105, 195
Carspecken, Margaret 38
Carspecken, Robert K. 38
Cartier, Edd 55–57
Cartmill, Cleve 20
Cartoon/Fantasy Organization (C/FO) 7
Cartoon Research 8
cartoons 3, 10, 110, 158–159, 190
Castlefall 38
Casual Rex: A Novel 27–29
Cat Rambo 79
Cats in Cyberspace 21
Cave Canem—Ein Felidae-Roman 66
cave paintings 3
Caveat Fuzzy 111
Central America 132
Chalk, Gary 137–139
Chambers, Whittaker 31–33
The Champion of Katara 63
Chandler, Raymond 190
Channel coast 143
Chanur Saga 135–137
Chanur 2
Chanur's Homecoming 135–137
Chanur's Legacy: A Novel of Compact Space 135–137
Chanur's Venture 135–137
Charlotte's Web 27, 45–47, 110

Charmed 20
Chasing the Spotlight 60
Chaucer, Geoffrey 22
Cheena, Yannarra 78
Cheetham, Anthony 143
Cherryh, C.J. 135–137
Cherryh, David A. 135–137
Chicago 51–53
children 9–11, 21, 27, 45, 56–57, 107–109, 120–122, 195
China 9, 48, 82, 167
Christian 26, 36, 166
Christopher, John 20
The Chronicles of Narnia 107–109
Chung, Sam **118**
Cinderella 103
City 23
civilization 24, 28, 33, 37–38, 49–51, 62, 78, 86, 91, 103, 111, 120–121, 122, 130, 136, 141–142, 149, 152–154, 159, 167, 176, 185, 194
Clan Apis 35–36
Clark, Alan M. 152–154
Clarke, Arthur C. 40
classic 12, 24, 45, 51, 96, 123, 158–159, 181–183, 185
CLAW 59
Claw the Way to Victory 47–49, **48**
Cleary, Beverly 11
Cleis Press 79–80
Close to Us 52
Coates, J.F.R. 78
coexist 24, 26, 50–51
collectable 8, 38
collection 4–5, 8, 12, 21, 30, 36, 43, 74–77, 80, 94–96, 185–186, 192–193
Collier's Weekly 30
Collins, Mick 38
The Color of Rain 37
columnist 29–30
comedy 9, 20, 43, 69, 83–84, 92, 113, 138, 191–192
comic books 1–2, 7, 10, 35, 63, 110, 146, 158–159, 172–173
Comic-Con 1, 7
comic strip 158–159, 191
Comics Buyer's Guide 8
Communist Party 25
community 1–5, 42, 54–55, 68, 97, 165–166
The Complete Chronicles of Narnia 108–109
computer 66, 141
computer graphic imagery (CGI) 172
ConFurence 29
Conly, Jane Leslie 120–122
Conly, Robert 120–122
Conroy, Samuel C. 82
Contract Negotiations 82

conventions 1, 7–8, 10, 11, 38, 51, 60, 66, 74, 75–80, 90
Conway, Dr. Samuel C. 78–79, 174
Cook, Kenneth 23
Cooner 103–104
copyright 100, 111
Cornell University 23
Cosmopolitan Book Corporation **148–150**
cosplay 7, 91
Coughlan, Stephen 52
Counsels, Councils, Consoles and Consuls 186
Coyote Season 124–125
The Cóyotl Awards vi, 5, 34, 36, 40, 43, 49, 60, 78–79, 80, 82, 89, 96, 101–102, 104, 114, 129, 135, 152, 165–166, 172–173, 198, 207–208, **207**; logo **208**; trophy **207**
The Cóyotl Awards Anthology 5
Crafter's Passion 161–163
Crawford, Robert 139–141
CreateSpace 11, 62–64, 92–94, 111–113, 116–117, **131–133**, **146–148**, 161–163, 166–170, 198–200
Cregar, Elyse 21
Crimson on Copper 95
Crisis on Doona 49
Critical Companions to Popular Contemporary Writers 179
Critical Explorations in Science Fiction and Fantasy 22
Cross of Valor Reception for the Raccoon, Tanner Williams, Declassified Transcript 52
Crucible 37
cruelty 9, 26, 58, 62, 96, 106, 138
Cub Scouts 100
Culdesac: A Novella from the War with No Name 118–120
culture 3, 44, 51, 125, 144, 165, 167–170, 185, 188
The Curators 78
Curless, Allan 137–139
Curtone, Ray "Stormcatcher" 172
Cuti, Nicola 55–57

dæmon 126
Danger in the Lumo-Bay 94
Dangerous Spirits 84
Dann, Colin 68
D'Arc: A Novel from the War with No Name 118–120
The Darkness of Dead Stars 78
Daughter of Shadows 193
Davis, Hank 185–186
DAW Books, 135–137, **155–157**
Day, Micheal **44**
A Day with No Tide 82

The Dead Lady of Clown Town 23, 185–186
deBrunoff, Jean 27
Decision at Doona 23, 49
Deity Theory 82
Delgado, Zayda vi
Delhi 115
Delmonico's Restaurant 187
del Rey, Lester 23
democracy 56–57
Denali 79
Denmark 26, 114
The Department Store of Hearts' Desires 186
Descent 47
Dev and Lee 133–135
DeviantArt 11
Dick, Philip K. 22
Dickson, Gordon R. 20, 23, 55–57
Dickson, H. Leighton 166–168
Diehr, Wolfgang 111
Diesel **122–123**
DiFilippo, Paul 20, 174
digital 78
The Digital Coyote 161–163
Dinosaur Mafia Mystery 28
diplomatic 48, 57
discovery 4
Discus Dog 47
Disney, Walt 27, 31, 33, 64, 100–101, 128, 192, 196
Distant Shores 78
Divine and Moral Songs for Children 26
Divisions 133–135
DNA 124–125, 154
Do-It-Yourself book publishing 11, 38
Dr. Birdmouse 20, 21
Dr. Dolittle 11
Doctor Rat 23
Doctor Who 128
Doggy Love 20, 21
Dogpatch Press 8
Dogs Extended 52
Dog's Life 20
Dogs of War 51–53
Dogs of War II: Aftermath 51–53
Dolphin's Way 23
Don't Blink 174
Doona 49
Doove, Bernard 168–170, **205**
Dorie, Sabrina 60
The Dorset Squirrels 142–144
Doubleday, Page & Co. 186–188
Douglas & McIntyre 177–179
Dowling, Lela 55–57
Downbelow Station 136–137
Drackus, Jaden 52
Drake, W.H. 99–101
drama 20–21, 28, 43, 61, 64, 78, 83, 125, 138, 155, 158–159, 182, 185

Index

Dreams Are for Vixens 193
Dressed Animals and Others 27
Dreyer, Kate 68–69
Drifting 174
Dryden, Alice "Huskyteer" 52, 78, 82
Dudman, Martin 61
Das Duell—Ein Felidae-Roman 66
duMaurier, Daphne 26
Duncton Found 53–55
Duncton Quest 53–55
Duncton Rising 53–55
Duncton Stone 53–55
Duncton Tales 53–55
Duncton Wood 53–55
Dwale 48–49, 52, 60, 78
dystopian 21, 36

Earth 56–57, 67
Earthman's Burden 55–57
The Easton Press 152
Eaton Collection of Science Fiction and Fantasy vi, 8
eBook 170
Ecuador 132
Eddy, Jeff 38
Edited by Fred Patten 5, **20–22, 36–38**, 51–53, 77–79, **82–84, 174–175**
editor 8
Egypt 3, 82
Eight Seconds and the Grace of God 49
electronic edition 11, 16, 59, 170
Embden, Michael **156**
Emergency Maintenance 78
emotions 181, 184, 188
encyclopedia 76
End of Ages 52
enemies 60, 62–63, 119, 172, 177, 189, 194, 199
ephemera 8
epic 54–55, 166–168
erotic 9, 59, 74, 131, 172–173, 176, 177–179, 198
espionage 177
Esquire 71
Etüden im Schnee 113–114
Europe 9, 20, 32, 86, 122, 195
The Evening Sun 29
The Ever Changing Palace 37
Every Breath Closer 95
Every Horse Will Do His Duty 52
evil 10, 54–55, 63, 78, 89, 138, 156
evolution 8, 26, 97
Evolver 78
exile 43
exotic 86, 89, 102, 113, 139–141, 151, 192
Experiment Seventy 78
exploration 86

Exploring New Places 8
extinction 119–120

fable 22, 113, 115
Fabulous Histories. Designed for the Instruction of Children, Respecting Their Treatment of Animals 10, 26, 57–58
Fair Trade 148
fairy 122, 187
The Faithful 23
The Fall of Eldvar 92–94
Fallen and Redeemed: Animals in the Novels of C.S. Lewis 27
Fallen Kitten Productions 127–129
False Doctrine 142
fame 60
Familiars 174
Family Bonding 78
The Famous Captain Walcott 16
fan-generated media 3
fandom 2, 7, 158–159
FANG 59–60
Fang, Claw, & Steel 37
Fangs of K'aath 12, 60–63, **62**
Fangs of K'aath II: Guardians of Light 60–63
Fantastic Furry Stories 37
fantasy 7, 10, 15, 17, 20–22, 27, 60, 87–90, 93, 120–122, 139–141, 148–150, 155–157, 166–168, 174, 177–179, 195
fanzine 1–2, 4, 7, 34, 36, 42–43, 61, 79, 169
farce 21, 56
Farmer Giles of Ham 27
The Fate of Mice 20
Fathers to Sons 52
Fauxpaw Publications 168
Fawkes, Wally 27
Feir, Bryan 78
Felicia and the Cult of the Rubber Nose 64
Felicia and the Tailcutter's Curse 63, 174
Felicia, Sorceress of Katara 63
Felicia: The Night of the Basquot 62–64
Felidae on the Road 64–66
Feline Online 21
Felipolis: Ein Felidae-Roman 66
Fennell, Amy 85–87
Fenrir's Saga 82
feral 124
festivals 22
Field Research 78
Field T. Mouse 52, 82
Fifth Avenue 187
Find the Beautiful 38
The Fire Bearers 80–82
The First Book of Lapism 43
First Chosen 82
The Fittest 23

Five Fortunes 90
Five Star/Thomson Gale 124–125
Flapper Era 148–150
Flayrah 8
Fles, Barthold 31–3
Flight of the Godkin Griffin 66–68
Flight of the Star Phoenix 169–170
Floating Dogs 23
Flook 27
Flower Power 98
Flowers for Algernon 23
FOE Money, SAD Money 186
Fogio, Phil 55–57
folk tales 9, 26, 62, 124, 140, 156
Fontaine, Kristin 174
Foofaraw 7
foreign 7, 112
Forest Gods 80–82
Forest Tales: A Chakat Family Journal 168–170
400 Rabbits 82
Four Satires 26
The Fox Maiden 193
The Fox of Richmond Park 68–69
Foxenawolf **206**
Foxhunt! 69–71
Foxy Lady 37
France 39, 57, 83, 115, 122
France, Anatole 22
Francis 71–73
Francis—Felidae II 66
Francis Goes to Washington 71–73
"Francis the talking-flying mule" 71–73
Frane, Kevin 141–142, 150–152
Fred Patten Special Collection on Science Fiction and Animation 8
Freddy the Pig 11
freelance 7–8
Freelance Familiars 128
Frenzeny, P. 99–101
Freud, Sigmund 22
frontier 3
Full Immersion 44–45
Full Pack (Hokas Wild) 57
funny 3, 8, 63–64, 71, 103, 118, 160, 173, 197
Funny Animal Liberation Front e.zine 159
Funny Animals and More: From Anime to Zoomorphics 8
Funny Animals in World War II Propaganda 8
Fur Plus 169
FurAffinity 11
FurPlanet Productions 5, 8, 11, 22, 51, 59, 77–79, **82–84**, 85–87, **89–90**, 94–96, **101–102**,

Index

103–104, 118, *129–131*, 131–133, *164–166*, *174–175*, 196–198, 212–213; logo *212*
furries 73
Furries Among Us: Essays on Furries by the Most Prominent Members of the Fandom *73–75*, 201
Furries Among Us 2: More Essays on Furries by Furries 73–75
furry community 3
furry fandom v, vi, 1–2, 4–5, 8, 9, 11, 12, 21, 23, 32, 36–38, 61, 66, 73–80, 111, 135–137, 181–183, 192–193
Furry Fandom Conventions, 1989-2015 8, *75–77*, 201
The Furry Future: 19 Possible Prognostications 77–79, 102
furry literature v, vi, 1, 137
Furry Nation: The True Story of America's Most Misunderstood Subculture 79–80, 201
Furry Specialty Publishers *211–216*
Furry! The Best Anthropomorphic Stories Ever 36–38
Furry! The World's Best Anthropomorphic Fiction 2, 36–38
Furry Writers Guild (FWG) 8
FurryPhile 10, 37, 192
fursona 38, 52, 60
fursuit 74, 79–80
Further Confusion 51
FURthest North Crew 37
FurVersion 37, 42, 192
Furword 75–76
The Future Is Yours 78
futuristic 21, 39–40, 43
Fuzzies and Other People 110–111
The Fuzzy Conundrum 111
Fuzzy Ergo Sum 111

G-rated 177
"Galactics" 152–154
galaxy 33–35, 56–57
Galford, Jim 92–94
Gallacci, Steve 8
Gallagher, Diana G. 18, 20
Gallico, Paul 13
Galsworthy, John 31–33
gambling 174
Game of Thrones 2
games 60–61, 111, 135, 161, 174, 181, 183
Garcia, Eric 27–29
Garman, Tess 133–134, *175*
Garou: Ein Schaf-Thriller 164
Gass, Nathanael 78
Gavet, Teagan 52, 60, *83*, *101*, 133, *175*
gay 5, 84–85, 134–135, 166, 176–177, 184
gender 52, 126, 170

genetics 66, 97, 102, 141, 152, 154, 170, 179
genitalia 170, 179
A Gentleman of Strength 48–49
Gerbasi, Kathleen C. *75–77*, 79
Germany 51–52, 66, 77, 114, 115, 146, 164
Geusz, Phil 37, 38, *43–45*, 170–172
Ghosts 95
Gibson, Roz vi, *21*, 78, 85–87, 209
Gladiator 146
Goal Publications 11, 213; logo *213*
God of Clay: The Fire Bearers: Book One 80–82, **80**
gods 3, 64, 67, 81–82, 82–84, 88–89, 96, 112, 115, 140, 141–142, 148, 156, 171
The Gods of Necessity 82
Gods with Fur: And Feathers, Scales, … *82–84*
The Godson's Triumph 66–68
The Going Forth of Uadjet 82
Going Home 52
Going to the Dogs 193
Gold, Kyell 1–5, 82, 83, 84–85, *133–135*, *164–166*, 174–175, *175–177*, 183–185
Golden Age 192
The Golden Ass 9, 22
The Golden Compass 125–127
The Golden Flight 142–144
Goldsworthy, Peter 23
Goodreads 60, 79
Goodridge, Ben 38, 59
Götergleich: Ein Felidae-Roman 66
government 56–57, 92, 121, 132, 195
Graduation Day 38
Grahame, Kenneth 16, 27, 43, 195–196
graphic novel 36, 63
Graphic Story Bookshop 7
Graveyard Greg 59
Great Apes 23
Great Depression 139–141, 148–150
Greece 22, 36, 82
greed 10, 43, 54–55, 58, 141
Green, Roland J. 20
Green Fairy 84–85
The Green Man Review 79
"greymuzzles" 52
Griffin, Rick 146–148
Griffin Ranger, Volume 1, Crossline Plains 85–87
Griffin Ranger, Volume 2, The Monster Lands 85–87
Grimm Brothers 187
Groat, Jim 79
Growing Fur 78

Guest of Honor 29
Gulliver's Travels 26
Gullwolf 52
Gunn, James 152–154

Hachimoto 78
Hall, Renee Carter 22, *89–90*, 172
Hall of Fame 8
Halloween 172–173
Hallsworth, Devin 52
Hammett, Dashiell 94
Hanes, Rich 69–71
Harbin, Taylor 52
hardcover 11
harmony 49
Harris, Joel Chandler 26
hate literature 10, 34
The Headlong Career and Woful Ending of Precocious Piggy 27
The Heart of a Dog 23
The Heavenly Horse from the Outermost West 87–89
Heaven's Reach 152–154
Heinlein, Robert A. 7, 21, 151
Hellhound 172
Helsinki 116–117
heresy 126, 187
hermaphrodite 169–170
Herriman, George 29–31
heterosexual 131, 158–159
Heyer, Georgette 122–123
high school 60, 181
High Steaks 127–129
Hilgartner, Beth 21
Hilton, Craig 38
Hindu 90, 115
His Dark Materials 125–127
Historimorphs 37
history 3, 5, 8, 22, 36, 74, 75, 79–80, 141, 174
Hitchcock, Alfred 26
A Hive for the Honeybee 35–36
Hoagland, Brock 38, 174
hobbyist 7, 80, 113
Hoch, Tarl "Voice" 172
Hofer, Jennie 38
Hogarth, M.C.A. 38, 65–68, 78, 174
Hoka! 55–57
Hoka! Hoka! Hoka! 55–57
Hokas Pokas! 55–57
homoerotica 59, 176
homosexual 59, 84–85, 131, 134–135, 158–159, 164–166, 176, 179, 183–184
Hood, Thomas 27
Hoodies and Horses 52
Hopkins, David 78
horror 20, 54–55, 60, 65, 94–96, 97, 172–173
The Horse and His Boy 108–109
Horwood, William 53–55, 143, 196

Index

Hosler, Jay 35–36
hostile 45, 56–57, 183
Hot and Sweaty Rex: A Dinosaur Mafia Mystery 27–29
House of Wax 95
How George Miles Almost Saved the World 37
Hubschmid, K. 52
Hughes Aircraft Company 7
Hugo Award 110–111, 135–137, 153, 183
human 19, 24, 27–28, 30, 33, 37, 44, 47, 54–55, 73, 81, 154, 158–159, 193–194
humanoid 44–45, 56–57, 62, 69–71, 81, 155, 171, 174, 191, 198
humor 9, 20, 29, 55–57, 64, 71, 78, 122–123, 125, 148–150, 192
Hunter's Fall 52
Huntress 89–90, **89**
Husky, Arthur 176
Huskyteer 47–48, 173
Hutchinson Children's Books 137–139

Ianus J. Wolf 94, 172–173
iBooks 2, 36, 38
idealistic 56–57
identification 3
If Only They Could Speak: The Pet Story 27
Ikegawa, Lance 79
Ikin, Van **22–24**
Iliad 9
An Illustrated History of Furry Fandom, 1966-1996 8
Imperium Lupi 91–92
import 7
In a Dog's World 131–133
In His Own Country 174
In Hoka Signo Vinces 56
In the Beginning 44–45
In Wilder Lands: The Fall of Eldvar 92–94
In Between 174
In the Line of Duty 174
inanimate 9
independence 3
India 9, 22, 99–101, 115, 167, 193
Indonesia 86, 103
Infinite Imagination 170
Infinity Shore 152–154
Inhuman Acts: A Collection of Noir 94–96
Inkpot Award 1, 7
Insect Play 26
instinct 35, 47, 125, 146, 154, 178, 180
integrity 54–55
intelligence 10, 11, 19–20, 22, 24, 28, 39, 47, 50–53, 56–57, 64, 67, 72–73, 86, 87, 95, 97, 110–111, 119, 121, 124–125, 128, 132, 144–146, 152, 154, 159, 170–171, 176, 180, 182–183, 185–186, 194, 199
interbreed 67
International Anthropomorphic Research Project 76
international trade 11
Internet 1, 4, 10, 11, 22, 23, 36, 37, 79, 158, 169, 183, 192
interspecies 21
interstellar 10, 19, 21, 34, 69–71, 78, 109, 131, 135–137, 147–148, 151, 154–155, 159, 168–170, 185, 193
Into the Desert Wilds 92–94
Ireland 35
Islam 166
The Island of Dr. Moreau: A Possibility 10, 96–97, **97**
Island of Lost Souls 96
Isolation Play 133–135
Italy 76–77

Jacks to Open 174
Jacobson, JJ vi
Jacques, Brian 122, 137–139
Jaffa Books **47–49**, 213–214; logo **213**
"Jane Doe" 26
Jansson, Tove 27
Japan 26, 72, 114, 115, 167
Japanese anime 7
Japanese manga 7, 61
Jaquays, Paul **122**
Jarlidium Press 214; logo **214**
Jekel, Pamela 100
Jenner, Janann V. 139–141
Jennie 13–14
Jerry Was a Man 21
Jewish 10, 20
Johanna T. 127
Jonathan Livingston Seagull—A Story 98–99
Journey to the West 9
Jovaik, Roland 173
Joy in Mudville 57
The Jungle Book 99–101
Jungle Books vi, 10, 27, 57, 100–101

Kafka, Franz 22
Kalin, Victor **109**
Kamui **165**
The Kanti Cycle 148
Kästner, Erich 26–27
Kaufman, Jonathan 38
Keller, Madison 52
Kenket 133–135
Keyes, Daniel 23
Kidd, Paul 4, 12, **60–62, 122–123**, 188–190
Kieffer, Bill 95
The Kif Strike Back 135–137
Killer Kitty 20

Killick 82
Kilner, Dorothy 10, 26, **105–107**
Kilworth, Garry 143
Kindle books 11, 80, 155
King Nobel the lion 9
Kipling, J. Lockwood 99–101
Kipling, Rudyard 10, 27, 99–101
Kipling Society vi
Kismet 78, **101–102, 102**
Kitchen, Allan 38
Kitsune Press 190
Klemp, Ronald W. 78
Knight, Barbara Anne 142–144
A Knight's Tale 47–48
Koa of the Drowned Kingdom 103–104
Kolkata 115
Koontz, Dean R. 179–181
Kotker, Joan G. 179
Kotzwinkle, William 23
Krazy Kat 30
Kritzer, Naomi 174
Kruse, Brandon 147
Kulp, John 52
Kurti, Richard 115–116
Kyle, Richard 7

Lackey, Mercedes **122–123**
La Faille, Eugene 22
La Fontaine, Jean de 22
Lally, Soinbhe 35–36
Lane, Eric 47–48
Las Vegas 60, 174
The Last Battle 108–109
Last Man Standing 52
The Last Unicorn 104–105
laughter 22
law 10, 87, 147, 166, 184
Lawrence, John 181–183
Lawson, Robert 110
A Leap Forward 48
Lear, Edward 27
legal 80, 111, 194
legend 14, 60, 81, 103, 156
Legion Printing & Publishing **20–22, 43–45**
Lenin, V.I. 25
Lensman 10
lenten fasting 22
The Leo Literary Awards 53, 77, 80, 86, 92, 102, 133, 208–210, **209**; logo **209**
lesbian 60, 67, 85, 158–159
Lettres de Coquefredouille 8
Lewis, C.S. 27, **107–109**
Libertation Game 161–163
liberty 54–55
library 11, 54, 69, 80, 127
Library of Congress 75
Life Achievement Award 7
The Life and Perambulation of a Mouse 10, 26, **105–107, 106**
the life and times of archy & mehitabel 30

Index

Life's Dream: The Journal of Pandora and Karl 168–170
Lightman, Alan 96
Lilliputian Life: The Mouse Story 27
Lily 16
Lime Tiger 52
Linebarger 23
The Lion, the Witch and the Wardrobe: A Story for Children **107–109**, *107*, 172
The Little Black Book of Furry Fiction 59
Little Fuzzy **109–111**, *109*
Little Monster 38
The Little White Book of Furry Fiction 59
Liu, Kim 37
the lives and times of archy and mehitabel 29–31
Lives of the Monster Dogs 23
Livingstone, Monika **61**
Lloyd-Webber, Andrew 192
Loewen, Alan 52, 82
Lofting, Hugh 11, 27
logo 76
London 69, 146
London, Jack 3
Long Beach, California 7
The Long Road Home 129–131
Lord Ikari 52
The Lord of the Rings 55, 156
Lorey, Dan 23
Los Angeles 7, 190
Los Angeles Fantasy Society (LASFS) 7
Lost on Dark Trails 129–131
Louvelex 42
love 54–55, 99, 112, 134, 158–159, 173, 179, 183
Love Match 134
The Loving Children 52
Lowd, Mary E. vi, 49, 52, 59, 60, 78, 82, 94–95, **131–133**, *207*
Lubin, Leonard 120–122
Lucius of Apuleius 22, 96
Lulu Press 4, 11, 154–155, 158–159, 193–195
Lunar Cavity 78
Luterman, Gre7g **146–148**
Luterman, H. Kyoht **146**
Lynch, David 197

MacBook Pro Computer 8
MacGregor 20, 21
Macguffin 101
magazine 8, 10, 27
The Magazine of Applied Anthropo morphics 8
The Magazine of Fantasy and Science Fiction 56–57
magic 9, 63, 93, 96, 103, 108, 111–113, 121–122, 124, 128–129, 174, 179, 193, 195

magazines 8–12, 20–22, 27, 30, 36–37, 52, 59, 192
The Magic of Desire 173
The Magician's Nephew 108–109
mainstream 3, 38, 113, 122
The Maltese Falcon 94
mankind 52, 101
Manxmouse 13
map 65–68, 91, 122–123, 135–137, 142–144, 155–157, 181, 198–200
Marge the Barge 49
Marie of Redwall 137–139
Marking Territory 127–129
Marmel, Mitch 79
A Marriage of Insects: A Novel of the World Tree 111–113
Marquis, Don vi, 27, 29–31
Mars 10
Marshall Plan 56–57
A Martian Odyssey 10
Martin, George R.R. 2
Martin, Watts 37, 78, 82, **101–102**, 159, 192–193
Martin the Warrior 137–139
Marx, Karl 25
Masefield 187
masquerading 7
Matched Up 52
mating 125
Mattimeo 137–139
mature 85
Maupin, Armistead 158–159
McCaffrey, Anne 23, 49
McCormick, Bill 52
McCoy, Elizabeth 38, 52
McDonald, Ian 23
McFarland & Co., Inc., Publishers vi, 8, **22–24**, **75–77**
McGregor, Ken 51
McIntosh, J.T. 23
McLeod, Lori vi
McMahon, Jim 14
McNally, T.S. 78
media 3
medieval 3, 22, 26, 47, 67, 121
Melanesia 103
melodrama 118, 123, 166–168
A Melody in Seduction's Arsenal 82
Melville, Chas. P.A. 38, 62–64, 174
Memoirs of a Polar Bear 113–114
Mendel, Gregor 66
Mephit Furmeet 170
Mercy to the Cubs: A Tale of the Furkindred 38
Merlino, Mark 7, 79
Messenger 38
Metamorphoses/The Golden Ass 9, 96
The Metamorphosis 22
metaphysical 143, 172
Methuen & Company 195–196

Mexico 7, 132
Meyers Konversations Lexikon 35
Middle East 61
Midwest FurFest 51
Midwesterners 193–195
MikasiWolf 48, 52, 78, 82
Milenkiewicz, Eric vi
Miles, Kylen Christine 38
Milholen, Layla vi
military 52, 62–63, 117, 119, 123, 124, 153, 183
Milne, A.A. 27
Minde, J.J. **209**
Mr. Ed 71
Mr. Limpet 71
Mitchell, Judith 87–89
Mitten, Cara 85–87
Miyagami, Kacey 168
MLP:FIM 77
The Model of a Judge 20
Molotov, V.M. 25
Monkey 22
Monkey Wars 115–116
The Monster in the Mist 52
Montmartre 85
Moomintroll 27
The Moon in Water 193
MoonDust: Falling from Grace 116–118
The Moons of Barsk 33–35
moral 9, 17, 26, 44, 57, 97, 106–107
More Terrible Than Chains: A.K.A. Leeana's Story 168–170
Morley, Christopher 186–188
Morphic Tales 37, 192
Morrison, William 20
Mort(e) **118–120**, *118*
Moscow 113
Moseley, Marshall L. 95
Mossflower 137–139
The Most Unforgettable Character I've Ever Met 48
Mother Nature 188–190
The Mouse and the Motorcycle 11
movie 10, 13, 79, 94, 96, 100–101, 105, 110, 121, 140, 171, 183, 190, 195, 198
Mrs. Frisby and the Rats of NIMH 120–122
Mullins, Tom 52
Munson, Russell 98–99
Murray Hill 187
Mus of Kerbridge 12, **122–123**, *122*
Musa Publishing 190–192
Muskrat Blues 94
Muslim 165–166
Mut 82
mutation 97, 153, 154
My Brother's Shadow 52

Index

mystery 4, 29, 43, 51, 64, 83, 86, 92, 94–95, 126, 176–177, 191–192
mysticism 99, 124–125
Mythagoras 10, 34, 37, 192
mythology 3, 9, 27, 54–55, 82, 84, 105, 122, 156, 182

Napoleon 57
The Napoleon Crime 57
Narnia 27
Native American 124–125, 130, 143, 192
nature 32, 36, 52, 54–55, 95, 124, 134, 140, 143–144, 176, 189, 195
Nazi Germany 25, 97, 146
NC-17 198
Nebula Award 34, 153
Needle, Jan 196
neofan 80
Nesbit, E. 27, 195
neurobiology 35
New Coyote 124–125
The New Delhi Times 115
New Directions Books 113–114
New York City 139–141, 195
The New York Tribune 30
New Zealand 52, 86–87, 151
Newbery, John 26
Newbery Medal 120–122
Newtype USA 8
Ng, Kapo 118
Niagara County Community College 76
niche markets 3
The Night the Stars Fell 52
Nightball 49
NightEyes DaySpring 52, 78, 82, 173
Nimble the mouse 10
Nivardus of Ghent 9
Noble 52
Noble, Ralph 64
noir 29, 65, 94–96
nonfiction works 3, 75–76, 201
non-human 11
Norse 82
Norstrilia 185–186
North America 79–80, 86, 129–131, 155
North American Fur 37
The Northern Approach 92–94
Northern Lights 125–127
Norton, Andre 7, 22
Nosy and Wolf 51
Number Nine 20
Nunnemacher, John 38, 183–185
The Nun's Priest's Tale 22
Nye, Jody Linn 49

Oakshadow, BanWynn 52, 82
O'Brien, Robert C. 120–122
Ocean Tigrox 78, 94–96, 209

Oceans 183
Of Storm and Furry: Contemporary Past 34
Of Storm and Furry: Peals and Vents 34
Off Leash 127–129
Off the Beaten Path **129–131**, *129*
Oklahoma 193–195
O'Kun, Tempe 196–198
Old-Dry-Snakeskin 60
Old Regimes 52
Oliver, Angela 52
Olympic Peninsula 124
on-demand publishing 3–4
On the Run from Isofell 82
Once a Year 173
One Hundred and One Dalmations 27
online 4, 8, 76, 192
Only Toys 27
Only with Thine Eyes 192
Origins 82
O'Riley, Rod 79
Orpheus and Eurydice 156
Orwell, George (Eric Blair) 10, **24–26**, 196
Osborne Collection of Early Children's Books vi
Osfer's Joint Publications 59
The Other Human Race/Fuzzy Sapiens 110–111
Other Trails Taken: A Chakat Family Journal, Book II 169–170
Other Worlds Science Stories 56–57
Otters in Space: The Search for Cat Havana **131–133**, *131*
Otters in Space II: Jupiter, Deadly 131–133
Otters in Space III: Octopus Ascending 131–133
Out of Position 5, **133–135**, *133*
out of the closet 134
Outcast of Redwall 137–139
Over Time 133–135
overpopulation 50–51, 144, 147
Oxford 126
Oz 195
Ozy and Millie 158–159

Pacific Northwest 124–125
The Pack 52
Paddington Bear 27
Padwolf Publishing 111–113
Painted Memories 38
The Palace of the Governor of Night 186
Palmer, Sara **175**
Palumbo, Donald E. **22–24**
Palwick, Susan 20
pamphlet 9, 106
paperback 7

parable 24–26, 62, 99
paradise 43, 60
paralyzed 8
Paris 177–179, 187
parody 9, 10, 20–21, 23, 26, 190–192
Parvin, Brian 11
pathos 20
Patten, Fred 1–2, 4–5, **20–22**, **36–38**, 51–53, **75–77**, **77–79**, **82–84**, **174–175**, *175*
Patten, Sherrill vi
Pauli, Frances 52, 82
Paull, Laline 35–36
Pawprints Across the Galaxy: Dogs in Science Fiction 22
Pawprints Fanzine 10, 37, 192
Payne, Michael H. 20, 37–38, 42–43, 82, 174
Pechet, Bill 177–179
Pendant of Fortune 176–177
Penguin Island 22
Pennsylvania 127
Père-Lachaise Cemetery 177–179
Perrault, Charles 26
Persia 22
Perth, Western Australia 12
pets 9, 13, 21, 105–107, 118–119, 127, 136, 139–141, 144, 172
Phantasia Press 135–137, 152–154
The Pharaoh's Throne 173
Philadelphia 195
philosophy 2–3, 22, 43–44, 98, 141–142
Phobophilia 173
The Phoenix and the Carpet 27
photo journalism 3
photographs 98–99
Ping Pong Diplomacy 47–48
Pinner, Erna 31–33
pioneers 8, 42, 66, 155
Piper, H. Beam **107–109**
Piper at the Gate 87–89
Pirinçci, Akif 64–66
Pittsburgh 60, 79
Play Little Victims 23
poems 30, 99
political 10, 56–57, 67–68, 71, 73, 77, 92, 111, 122, 126, 128, 132, 153, 172, 177, 182, 198–199
popular culture 3, 79
porn 77
Port in a Storm 38
Posner, Matt 38
postwar 56–57
Potter, Beatrix 21, 27
Potter, Daniel 127–129
Poyser, Victoria 55–57
Pratt, Theodore 71
Pravda 25
The Precession of the Equinoxes 82

predator 54, 180, 182
prehistoric 3, 22
prejudice 15, 43, 52, 155
press 3, 4
Price, Garrett 71–73
The Pride of Chanur 135–137
Prince Caspian: The Return to Narnia 107–109
print-on-demand 4, 158–159
The Prisoner's Release and Other Stories 176–177
Prodigal Son 44–45
Prohibition 31, 148–150
propaganda 25
Propp, Vladimir 22
proselytize 43–44
prosperity 56–57
proto-fans 11, 20, 30, 31–33, 101, 107
pseudonym 38, 52, 60, 71, 83, 122
psychological 19, 42–43, 171
public library 7, 14, 116, 184
public perception 79
Publishers Weekly 29
Puffin Books 183
Pullman, Philip 125–127
pun 76
Puss in Boots 26
puzzle 119
Pylman, R.S. 158–159

The Queen's Confederate Space Marines 52
Questor's Gambit 82

R-rated 174
Rabbit Valley Publishing 172–173, 214–215; logo **215**
The Raccoon's Bookshelf 170
racial 26, 154
Racso and the Rats of NIMH 120–122
Radcliffe, John vi
Rainbow Award 5
RainFurrest 90
Rango 195
Rankin/Bass Productions 105
Rat's Reputation 38, 42–43
Raven Blackmane 37
Raven's Lair website 37
RAWR 5
Reaver, Miles 52
Rechan 172, 209
Recruiting 38
Red Devil 84–85
Red Engines 52
red herrings 194
Reed, John 26
refugee 20
Regency 177
Reichert, Mickey Zucker 20
reincarnation 30, 177–179
relationships 3, 60

religion 10, 42–43, 48, 54–55, 65, 67, 70–71, 83, 89, 97, 119, 126, 128, 131, 134, 141–142, 143–144, 155, 156, 158–159, 165, 174, 181–182, 184, 187, 189, 194, 199
Remembrance 52
Repas du Vivant 38
Repast (A Story of Aligare) 82
Repino, Robert **118–120**
reprint 2, 11, 20–21, 23, 26, 30, 37–38, 146–148, 170, 192–193
The Rescuers 10, 27
resistance 60
Respect the Sea 38
respectable 10
restrictions 11
retrospective 2
revenge 26, 63, 130
review 4, 5, 7–8, 10, 25, 29, 76, 79, 96, 115–116, 129, 139–141, 147, 156, 159, 177, 179
revolution 24–25, 185
Rex Collings Ltd. **181–183**
Richardon, Bill 177–179
rights 39–40
Ring of Swords 2
risqué 9
River Man 20
The Road to the Catmaster 186
ROAR 59
Roaring Twenties 148–150
Roberts, Adam 38–40
Robertson, Graham 195–196
Robin Hood 100
Robopocalypse 118
Rochefort, Patrick 48, 49
Rodgers and Hammerstein 195
Rodriguez, Jenn Pac **48**
Roger Rabbit 28
Rogers, Bill "Hafoc" 172
Rohmann, Eric 125–127
Roman de Reynard (Romance of Reynard the Fox) 3, 9, 22, 26
romance 2, 4, 14, 19, 43, 60–61, 69, 71, 78, 83, 104, 112, 118, 123, 131, 144–146, 172–173, 177, 179–180, 192–193, 197
Rome 22
Roof Books 26
Roosevelt, Franklin Delano 31
Rosettes and Ribbons 38
Rowrbrazzle 1–2, 8, 12, 37, 61
R-T, Margaret, and the Rats of NIMH 120–122
Ruddertail, Skip 59
Rukis 84, **129–131**, 133–135
RusFURence 76
Russia 76

Sabatini, Rafael 122
Sabretoothed Ermine **73**, 127
Sabrina the Teenage Witch—Salem's Tails 20

sacred 115
Sacrifice 52
St. Ailbe's Hall 174
St. Augustine 9
Saint-Cloud, Pierre de 9
St. Kalwain and the Lady Uta 60
St. Martin's Press 190–192
Saki 22
Salamandastron 137–139
Salten, Felix 31–33, 40
Salve Roma!—Ein Felidae-Roman 66
Salzmann, Siegmund 31–33
San Diego 139–141
San Diego Comic-Con 7
San Jose, California 51
Sandeagozu 139–141
Sanskrit 193
Sasya Fox 159–161
satire 10, 21, 26–27, 187
The Saturday Evening Post 30
The Savior of Dragondom 60
Scars 52
Schandtat—Ein Felidae-Roman 66
Schism 44
Schnee, Kris 52, 82, 161–163
Schoen, Lawrence M. 33–35
scholar 22–23, 27, 79
Scholastic Childrens' Books 125
Schurman's Trek 20, 21
science fiction 1–2, 7, 11, 20–22, 34, 40, 55–57, 97, 101–102, 109, 116–118, 120–122, 135–137, 143, 146–148, 151, 166–170, 174, 179, 185–186, 194
Science Fiction Book Club (SFBC) 55–57
Science Fiction Chronicle 143
scientist 20, 36, 65–66, 76, 124, 152, 154, 171
Scotland 26
scoundrels 60
Scrabble 181
Searska GreyRaven 52
Secker & Warburg **24–26**, **144–146**
Second Chance: Furmankind II 154–155
The Second Jungle Book 99–101
The Second Wave 142–144
Secret Weapon 38
secrets 60, 183–184, 191–192
Seeing Things 193
Sekhmet **89**
Self, Will 23
self-publish 4, 16, 63, 143, 146–148
Sendak, Maurice 27
sequel 66, 83, 100, 102, 108, 111, 120–122, 131, 135–137, 143–144, 148, 155, 160, 164, 196
The Sequence 78

Index

series 2, 4, 55, 61, 67, 73, 81, 83, 94, 108–109, 118–120, 128, 133–137, 138, 148, 158–159, 166–170, 175, 183, 197
Seton, Ernest Thompson 27
The Seventh Chakra 141–142
Sewell, Anna 26, 40–42
sex 74, 83, 124, 159, 170, 173, 180, 183, 198
SFWA 79
Shadow of the Father 176
Shadows of Novoprypiatsk 142–144
Shaikman, Axel 38
Sharp, Margery 10, 27
Shaw, Bruce **22–24**
Shells on the Beach 52
The Sheriff of Canyon Gulch 56
Sherlock Holmes 57
The Shrine War 52
Siberia 114
Sibley, Brian 108
Silly Symphonies 31
The Silver Chair 108–109
The Silver Tide 142–144
Silverberg, Robert 185
Simak, Clifford D. 23
Simpson, D.C. "Rain" 158–159
Singapore 52, 83
The Singing Tree 11
Sirius: A Fantasy of Love and Discord 23, **144–146**, *145*
Six 174
Sixth Column 7
Skeleton Crew **146–148**, *146*
Slate 196–198
slave 61, 93, 123, 153, 157, 160, 185
Slip-Wolf 52, 82, 95
Slough 172
Slovenia 52
small press publishers 3, 11, 12, 36, 47, 51
Small World 146–148
Smith, Cordwainer 22–23, 185–186
Smith, Dodie 27
Smith, Edward Elmer "Doc" 10
Smith, Terrie 188–190
Smith, Thorne **148–150**
A Snapshot from Fayetteville 38
The Snow Goose 13
Snow in the Year of the Dragon 167–168
Snowballs Chance 26
Snowfox Press 159–161
socialism 26
society 3, 24, 29, 34, 39–40, 43, 58, 155, 166, 168–171, 178, 183, 188–190, 194, 199
sociopath 96
Socrates 20
Sofawolf Press 2–4, 8, 11, **36–38**, 42, 66–68, **80–82**, 84–85, **133–**

135, 141–142, ***175–177***, 183–185, 192–193, 215; logo **215**
softcover 11
Soho Press **118–120**
soldier 52
Solus Lupus 95
The Son of Goulon Stumptail 52
Son of the Blood Moon 172
Songs in the Year of the Cat 166–168
sorcery 174
Soukup, Martha 20
The Sound & the Furry: The Complete Hoka Stories 55–57
South America 96
Southern Sea 103–104
souvenir book covers 11, 76
Soviet Union 24–25, 113–114, 115–116, 180
space 4, 56–57, 69–71, 101, 117, 152–154, 161, 168–170, 185, 193
space opera 4, 69, 71, 135–137, 159–161, 174
specialty press 3, 11, 24, 60–61, 76, 175, 190
species 34, 38, 43, 66–67, 86, 106, 111–113, 116–118, 122, 132, 136, 138, 144, 152–154, 158–159, 173–176, 181, 184–185, 193
spirit 44, 54–55, 141–142
sports 47–49, 84, 133–135, 183, 189
Stalin, Josef 24–25, 116
Stanton, Mary 87–89
Stapledon, Olaf 23, ***143–146***
The Star Mouse 20, 23
Star Prince Charlie 55–57
Star Trek 2, 94–95
Star Trek Voyager 20
Starfire Publishing 170
Startide Rising 152–154
Startling Stories 23
State University of New York 76
status quo 43
steampunk 3
Steele, James L. 47, 82
Steele, Thomas "Faux" 52
Stern, David 71–73
Still Life, with Espresso 193
Stone, Stephanie "Cybercat" 168
Stone Bridge Press 8
The Story of Dr. Dolittle 27
The Story of the Robins 10, 58
The Story of Walt Disney's Motion Picture: The Jungle Book, Adapted from the Mowgli Stories by Rudyard Kipling 100
storytelling 3–4
The Stray Lamb **148–150**, *149*
Streamline Pictures 7
Streams 183
Strike, Joe 79–80
Strike but Hear Me 52

stroke 5, 8
Stuart Little 27
subculture 9, 12, 37–38, 75, 79–80
The Subtle Knife 125–126
Succession 52
suicide 179
Sullivan, C.W. III **22–24**
Summerhill 150–152
Sun Wu-kung 9
Sundiver 152–154
Sunset of Lantonne 92–94
superheroes 7, 174
Superman 146
¡Supermen South! 7
supernatural 9, 125, 156, 172, 198
The Surface Tension 52
surgically made 60
Susman, Tim 37, 38, 60, 209
suspense 19, 28, 61, 64, 69, 88, 172, 179
suspicion 86
Sutherland, Todd G. 38
Suzukawa, Vince 176
Swallowtail & Sword: The Scholar's Book of Story and Song 167–168
swashbuckling 2
Sweden 52, 83
Swift, Jonathan 26
Swycaffer, Jefferson P. 38, 52, 82
symbolism 100
Sythyry's Journal: A World Tree Chronicle of Transaffection, Adventure, and Doom 111–113

T-shirt 76
Tabsley **73**
Tailchaser's Song **155–157**
Tails of the City 158–159
Tales from the Chakat Universe 169–170
Tales from the Tai-Pan Universe 37
Tales from Watership Down 181–183
Tales of the City 158–159
Tales of the Firebirds 134–135
Tales of the Willows 196
talking animals 9–10, 16–17, 20, 26–27, 37, 40, 45, 57–58, 61, 68, 105, 108–110, 115, 125, 128–129, 182, 195
Tampa, Florida 193
Taurin Fox 176
Tears of the Sea 52
technology 124–125, 132, 147, 158–159, 169, 170–172, 179, 194–195
telepathy 140, 180
Televassi 52, 82
television (TV) 7, 10, 20, 45, 47, 74, 79, 118, 158–159, 172, 197
Ten Thousand Miles Up 148

Tenniel, John 16–17, 27
TFC Trickompany Filmproduktion GmbH 66
That Exclusive Zodiac Club 82
Thebe and the Angry Red Eye 78
theme 1, 22, 51–53, 60, 77–79, 82, 85, 134–135, 146, 172–174, 176
Theme Park Press 8
Theta 159–161
The Things We Do for Love 173
The Third Jungle Book 100
Thomasina, the Cat Who Thought She Was God 13
Thousand Leaves 142
Thousand Tales: How We Won the Game 161–163
Thousand Tales: Learning to Fly 161–163
threats 36, 138, 172, 179
The Three Days of the Jackal 82
The Three Little Pigs 31
Three Minutes to Midnight 82
III Publishing 26
The Third Variety 52
thriller 67, 117–118, 142, 151, 179
Through the Looking-Glass 1, 10, 16–18
Thurston Howl **73–75**, 209
Thurston Howl Publications (THP) 11, 52, **73–75**, 146–148, 215–216; logo **216**
Thy Servant, a Dog 27
The Tiddlywink Warriors 56
Tilley, R. Sugden 31–33
The Time He Desires **164–166**, **165**
The Time Machine 96
time-travel 151
Timpf, Lisa 52
Tinseltown 190
To Journey in the Year of the Tiger 166–168
To the Magic Born 37
To the Reader ... 82
To Walk in the Way of Lions 166–168
Tobermory 22
Tod, Michael 142–144
Tokyo 171
Tolkien, J.R.R. 22, 27, 63, 157
Tommy Trip's History of Birds and Beasts 26
Ton Inktail 116–118
Tony Greyfox 78, 95
'toon (cartoon) 190–192
Tooth, Claw and Fang 52
Top of the Mountain 38
Tor Books 34, 42
The Torch 60
Toronto Public Library vi
torture 10, 65, 96, 107
Tow 78
toy 78

Tracer, Jessie "Electric Keet" **208**
tragedy 69, 71, 83, 92, 116, 126, 138, 146, 185, 189, 192
Transformations: A Forest Tales Story 168–170
Transmutation NOW! 170–172
transvestite 85
Traveling Music 192
The Traveling Musicians 26
travelogue 43
treason 177
Treaty at Doona 49
Treaty Planet 49, 51
Trial by Error 52
TrianglePascal 47, 49
Trick or Treat 172–173
Trick or Treat, Volume 2: Historical Halloween 172–173
trilogy 125–127, 129–131, 131–133, 134, 135–137, 138, 143, 152–154, 183
Trimmer, Mrs. [Sarah] 10, 26, 57–58
Trinity Church 187
Trinka and The Robot 78
Trotsky, Leon 25
Turner, Buck C. 59
TSR Books **122–123**
Turrittin, Tom 38
Twain, Mark 16
2040: Reconnection: A "Thousand Tales" Story 161–163
Twin Peaks 197
Two If by Sea 52

Umbra's Legion: Charo's Obol 52
unauthorized 26, 100, 111, 196
Uncovered 133–135
Under Old Earth 185
Undiplomatic Immunity 57
unicorn 27
United Kingdom 83
United Nations 56–57
United Publications 11, **60–62**
United States (U.S.) 1, 7, 11, 48, 52, 56–57, 71, 79–80, 83, 100, 116–117, 120, 125–127, 139–141, 143, 164–166, 171, 180, 195–196
Universal Pictures 73
Universe Science Fiction 56–57
University of California, Los Angeles (UCLA) 7
University of California, Riverside Rivera Library vi, 8
Unrealty 172
Uplift Storm Trilogy 152–154
Uplift Trilogy 152–154
Uplift Universe 152–154
The Uplift War 152–154
"uplifted" 152
Ursa Major Awards (UMA) 4, 5, 8, 29, 37, 49, 52, 60, 63, 68, 74–77, 78–80, 82, 89, 101–102, 111, 125, 129, 131–133, 135, 141–142, 158–159, 170, 177, 183–185, 198, 205–207, **206**; logo **206**
Ursa Major Awards (UMA) Trophy 205–207, **206**
The Ursa Major Awards Anthology: A Tenth Anniversary Celebration **174–175**

Valisca, Ashe 59
vampire 193
Vance, Alex 59
Van Den Vos Reynaerde (About Reynard the Fox) 10
Van Genechten, Robert 10
vengeance 119
Vernon, Ursula **37**
Vertical Blanking 193
victim 65–66, 106
Victorian 3, 17, 40, 60, 126
video 7, 66, 161, 166
Villard Books 190–192
violence 23, 65, 69, 86, 131, 158–161, 189
virtue 9
Vision Books 11
Vision Novels 188–190
Vivian 78
vivisection 10, 96–97
The Vixen Sorceress 63
Vlach, Heidi C. 82
vocabularies 10
Volle 83, **175–177**, **175**
Voltaire 22
Vootie! 1
The Voyage of the Dawn Treader 107–109

Waiting for Gertrude: A Graveyard Gothic 177–179
Wall Street 148, 187
Wan, Adam 176
war 9, 31, 51, 53–55, 56–57, 64, 68, 69–71, 94, 116–118, 116, 118–119, 122, 130, 136, 146, 170–171, 199
War of Attrition 52
The War with No Name 118–120
War with the Newts 23
Warner Bros. 94
Washington state 125
Watchers 179–181
Watching Anime, Reading Manga: 25 Years of Essays and Reviews 8
Watership Down 1, 10, 54, 87–89, 115, 142–144, 156, **181–183**, **183**, 196
Waterways 183–185
Watt, Isaac 26
Watt-Evans, Lawrence 37
We the Underpeople 185–186
Weasel Presents: Tales from Argaea 176

Index

Weasel Press 216; logo *216*
webcomic 63
website 76, 158–159, 168–170
Weinbaum, Stanley G. 10
weirdest 177–179
Wells, H.G. 10, **96–97**
Western 193–195
The Wharf Cat's Mermaid 60
What Alice Found There 10, 16
Where the Blue Begins 186–188
Where the Wild Things Are 27
Whimpers Law 38
A Whisper of Wings 4, 188–190
White, E.B. 27, 45–47, 110
White, Mel 38
White, Yoté 173
White Fang 3, 40
The White Fox 11
Whitlock, Ross 60
Who Censored Roger Rabbit? 190–192
Who P-P-P-Plugged Roger Rabbit? 190–192
Who Wacked Roger Rabbit? 190–192
whodunit 190–192
Why Coyotes Howl 192–193
Wiese, Kurt 31–33
WikiFur 76

Wikipedia 68
Wild Night 172
Wild West Show 193
Wild Wood 196
A Wilder West 193–195
Williams, Cherry vi
Williams, Chris "Sparf" 60
Williams, Garth 45
Williams, Tad **155–157**
Williams, Tanner 52
Wills, Tod 198–200
Wilson, Daniel H. 118
The Wind in the Willows 1, 16, 27, 43, 180, 195–196
Windfall 196–198
Wings 38
Wings of Faith 82
Winkle, Michael D. 52, 82
Winnie the Pooh 27
Wish 23
The Wishing Tree 22
The Witch Doctor 173
Without Evidence 193
Wolf, Gary K. 28, 190–192
Wolf, PJ 47
Wolfe, J.N. 52
Wolves in Winter 52
Wonder Stories 10
Wong, Conrad 38
The Woodstock Saga 143–144

World Science Fiction Convention 7–8
The World Tree Role Playing Game 111–112
World War II 20, 71, 144–146
worldwide 3, 76
Worsel the Velantian 10
A Wrath of Trees 198–200
writing workshops 4–5
Wu Ch'eng-en 9, 22
Wylie, Philip 146
Wyman, Vicky M. 38
Wynoochee Valley 125

Yamavu **77**
Yarf! The Journal of Applied Anthropomorphics 8, 10, 37, 78, 192
Yesterday's Trickster 82
Yo Ho Hoka! 20, 56
Yoko Tawada 113–114
Young, Harding 20
YouTube 198

Zhivago **80**
Zhu Bajie 9
zine (fanzine) 1
zoo 14–15, 69, 114, 139–141
Zoomorphica 10, 37, 192
ZU 63